SPITFIRE
ACE OF ACES
The Wartime Story of Johnnie Johnson

DILIP SARKAR
MBE FRHistS

AMBERLEY

For Johnnie

Author's Note

Throughout the text I have referred to German *Messerschmitt*
fighters by the abbreviation 'Me' (not 'Bf', which is also correct),
or simply by their numeric designation, such as '109' or '110'.
Likewise the Focke-Wulf 190 becomes the 'FW 190' or simply
'190'. Also, the direct quotes from Johnnie Johnson are from a
combination of sources, including taped conversations between us.
These I have not edited but reproduced as spoken – warts and all!

This edition first published 2014

Amberley Publishing
The Hill, Stroud,
Gloucestershire, GL5 4EP

www.amberley-books.com

Copyright © Dilip Sarkar 2011, 2014
Unless otherwise indicated, all
photographs are courtesy Paula and Chris
Johnson and/or Dilip Sarkar Archive.

The right of Dilip Sarkar to be identified
as the Author of this work has been
asserted in accordance with the
Copyrights, Designs and Patents Act
1988.

ISBN 978 1 4456 1713 8

British Library Cataloguing in
Publication Data.
A catalogue record for this book is
available from the British Library.

Typesetting and Origination by
Amberley Publishing.
Printed in the UK.

Contents

	Glossary	4
	Introduction	7
1	First Blood: Prelude to Excellence	9
2	The Bader Factor: Tangmere Wing	41
3	Bader's Bus Company: Still Running	81
4	Squadron Commander: Rhubarbs & JUBILEE	93
5	Wing Commander (Flying): Greycap Leader	112
6	127 Wing: Tactical Air Force	174
7	Staff Appointment: 'My Closest Shave of the War'	194
8	144 Wing: Shot & Shell	198
9	D-Day: 'Looking Down into Hell'	228
10	Normandy: Overtaking the Sailor	236
11	Normandy: Top-Scoring Fighter Wing	255
12	Normandy: Search & Destroy	262
13	127 Wing: The Long Trek	285
14	Johnnie Johnson: Top-Scoring RAF Fighter Pilot	296
15	Conclusion: 'A Marvellous Life'	300
	Appendix: Johnnie Johnson's Aerial Combat Claims	312
	Acknowledgements	314
	Bibliography	315
	About the Author	319
	Other Books by Dilip Sarkar	319

Glossary

AAF	Auxiliary Air Force
AASF	Advance Air Striking Force
A&AEE	Aircraft & Armament Experimental Establishment
ABC	Airborne Cigar
ACM	Air Chief Marshal
AFV	Armoured Fighting Vehicle
ADGB	Air Defence of Great Britain
AEAF	Allied Expeditionary Air Force
AFC	Air Force Cross
ALG	Advance Landing Ground
AOC	Air Officer Commanding
ASI	Air Speed Indicator
ASR	Air Sea Rescue
AVM	Air Vice-Marshal
BEF	British Expeditionary Force
CBC	Canadian Broadcasting Company
CIGS	Chief of the Imperial General Staff
DFC	Distinguished Flying Cross
DSO	Distinguished Service Order
E/A	Enemy Aircraft
CAS	Chief of the Air Staff
CBOD	Combined Bomber Offensive Directive
CFI	Chief Flying Instructor
CFS	Central Flying School
CO	Commanding Officer
EFTS	Elementary Flying Training School
FTS	Flying Training School
HQ	Headquarters
IAS	Indicated Air Speed
LAC	Leading Aircraftman
MC	Military Cross

MET	Motor Enemy Transport
MGB	Motor Gun Boat
M/T	Motor Transport
NCO	Non-commissioned Officer
ORB	Operations Record Book
OTU	Operational Training Unit
PSP	Pierced Steel Planking
RAF	Royal Air Force
RAFVR	Royal Air Force Volunteer Reserve
RCAF	Royal Canadian Air Force
RCM	Radar Counter Measures
RDF	Radio Direction Finding, radar
RE	Royal Engineers
RN	Royal Navy
R/T	Radio Telephone
RV	Rendezvous
SAS	Special Air Service
SASO	Senior Air Staff Officer
SCU	Servicing Commando Unit
SHAEF	Supreme Headquarters Allied Expeditionary Force
TAF	Tactical Air Force
TOT	Time On Target
USAAC	United States Army Air Corps
USAF	United States Air Force
VC	Victoria Cross
VHF	Very High Frequency
WAAF	Women's Auxiliary Air Force
W/C	Wing Commander

GERMAN TERMS

Experten	Fighter aces
Festung Europa	Fortress Europe
Geschwader	The whole group, usually of three *Gruppen*
Geschwader Kommodore	The group leader
Gruppe	A wing, usually of three squadrons
Gruppenkommandeur	The wing commander

Jagdgeschwader	Fighter group, abbreviated JG
Kanalgeschwadern	Groups based on the Channel coast
Kanaljäger	Fighter pilot based on the Channel coast
Katschmarek	Wingman
Jagdbomber	A fighter-bomber, or *Jabo*
Jagdflieger	Fighter pilot
Jagdfliegerführer	Commander-in-Chief of Day Fighters
Jagdwaffe	German fighter force
Oberkommando der Wehrmacht	'OKW', the German armed forces high command
Rotte	A pair of fighters, comprising leader and wingman, into which the Schwarm broke once battle was joined
Schwarm	A section of four fighters
Stab Schwarm	The staff flight
Staffel	A squadron
Staffelkapitän	The squadron leader
U-bootwaffe	The submarine force
Zerstörer	Destroyer

Each *Geschwader* generally comprised three *Gruppen*, each of three *Staffeln*. Each *Gruppe* is designated by Roman numerals, i.e. III/JG 26 refers to the third *Gruppe* of Fighter Group 26. *Staffeln* are identified by numbers, so 7/JG 26 is the 7th *Staffel* and belongs to III/JG 26.

Certain rank comparisons may also be useful:

Feldwebel	Sergeant
Hauptmann	Squadron Leader
Leutnant	Pilot Officer
Major	Wing Commander
Oberfeldwebel	Flight Sergeant
Oberleutnant	Flight Lieutenant
Oberst	Group Captain
Unteroffizier	Corporal, no RAF aircrew equivalent

Introduction

As a child growing up during the 1960s in post-war Britain, the Second World War remained omnipresent. Family members, neighbours, had all been involved in this epic conflagration. Feature films on the subject abounded, compulsory weekend viewing being such films as *633 Squadron*, *The Dambusters* and, of course, the incredible story of the RAF's legless fighter ace Douglas Bader, *Reach for the Sky*. There were plastic scale models, too, those made by Airfix being especially popular and well stocked by newsagents and toy shops. After the release of the film *Battle of Britain* in 1969, when I was eight years old, demand for model Spitfires soared. The 1/72nd scale offering from Airfix, though, was not a Battle of Britain machine but a later mark. This aircraft had green and grey camouflage, a four-bladed propeller and cannons. On the fuselage was painted a maple leaf motif and the letters 'JE-J'. The instructions told me that this was Supermarine Spitfire Mk IX EN398, flown by Wing Commander James Edgar 'Johnnie' Johnson at Kenley in 1943, who became the top-scoring RAF fighter pilot of the Second World War. I made this kit many times, and wanted to learn more about my hero, Johnnie Johnson. A couple of years later I read Paul Brickhill's *Reach for the Sky*, followed by Johnnie's own autobiography *Wing Leader*. This was all great stuff, but I had no idea then that in years to come, as a professional historian and author, I would actually get to know the men from history's pages – and Johnnie Johnson would become my friend.

Johnnie's distinguished record in war and peace marks him out as a remarkable man. All of those achievements, though, tell us very little about the man himself. There was so much more to Johnnie than these tangible things. A natural-born hunter and leader, Johnnie was fascinated by the subject of leadership. He possessed great charisma, enormous charm – with a presence to match. Gregarious and loyal, Johnnie made snap decisions about people and was never wrong – instinctively he knew whether or not you were 'reliable'. He did not, though, suffer fools. The greatest thing about Johnnie to me, that I could so relate to personally, was his boundless enthusiasm for all he did. This, more than anything else, was inspirational to me. It has been said that Johnnie was blessed with the unique ability to ignite the spirit and get the best out of people. That to me, and to Chris, Johnnie's second son, is the most fascinating and endearing aspect of this great man's life.

Throughout the 1990s, I was a regular visitor to Johnnie's home near Buxton in Derbyshire. For hours we would sit in his den, recording interviews, going over the text of *Wing Leader* and through his pilot's flying logbook, picking out detail, a story here, an emphasis there. It was great fun, and sometimes I had to pinch myself. The 'AVM' became a regular guest at the various high-profile events I organised at that time, book signings, air war symposiums attended by enthusiasts from all over the world. Johnnie loved it, being in the company of those who shared his passion for flying and fighting in the Spitfire. Best of all he revelled in the company of others who had shared the 'Great Adventure'. I met or corresponded with many of Johnnie's pilots, which not only helped me recreate the experience of flying with him on paper, but gave me new insights into what made the 'Boss' tick. The result is this book. So, read on – and be *inspired*!

Dilip Sarkar MBE FRHistS BA (Hons)
Worcester, February 2011

First Blood:
Prelude to Excellence

James Edgar Johnson was born on 9 March 1915, at Barrow-upon-Soar in rural Leicestershire. The new arrival's parents were Alfred Edgar and Beatrice May Johnson, who dubbed their eldest son 'Jim'. Mr Johnson was an officer in the Leicestershire Constabulary, stationed in Melton Mowbray, where the family lived at Welby Lane. Young Jim first attended the town's Camden Street Junior School. A few years later the Johnsons were blessed with another son, Ross, who recalled his elder brother, now known to all as 'Johnnie':

> There is no doubt that a great influence on my brother was our Uncle Charlie, who was our mother's brother. As Second Lieutenant E. C. Rossel he had won a Military Cross serving with the Royal Fusiliers in the Great War. Afterwards he went off to Malaya and managed a 3,000-acre rubber plantation. During his trips home Uncle Charlie always stayed with us, inspiring Johnnie through his tales of derring-do and travel. To us, Uncle Charlie was an exotic and romantic character. Early on it was Uncle Charlie who recognised some potential in Johnnie and paid for him to board at Loughborough Grammar School. As our father was a police officer, which was not a well paid job in those days, our parents could never have afforded this. As a youngster Johnnie was always in trouble, always up to something. I remember once that he nearly got expelled for refusing to take a beating for some misdemeanour or other. It wasn't that he was afraid, just that he felt very strongly that it was unjustified. He was very principled and simply dug his heels in.
>
> Locally Johnnie was great friends with Len Leader, who was his mentor, really. He was obsessed with speed and joined the Melton Car Club with George Houghton. The only problem was that unless he took the Old Man's car without him knowing, Johnnie was the only member who didn't actually have a car! Not only

was he into fast cars, but equally pacey girls as well! That he became interested in flying, therefore, was no surprise.

Before the war our father was the police inspector at Melton Mowbray. One evening the British Union of Fascists had a licence for a meeting at the Town Hall, where Sir Oswald Moseley spoke. The licence expired at 10 p.m., and on the dot Inspector Johnson went in, alone, and closed the meeting, saying to Moseley 'You've had your time, now get out'. That took courage.

After leaving school Johnnie graduated as a civil engineer at University College, Nottingham. Thereafter he was articled to Mr W. H. Jarvis, the Borough Surveyor at Melton Urban Council before taking an appointment at Loughton in Essex. By then Johnnie was twenty-two, the year 1938 and the time of Munich. Since 1933, when Adolf Hitler became Chancellor of Germany, the shadow of major conflict had fallen over the world for the second time in the twentieth century. Slowly but surely Hitler and the Nazis dismantled the Versailles Peace Treaty of 1919, through which the victorious Allies sought to prevent Germany ever rising again as a military power. The redefined map of Europe after the Paris Peace Conference, however, caused many more problems than it resolved, creating significant ethnic minorities within new nations. The Sudetenland of Czechoslovakia, with a high proportion of German inhabitants, was a case in point. Having already remilitarised the Rhineland and united with Austria – both forbidden by Versailles – Hitler reclaimed the Sudetenland, an area crucial to Czechoslovakian security given that it contained the country's fortified border defences. Britain, France and Italy, however, did nothing. Indeed, the Czechs were not even invited to attend the Munich Conference on 30 September 1938, at which the Sudetenland was ceded to Germany. The British Prime Minister, that great champion of appeasement, Neville Chamberlain, returned to Heston airport triumphantly brandishing his piece of paper bearing his own and Hitler's signatures and which guaranteed 'peace for our time'. It was not, of course, to be. In March the following year Hitler occupied the remainder of Czechoslovakia, providing a clear indication of how sinister and unlawful his territorial ambitions really were. It was against this backdrop that Johnnie and countless other young men got on with their lives and considered an uncertain future.

A keen and aggressive sportsman, while working and living in Essex Johnnie played rugby for Chingford,

> enjoying some excellent games and the company of a very spirited collection of young men, most of whom were already serving in one or another of the various Territorial organisations. In one game, against Park House, I was brought down heavily on a frozen surface and broke my right collar-bone. Although I didn't know it at the time, the break was improperly set and the nerves to the forearm were imprisoned below the bone.

Later, this would have serious consequences – nearly ending Johnnie's flying career before it had barely begun.

Before Munich Johnnie had started taking flying lessons, at his own expense, and applied to join the Auxiliary Air Force (AAF), which had been founded in 1924 and based upon the territorial concept. At this time, however, Britain remained an extremely hierarchical society. For example, all officers were former public schoolboys, representing the top 5.2 per cent of Britain's social pyramid. If officers generally represented a social elite, however, those of the AAF were the elite of an elite. Hugh 'Cocky' Dundas, a trainee solicitor from the West Riding and, according to Johnnie, 'related to half the bloody aristocracy in Yorkshire', joined the AAF in 1938:

> In all the history of arms there can seldom have been a body of men more confident and pleased with themselves than the pilots of the AAF. We wore a big brass 'A' on the lapels of our tunics … The regulars insisted that the 'A' stood for 'Amateur Airmen', or even 'Argue and Answer Back'. To us they were symbols of a very special club. The pilots of the AAF were lawyers and farmers, stockbrokers and journalists; they were landowners and artisans, serious minded accountants and unrepentant playboys.

What they were not, however, were humble policemen's sons. Johnnie:

> I went along for this interview and the senior officer there, knowing that I came from Leicestershire, said 'With whom do

you hunt, Johnson?'

I said 'Hunt, Sir?'

He said 'Yes, Johnson, hunt; with whom do you hunt?'

I said 'Well, I don't hunt, Sir, I shoot.'

He said 'Oh, well thank you then, Johnson, that will be all!'

Clearly the fact that I could shoot game on the wing impressed him not one bit. Had I been socially acceptable, however, by hunting with Lord so-and-so, things would have been different, but back then, that is what the Auxiliaries were like, and do not forget that many members were of independent means, which I certainly wasn't!

After Munich it was clear that war with Nazi Germany was inevitable, and, perhaps naively, Johnnie reapplied to the AAF:

I was curtly informed that sufficient pilots were already available but there were some vacancies in the balloon squadrons. Was I interested in this vital part of the defence organisation? I replied, with similar brevity, that I was not at all interested in flying balloons!

Britain now stepped up its reluctant rearmament programme. By 1939 there were twenty AAF squadrons, for example, and the University Air Squadrons (UAS) provided another 500 trained officer pilots for the RAF. In 1934 the Expansion Plan began raising the establishment of Home Defence squadrons to fifty-two by 1940. Nonetheless, in 1936, Expansion Scheme 'F' recognised that there remained an insufficient reserve. This led to the creation of the RAF Volunteer Reserve (VR). The official monograph on RAF Flying Training during the Second World War states that the RAFVR would

have a wide appeal based upon the Citizen Volunteer principle with a common mode of entry and promotion and commissioning on merit … So far as aircrew training was concerned, the system was based upon local town centres for spare time ground training and upon aerodrome centres associated with the town centres for flying training at the weekend, also for a fortnight's annual camp.

According to Air Ministry Pamphlet 101, published in November 1939:

> Entry into the General Duties (Flying) branch of the RAFVR is normally through the ranks, commissions being given by selection, either on completion of flying training or subsequently, but past or present members of UAS who hold proficiency certificates will be eligible for consideration for appointment to commissions on entry.

All volunteer aircrew were automatically made sergeants, with the possibility of a commission based – apparently – not on an elitist background but on the basis of ability. The VR provided, therefore, a unique opportunity for many young men from ordinary educational and social backgrounds to fly. Inspired by several Chingford teammates who had already joined the VR, Johnnie applied. Unfortunately the outcome was disappointing: for the time being there were more applicants than vacancies. Johnnie was advised that in the event of further expansion the VR would contact him. There, having failed to get accepted by either the AAF or VR, Johnnie's story could easily have ended on an unremarkable note.

Disappointed but still keen to serve his country and play his part in the conflagration about to once more consume the globe, Johnnie decided to join the mounted Leicestershire Yeomanry. One reason he was so keen to join a part-time service unit, in this case one of the Territorial Army (TA), was because Johnnie's was a reserved occupation. Looking ahead, when war came the young civil engineer had no intention of seeing out the duration 'building air-raid shelters or supervising decontamination squads'. Although not interested in fox hunting – a strong tradition of rural Leicestershire – Johnnie had learned to ride at an early age. Passing an interview with the local troop commander, Johnnie soon found himself both in khaki and in the saddle. In his memoir *Wing Leader*, he described Yeomanry service 'as a very happy affair' during which were spent 'many enjoyable days charging over the countryside'. Years later, Johnnie elaborated: 'Yes, but it was all very well being on the back of a bloody great horse! One day two Spitfires flew overhead and I thought "Christ, that's more like it, get me out of the saddle of this bloody great thing!"' Indeed, Johnnie's Yeoman comrade Dick

Black, a Leicestershire farmer and noted steeplechaser, remembered
that 'Whilst at Burleigh Park on annual camp we went to the airfield
at nearby Wittering to see some new Hawker Hurricanes. Johnnie
said "If I've got to fight Hitler I'd sooner fight him in one of those
than on a bloody great horse!"' Fortunately, with this enduring
ambition to fly in mind, upon Johnnie's return to Loughton he was
awaited by a letter from the Air Ministry: the VR was being further
expanded and James Edgar Johnson was invited to attend a medical
at the organisation's headquarters in Store Street, London. As
Johnnie said, 'That was great news.' Greater news still was passing
and being sworn in as a sergeant-pilot under training. No longer
was Johnnie Johnson haunted by the spectre of either going to war
on horseback or, worse, remaining a surveyor when war came.

Johnnie began flying training at weekends at Stapleford Tawney,
a satellite of the Fighter Command Sector Station at North Weald.
Tuesdays and Thursdays were consumed by lectures at Store Street on
such subjects as navigation, airmanship, armament and signals. The
students were forcefully reminded that ground instruction, although
less exciting, was equally as important as that in the air, and that
in the event of ground studies being neglected the dreaded 'chop'
would result. Johnnie now found that with his time divided between
his full-time civilian job and training with the VR, he was 'fully
occupied'. The atmosphere of the VR was entirely to the gregarious
young Johnson's liking: 'Our ranks were made up from every walk
of life, including farmers, engineers, stockbrokers, articled pupils,
bank clerks and young men who were beginning their professional
careers.' Whereas officers, and the vast majority of pilots, therefore,
in both the regular service and AAF had a public school background,
the VR was arguably a grammar schoolboys' air force. Nonetheless,
even in the VR only former public schoolboys were considered
for an immediate commission. Everyone else, including Johnnie,
began with the non-commissioned rank of sergeant, the prospect
of being commissioned based not upon a privileged background
but on ability. This is crucial both to Johnnie's story *per se*, and to
contextualising his subsequent achievements.

Taught by retired service pilots of 21 Elementary & Reserve
Flying Training School (E&RFTS), the young reservists received *ab
initio* air experience on the ubiquitous Tiger Moth biplane. In late
August 1939, members of the VR were mobilised. Johnnie reported

accordingly to Store Street but was simply told to go home and there await orders. On 1 September 1939, Hitler invaded Poland, thus beginning the Second World War. While the Poles suffered the world's first demonstration of shocking *Blitzkrieg* tactics, Britain and France gave the *Führer* an ultimatum: withdraw from Poland or suffer the consequences. Hitler was unmoved. On 3 September 1939, Britain and France, therefore, declared war on Nazi Germany. The RAF was now fully mobilised, fighter and light bomber squadrons immediately landing in France to form the Advanced Air Striking Force (AASF), which was required to support the British Expeditionary Force (BEF). Once more Johnnie reported to Store Street. Soon after hearing the Prime Minister's historic broadcast announcing that the country was again at war with Germany, Sergeant 754750 J. E. Johnson and several hundred other VR sergeant-pilots under training were entrained for Cambridge. Their destination was 2 Initial Training Wing (ITW), the young sergeants being billeted in various of the town's famous university colleges until the administrative and logistical process found them all places at various flying training schools. Johnnie:

> One day a few elderly officers interviewed us about what we wanted to become – bomber, fighter, reconnaissance or training pilots. These old officers had lunched well and, clearly bored, found tedious the fact that everyone wanted to be a fighter pilot – except me. I said that being a civil engineer I had knowledge of surveying, topography and mapping, and therefore felt that I could be more useful in a reconnaissance role. The Wing Commander agreed – but I became a fighter pilot!

After 'square bashing', by December 1939, Johnnie was a pupil at 22 Elementary Flying Training School (EFTS), Cambridge, undergoing initial service flying training. That month he flew just three times, and eight in January 1940, all as second pilot. On 29 February 1940, however, Sergeant Johnson soloed on Tiger Moth N6635, a significant flight of 15 minutes. On 15 March, following further dual and solo flights, Johnnie passed Pilot Officer Russell's Flight Commander's Test. A more intensive test, lasting 50 minutes and comprising a variety of exercises, taken by a Flight Lieutenant Lawrence, was passed on 24 April, as was a similar Chief Flying

Instructor's (CFI) test on 6 May. The following day saw Johnnie's first
two night flights, indicating growing competence and confidence.

Across the Channel, Lord Gort's BEF still sat out what had been
dubbed 'The Phoney War'. After the great flurry of activity when
war broke out, which saw Britain's armed forces mobilised and
on full alert, events had stagnated. The dreaded 'knock-out blow'
on England was not delivered by German bombers. Hitler's forces,
having quickly conquered Poland, remained behind the Third
Reich's borders. The Belgian King – naively determined to remain
neutral – had refused the BEF permission to enter his country in
September 1939 to fortify Belgium's border with Germany. Instead
Gort had to dig in along the Franco-Belgian border, while the
French put their faith in the substantial underground concrete
fortifications of the Maginot Line – howsoever incomplete this
defensive network was. Then, on 10 May 1940, without warning,
Hitler attacked the West, invading Holland, Belgium, Luxembourg
and France. Immediately the Belgians called for help, leading to
the BEF having to leave their carefully prepared positions and
pivot forward some 60 miles across unfamiliar and unprepared
ground. Two days later Liege fell, and *Panzers* crossed the Meuse
at Dinant and Sedan. Meanwhile the BEF expected to meet the
German *Schwerpunkt* – point of main effort – which appeared
to be following the same route, south-west through Holland and
into Belgium, as in the Great War. In fact it did not. Holland
was certainly attacked – the Dutch Air Force being wiped out on
the first day – but the main enemy thrust was cleverly disguised.
With Allied eyes firmly focussed on the Belgian–Dutch border,
Panzergruppe von Kleist successfully negotiated the Ardennes
Forest – supposedly impassable to armour – much further south.
German armoured columns then poured out of the forest, bypassing
the Maginot Line, rendering it useless. The *Panzers* then punched
upwards, towards the Channel coast – ten days later the Germans
had reached Laon, Cambrai, Arras, Amiens and even Abbeville.
Indeed, Erwin Rommel's 7th *Panzer* covered ground so quickly
that it became known as the 'Ghost Division'.

The effect on the Allies was virtual paralysis, so shocking was the
assault, unprecedented in speed and fury. Civilians in Britain were
equally stunned – not least after the bombing of Rotterdam on 14
May, which reportedly caused 30,000 civilian fatalities (although

post-war estimates put the death toll at nearer 3,000). Before the war, the British Prime Minister had warned the House of Commons that 'the bomber would always get through'. Following the devastation of Guernica by German bombers during the Spanish Civil War and Warsaw's similar fate in the Battle for Poland, Rotterdam appeared to confirm Baldwin's ominous and pessimistic prophecy. With the AASF squadrons suffering combat casualties, the amateurs of the VR under training would soon be urgently required by front-line squadrons. Consequently the training of RAF pilots immediately adopted an infinitely more serious and urgent emphasis. On 24 May 1940, Johnnie's *ab initio* flying training at Cambridge was successfully completed. His ability as a pupil pilot and pilot-navigator was assessed as 'Average'. The following day Sergeant Johnson was posted to 5 Service Flying Training School (SFTS) at Sealand, near Chester, there to fly monoplanes for the first time.

On 2 June, Johnnie made his first flight from Sealand as second pilot in Miles Master N7454 flown by a Sergeant Broad. His fourth flight that day was solo on the Master, as were the majority of subsequent flights at Sealand. These largely comprised such exercises as instrument flying, navigation, 'precautionary flying' and practising forced landings. On 25 June came a lengthy cross-country exercise, from Sealand to South Cerney, via Little Rissington, in the Cotswolds, and return. Night-flying also featured heavily in the programme, which concluded on 7 August. With another 'Average' assessment stamped in his Pilot's Flying Logbook, Johnnie had now won his 'wings' and was a qualified service pilot. With a total of 55 hours and 5 minutes solo flying time, on 10 August Johnnie was commissioned 'for the duration of hostilities' as a Pilot Officer in the General Duties Branch of the RAF. The pressure of mounting casualties meant that advancement was no longer purely influenced by the socio-educational prejudice that had shaped the pre-war service. For Johnnie this was the first step up what would be a long ladder.

By this time there had been significant developments in the air war. The German invasion of the West had totally overwhelmed and defeated the shocked Allies. The sky was dominated by German fighters, which took a heavy toll on the AASF. Casualties mounted rapidly. With great foresight, however, Air Chief Marshal Sir Hugh Dowding refused to send precious Spitfires – which were all too few in number – to France, where they would be wasted in a battle already lost. Only the inferior, though more numerous, Hawker Hurricane therefore operated across the Channel. On 26 May 1940, by which time the collapse of the Belgian Army to the north and the French to the south had left the BEF in danger of envelopment, the decision was reluctantly made for Gort's force to retire and be evacuated from Dunkirk. A great combined operation was rapidly under way to bring the survivors home. To Air Vice-Marshal Park, the commander of Fighter Command's 11 Group, responsible for the defence of London and the South East, was given the task of providing aerial cover to the seaborne evacuation. To this battle, Spitfire squadrons were committed – and over the French coast met the German Me 109 fighter for the first time. In these combats the Spitfire acquitted itself well, earning the respect of the German fighter pilots, who realised that this machine was a match for their own aircraft. By 4 June some 340,000 troops had been rescued and the evacuation ended. On 22 June, France formally surrendered.

Hitler's advance to the Channel coast was as unprecedented as it was unexpected. Hitherto it was expected that any aerial attack on England would approach the east coast, across the North Sea, and be made by bombers operating from bases in Germany. Consequently the RAF tacticians had written a manual of air fighting geared up entirely to meeting such a threat, involving squadrons of Spitfires and Hurricanes attacking slow-moving bombers able to take little or no evasive action. The favoured Fighter Command formation was the 'vic' of three aircraft flying in close formation. Each fighter was armed with eight machine-guns, the reasoning behind the 'vic' being that twenty-four guns could be brought to bear. An RAF fighter squadron comprised twelve operational aircraft, the unit divided into two flights, 'A' and 'B', each commanded by a flight lieutenant and comprising six aircraft each. The flights were then subdivided into two sections of three, each colour coded, such as Blue or Red Section. Air exercises before the war had been totally unrealistic, Bomber Command's aircraft obligingly flying straight and level while Spitfires and Hurricanes eagerly took their turn to 'attack' these sedate targets. Given the high speed achievable by the new monoplane fighters, the tacticians did not, in fact, anticipate fighter-to-fighter combat as in the Great War. The speeds now involved, they believed, were simply too great for this to be possible. Consequently there was little or no consideration given to evolving fighter-to-fighter tactics. The events in France, however, indicated very clearly that this was a most negligent oversight. The Germans, though, had worked out their fighter tactics in Spain, Werner Mölders rapidly appreciating that, due to the high speeds involved, fighters needed space. He worked out a line-abreast formation, known as the *Schwarm*, in which each aircraft was 200 metres apart. Pilots were, therefore, able to concentrate on searching the sky for the enemy – rather than concentrating on close formation flying as in the RAF three-ship 'vic'. Moreover, when battle was joined the *Schwarm* broke into two *Rotten*, each *Rotte* (pair) comprising a leader and a wingman. While the leader pounced on the enemy, he was protected by his wingman. In France, and over Dunkirk, Fighter Command had suffered from this tactical deficiency. Unfortunately it took a long time – and many casualties – for the RAF to catch up.

Hitler's surprise acquisition of airfields in the Pas-de-Calais changed everything. Southern England – even London – was now within range of enemy fighters. The *Luftwaffe* was equipped with two types: the single-engined Me 109E, which was superior to the Hurricane but a match for the Spitfire, and the twin-engined Me 110, *Reichsmarschall* Göring's much vaunted *Zerstörer* (destroyer). While the 109 enjoyed certain technical advantages over the Spitfire, including a fuel-injected engine and a constant-speed propeller (although the latter was rectified during the summer of 1940), the 110 proved a failure. Although this twin-engined machine enjoyed reasonable range, its lack of manoeuvrability and speed made it easy prey for the more nimble and faster RAF single-engined fighters. Perceived to be a useful long-range bomber-escort fighter, the 110 proved woefully inadequate in this role to the extent that it required protection itself. Although the 109, like the Spitfire and Hurricane designed as a defensive fighter, only had sufficient fuel for 20 minutes' flying time over the British capital, this fact alone changed the entire tactical scenario. No longer could Fighter Command simply expect unescorted bombers ponderously approaching over the North Sea. Instead the bombers could approach from their new bases in Northern France – escorted by the dangerous 109. Naturally the *Oberkommando der Wehrmacht* (OKW) intended to exploit their advantage to the full – by mounting a seaborne invasion of South East England, codenamed Operation *Seelöwe* (Sealion). As a prelude to this ambitious and unprecedented combined operation, the *Luftwaffe* was tasked with achieving aerial supremacy over England. So far undefeated, Göring was sublimely confident and estimated that Fighter Command would be annihilated in three weeks. Air Chief Marshal Dowding, however, disagreed, believing that he could hold out 'for some time, if not indefinitely'.

The German air assault on England, which became known as the Battle of Britain, began on 10 July 1940. This first phase saw intensive skirmishing by the opposing fighter forces over Channel-bound convoys. The enemy probed British coastal defences, *Stuka* dive-bombers attacking radar installations along the south coast. On 8 August the Germans intensified these operations. Fortunately the enemy did not fully appreciate the significance of radar – which played a crucial role in Dowding's System of Air Defence. Consequently attacks against these all-important targets – which provided Fighter Command's Controllers with early warning of approaching hostile raids – were not pressed home sufficiently to break the chain of stations protecting Britain with their invisible beams. Nonetheless the air fighting was heavy, substantial losses being suffered by both sides. While the supply of replacement aircraft was never to cause Dowding concern, even when the Supermarine Spitfire factory at Southampton was successfully bombed and production halted, what was a paramount concern was the loss of pilots. These were, of course, all fully trained and operational. Many had already experienced aerial combat over France. Such men could not easily be replaced. More than ever, therefore, the training of pilots was of paramount importance. To increase the flow of combat-ready pilots to the squadrons, the system was both changed and shortened. Until recently the fighter squadrons themselves had provided operational instruction. The pressure of combat operations, however, dictated that this long-established practice was no longer possible. Consequently the OTUs were created to provide this experience. Upon completion of their service flying training, newly qualified pilots would be posted to one of three OTUs, there to receive instruction on either the Spitfire or Hurricane. Although at this time there was only a third as many Spitfires equipping Fighter Command than Hurricanes, it was clear that the Spitfire was superior, due to its high-altitude capability, and would ultimately become Fighter Command's mainstay. Two of the OTUs, therefore,

No. 5, at Aston Down, near Stroud in Gloucestershire, and No. 7, at Hawarden near Chester, were Spitfire schools. No. 6, at St Athan in South Wales, provided Hurricane experience. For Pilot Officer Johnnie Johnson a dream came true when, upon completion of his course at Sealand, he was posted to 7 OTU – to fly Spitfires.

Having been checked out for 10 minutes in a Miles Master by Flying Officer Baldie, Johnnie's first Spitfire flight took place on 19 August 1940 – while the Battle of Britain was in full swing. The flight lasted an hour, and, according to Johnnie, 'was one to remember'. Of this landmark occasion he wrote:

I trundled awkwardly over the grass surface swinging the Spitfire from side to side with brakes and bursts of throttle ... I reached the very edge of the airfield, and before turning into wind carried out a final cockpit check. I swung her nose into the wind. Throttle gently but firmly opened to about four pounds of boost. She accelerates very quickly, much faster than the Master. Stick forward to lift the tail and get a good airflow over the elevators. Correct a tendency to swing with coarse rudder. No more bouncing about. We can't be airborne yet! Yes, we are, and already climbing into the sky. Things move fast in a Spitfire! Wheels up. Pitch control back and throttle set to give a climbing speed of 200 mph. Close the hood. After a struggle, during which the nose rose and fell like the flight of a magpie, I closed the perspex canopy and the cockpit seemed even more restricted than before. I toyed with the idea of flying with the hood open, but I could not fly or fight at high altitudes in this fashion and I must get acquainted with every feature of the plane. I carried out an easy turn and tried to pick up my bearings. Not more than four or five minutes since take-off, but already we were more than twenty miles from Hawarden. I flew back, gaining confidence with every second. A Master looms ahead and slightly below. I overtake him comfortably, and to demonstrate my superiority attempt an upward roll. I forget to allow for the heavy nose of the Spitfire with sufficient forward movement of the stick and so we barrel out of the manoeuvre, losing an undignified amount of height. Better concentrate on handling characteristics and leave aerobatics for another day.

Johnnie's subsequent landing was not the best, leading to further dual instruction in the Master with Flight Lieutenant Powell. Nonetheless, Johnnie Johnson had achieved his ambition: to fight Hitler from the cockpit of a Spitfire, instead of 'on the back of a bloody great horse!'

At Hawarden, Johnnie embarked upon an intensive training programme, flying every day and making up to four training sorties daily. These included such exercises as 'Handling', in which the pilot became familiar with the Spitfire, plenty of formation flying practice, learning how to use the Radio Telephone (R/T) system to communicate with both ground control and other aircraft, 'Attacks', 'Battle Climbs', 'Aerobatics and Dog Fighting', and navigation. On 28 August 1940 the course was complete. By that time Johnnie had flown a total of 205.35 hours on service types – 23.50 on the Spitfire while at Hawarden. Throughout the Battle of Britain, the length of OTU courses was frequently reduced, so as to rush replacement pilots through to the fighter squadrons. By this time the usual number of Spitfire flying hours provided by OTUs was ten, so 23.50 was a respectable amount of flying time indeed. After their time at OTU, pilots were posted to operational fighter squadrons. At this time the air defence of Great Britain was organised by way of fighter groups: 10 Group covering the West Country and South Wales, 11 Group protecting London and the South East, 12 Group defending the industrial Midlands and the North, and 13 Group Scotland and Northern Ireland. Clearly, now that the *Luftwaffe* was able to operate from bases in northern France, the main assault was focussed on 11 Group. Consequently Fighter Command operated a system whereby squadrons were cleverly rotated in and out of the battle zone. This was essential for several reasons. Firstly it meant that the British fighter force was not entirely or largely concentrated in the South East, where it could be destroyed. Secondly this provided protection for other important targets throughout the country – Dowding could never be sure, of course, where the enemy would attack, and on 15 August the wisdom of this strategy became evident when the enemy attacked Newcastle and Sunderland from bases in Norway. Not expecting to meet opposition, the *Luftwaffe* was roughly handled by Spitfires and Hurricanes based in northern England. The North, however, being beyond the range of Me 109s, was only troubled by lone or small formations of bombers. The tempo of fighting was, therefore, entirely different to the hectic cut and thrust over southern England. Consequently Dowding was able to rotate squadrons depleted in combat to rest and re-fit in the North. The place of these battle-weary units was taken in the front line by units from the North and which were at full strength. Ideally OTU fresh pilots would be posted to a unit re-fitting in the North, where they could gain more operational experience before heading south and to the battle proper – but this was not always possible. When postings appeared on the board at Hawarden that last week of August 1940, Pilot Officer Johnson and two other fledgling Spitfire pilots found themselves preparing to join 19 Squadron at Fowlmere in the Duxford Sector of 12 Group. They arrived on 3 September – on which day the Second World War was exactly one year old.

Duxford, near Cambridge, lay to the north-east of London, in East Anglia. The job of 12 Group's pilots was to protect convoys off the east coast, cover 11 Group's airfields whilst Air Vice-Marshal Park's fighters were engaged further forward, and defend the industrial Midlands and the North in the event of attacks on targets in those geographic areas. 19 Squadron was a regular fighter squadron with a fine record. Indeed, on 4 August 1938, 19 Squadron had received the RAF's first Spitfire, over the next few weeks converting from Gloster Gauntlet biplanes to the new eight-gun Supermarine monoplane. Thus 19 became the RAF's first Spitfire squadron. On 26 May 1940, however, the unit was mauled by Me 109s over Calais, when the Commanding Officer (CO), Squadron Leader Geoffrey Stephenson, led his Spitfires in a textbook Fighter Command Attack, in tight sections of three and throttled right back to match the slow speed of their *Stuka* prey. Unfortunately the Spitfires, in a hopeless tactical position, were bounced by high-flying Me 109s. Stephenson himself was shot down and captured, and Pilot Officer Watson was killed. Thereafter, throughout the Dunkirk fighting, the Squadron was led by the commander of 'A' Flight, Flight Lieutenant Brian Lane, who subsequently received a well-earned DFC for his efforts. A regular career officer without combat experience, however, Squadron Leader Phillip Pinkham AFC, was selected to replace Stephenson. 19 Squadron, though, had been re-equipped with the experimental Spitfire Mk IB, armed not with the normal eight machine-guns but with two 20-mm cannon. The new weapon proved problematic, and while Pinkham busied himself with evaluating and reporting on the problem, Lane continued to lead the unit in the air.

When the Air Ministry considered what armament it required the new RAF monoplane fighters to have, it had been decided that eight wing-mounted, rifle-calibre machine-guns were appropriate. In Germany the Me 109 had initially been armed with two 7.62-mm machine-guns located on top of the engine block, firing through the propeller arc. The German designers were disconcerted by news that the RAF fighters would be so comparatively heavily armed, but, as the 109's wing section was so thin, could not add extra machine-guns. Instead the Germans decided to wing-mount two 20-mm Oerlikon cannon, the ammunition drums of which were accommodated by way of external blisters on the upper and lower wing surfaces. This expedient proved significant. The missile fired by such a cannon is substantial, and can be ball, tracer or high explosive. The weapon's range is greater than a .303-calibre machine-gun. The rate of fire, however, is substantially slower than a machine-gun, requiring greater accuracy, but this disadvantage is easily offset by the weapon's potential destructive power. The fitting of cannons to the Me 109 proved to be far-sighted, and in this respect, as with the lack of fuel injection and constant-speed propellers, the RAF fighters were initially at a disadvantage. Indeed, cannon would have proved greatly advantageous during the Battle of Britain for attacking heavily armoured bombers, so it was a matter requiring urgent resolution and hence 19 Squadron's trialling the Mk IB. The problem was that the Spitfire's wing section was also thin, too thin to accommodate the Hispano-Suiza cannon's ammunition drum. Consequently the weapon was side-mounted, to lie flush within the wing, and belt-fed from an ammunition tray. In combat, however, the harsh g-forces involved meant that the wings flexed and became temporarily distorted – impeding the feed of rounds or ejection of spent cases. This jammed the cannon. As the Mk IB was only armed with cannon, and pilots frequently experienced stoppages in both guns, this clearly placed the pilot in an extremely dangerous position. After some frustrating weeks, morale suffered and it was clear that the position was untenable. Air Chief Marshal Dowding himself flew to Fowlmere and, after listening to the pilots' complaints, authorised that the Mk IBs be replaced with machine-gun-armed Mk IAs from Hawarden. In due course the matter was, fortunately, successfully resolved by way of correctly mounting the cannon and, as in the 109, accommodating the ammunition drum by way of external blisters. Moreover, it was decided that, again like the 109, the Spitfire should benefit from both cannon and machine-gun armament, each wing housing one cannon and two machine-guns. In this way the RAF pilots, like their German enemy, enjoyed the best of both worlds.

Such, then, was the position on 19 Squadron when Pilot Officer Johnson reported for duty. The cannon Spitfires were in the process of being exchanged with Mk IAs, this being completed on 4 September. More confident in their machine-gun-armed Spitfires, the Squadron's pilots were anxious to get at the *Luftwaffe*; they were less enthusiastic to wet-nurse new pilots. Johnnie recalled that:

> even though I had 23.50 hours on Spitfires, I wasn't really going to be any use to 19 Squadron until I had 50. And because these chaps were engaged in active operations against the enemy, they simply had not the time or inclination to provide further instruction to we three replacements. With little to do we three breakfasted at Duxford before driving over the Fowlmere satellite, where 19 Squadron was based. There we would hang around all day listening to the pilots talking about their fights, talking to the groundcrews and anyone else who would listen. We did odd errands for the Squadron Adjutant, like driving the Squadron transport into Cambridge to buy him razor blades, or helping him sort out the possessions of dead pilots. It was depressing. On paper we were members of 19 Squadron, but we were far from being admitted to their select and exclusive ranks, and with each day the gulf seemed to get wider.

On 5 September, Squadron Leader Pinkham led 19 Squadron into battle for the first time since taking command of the unit the previous June. In a melee over Kent, the 25-year-old career officer was shot down and killed in combat with Me 109s. That day, while 19 Squadron's CO was still 'missing', his fate unknown, Johnnie and his fellows were called for by the Squadron Adjutant and told to report to 616 Squadron. This unit, he explained, had been heavily engaged while flying from Kenley in 11 Group, but had been withdrawn to the quieter Coltishall Sector in Norfolk.

Unlike 19 Squadron, 616 would, he assured, have time to train inexperienced pilots before returning to a front-line sector station. Upon conclusion of the interview the Adjutant's telephone rang. He took the call, then looked up at the three pilots standing before him: 'They've found the CO. Probably dead when he crashed. Well, good luck with 616.' Command of 19 Squadron now, at last, passed to the exceptional and popular Brian Lane. As the Squadron mourned Pinkham's loss but celebrated Lane's promotion, Johnnie packed and left for Coltishall. Ironically, 616 was an AAF unit. Because these squadrons were locally raised, when they suffered casualties morale was badly affected. Replacements came from a variety of sources: regular airmen and, significantly, sergeant and officer pilots, like Johnnie, from the VR; foreign nationals, such as free Poles, Czechs, French and Belgians, not to mention Commonwealth pilots and even volunteers from neutral America, were also absorbed into these and regular RAF fighter squadrons. In a relatively short period of time, therefore, the whole identity of these hitherto socially elite AAF squadrons was completely changed, becoming both socially and racially diverse. So, several years after having been rejected by the AAF, Pilot Officer Johnson found himself posted to fly Spitfires with the AAF's 'South Yorkshire' Squadron.

At Coltishall, on 6 September 1940, Johnnie reported to his new CO, Squadron Leader H. F. 'Billy' Burton DFC, a veteran with a shared He 111 destroyed and another probably destroyed to his credit. Having fought over Dunkirk as a flight commander in 66 Squadron, on 3 September 1940 Burton had been promoted to Acting Squadron Leader and given command of 616 Squadron. The Squadron had been hotly engaged flying from Kenley in 11 Group, where it arrived from Leconfield in Yorkshire on 19 August. Badly led by Squadron Leader Marcus Robinson, over the next few days 616 Squadron was virtually annihilated. By the time the Squadron flew out of Kenley, Coltishall bound, on 3 September, the unit had lost eleven Spitfires destroyed and three damaged; five pilots had been killed, six wounded and one captured. Upon arrival at Coltishall only eight members of the company that had arrived at Kenley only a few days previously remained operational. Burton had been tasked with rebuilding and training the unit – the morale of which, needless to say, was low. Johnnie:

I did not like the atmosphere. The veterans kept to themselves and seemed aloof and very remote. Even to my inexperienced eye it was apparent that the quiet confidence of a well-led and disciplined team was missing from this group. There was a marked difference between the bunch of aggressive pilots I had met at Fowlmere and these too silent, apprehensive men.

Burton, however, immediately impressed:

Billy was a regular officer who had won the Cranwell Sword of Honour in 1936 ... he was an outstanding product of the Cranwell system. Exacting in his demands, he was always full of vitality and enthusiasm. I liked him at first sight and have never served under a better or more loyal officer.

Half an hour after this initial interview, Johnnie was airborne for 50 minutes in Spitfire X4055, being put through his paces by Squadron Leader Burton. Afterwards, the CO concluded that Johnson's performance was 'Not bad', but emphasised the need to keep a constantly good lookout. Johnnie:

No-one, so far, had really talked to us about tactics. We were, of course, very keen to know what it was like fighting the Me 109, and how to best shoot one down. At training school we virtually had to cajole instructors into imparting knowledge, and whilst at Duxford had listened keenly to what the Spitfire pilots of 19 Squadron and the Czech Hurricane pilots of 310 had to say – but this was all in the informal environment of either dispersal or the Mess. After that flight with Billy, though, he talked to me about the difficulties of deflection shooting and the technique of the killing shot from the line-astern or near line-astern positions; the duty of the number two whose job was not to shoot down aircraft but to ensure that the leader's tail was safe; the importance of keeping a good battle formation and the tactical use of sun, cloud and height. Here was a man, I thought, who knew what he was about, and under whose leadership we might actually get somewhere.

Over the next few days Johnnie flew various training flights, including aerobatics, formation practice, practice attacks, and air-to-ground firing. His logbook also clears up an ambiguity: Pilot Officer J. E. Johnson did indeed qualify for the coveted Battle of Britain Bar to the 1939–45 Star. For reasons as will shortly be explained, Johnnie saw no action during the Battle of Britain, which lasted from 10 July to 31 October 1940. When later assessing the criteria for award of the Battle of Britain Bar, the Air Ministry decreed that eligibility was dictated by having been on the strength of one of the seventy-two units deemed to have participated, and having made at least one operational flight between the relevant dates. On 11 September 1940, Johnnie flew Spitfire X4330 on a 15-minute 'X-Raid Patrol', thus qualifying for the Battle of Britain Bar and therefore inclusion among the names of Churchill's fabled 'Few'. An X-Raid was an unidentified radar plot, as yet unconfirmed as either hostile or friendly. Frequently the 'bogey' turned out not to be a 'bandit', i.e. an enemy aircraft, but a friendly machine going about its legitimate business. A patrol in pursuit of an X-Raid, therefore, could have three outcomes: interception of either an enemy or friendly aircraft, or no contact whatsoever. In this case it is assumed that the patrol was inconclusive. Nonetheless, this was an operational patrol which therefore qualifies Johnnie as a *bone fide* Battle of Britain pilot.

On 14 September 1940 Pilot Officer Johnson and a number of his squadron mates were enjoying a few pints in the Bell public house at nearby Norwich. The party was abruptly ended by the arrival of RAF policemen recalling all RAF personnel to their airfields immediately. Back at Coltishall, Johnnie discovered that Alert No. 1 – 'invasion imminent and probable within twelve hours' – had been issued. The nation's defences were being brought to the highest state of readiness, and an atmosphere of confusion prevailed at Coltishall. The whereabouts of Squadron Leader Burton were unknown, so Johnnie left the crowded ante-room to telephone dispersal, where he thought the CO and his flight commanders may be. As he hastened along the hallway to use the telephone, he almost collided with a squadron leader who purposefully stomped along with an awkward gait. It was to prove a significant meeting. Johnnie:

> His vital eyes gave me a swift scrutiny, at my pilot's brevet and one thin ring of a pilot officer. 'I say old boy, what's all the flap about?' he exclaimed, legs apart and putting a match to his pipe.
> 'I don't really know, Sir,' I replied. 'But there are reports of

enemy landings.'

The Squadron Leader pushed open the swing doors and stalked into the noisy, confused atmosphere of the ante-room. Fascinated, I followed in close line-astern because I thought I knew who this was. He took in the scene and then demanded in a loud voice, and in choice, fruity language, what all the panic was about. Half a dozen voices started to explain, and eventually he had some idea of the form. As he listened, his eyes swept round the room, lingered for a moment on us pilots and established a private bond of fellowship between us.

There was a moment's silence whilst he digested the news. 'So the bastards are coming. Bloody good show! Think of all those targets on those nice flat beaches. What shooting!' And he made a rude sound with his lips which was meant to resemble a ripple of machine-gun fire.

The effect was immediate and extraordinary. Officers went about their various tasks and the complicated machinery of the airfield began to function smoothly again. Later we were told that the reports of enemy landings were false and that we could revert to our normal readiness states. But the incident left me with a profound impression of the qualities of leadership displayed in a moment of tension by the assertive Squadron Leader. It was my first encounter with the already legendary Douglas Bader.

Douglas Bader was legendary indeed. A Cranwell graduate, this gifted aerobatic pilot – in spite of having been warned by his flight commander – crashed at Woodley airfield near Reading on 14 December 1931 while attempting a slow roll in a Bristol Bulldog. In his logbook Bader simply wrote that the blameworthy incident was a 'Bad show'. Indeed it was: the 21-year-old pilot was so badly injured in the crash that both legs were consequently amputated – one above the knee, the other below. Incredibly, Bader overcame this disability, learning to walk on 'tin' legs and even passed a flying test at the CFS. Unfortunately King's Regulations did not provide for limbless pilots, and so Bader was offered a chair-borne role. This he was unprepared to accept and so, with a heavy heart, left the service he loved so much in 1933. That year, though, Adolf Hitler and the Nazis came to power in Germany, beginning the countdown to the Second World War. At the time of Munich, Bader, by now a married man, offered his services to the Air Ministry as a trained pilot. This was declined. In March 1939, when Hitler invaded the remainder of Czechoslovakia, Bader tried again. Although another refusal ensued, this time the decision was tempered with the possibility of acceptance in the event of war. The declaration of war against Germany on 3 September 1939 was, therefore, Bader's salvation. On 18 October 1939, Bader arrived at the CFS Upavon for another flying test – acceptance of his services being conditional upon passing this. The examiner was an old Cranwell chum, Squadron Leader Rupert Leigh, the test being conducted in an American Harvard aircraft. This was a problem for Bader because all American aircraft have brakes operated by foot pedals. As this required flexing the ankles, Bader was unable to use foot brakes. Fortunately Leigh was sympathetic and dabbed the foot brakes himself. Bader passed the test, therefore, and the following month reported to the CFS Refresher Squadron. On 20 December, Flying Officer Bader soloed on the Hawker Hurricane, undertaking 'Circuits and low-flying'. Upon conclusion of the course, Bader's ability as a pilot was assessed as 'Exceptional'.

While at the CFS, Bader flew over to Duxford in a Hurricane. There he rekindled acquaintance with the Station Commander, Group Captain A. B. 'Woody' Woodhall, who introduced him to the 12 Group Air Officer Commanding (AOC), Air Vice-Marshal Trafford Leigh-Mallory. According to Woodhall:

> Over lunch Douglas used all of his considerable charm to persuade 'LM' to take him into one of his operational fighter squadrons. After lunch Douglas put on a most finished display of aerobatics, and this finally decided 'LM'. Douglas was posted almost at once to 19 Squadron at Duxford, which was commanded by his old Cranwell friend Geoffrey Stephenson. Douglas impressed us all with his terrific personality and amazing keenness and drive. I have never known his equal. Flying was his supreme passion and his enthusiasm infected us all.

On 7 February 1940, Flying Officer Bader was posted to fly Spitfires with 19 Squadron – this happy circumstance having been greatly assisted by his Cranwell connections.

Flying the Spitfire, however, was a different proposition to the biplane fighters Bader had flown in the 1930s. By now, Spitfires were being fitted with the two-pitch de Havilland propeller, providing the benefit of fine pitch for take-off and coarse for cruising. The biplanes and Hurricanes that Bader had hitherto flown had fixed pitch airscrews, so this improvement was new to him. Moreover, the new monoplanes also had retractable undercarriages. These technical advances caused Bader problems: Bader was 'embarrassed' on one occasion when he forgot to raise his Spitfire's undercarriage, and crashed another aircraft when he failed to select fine pitch upon take-off. Nonetheless, his old Cranwell chum Squadron Leader Stephenson endorsed his performance on the Spitfire as 'exceptional'. Being junior to Stephenson, his former Cranwell and squadron equal, however, did not suit: Bader therefore persuaded another Cranwell contemporary, Squadron Leader 'Tubby' Mermagen, CO of Duxford's other Spitfire squadron, 222, to take him as a flight commander. On 16 April 1940, therefore, Douglas Bader was promoted to Acting Flight Lieutenant and posted to command Mermagen's 'A' Flight.

Bader was serving with 222 Squadron when Operation DYNAMO began, the air operation supporting the Dunkirk evacuation. Operating from Hornchurch on 1 June 1940, Bader claimed his first victories when he destroyed an Me 109 and damaged a 110 over the French coast. On 23 June, Flight Lieutenant Bader crashed another Spitfire while landing at night, but yet again his logbook was endorsed 'exceptional' – this time by Cranwell contemporary Squadron Leader Mermagen. Indeed, Mermagen and Wing Commander Woodhall recommended to Air Vice-Marshal Leigh-Mallory that the buccaneering and energetic Bader was just the man to restore morale to the Canadian 242 Squadron – a Hurricane unit having had a particularly bad time during the Battle of France. On 2 July, Bader was promoted to Acting Squadron Leader and took command of 242 at Coltishall, another sector station in Leigh-Mallory's 12 Group.

Upon arrival at Coltishall, the disgruntled Canadians were unimpressed to discover that their new CO had no legs. In an after-dinner speech some years later, Bader himself described events:

> The AOC told me that the 242 (Canadian) Squadron was a pretty brassed-off bunch, they lacked discipline and thought that I might

be some use in getting the thing straight. So I rushed off thinking
that this would be absolutely splendid – but when I got to the
station where this squadron was I had some difficulty getting
in because the chap on the gate said 'What's the password?', to
which I replied 'You stupid prick, I don't know!' I found myself
the following morning in conjunction with my Adjutant, an
elderly gentleman of the finest class who had been Member for
the Isle of Wight for the past plus 500 years, and fought in World
War One, he took me into a dispersal hut where these chaps were
lying about on beds, wearing Mae-Wests and flying clothes, and
all reading comic strips. He said 'Gentlemen, this is your new
Squadron Commander, Squadron Leader Bader', and for some
extraordinary reason, because I had been trained at the RAF
College Cranwell, I thought they might stand up – in fact some
of them lowered their comics, looked over the top, obviously
didn't care for what they saw, put the comics back up and went on
reading! There was one chap who was lying with his back to me.
He actually turned over, had a look, then turned back again and
went on reading! I then told then Adjutant that I wanted to see all
of the pilots in my office in half an hour's time. They arrived and
I gave them what I thought was a reasonable three-minute talk.
When I finished I said 'Has anybody got anything to say?' There
was a long silence, then from the back a voice said 'Horseshit!'
Again, they hadn't taught me at Cranwell what to do in such a
situation! As I was getting rather red around the neck and face,
and was about to make a bloody fool of myself, the same voice
added 'Sir!'

Bader's response was typical of his dynamic and aggressive personality:
for the next hour and ten minutes he provided a daredevil demonstration
of aerobatics over the airfield. Upon conclusion, there was clearly
no suggestion that this legless officer was a 'passenger'. Indeed, as
Wing Commander Woodhall wrote: '242 Squadron soon became an
enthusiastic team led by their single-minded and swashbuckling CO.'
This was the first real example of Bader's style of leadership at its best:
on 9 July 1940, 242 Squadron was declared fully operational. The
following day, the Battle of Britain officially began: one day later, it
was the 'passenger' who chalked up 242 Squadron's first aerial victory
– a Do 17 reconnaissance bomber destroyed off Cromer.

At Coltishall, however, Bader soon became frustrated at the lack of action and monotonous patrols over convoys chugging around the east coast. Off the south-east coast, however, the action was becoming increasingly fierce, as the fighter forces of both sides clashed over Channel-bound convoys. As the enemy air assault continued, 11 Group became stretched, but Air Vice-Marshal Park maintained his policy of intercepting raids with small formations of fighters. This was to preserve his fighters, preventing them being destroyed en masse. It was also in compliance with Air Chief Marshal Dowding's System of Air Defence. So a situation developed where the pilots of 11 Group were hotly engaged, sometimes several times a day, while those in 12 Group, including Bader, kicked their heels around awaiting the call to scramble – which rarely came. And so, while Spitfires and Hurricanes were embroiled in deadly combat over southern England, 12 Group had no choice but to continue their monotonous convoy patrols, occasionally intercepting small formations of or lone German bombers. They were, however, providing an essential reserve. Fighter Command had always to maintain a substantial reserve to counter any threat to the Midlands and industrial North. Indeed, the System also provided for 12 Group's fighters to move forward and patrol 11 Group's airfields in the event of Park's fighters being committed to battle further south. This was, of course, essential, as the airfields had to be kept secure. To Bader, however, this scenario was unacceptable – as he was just not getting the action he craved.

On occasion, 242 Squadron flew south, to Duxford, and there awaited the call to reinforce 11 Group. On 30 August 1940, 242 Squadron was patrolling at 15,000 feet over North Weald as a precautionary measure given that sixty He 111s of I/KG 1 and II/KG 53 had crossed the coast north of the Thames. The bombers soon separated, I/KG 1 heading for the Vauxhall Motor Works and aerodrome at Luton while II/KG 53, being the larger formation, flew westwards towards the Handley Page Aircraft Factory at Radlett. Vectored towards II/KG 53, 242 Squadron soon saw the biggest raid it had so far encountered – this aerial armada being nothing like the small numbers of bombers previously encountered. Attacking from the tactically advantageous up-sun position, 242 Squadron engaged. After the subsequent 'party', Bader's pilots claimed seven Me 110s destroyed and three probables,

and five He 111s destroyed. It was an impressive score, leading
to numerous congratulatory signals. Air Vice-Marshal Leigh-
Mallory telephoned 242 Squadron's CO personally, during which
conversation Bader put to his AOC that had he commanded more
fighters then the execution would have been greater. Leigh-Mallory
– who although commanding a fighter group had no personal
experience as a fighter pilot, and, the evidence proves conclusively,
had a poor appreciation of the tried and tested System – agreed.
Arrangements were made for 242 Squadron to operate in future
out of Duxford, Bader leading a formation comprising not only his
Canadians but also the Czech 310 Hurricane Squadron, and the
Spitfires of 19 Squadron. The theory was, therefore, that a wing
of thirty-six 12 Group fighters would sally forth to engage the
enemy over 11 Group. The problem was that Bader's theory was
flawed from the outset: contrary to his belief in the heat of battle
– remembering that this huge formation was unlike anything 242
had previously encountered – 242 was not, in fact, the only RAF
fighter squadron engaged. In reality, the Hurricanes of 11 Group's
1, 56 and 501 Squadrons were all engaged and scored kills, as did
the Spitfires of 222 Squadron. Indeed, recent research indicates
that only two Me 110s were definitely destroyed by 242 Squadron.
Although the confused air fighting involved makes it impossible to
be certain regarding any further claims, that is not to say that 242
did not destroy more – but Bader's pilots certainly did not destroy
anything like the number with which they were credited without
question. The reason for this is because the greater the number of
fighters engaged, the more confused the fighting becomes – several
pilots, for example, can attack the same enemy aircraft oblivious
to the presence of their comrades, meaning that particular enemy
aircraft becomes multiplied on the balance sheet. Nonetheless,
both Leigh-Mallory and Bader were convinced that large fighter
formations were the way forward – as it certainly was so far as
getting 12 Group into the battle proper was concerned.

On 7 September 1940, Bader led the so-called 12 Group or
Duxford Wing into action for the first time. On this day the Germans
began bombing London round the clock. Bader's Duxford fighters
were ordered off to patrol North Weald and sighted another large
enemy formation. Bader's Wing, however, was below the raiders
and forced to climb over the Thames Estuary at full throttle to

intercept. While at this tactical disadvantage, however, the 12 Group fighters were attacked by Me 109s – lethal enemy fighters not present when 242 Squadron were engaged on 30 August. Under such an attack it proved impossible to maintain cohesion. The Wing split up, Bader's pilots attacking individually. Again, however, 12 Group's claims were impressive on paper: twenty destroyed, five probables and six damaged, offset against two Hurricanes destroyed (one pilot killed), and three more damaged. Again, though, research indicates that the destruction of but six enemy aircraft can definitely be accredited to the Duxford Wing, representing an over-claiming factor of three to one. This pattern continued throughout the Battle of Britain – providing a completely false impression, therefore, of the value of 'Big Wings'. At the time, however, the tactic found favour with influential officers of air rank as well as politicians, all keen to defeat the *Luftwaffe* in the most efficient possible way. Bader's Duxford Wing – to which was soon added another two squadrons – appeared to provide that opportunity. By comparison, 11 Group's claims were much smaller – suggesting that mass fighter tactics were more effective than the tactics employed by Air Chief Marshal Dowding's System and used by 11 Group's Air Vice-Marshal Park. The evidence, now that historians have had the time and opportunity to cross-reference combat claims with actual German losses, confirms that 12 Group's claims were highly inflated, while 11 Group's were infinitely more accurate. This means that the tactics used by Dowding and Park were entirely correct – while those propounded by Douglas Bader – a comparatively junior and inexperienced squadron leader, supported by his AOC, Air Vice-Marshal Leigh-Mallory – were not.

This, then, was the state of play at that first meeting between Pilot Officer Johnson and Squadron Leader Bader at Coltishall, amid the panic of an invasion scare. Bader's reaction was another example of his unique style of leadership, which, although brash and buccaneering in many respects, was undoubtedly inspirational when it mattered most. Bader would soon become a huge influence on the young Johnnie Johnson, who in due course joined Bader's inner circle. Both men were great leaders, but each, as we will see, led in very different ways. As Johnnie said, 'Leadership is a gift. You can learn the mechanics at staff college, of course, but that final indefinable bit that makes a great leader is a gift, like that of a great artist or writer.' Bader had that gift. So, it would later transpire, did Johnnie Johnson – who was himself greatly impressed and inspired by his first chance encounter with Douglas Bader.

The feared German invasion of southern England fortunately never came. On 15 September 1940, though, Fighter Command faced its greatest test so far, as the enemy launched repeated heavy attacks against London and other targets. For 616 Squadron, rebuilding to full-strength at Kirton-in-Linsey in 12 Group, there would be no action on that great day, still celebrated annually as 'Battle of Britain Day'. Johnnie flew three times: a squadron practice battle climb, and air firing practice at Manby. There was, however, a problem concerning the young pilot from Leicestershire, one which was threatening to destroy his flying career. Johnnie:

> At this time my right shoulder was causing me a great deal of anxiety. I had a minor crash at Sealand during training which had wrenched it badly. The old rugby injury collar-bone break was very sore. I had to be carefully when donning my parachute and tightening the cockpit harness. I started packing the shoulder with cotton wool, but that wasn't all: the fingers in my right hand sometimes felt cold and life-less. The Spitfire's fabric ailerons, however, dictated that stick pressure in a dive was so high that it took a lot of strength to control the aircraft. This aggravated the shoulder injury. Whenever I could I held the control column in my left-hand, usually used for controlling the throttle, but if the CO or Ken Holden, the senior pilot officer, gave me dog-fight practice I had also to use my right hand – as this was very much a two-handed business. I began landing the aircraft with my left-hand, but this was dangerous because sometimes you needed a quick burst of throttle to ease her down. It was a difficult situation. Every day the condition got worse, whilst daily acceptance by the veterans increased – the formal 'Johnson' had by now changed to the warmer 'Johnnie', which stuck with me ever after. So I didn't want to see the doctors for fear of being taken off the squadron. I remembered that before playing rugby again I had a course of massage and heat-treatment, and hoped re-visiting this might do the trick. So I took a young doctor into my confidence in the Mess. He kindly took me to sick quarters for an off-the-record examination – but whilst this was in progress the Senior Medical

Officer (SMO) appeared. They both told me to continue packing the shoulder with cotton wool, and were charming – but I went away with an uneasy feeling. The following day Billy Burton sent for me and, in frosty silence, accompanied me to the Station Commander's office. He, Stephen Hardy, told me that the doctors had reported the fact that I was supposedly suffering from an unspecified affliction to the right shoulder. As this had clearly not troubled me during training, he was considering transferring me to instruct on genteel Tiger Moths at an EFTS. Disaster. The matter was clearly distasteful to him and I immediately realised why: I was suspected of being 'lacking in morale fibre' (LMF) – cowardice, effectively. Hardy gave me a choice: become an instructor or go under the knife. Without hesitation I said 'When can I go into hospital, sir?' This broke the tension.

Arrangements were made immediately for Johnnie to have treatment at the RAF Hospital in Rauceby, Lincolnshire. Pilot Officer Johnson left for Rauceby on 20 September, undergoing a painful but successful corrective operation soon afterwards. Before leaving Kirton, Squadron Leader Burton had promised to take Johnnie back once he was fit: 'It was a second chance. All I wanted was to live and fight with men like Billy Burton and Ken Holden, so I was very grateful and happy indeed to return to 616 Squadron on 28 December 1940.' It was certainly a close call – which so nearly ended the career of the man who would ultimately become the RAF's most outstanding fighter pilot, and, so some say, wing leader, of the 1939–45 war.

On New Year's Eve 1940, Squadron Leader Burton checked out Pilot Officer Johnson in Magister L8151. Johnnie's fitness to fly was approved after a 45-minute flight practising circuits and landings. Johnnie was posted to 'A' Flight, commanded by Ken Holden, who was now a flight lieutenant. Indeed, there had inevitably been many changes on the squadron in Johnnie's absence. On 19 September, 616 Squadron – by then considered operational once more – relieved 611 Squadron in Douglas Bader's 12 Group Wing. On various occasions thereafter, the squadron flew from Kirton and operated from Fowlmere, near Duxford, with the sector's other Spitfire squadron, 19, to which Johnnie had initially been posted. On 27 September, while flying with the Wing, 616 Squadron lost its last pilot to die in the Battle of Britain. Two days later, enemy attacks were considered sufficiently reduced for 616 to return to Kirton and discontinue operations from Duxford. Although the association was a short one, it would prove significant the following year, when, as we will see, 616 became very closely associated with Douglas Bader – having made his acquaintance during this handful of Battle of Britain sorties.

New Year's Day 1941 saw Johnnie fly the Magister thrice more. His final flight that day was in Spitfire K9996, described as 'handling' and lasting an hour. Numerous further training flights followed, significantly including a 'Wing Patrol' with other 12 Group squadrons out of Wittering on 14 January. As previously explained, the idea of using large formations of fighters had been argued by Douglas Bader, leading to him achieving the support of his AOC, Air Vice-Marshal Leigh-Mallory. Subsequently Bader had frequently led a wing of between three and five squadrons from Duxford, the combat claims of which were highly impressive – although research has since proven that they were not in fact. Soon after the Battle of Britain, some say because of the heated controversy that consequently broke out over tactics, Air Chief Marshal Dowding and Air Vice-Marshal Park were respectively replaced by Air Chief Marshal Sholto Douglas and Air Vice-Marshal Leigh-Mallory. Both men endorsed the idea that wings should become standard operating procedure, in both attack and defence. During late 1940 a new policy was decided of 'Leaning in France', i.e. taking the war offensively across the Channel to the Germans the following 'season'. These sorties were initially very limited. The first was flown by two Spitfires of 66 Squadron on 20 December 1940, which attacked an enemy airfield at either Berck or Le Touquet on the French coast. The idea was that these operations, called simply 'Rhubarbs', were to be carried out by either single fighters or formations not exceeding six, using low altitude and cloud cover to escape detection. The purpose of Rhubarbs was to 'attack and destroy enemy aircraft, or, if impractical, suitable ground military objectives'. Although the tempo of such operations increased, the RAF fighters failed to draw the *Luftwaffe* to battle. Rhubarbs were therefore used simply for opportunist 'seek and destroy' missions. On 9 January 1941, however, five RAF fighter squadrons swept over France in wing formation. Once more the enemy very sensibly failed to respond, German fighter tacticians appreciating full well that an enemy fighter is only dangerous if intercepted. Far better, therefore, to remain on the ground – letting the RAF waste fuel on harmless sweeps overhead. Nonetheless, these early offensive operations in wing strength, and the fact that home-based fighter squadrons were practising flying together in such formations, provide an indication of what lay ahead.

On 22 August 1940, 616 Squadron's Pilot Officer Hugh 'Cocky' Dundas had been shot down over Dover by none other than Major Werner Mölders – the so-called 'Father of German Air Fighting' himself – baling out, wounded. One of the squadron's original auxiliary members, Dundas returned to 616 on 13 September, by which time the depleted unit had been withdrawn from Kenley to re-fit at Kirton. Dundas was also a member of Flight Lieutenant Ken Holden's 'A' Flight. On 15 January 1941, Dundas, by then a flying officer, was on the board to lead Red Section. At 1342 hours, the section was scrambled, with Johnnie flying Red Two, to patrol a convoy passing 34 miles off North Coates. At 15,000 feet over the convoy, the Controller alerted Red Section that an enemy aircraft was approaching from the east. Cleverly, the Controller climbed the pair of Spitfires to 16,000 feet and positioned them to attack from out of the sun. Johnnie's combat report described events:

> The enemy aircraft (E/A) was sighted at about 1420 hours and Red One ordered line astern and dived to attack E/A. The latter went into a steep dive, turning towards the East. As soon as Red One had delivered his attack, I followed in and gave two bursts of five and four seconds, from astern and starboard, allowing for deflection and aiming for the nose of the aircraft. During this time I experienced return fire and broke away at 200 yards to starboard and climbed round to position my second attack. I again opened fire at 300–100 yards from the same position as before, and gave a five second burst and broke away to port. This time I experienced no return fire. After breaking away from this attack I lost sight of the E/A and Red One, so returned to base, landing at 1446.

Back at base, the Squadron 'Spy', Flight Lieutenant E. P. Gibbs, credited Flying Officer Dundas and Pilot Officer Johnson with a half share each of a damaged Do 17. Years later, Johnnie added that:

> Already our listening services had intercepted a distress signal from the Dornier to its base in Holland, and it seemed doubtful that it could struggle back to the Dutch coast. As we had not seen it crash into the sea, we couldn't claim it as destroyed or, indeed, probably destroyed. So we had to content ourselves with sharing a 'damaged' Do 17.

In his logbook, Johnnie conciliatorily added 'Believed destroyed'.

Whatever the enemy bomber's fate, it had been a significant engagement given that, as Johnnie wrote, 'this incident marked the beginning of my personal score against the *Luftwaffe*'. It would be the first of many combats with German aircraft – but the only time Johnnie would engage an enemy bomber. With this experience under his belt, and another 16.35 flying hours on Spitfires recorded in his logbook that first month of 1941, Johnnie and his fellows in 616 Squadron looked forward to the fast approaching 'season' of better weather. Little did they know how dramatic the months ahead would be.

2

The Bader Factor:
Tangmere Wing

February 1941 saw a continuation of training flights for the pilots of 616 Squadron at Kirton. At this time the night Blitz of winter 1940/41 was in full swing. British nocturnal defences remained embryonic and inadequate, enemy bombers operating largely unmolested under cover of darkness. Desperate measures were introduced, including so-called 'Fighter Nights', in which the sky over British cities was filled with Spitfires and other day-fighters. None of these aircraft, though, had any airborne radar to assist interception, the idea being simply that with so many fighters crowding the night sky, some pilots at least would contact the enemy. The Spitfire, however, was not designed as a night-flying aircraft, one problem being that the two rows of exhausts either side of the engine cowling and in front of the pilot spoiled his night vision. Although the odd bomber was encountered and destroyed, overall the tactic was unsuccessful. The pressing of Spitfires into this role, however, explains the increasing amount of nocturnal training flights made by 616 Squadron during this period. Johnnie's logbook, for example, records many of these sorties, especially 'dusk landings'. Daytime wing practices and general dog-fighting skills, however, were a daily feature. Indeed, on 22 February, Johnnie flew Spitfire R6611, 'QJ-F', out of Wittering, recording in his personal log that the 'Duty Wing ... attacked Me 110 from 24,000 to 7,000 feet', damaging the intruder.

In late February came exciting news: the squadron was moving – south. Johnnie:

Billy Burton told us that we were going back into the line, and if all worked out we would remain in the south for the spring and summer – which, due to the better weather, was the air-fighting 'season' we all looked forward to. Speculation was rife as to our destination: would it be Kenley, Biggin Hill, North Weald or

Hornchurch? No. It was Tangmere, a famous fighter station on
the South coast, near Chichester and on the Channel coast.

On 26 February, 616 Squadron flew south, relieving 65 Squadron
at Tangmere. The two units exchanged aircraft: in a secondary
role, 616 Squadron had flown obsolete Spitfire Mk IAs of Battle
of Britain vintage, while at Tangmere 65 Squadron were operating
the new Mk IIA. By this time Johnnie had flown 10.40 operational
hours and had fired his guns in anger:

> We very much welcomed the prospect of getting stuck in from
> Tangmere. Billy told us that if the Germans resumed their air
> assault on Britain we would 'have our work cut out'. If not, then
> we would be taking the war to them, across the Channel.

Throughout this winter, Fighter Command was reorganised for the
coming season. At the end of 1940, Fighter Command's strength
was 1,243 pilots. By early 1941 that figure had increased to 1,665.
The huge Castle Bromwich Aircraft Factory was also producing
Spitfires at full capacity. Spitfire production in 1940 had totalled
1,246, increasing to 2,518 in 1941. Moreover, the Hurricane's
deficiency as a high-altitude fighter meant that the Spitfire now
ruled supreme: the Hawker fighter was withdrawn for use in
secondary roles at home or service overseas, while the Spitfire
became the mainstay. As previously mentioned, Fighter Command's
new masters, Douglas and Leigh-Mallory, were keen to encourage
an offensive outlook; as the latter said: 'We have stopped licking
our wounds. We are now going over to the offensive. Last year the
fighting was desperate. Now we are entitled to be cocky.' Although
Fighter Command's new masters were exponents of mass fighter
tactics, their squadrons practising operating in wing formations
from the sector stations, there was no formal arrangement as
to who would lead each wing. During these early sorties, wings
were generally led by the senior squadron commander, but there
was no dedicated wing leader or wing mentality. Leigh-Mallory
recognised that change was required. On 7 December 1940, he
shortlisted suitably experienced officers for appointment as the
first formal wing leaders. This new post would be officially known
as 'Wing Commander (Flying)'. Each sector station was to have its

own wing of three Spitfire squadrons, under the overall control of the wing commander. When 616 Squadron arrived at Tangmere, however, the new Wing Leader had yet to be appointed.

The pilots of 616 Squadron spent their first day at Tangmere visiting the operations room, meeting controllers and being briefed on current enemy tactics by intelligence officers. While the Spitfire Mk II was an improvement over the Mk I, enjoying the benefits of a more powerful engine, which ran on 100 as opposed to 85 octane petrol, providing an extra 2,000 feet of ceiling, the Germans were now operating the curvaceous Me 109F, which was superior to the more angular Me 109E of Battle of Britain days. Sufficiently updated, during their first few weeks at Tangmere, nothing much changed for 616 Squadron, which continued the usual training flights. These were interrupted only by the occasional, uneventful wing sweep over the Channel or French coast, or a convoy patrol. On 17 March 1941, however, there was exciting news. Johnnie:

> Billy Burton strode into dispersal with some momentous news: 'Listen, you chaps. Fighter Command is appointing wing commanders to lead the wings. The first two have been selected. 'Sailor' Malan is going to Biggin and Douglas Bader is coming here! He has just been on the blower and will fly with us. We shall be in the thick of all the scrapping. He arrives tomorrow.'

The other Spitfire squadrons at Tangmere were 145 Squadron, commanded by Squadron Leader Jack Leather, and Squadron Leader John Ellis's 610. Neither CO was an Old Cranwellian, whereas Squadron Leader Burton was. Moreover, neither 145 nor 610 Squadrons were known to Wing Commander Bader – whereas 616 had flown in his 12 Group Wing during the Battle of Britain. He trusted Burton, a fellow Cranwellian, and knew the squadron – hence why he chose to lead the Tangmere Wing at the head of Burton's unit.

Although 145, 610 and 616 Squadrons were known as the Tangmere Wing, they were not actually based at that sector station, but dispersed at nearby satellites: 610 and 616 at Westhampnett (now Goodwood), and 145 at Merston. Sergeant Alan Smith was at readiness in 616 Squadron's dispersal on 18 March 1941:

I heard the roar of a Spitfire. It dived low, climbed, did a half-roll, lowered its undercarriage whilst inverted, rolled out, side-slipped and made a perfect landing. Out of the cockpit climbed Wing Commander Douglas Bader – who walked with his distinctive gait into our dispersal. He announced himself, said that he would be leading the Tangmere Wing, and would do so with 616 Squadron. He knew Flying Officer Cocky Dundas and Pilot Officer Johnnie Johnson, and said: 'You'll be Red Three, Cocky, and you, Johnnie, will be Red Four.' Looking around he caught my eye and said 'Who are you?'

'Sergeant Smith, sir.'

'Right, you fly as my Red Two and God help you if you don't watch my tail!' I couldn't believe my ears! It was like God asking me to keep an eye on heaven for him!

The following day, Wing Commander Bader led his new Wing on a Channel sweep. Johnnie flew as Red Three in 'Dogsbody Section', recording in his logbook 'Look Out!!', which requires explanation. Johnnie:

We flew in line-astern formation, each squadron in sections of four. Cocky was Red Two, Bader, of course, Red One, and Pilot Officer 'Nip' Hepple brought the rear as Red Four. As we climbed across the Channel I spotted three 109s only a few hundred feet higher than us, travelling in the same direction. They hadn't seen us and 145 Squadron, which was higher than the 109s, were perfectly positioned to attack. I should have calmly reported over the R/T the number, type and position of the enemy. I did not do so. In my excitement I simply shouted 'Look out, Dogsbody!' (this being the Wing Commander's radio call sign). This represented a warning of utmost danger, of being bounced. The other pilots took rapid evasive action, breaking in all directions. Our tight formation was reduced to a shambles, and we returned to Tangmere individually. Bader came into our dispersal and angrily said 'Now who's the clot who shouted "Look out"?' I admitted that it was me. 'Very well. Now tell us what we had to "Look out" for?'

'Well sir, there were three 109s a few hundred feet above…'

'Three 109s! We could have clobbered the lot! But your girlish scream made us think there were fifty of the brutes behind!' This humiliating public rebuke hurt deeply, but it was well justified. Douglas, though, was always quick to forgive and gave me an encouraging grin as he stomped out of dispersal. It was a lesson in leadership that I never forgot.

Due to Johnnie's error, the Tangmere Wing's first operation had been a dismal failure. Suffice it to say that in future the warning 'Look out' would not be used.

Johnnie's logbook during this period indicates a number of patrols seeking German bombers over base. At 0055 hours on 10 April, a Ju 88 successfully attacked the wing: five airmen were killed and fourteen wounded. Much damage was also caused. On 15 April 1941 the Tangmere Wing once more swept high over the Channel, escorting bombers back from France, but did not meet the enemy. Such operations would become an increasing feature of the Tangmere Wing pilots' lives. Fighter sweeps over north-west France had failed to provoke the required reaction from the *Luftwaffe*. It was therefore decided to add a small force of light bombers, usually Bristol Blenheims of 2 Group, Bomber Command, to the formation. Raids were to be mounted against such targets as enemy airfields, power stations and railway marshalling yards, meaning that the German fighters would have to respond. The RAF bombers were to be escorted by great numbers of Spitfires, which would, it was hoped, destroy the enemy en mass. Codenamed 'Circus', these were complex operations requiring much planning and co-ordination at Fighter Command level, because fighters from 10, 11 and 12 Groups were involved. This was in direct contrast to the so-called 'Rhubarb', which could simply be initiated by a flight commander. In the Circus scenario fighter wings were given specific responsibilities:

- Close Escort – This wing literally surrounded and remained with the bombers at all times.
- Escort Cover – A wing that protected the Close Escort.
- High Cover – Positioned to prevent enemy fighters bouncing the Close and Escort Cover wings.
- Top Cover – Geographically restricted to the bombers' route, but with a roving commission to sweep the sky in advance of the main formation.

- Target Support – Independently routed fighters flying directly to and covering the target area.
- Withdrawal Cover – Fighters supporting the return flight, by which time escorting fighters would be running low on fuel and ammunition.
- Fighter Diversion – A wing, or even wings, engaged on a diversionary sweep to keep hostile aircraft away from the target area during 'Ramrod' operations – similar to a Circus but aimed at the destruction of a specific target, as opposed to a mere nuisance raid.

Circus Number One had been undertaken on 10 January 1941. Two RAF fighters were lost; although there were several claims for the destruction of German fighters, not one Me 109 was, in fact, lost. It was an ominous start to the 'Non-Stop Offensive' and would soon become an all too common scenario. Involving so many aircraft, which milled around over Beachy Head as squadrons and wings formed up, these huge formations became appropriately known as 'Beehives'. On one occasion, for example, Pilot Officer David Cox, a Spitfire pilot with 19 Squadron, participated in a Circus to the German airfield at St-Omer: 'It was an incredible sight: one Stirling bomber escorted by 200 Spitfires!' On 21 April the Tangmere Wing escorted eighteen Blenheims to Le Havre, but the bombers were unable to locate their target. Running low on fuel, Wing Commander Bader reluctantly waggled his wings as a signal for the Wing to return across the sea to England – leaving the bombers to their fate. It must be remembered that the RAF fighter pilots had to contend with two sea crossings on these flights, and yet the single-engined Spitfire was neither designed nor intended as a long-range fighter. This lack of range, of course, severely restricted the depth of penetration into enemy-occupied France. Sergeant Bob Morton recalled that during the return flight from Le Havre the pilots of 616 Squadron had:

> concentrated more on our fuel gauges than keeping lookout. Only a stream of golden rain past my canopy, and the sight of my number two rearing up out of control, alerted me that I was being attacked! I shouted a warning to the Squadron before turning steeply in time to see two Me 109s haring back to France. There

was no point trying to catch them so I concentrated on my number two, Sergeant Sellars. I saw that he had baled out and was floating above a mass of creamy foam that I later came to associate with a ditched aircraft. I circled him for a time, providing a fix, then made for home before my petrol ran out. I later learned that whilst I circled Sellars Flight Lieutenant Colin MacFie had protected me. In spite of Air Sea Rescue (ASR) resources, and a search of the area by the entire squadron immediately after re-fuelling, Sellars was never found.

Sergeant Sellars, of 'B' Flight, had been shot down by *Leutnant* Votel of I/JG 2, some 20 miles south of the Isle of Wight. The operation had been a long flight, lasting 1 hour and 50 minutes, which pushed the endurance envelope somewhat. Afterwards, Johnnie participated in the search for Sellars, that flight lasting 1 hour and 20 minutes. That night, the Spitfire pilots went to bed exhausted.

The following day, Group Captain 'Woody' Woodhall arrived at Tangmere, pending taking over as Station Commander and 'Boss Controller' on 24 April. Woodhall had been Station Commander at Duxford during the Battle of Britain, during which time he had controlled Bader's 'Big Wing'. Air Vice-Marshal Leigh-Mallory was putting his old team back together. Woodhall, who would later play a crucial role in the ferocious air battles over Malta, was undoubtedly the most outstanding fighter controller of the war. In high-stress situations over the Channel or enemy-occupied France, many a Spitfire pilot would have occasion to be grateful for Woodhall's calm and steady voice in their headphones – inspiring confidence and providing reassurance. He would constantly monitor weather conditions, such as changing head winds or the sudden appearance of low cloud that shrouded British airfields, advising the Wing accordingly. When the Spitfires landed, Woodhall would always be waiting at Westhampnett to debrief the sortie with Wing Commander Bader and his squadron commanders. In the Mess, Group Captain Woodhall was frequently at the centre of boisterous parties, playing his accordion or saxophone with some talent!

The Tangmere Wing's official radio call sign was 'Greenline Bus' – soon unofficially known as 'Bader's Bus Company'. Woodhall's Tangmere Control became 'Beetle, the Beachy Head rendezvous point 'Diamond'. Sergeant Ron Rayner:

There would be this mass of Spitfires orbiting Diamond, going
round and round in circles over the English coast until everyone
was together. Then Bader would say 'Okay, we're going', and the
Beehive would then proceed across the Channel to France. The
position of the sun, as ever, was crucial, dictating the Beehive's
route. During morning operations, for example, the Beehive
would cross the French coast, both in and outward bound,
over Gravelines, to the north-east. In the afternoon it would
cross further to the south-west, near Boulogne or Le Touquet,
codenamed 'Golf Course', after the upmarket coastal resort's
famous course. Between 1100 and 1400 hours the sun was high
– therefore favouring the German fighter pilots who flew from
such airfields as that near St-Omer – the 'Big Wood'. The French
coast was also a dangerous flak belt. Once battle was joined,
wings inevitably scattered, standing orders being issued that if
separated over France, pilots should dive for the deck and come
home immediately. In Woodhall's Operations Room worked the
'Beauty Chorus', plotters of the Women's Auxiliary Air Force
(WAAF) who pushed around counters, representing friendly and
hostile aircraft, on a large map table. A tannoy system enabled
them to hear the action when battle was joined. On occasions,
however, the oaths uttered by men in combat were considered
unsuitable listening for female hours, and Woodhall often
switched off the tannoy.

Johnnie:

> Well Douglas was very 'salty', you know, always 'effing and
> blinding'. Woodhall would shout up and say 'Come on, Douglas,
> I've got WAAFs down here', and Bader would just reply 'Oh its
> all right, Woody, they don't mind, I'll just come and see 'em and
> apologise!'

In addition to Woodhall's arrival, that April there were soon other
changes in the Tangmere Sector, as Bader began reorganising his
new command, putting 'his people' in place. Ken Holden of 616
was promoted to command 610, and the Canadian Stan Turner,
previously one of Bader's flight commanders in 242 Squadron (and
he of 'Horseshit!' fame), replaced Leather as CO of 145. Charles

Bush and Denis Crowley-Milling, both of whom had flown with Bader during the Battle of Britain, were also brought in from 242 Squadron to command flights in Holden's 610 Squadron, as was Charles Arthur, who was given one of Turner's flights. The Tangmere Wing was now ready to go to war in earnest.

On 23 April, Johnnie flew the dawn patrol over 'Diamond'. Other Tangmere Wing aircraft flew Rhubarbs, in pairs, over France. Flying Officer Dundas and Sergeant Mabbett of 616 Squadron's 'A' Flight returned safely following an uneventful prowl around the Abbeville area. Then Flight Lieutenant MacFie and Sergeant McDevette of 'B' Flight went over the Channel to the Cherbourg peninsula. There MacFie strafed Maupertus airfield, machine-gunning seven JG 2 Me 109s that were scrambling to intercept the Spitfires. McDevette, however, was never seen again. Johnnie:

> As previously explained when I began flying Spitfires no-one seemed to want to talk about tactics. Although Billy Burton had given basic advice after our first flight together, even he later rebuked me for talking 'shop' in the Mess when once I began inquiring how best to get on the tail of a 109. Douglas Bader, though, was different.

On the morning of 5 May, Johnnie was at dispersal preparing to fly a couple of air tests, when Wing Commander Bader came in. After a discussion concerning the relative night-flying merits or otherwise of the Spitfire and Hurricane, the Wing Leader decided that he and Pilot Officer Johnson would slope off on an impromptu flight across the Channel to 'see if we can bag a couple of Huns before lunch'. A few minutes later the two Spitfires were streaking towards France in line-abreast formation. Johnnie:

> I could hardly believe that I was flying as wingman to this legendary pilot. But there he was only a few yards away with his initials and wing commander's pennant painted on the fuselage of his Spitfire. There would be no reporting mistakes this time.

Unfortunately Woodhall vetoed the unauthorised sortie, recalling 'Dogsbody' to Tangmere and uttering 'a strong oath that stung the ears of the Controller and startled the WAAF plotters!' Instead,

Wing Commander Bader taught Johnnie, at last, how to get on the tail of a 109. Indeed, as Johnnie later wrote, according to the 'Wingco', there was 'Nothing to it. A piece of cake!'

Tactics, though, remained a vexing issue for Fighter Command. Johnnie: 'We had seen, of course, the Germans flying in these loose, strung out, line abreast formations, like a pack of hunting dogs, lean and hungry looking.' On the evening of 7 May, Bader and his pilots sat up late into the night, discussing tactics in the Mess. Flying Officer Cocky Dundas:

> We expressed our dissatisfaction with formations adopted in the past ... the half pints went down again and again whilst we argued the toss. I suggested that four aircraft flying in line abreast, each at least fifty yards apart, could never be bounced from behind. The Spitfires on the right would cover the tails of those on the left, and vice versa. No enemy could therefore approach unseen, but if attacked the formation could break upwards, one pair to port, the other to starboard. This was, of course, similar to the tactics worked out by Mölders in Spain.

The following morning found Dundas nursing a hangover at breakfast, when in strode the teatotal Bader in rude health: 'He told me that he had been thinking about my idea and had decided to try it out. I nodded in weak agreement but was somewhat startled when Bader added "This morning"!' Soon two pairs of Tangmere Spitfires – Squadron Leader Woodhouse and Sergeant Maine (of 610 Squadron), and Wing Commander Bader flying with Flying Officer Dundas, were prowling up and down, 26,500 feet above the Dover Straits. This effort to provoke an attack from marauding 109s succeeded: six 109s of *Stab*/JG 51 – coincidentally led by Major Werner Mölders himself – approached the Spitfires from the rear and at the same height. Bader held the formation together, the Spitfires continuing as if blissfully unaware of their peril. At what he considered the optimum moment, Bader shouted 'BREAK!' The Spitfires immediately whipped round, the pilots nearly blacking out, so steep was the turn. Dundas levelled out but there was no sign of the enemy. The break had, in fact, been mistimed, as the manoeuvre was intended to reverse the antagonists' position. Suddenly Dundas's Spitfire was raked with cannon fire. Thick smoke immediately engulfed the cockpit, the Spitfire pilot taking what evasive action his damaged aircraft permitted. Protected by Woodhouse, Dundas limped back across the Channel to the coastal airfield at Hawkinge, where he safely crash-landed. It was the second and final time that Dundas was shot down by the so-called 'Father of German Air Fighting'. Sergeant Mains had faired better, damaging a 109 before hitting a second, which crashed in the sea.

After Dundas had been collected from Hawkinge in the station Magister, Bader held a debrief at Westhampnett. In spite of Dundas having been shot down, the benefits of the line-abreast formation in helping to prevent a surprise attack had been proven. The fault on this first occasion lay with the Wing Leader, who had mistimed the break. Consequently one or more enemy fighters remained behind the Spitfires when they had come out of their turn. The Tangmere Wing now started experimenting greatly with this idea, which was soon perfected and known as either the 'Finger Four' or 'Crossover Four', on account of the fact that in plan view the fighters occupied positions similar to the fingers of an outstretched hand, and because the pairs literally crossed over in the turn. Eventually the formation was adopted universally throughout Fighter Command – for which Wing Commander Bader and Flying Officer Dundas can take credit. This was a significant development so far as RAF air fighting was concerned. As Johnnie said, 'We all learned a tremendous amount from Douglas, who had the ability to impart his knowledge and ideas on tactics.'

On 15 May 1941 Johnnie flew his usual mount, Spitfire P7837, on a 'Nuisance Raid – France' with Squadron Leader Burton. This was essentially a Rhubarb, during which operation the Spitfire pilots swept over the French coast at 4,000 feet. Their intention was to find a suitable ground or sea target, but no suitable opportunity presented itself. The Germans had been quick to implement counter-measures against these sorties. Decoy targets were common, the unwary suddenly being fired upon by numerous well-hidden flak guns. The Spitfire's mighty Merlin engine was cooled by glycol, stored in a small tank, which, together with the all-important radiator was exposed to ground-fire during these low-level attacks. Just one rifle-calibre machine-gun bullet hitting either the glycol tank or radiator resulted in a seized engine. Rhubarbs, therefore, were hazardous indeed. Also, attacking vehicles in France caused some pilots concern; Ron Rayner: 'How could we be sure that we were strafing enemy transports – or was our target really the local French doctor on a trip to treat a patient?' Johnnie:

> I loathed Rhubarbs. In addition to the obvious dangers presented by flak, we had also to consider letting down through low cloud over France – with no accurate knowledge of the cloud base's altitude. To me the great risk seemed disproportionate to whatever damage we inflicted on these stupid raids.

Indeed, many pilots and experienced leaders were lost on Rhubarbs, including such aces as Wing Commander Paddy Finucane and Flight Lieutenant Eric Lock, both of whom were killed, and Wing Commander Robert Stanford Tuck, who was captured. These were all men that Fighter Command could ill afford to lose, so it is unsurprising that Johnnie viewed Rhubarbs with a 'deep, dark hatred'.

On 20 May, while flying the Magister from Wittering back to Tangmere, Johnnie forced-landed at Burton Lazaars, near Rutland in his home county of Leicestershire. At an aircrew reunion in Canada during 1970, Johnnie told the story of that incident:

> We had on the station a little communications aeroplane called the *Maggie*, the Miles Magister. One Friday I went to my CO, Billy Burton, and asked to borrow the *Maggie* to slip up to Nottingham and see my girlfriend for the weekend. He said, 'Yes, alright, be back on Monday morning in time for readiness.' Well I did one of those stupid things: I forgot to re-fuel the aeroplane before taking-off from Nottingham on the Monday morning. I had just got a few miles south of Nottingham when the engine cut dead and with my usual skill and aplomb I managed to put it down in a field without a scratch, rang up the local RAF airfield – they sent the bowser down. I topped up and proceeded to Tangmere, but instead of getting there for ten o'clock readiness it was lunchtime when I arrived. My CO was rather displeased with Pilot Officer Johnson and said, 'It's not the *Maggie* and running out of petrol and that sort of thing, it's being late. You're in front of the Wing Commander first thing tomorrow morning.' I was instructed to bring my logbook. The following morning we were marched in

front of the great man, Johnson with his logbook. I then had to relate the sorry tale of not refuelling the Maggie, and I received a great bollocking from Douglas, who then reached out for the logbook and wrote something in it. There was a sort of eloquent silence and I suddenly realised that we might be parting company, if you know what I mean, and that I might be thrown out of my squadron, which would have been the most dreadful thing. But as Wing Commander Bader handed the logbook back, he just uttered one single, sharp, expressive four-letter word. Then I knew that all was well and that I should remain with the Tangmere Wing!

To this, part of a speech after a dinner attended by both General Adolf Galland and Group Captain Sir Douglas Bader, the latter responded, 'The four letter word that I called him ... he was, in fact, at the time!'

June 1941 saw the tempo of fighting increase. On 17 June, Johnnie was leading Yellow Section and intercepted a pair of Me 109Fs. Although both Johnnie and his Yellow Two opened fire, the combat was inconclusive and no claims were made. This was, of course, just a few days before Hitler's surprise invasion of the Soviet Union on 22 June. By this time only two German fighter groups remained on the Channel coast, the rest sent eastwards for the next assault. *Oberleutnant* Adolf Galland was *Kommodore* of JG 26, based in and around the Pas-de-Calais, and Major Wilhelm Bathasar's JG 2 was located around Cherbourg. Between them these *Kanaljäger* were responsible for defending the Nazi empire from the Netherlands south to the Bay of Biscay. In overall command was the *Kanalfront Jagdfliegerführer*, General Theo Osterkamp – who had achieved the rare distinction of having already become an ace in both world wars. Osterkamp's brief to both of his *Kanaljagdgeschwardern Kommodoren* was simple: inflict maximum losses upon the enemy while preserving their own limited forces in the process. Although due to the presence of bombers RAF Circus operations could not be ignored by the *Luftwaffe*, there were no targets in France of sufficient importance to lure the enemy into a rash charge. Instead the German fighter pilots had the luxury of only engaging when they possessed the tactical advantage of height, sun and numbers. Moreover, unlike during the fighting over England of the previous summer, it was now the RAF fighter pilots undertaking a two-way sea crossing and operating at the limit of their range. Also, when shot down or forced to land in France for whatever reason, more often than not RAF pilots were captured. The Germans, like Fighter Command's pilots fighting over England in 1940, were operating over territory they controlled.

The Me 109F was an excellent fighter aircraft. The new German fighter had redesigned radiators, flaps and ailerons, and a slightly greater wingspan than its predecessor, with rounded wingtips, a streamlined nose profile, and no tail-struts. The DB601E used a lower-octane fuel, producing a top speed of 390 mph at 22,000 feet, a service ceiling of 37,000 feet and a range of 440 miles. An ingenious nitrous oxide injection pack, known as 'Ha Ha', was added to the Me 109F-2, giving exceptional emergency boost. The *Franz* was armed with two engine-mounted MG 17 machine-guns, their rate of fire being 1,180 rounds per minute, and provision was made for a single 15- or 20-mm cannon to fire through the propeller boss. Such weapons had a much slower rate of fire, however – that of the 15-mm Mauser MG 151 cannon, for example, being 700 rounds a minute. The benefits of cannon had long been recognised by the *Luftwaffe*, and in this respect the RAF had only recently caught up. After 19 Squadron's trials and tribulations with the unsuccessful cannon-armed Spitfire Mk IB during the Battle of Britain, the difficulties of mounting cannon in the Spitfire's thin wing section had at last been overcome. As a precaution against stoppages, however, and to provide pilots with the benefit of both the higher rate of fire provided by machine-guns, which required less accuracy to be effective, and hard-hitting but slower-firing cannon, the Spitfire Mk IIB was armed with four machine-guns and two cannon.

The Spitfire was now, therefore, much more heavily armed than the Me 109F, a matter which caused controversy among the *Jagdfliegern*. Galland argued that such light armament was useless against the new and more heavily armoured Spitfires, and that wing-mounted cannons, as fitted to the Me 109E, were better for inexperienced pilots because the 'spread' achieved required less accuracy than weapons tightly grouped together in the F's nose. Mölders, conversely, favoured the lighter armament on the grounds that it saved weight and thereby increased agility. In action, some

Experten actually chose just to use the single cannon, ignoring their two machine-guns completely. Interestingly, across the Channel RAF fighter pilots were engaged in a similar debate. Wing Commander Bader was against the fitting of cannon for similar reasons to Galland favouring a combination of wing- and nose-mounted armament. Eight machine-guns, as fitted to the original Spitfires and Hurricanes, were harmonised as per the pilot's personal preference to converge at a given point, producing a cone of fire. The spread achieved by eight guns, depending on harmonisation, could be likened to the shotgun effect. Cannon, however, with a much slower rate of fire, required much greater accuracy. Machine-guns, Bader considered, were more forgiving to novice fighter pilots and more likely, therefore, to achieve the required result than cannon. Nonetheless, the combination of both cannon and machine-gun became standard armament for RAF fighters.

The Spitfire was also being improved in another important respect at this time: having hitherto fitted the Spitfire with fabric-covered ailerons, Supermarine engineers at Hamble airfield near Southampton were fitting metal ailerons, making the aircraft easier to control at high speeds. Jeffrey Quill, the Supermarine Test Pilot, remembered that 'the word swept round Fighter Command like wildfire and in no time the air around Hamble was thick with the Spitfires of wing leaders and squadron commanders all trying to jump the queue to get their aircraft fitted with the new metal ailerons – Douglas Bader leading the hunt!' Pilot Officer Johnson flew his Spitfire, P7837, 'QJ-C', to Hamble for conversion to metal ailerons on 20 June, returning the same day. By now, the Tangmere Wing was flying sweeps and bomber escorts over France on a daily basis. Johnnie:

> My job as one of two wingmen in Dogsbody Section was to protect the remainder of the Section from a flank or stern attack. Sergeant Alan Smith was the other wingman and did likewise from his position on the port side. My head, therefore, was usually turned to the left or strained right round so that I could watch our vulnerable rear. We had little idea of what lay ahead, but knew from radio chatter and our own manoeuvres when Bader was wading into a gaggle of 109s. We had to watch our leader, and resist the natural instinct to personally break formation

to chase a 109. The Squadron's total of kills and the scores of certain individual pilots increased. A combination of my role as a wingman and the fact that it seemed as if there just wasn't time to single out an opponent from the maelstrom of fighters as we jockeyed and vied for an opening, meant that I was slow to score. It was an acutely frustrating time.

Alan Smith, Dogsbody Two, adds:

> If you cannot be a leader then be the best possible number two, and that means several things. The protection of your leader is paramount. His job is to shoot down the enemy whilst you must protect his tail. Stick to him like glue. Be constantly alert for the 'Hun in the sun'. Early warning equates with longer life. The 'Finger Four' formation introduced by Douglas Bader was ideal for cross-over and a vast improvement on previous formations.

As Johnnie said, 'We number twos were actually serving a privileged apprenticeship under the Master himself.'

On 26 June, Wing Commander Bader led his Wing to Redhill in Surrey, from which sector station the Tangmere Spitfires participated in Circus 24. Crossing the French coast at Gravelines, 'Dogsbody' was warned of twenty-four Me 109s to the south-east. Simultaneously these 'bandits' were sighted in front of the wing, in the usual loose line-abreast formation. The 109s then turned, climbing to attack 610 Squadron from the rear. Immediately the battle was joined; Johnnie, flying as Dogsbody Four, reported that after the initial contact,

> I became detached from Wing Commander Bader's Section at 15,000 feet, through watching three Me 109s immediately above me. I saw them dive away to port and almost immediately afterwards saw an Me 109E coming in from my starboard side, which flew across me about 150 yards away, turning slightly to port. I immediately turned towards the E/A and opened fire, closing to 100 yards. After two one-second bursts, the E/A jettisoned hood, rolled over and the pilot baled out, his parachute opening almost immediately. I then broke away as there were other E/A about. I estimated I was over Gravelines when I was in combat

... I then joined up with Flying Officer Scott of 145 Squadron
and landed at Hawkinge for re-fuelling.

Johnnie's victory – his first 100 per cent confirmed personal kill
– had been witnessed by several pilots of 145 Squadron. He had
fired 278 machine-gun rounds (his Spitfire Mk IIA, P7837, having
no cannon). His victim was one of five Me 109Fs lost that day by
JG 2.

On 1 July, the Tangmere Wing swept inland over France as far
as Béthune, another long flight of an hour and a half. Johnnie
attacked a 109F that was 'squirting' at Dogsbody Section,
but saw no apparent result. Three days later the Wing orbited
St-Omer on Circus 32. Johnnie's combat report described
events:

I heard Wing Commander Bader instruct his Section to break. As
I was immediately behind, I broke away steeply to the left and
after two tight turns saw an Me 109E firing at me, but no fire
hit me owing to the tightness of the turn. The E/A broke away to
port in a fairly medium dive. I followed him down and gave him
a short burst and observed glycol coming out of it. I then broke
away as there were other 109s in the vicinity, finally returning to
base at 1600.

Having expended eight-nine rounds, Johnnie was credited with
a 'damaged'. On 4 July, Johnnie scored again. On that day the
Tangmere Wing provided Target Support to six Stirlings bombing
Lille. Johnnie:

I was Yellow Three returning from Lille ... when I became
separated from the rest of the Section. I then joined up with
Wing Commander Bader and Sergeant Smith. We were attacked
separately by 109s on the journey out and on one occasion I
saw a 109E about 300 yards behind us, coming up to deliver an
attack. I shouted to the Section to break and did a steep climbing
turn to the right. The E/A climbed straight up and I came down
from his starboard side, underneath him. I pulled the stick back
and delivered an attack into the underside of the E/A at about
seventy-five yards range (slight deflection). Just as I was on the

point of stalling, the E/A exploded into bits with black and yellow
smoke coming off it. I later re-joined Wing Commander Bader
and Sergeant Smith, and we were attacked again. After breaking
up, as instructed by Wing Commander Bader, I saw a 109 going
down with glycol flames and black smoke pouring out. This was
probably the E/A Wing Commander Bader attacked as I did not
shoot at it.

Again, these enemy aircraft were from JG 2. July was proving to be
a busy month for the Tangmere Wing.

On 8 July, the Tangmere Wing flew Target Support once more,
this time on Circus 38. Johnnie wrote in his logbook, 'One Stirling
shot down by ack-ack'. Four Stirlings had, in fact, split into two
pairs, each attacking a different target. The Stirling destroyed was
hit by flak on the way out – only two of the crew baled out before
their big bomber crashed on houses. As the 616 Squadron diarist
recorded, 'It was not a very pleasant sight to watch.' The next
day Bader led the Wing on yet another Circus. 616 Squadron
was engaged by 109s, Squadron Leader E. P. Gibbs, the 'Aerobatic
King', and Sergeant Bob Morton being shot down – both were
captured. Johnnie fired at an enemy fighter during the swift
punch-up, but made no claim. This day also saw Squadron Leader
Burton test a new Spitfire, P8707, a cannon-armed Mk VB. He
wrote in his logbook, 'Cannon firing. Nearly hit a boatload of
fishermen!' On 10 July, Johnnie flew this aircraft, practising firing
cannon and machine-guns. He missed a big fight over Béthune, in
which Dogsbody Section claimed two 109s destroyed and three
probables. Johnnie scored again on 14 July, when the Tangmere
Wing flew on Circus 48 to St-Omer. A section of 610 Squadron
Spitfires were attacked over St-Omer, without loss, as was 145
Squadron, the CO of which, Squadron Leader Turner, engaged
three 109s, damaging one. Johnnie:

I became separated from the Squadron when over the target so
decided to fly with the Beehive during the return flight. When
about twenty-five to thirty miles from the French coast and flying
at 1,500 feet above and behind the Beehive, I saw three aircraft
in line astern to the south-west. I then turned inland, above and
behind the three aircraft which I then identified as Me 109Fs.

I made a quick aileron turn and attacked number three from below and behind, when I was climbing. I gave a second burst with cannon and machine-gun at 150 yards range and saw the tail blown off. The E/A went into an uncontrollable spin. I am claiming this E/A as destroyed. I then broke away as my Number Two had lost me. When over the French coast at 10,000 feet I saw an Me 109E over Étaples, diving steeply. I gave chase. It pulled out at 2,000 feet and flew straight and level. I drew up and gave a short burst at 150 yards range. I thought I saw something break away from the starboard wing of the E/A, but cannot be certain as my screen was covered in oil from the E/A in the first engagement. I therefore make no claim in this second engagement.

The 109 that Johnnie definitely destroyed was probably that flown by *Unteroffizier* R. Klienike of III/JG 26, who was reported missing.

By now Johnnie was an established member of Wing Commander Bader's 'inner sanctum':

Douglas and his wife, Thelma, rented the 'Bayhouse', some five miles from Tangmere and their door was always open to us. About once or twice a week we motored there and always found the Wing's inner-sanctum gathered about our leader. The conversation rarely strayed far from our limited world of fighters and air fighting. Sipping his lemonade, Bader analysed our recent fights, discoursed on the importance of straight shooting, on the relative merits of machine-guns and cannons, on the ability of our opponents (whom he always held in contempt), on the probable destiny of the pilot who flew with his head in the office and of our own dreadful fate should we ever lose sight of him in combat. He was dogmatic and final in his pronouncements – nobody argued with him. It was a great privilege for us junior officers to be taken into the confidence of a wing commander, and in this fashion the three squadrons were blended into the Tangmere Wing. It was a very exciting and inspiring time down at Tangmere that unique summer. Bader, the great man with both DSO and DFC, I was just a mere pilot officer, but he treated us all as equals. He was a great leader. It was certainly inspirational being led by this dynamic and aggressive man, possessed of incredible energy and drive. Over France he would be chatting away to 'Woody'

on the R/T, organising squash courts ready for his return – and
this from a man without legs! On some occasions when we were
homeward bound from an operation, Bader would get out his
pipe, light a Swan Vestas match on the dashboard, and sit there
puffing away with the hood open – this whilst flying an aircraft
full of highly inflammable 100 octane petrol! You could see him,
sat there, puffing away. Incredible. When he lit up we used to veer
away and keep our distance, I can tell you!

Such disregard for danger was perhaps reckless – but served only
to raise morale and convince the Tangmere Wing's pilots that their
legendary leader was indestructible. Johnnie:

> He'd come stomping into dispersal and say to Billy Burton 'What
> are we doing today then, Billy?'
>   Billy might respond 'Well the Form "D" (operational order)
> has come through, Sir, but we're not on it. The other wings are
> but not us.'
>   Bader would say 'Right, we'll see about that! I'll have a bloody
> word with "LM".'
>   He would then personally ring the AOC and, lo and behold,
> we would be on ops!

High summer of 1941 at Tangmere was undoubtedly a stirring time,
though sadly punctuated with the names of the dead.

The afternoon of 21 July saw the Tangmere Wing engaged
on Circus 55, its second escort mission of the day. After making
landfall at Le Touquet, the three squadrons split up and swept
independently. Johnnie was flying as Red One, his number two
being Sergeant Sidney 'George' Mabbett. Near the target area,
24,000 feet over Montreuil, Johnnie positioned his section to
starboard and slightly above and behind Dogsbody Section. Six
Me 109s were sighted, flying eastwards. Wing Commander Bader
swung his section around so as to attack the enemy fighters from
the rear. Johnnie:

> I then brought my Section slightly below and almost abreast of
> Dogsbody Section, and at this stage my Number Two was with
> me. When about 250 yards from the enemy formation I saw

Dogsbody Four (Pilot Officer Hepple) open fire at the right-hand 109 – which emitted glycol fumes but continued to fly straight, carrying out gentle swings to port and starboard. Unfortunately I did not hear the order to break and pressed home my attack on the right-hand E/A from 150–200 yards. After two short bursts (eight machine-guns) the nose of E/A dropped slowly and it eventually went into a vertical dive, the white glycol fumes giving way to thick black smoke. I then broke away and did not see E/A again. My Number Two was not seen again after this engagement. Very accurate flak experienced when crossing on return journey'.

Pilot Officers Johnson and Hepple were credited with a shared probable. The emission of white smoke from their victim is noteworthy, however. White fumes indicate damage to the coolant system, without which, of course, the aircraft's engine overheats and seizes. Conversely, black smoke could be one of two things: nothing untoward and simply exhaust emissions due to sudden use of increased throttle, or serious engine damage. As the 109 enjoyed the benefit of fuel injection, as opposed to the Spitfire's Merlin engine which had a gravity-fed carburettor, it was able to outpace RAF fighters in the dive. That being so, the German fighter pilots' standard evasive manoeuvre was a steep, high-speed dive. Ramming the throttle forward, the German would dive suddenly and sharply – the sudden use of full throttle producing black smoke emissions from the engine's exhaust ports – giving the impression that the target had been hit, damaged, and was crashing. These combats took place at relatively high altitude, often above a layer of cloud. An enemy aircraft undertaking such a manoeuvre, therefore, would level out beneath the cloud base, having lost its pursuers and none the worse for the experience. To all intents and purposes, however, the enemy machine – seen diving sharply at high speed and emitting black smoke – appeared to have been destroyed. This is one reason why Fighter Command over-claimed so much. The emission of white smoke, though, gave clear confirmation that the target had indeed been damaged and may not, therefore, make it home. There is no question, therefore, that the 109 hit by Johnson and Hepple during this combat was very badly damaged. Another factor was aircraft identification. With combats involving so many machines, all moving very fast indeed and similar in appearance – the more

curvaceous Me 109F, for example, looked very similar to the Spitfire
– mistakes were bound to happen. There are numerous recorded
instances of so-called 'Friendly Fire'. Indeed, after this particular
combat Squadron Leader Burton wrote in his logbook: 'Should
have shot down a 109 but failed to open fire till too late owing to
uncertainty of identity.'

Johnnie's missing Red Two, Sergeant Mabbett, had been hit by
Unteroffizier Gottfried Dietze of 2/JG 26. It was the German's first
kill, and 'Mabb's' Spitfire was hit in the cockpit area by cannon fire.
Fatally wounded, Red Two managed to make a successful wheels-up
forced-landing near St-Omer. Sadly the young rugby player from
Cheltenham died almost immediately afterwards. So impressed
with his skilful flying when so badly wounded, the Germans buried
Sergeant Mabbett with full military honours.

During the evening of 23 July, Wing Commander Bader
and the Tangmere Wing were up on yet another Circus, which
was again their second operation that day. From the point of
crossing the French coast over Le Touquet, the Spitfires came
under constant attack from JG 26 Me 109s. The Spitfires were
immediately split up into their fighting pairs. As the usual scrap
commenced, another fifty 109s could be seen holding off in the
distance, their leader awaiting the perfect moment to join the fray.
610 Squadron's diary records that 'all engagements were terrific
dogfights'. Wing Commander Bader and Flight Lieutenant Dundas
– now commander of 616 Squadron's 'A' Flight – shared a 109
destroyed, Flying Officer 'Buck' Casson destroyed another while
Pilot Officer Johnson damaged a third. 616 Squadron had scored
its 50th combat claim in this fight, and the Tangmere Wing's 500th.
Johnnie wrote in his logbook that there were 'More 109s about
than ever before. Wing engaged almost whole time over France'.
Interestingly, *Oberst* Adolf Galland, the *Kommodore* of JG 26 and
among Germany's most exceptional fighter pilots, was wounded in
this engagement – while attacking a Spitfire another RAF fighter
hit him from behind, his life saved only by the steel armour plate
protecting his head.

In spite of the high number of offensive operations flown daily,
training flights continued. Over the next few days Johnnie practised
'Surprise attacks', noting in his logbook on 25 July that he had been
'shot down by Buck'. Other flights included escorting a Lysander

over the Channel, searching for a ditched Blenheim, and escorting a destroyer 'shelling French coast'. On 28 July more change was afoot at Tangmere: 145 Squadron was pulled out of the line and replaced with Squadron Leader Lionel Don Finlay DFC's 41 Squadron, which based itself at Merston. This changed the wing's identity. The team that had developed and strengthened bonds of shared experience and understanding was now no more. Finlay, a former Olympic gold medallist, was an unpopular commander in spite of being a successful fighter pilot. On 1 August, in fact, Finlay was promoted to wing commander and replaced as 41 Squadron's CO by Squadron Leader L. M. 'Elmer' Gaunce DFC, who had flown Hurricanes with 615 Squadron during the Battle of Britain. Gaunce had been rested from operations since December 1940, however, so the nature of the current fighting was all new to this Canadian squadron commander. 41 Squadron had flown with distinction from Hornchurch during the Battle of Britain, and had since rested and refitted at Catterick. It was now at the base of a steep learning curve.

On 30 July, Johnnie tested the cannons of a new Spitfire Mk VB, W3334. This aircraft replaced his Mk IIA, P7837, and would be his regular mount for the next few days. Poor weather throughout the week ahead prevented wing operations, although various pairs of Spitfires were despatched to France on Rhubarbs. On 7 August, Wing Commander Bader led the Tangmere Wing, including, for the first time, 41 Squadron, on a Circus to Lille. Orbiting between Merville and Le Touquet, the Wing was pounced upon by a large formation of 109s. Curiously, when the Wing wheeled around to meet the threat, the 109s dived away without pressing home their attack. Other enemy formations, though, did engage, and there were losses on both sides. Sergeant Bob Beardsley flew with 41 Squadron that day:

> I was leading a Section of four, rear cover, and we were the Wing's low squadron that day. As I looked to my rear-left, I saw a 109 closing on my port sub-section, so close that the cannon aperture in the propeller boss was very apparent! I called 'Break, port!', and we all went hard at it. The attacking aircraft had not fired, but I called the Wing Leader to report that we had been attacked by 109s. To my amazement, Wing Commander Bader responded 'Only Hurricanes, old boy!'

I, however, failed to see the joke! The next second the whole
Wing was engaged – I saw no more 'Hurricanes'! When the
lead squadron was attacked, Bader did actually say 'Sorry old
boy!'

It was yet another example of the difficulties regarding aircraft
identification – and clearly even the 'Master' could make mistakes.

On the morning of Monday 9 August 1941, the teleprinter
clattered away at Tangmere. The daily Form 'D' came through
from 11 Group HQ, detailing the Wing's task for that day. This
was another complex Circus, No. 68, involving many aircraft
to Gosnay. The Tangmere Wing was to provide Target Support.
Sergeant Alan Smith, Wing Commander Bader's usual 'Dogsbody
Two', had a head cold and so was unable to fly. Imminently to
be commissioned, and as his name was not 'on the board', Smith
prepared to go into London and buy a new uniform. His place
as the Bader's wingman was taken by a New Zealander, Sergeant
Jeff West, a pilot with one and a half Me 109s destroyed and one
damaged to his credit. West was not without experience: frequently
that summer he had flown Number Two to Flight Lieutenant E.
P. Gibbs, until that officer was shot down over France on 9 July
1941. For this Target Support sortie to Gosnay, Dogsbody Section
therefore consisted of:

- Dogsbody – Wing Commander Douglas Bader
- Dogsbody 2 – Sergeant Jeff West
- Dogsbody 3 – Flight Lieutenant Hugh Dundas DFC
- Dogsbody 4 – Pilot Officer 'Johnnie' Johnson

Also leading 'Finger Fours' within the 616 Squadron formation of
three sections would be the squadron commander, Squadron Leader
Billy Burton (Yellow Section), and the 'B' Flight commander, Flight
Lieutenant Buck Casson (Blue Section). Across the other side of the
airfield, Squadron Leader Ken Holden DFC and his 610 Squadron
also prepared for the morning sortie.

Take-off came at 1040 hours, Dogsbody Section leading
Westhampnett's Spitfires on yet another sortie into very hostile
airspace. High over Chichester, Squadron Leader Holden swiftly
maneuvered 610 Squadron into position above and slightly to port

of 616. As Target Support, the Wing had no bombers to meet prior to setting course for France, although the Spitfires were still routed out over Beachy Head. As the Wing left Chichester, however, there was no sign of 41 Squadron.

The Beachy Head Forward Relay Station recorded the Tangmere Wing's R/T messages that day. As the Wing neared 'Diamond', 41 Squadron had still not appeared. Group Captain Woodhall, at Tangmere, was the first to speak, making a test call:

'Dogsbody?'
'OK, OK.'

Bader then made R/T test calls to the commanders of both 610 and 41, using their Christian names as was his usual practice:

DB: Ken?
Ken Holden (KH): Loud and clear.
DB: Elmer?

There was no response from Squadron Leader Gaunce, which provoked an acerbic remark from the Wing Leader to 'Woody'. Unable to wait, 616 and 610 Squadrons set course for France and Gosnay, adopting their battle formations in the process. Still climbing, Wing Commander Bader waggled his wings insistently, indicating that 'Dogsbody 3', Flight Lieutenant Dundas, should take the lead. Dundas slid across, tucking his wingtip just two or three feet from Bader's. From this close proximity, Dundas saw the Wing Leader mouth two words: 'Airspeed Indicator', meaning that the instrument on Spitfire Mk VA W3185 was unserviceable. The Wing had to climb at the right speed to ensure Time on Target (TOT) at the appointed time, which was crucial. Dundas gave a 'thumbs up' and moved forward to lead the Spitfires to France. On the rear of his hand he had fortunately written the time at which the Wing was due over the French coast in addition to the speed which had to be maintained. The 21-year-old Flight Commander then 'settled down to concentrate on the job'.

Dundas later recalled that the 'sun was bright and brilliant, unveiled by any layer of high haze or cirrus cloud'. Realising that the white cumulus cloud below provided a background which would immediately reveal the silhouettes of any aircraft, Dundas correctly anticipated that under such conditions 'Dogsbody' would wish to climb as high as possible, and so adjusted both his throttle setting and rate of climb accordingly, taking the Spitfires up to 28,000 feet. Then, more radio messages:

> DB: Ken and Elmer, start gaining height.
> KH: Elmer's not with us.
> *Unidentified, garbled voice on the R/T, believed to be Squadron*
> *Leader Gaunce.*
> DB: Elmer from Dogsbody. I cannot understand what you say, but we are on our way. You had better decide for yourself whether to come or go back.

Following the last radio transmissions, at least the Wing was now aware that more Spitfires were bringing up the rear, even if some distance away. The Spitfires cruised over the Channel, towards France, with 610 Squadron above and behind 616. Dundas led the Wing over the French coast right on cue (although there is conflicting evidence regarding whether the coast was crossed south of Le Touquet, known as the 'Golf Course', or Boulogne, slightly further north). This crucial timing observed, Bader accelerated ahead and informed 'Dogsbody 3' over the R/T that he was resuming the lead. The Spitfires' arrival over the coastal flak belt was greeted by dangerous little puffballs of black smoke, making the formation twist and turn. 'Beetle' then called 'Dogsbody', informing Wing Commander Bader that the Beehive itself was 'on time and engaged'. As the Spitfires forged inland, therefore, some distance behind them the bombers and various cover Wings were now bound for France and action.

Slightly below the condensation trail level, a 610 Squadron pilot reported seeing contrails 'above and to our left'. Squadron Leader Holden consequently led the squadron higher still while 'Beetle' (B) reported:

> B: Dogsbody from Beetle. There are 20 plus five miles to the east of you.

DB: OK, but your transmitter is quite impossible. Please use the other.

B: Dogsbody, is this better?

DB: Perfect. Ken, start getting more height.

KH: OK, Dogsbody, but will you throttle back? I cannot keep up.

DB: Sorry Ken, my airspeed indicator is u/s. Throttling back, and I will do one slow

left-hand turn so you can catch up.

KH: Dogsbody from Ken, I'm making smoke [contrails] at this height.

DB: OK, Ken, I'm going down very slightly.

Beetle then advised Dogsbody of more bandits in the vicinity. 616 Squadron's Flying Officer Roy Marples (RM) saw the enemy first.

RM: Three bandits coming down astern of us. I'm keeping an eye on them, now there are six.

DB: OK.

B: Douglas, another twelve-plus ahead and slightly higher.

RM: Eleven of them now.

DB: OK, Roy, let me know exactly where they are.

RM: About one mile astern and slightly higher.

B: Douglas, there is another forty-plus 15 miles to the north-east of you.

DB: OK Beetle. Are our friends where they ought to be, I haven't much idea where

I am.

B: Yes, you are exactly right. And so are your friends.

RM: Dogsbody from Roy. Keep turning left and you'll see 109s at nine o'clock.

DB: Ken, can you see them?

KH: Douglas, 109s below. Climbing up.

By this time, 616 and 610 Squadron had progressed into a very dangerous French sky indeed, Beetle having already reported some seventy-two bandits, representing odds which outnumbered the Spitfires by nearly three to one. Clearly, this was not to be an uneventful sortie. Tension mounted, the Spitfire pilots switched on their gunsight reflectors and gun buttons to 'Fire'. Anxiously they searched the sky, an ever-watchful eye being kept on the 109s positioned 1,000 feet above the Wing, waiting to pounce. Bader himself dipped each wing in turn, scrutinising the sky below for the 109s reported by Ken Holden.

> DB: I can't see them. Will you tell me where to look?
> KH: Underneath Bill's section now. Shall I come down?
> DB: No, I have them. Get into formation. Going down. Ken, are you with us?
> KH: Just above you.

As Dogsbody Section dived on the enemy, Flight Lieutenant Casson followed with three other aircraft of 'B' Flight. Dogsbody Three, Flight Lieutenant Dundas, had 'smelt a rat' in respect of the *Schwarm* of 109s that Dogsbody Section was now rapidly diving towards. Finding no targets to the Section's right, Dogsbody Four, Pilot Officer Johnson, skidded under the Section and fired at an Me 109 on the left. By this time the whole of Dogsbody Section was firing, although Dundas, still unhappy and suspecting a trap, had a compelling urge to look behind. Suddenly Pilot Officer 'Nip' Hepple shouted over the R/T: 'Blue Two here. Some buggers coming down behind, astern. Break left!'

The Spitfire pilots hauled their aircraft around in steep turns. The sky behind Dogsbody Section was full of Me 109s, all firing – without Hepple's warning the Spitfires would have been instantly nailed. As the high 109s crashed into 616 Squadron, Squadron Leader Holden decided that it was time for his Squadron to join the fray and reduce the odds. Informing Flight Lieutenant Denis Crowley-Milling of this decision, Holden led his Spitfires down to assist. Flight Lieutenant Casson, following Bader's Section, was well throttled back to keep his flight together. Also attacking from the rear, Casson managed a squirt at a *Rotte* of 109s. Flying Officer Marples, number three in Casson's Section, then shouted a warning of even more 109s diving upon the Wing, while Squadron Leader Billy Burton urged the Spitfires to 'Keep turning' – thus preventing the 109s (which could not out-turn a Spitfire) getting in a shot. Suddenly the organised chaos became a totally confused maelstrom of twisting, turning fighters:

'BREAK! FOR CHRIST'S SAKE, BREAK!'

The Spitfires immediately 'broke' – hard. Johnnie:

> There was this scream of '*Break!*' – and we all broke, we didn't
> wait to hear it twice! '*Round*', then a swirling mass of 109s and
> Spitfires. When I broke I could see Bader still firing. Dundas was
> firing at the extreme right 109. There was some cloud nearby
> and I disappeared into it as quick as possible! I couldn't say how
> many aircraft were involved, suffice to say a lot. It seemed to me
> that the greatest danger was a collision, rather than being shot
> down, that's how close we all were. We had got the 109s we were
> bouncing and then Holden came down with his section, so there
> were a lot of aeroplanes. We were fighting 109Fs, although there
> may have been some Es amongst them. There was an absolute
> mass of aeroplanes just 50 yards apart, it was awful. I thought
> to myself 'You're going to collide with somebody!' I didn't think
> about shooting at anything after we were bounced ourselves, all
> you could think about was surviving, getting out of that mass of
> aircraft. In such a tight turn, of course, you almost black out, you
> cannot really see where you are going. It was a mess. I had never
> been so frightened in my life, never!

Chased by three Me 109s, the closest just 100 yards astern, Pilot
Officer Johnson maintained his tight turn, spiralling down towards
the safety of a nearby cloud into which his Spitfire dived with over
400 mph on the clock. Pulling back the throttle and centralising the
controls, the altimeter stabilised, but the Spitfire stalled. Beneath
the cloud, Dogsbody Four recovered control. Having requested and
received a homing course for Dover, Johnnie headed rapidly for
England. Over the R/T, Pilot Officer Johnson could still hear 616
and 610 Squadrons' running battle:

> 'Get into formation or they'll shoot the bloody lot of you!'
> 'Spitfire going down in flames, 10 o'clock.'
> 'YQ-C [616 Squadron Spitfire]. Form up on me, I'm at three
> o'clock to you.'
> 'Four buggers above us.' [From Hepple]
> 'All Elfin aircraft [616 Squadron] withdraw. I say again, all Elfin
> aircraft withdraw.'
> 'Use the cloud if you're in trouble.' [From Billy Burton]

'Are you going home, Ken?' [From Burton]

'Yes, withdrawing.' [From Holden]

'Ken from Crow. Are you still about?'

'I'm right behind you, Crow'.

'Are we all here?'

Two short.'

'Dogsbody from Beetle. Do you require any assistance?'

'Beetle from Elfin Leader. We are OK and withdrawing.'

'Thank you Billy. Douglas, do you require any assistance? Steer three-four-zero to the coast.'

The silence from 'Dogsbody' was ominous. Flight Lieutenant Casson remembers:

I watched Wing Commander Bader and 'A' Flight attack and break to port as I was coming in. I was well throttled back in the dive, as the other three had started to fall behind and I wanted to keep the flight together. I attacked from the rear, and after having a squirt at two 109s flying together, left them for a single one which was flying inland alone. I finished nearly all of my cannon ammunition up on this boy, who finally baled out at 6,000 feet, having lost most of his tail unit. The other three 'B' flight machines were in my rear and probably one of the lads saw this. I climbed to 13,000 feet and fell in with Billy Burton and three other aircraft, all from 'A' Flight. We chased around in a circle for some time, gaining height all the while, and more 109s were directly above us. Eventually we formed up in line abreast and set off after the Wing. Billy's section flew in pairs abreast, so I flew abreast but at about 200 yards to starboard. We were repeatedly attacked by two Me 109s which had followed us and were flying above and behind. Each time they started diving I called out and we all turned and re-formed, the 109s giving up their attack and climbing each time.

About fifteen miles from the coastline I saw another Spitfire well below us and about half a mile to starboard. This machine was alone and traveling very slowly. I called up Billy on the R/T and suggested that we cross over to surround him and help the pilot back as he looked like a sitting duck. I broke off to starboard and made for the solitary Spitfire, but then, on looking back for Billy and the others, was amazed to see them diving away hard to the south-west for a low layer of cloud into which they soon disappeared. I realised then that my message had either been misunderstood or not received. Like a greenhorn, I had been so intent upon watching Billy's extraordinary disappearance to the left, and the lone Spitfire to my right, I lost sight of the Me 109s that had been worrying us. I remember looking for them but upon not discovering their position assumed that they had chased Billy instead. I was soon proved wrong, however, when I received three hits in both fuselage and wing. This occurred when I just broke for some cloud at 5,000 feet, which I reached but found too thin for cover, and was pursued by the 109s.

I then picked out two more 109s flying above me and so decided to drop to zero feet, fly north and cross the Channel at a narrow point as I was unsure of the damage sustained and the engine was not running smoothly. I pressed the teat and tried to run for it, but the two Me 109s behind had more speed and were rapidly within range, whilst the other two flew 1,500 feet above and dived from port to starboard and back, delivering quick bursts. Needless to say I was not flying straight and level all this time!

In the event I received a good one from behind, which passed between the stick and my right leg, taking off some of the rudder on its way. It passed into the petrol tank but whether the round continued into the engine I do not know. Petrol began leaking into the cockpit, oil pressure was dropping low, and with the radiator wide open I could smell the glycol overheating.

As the next attack came, I pulled straight up from the deck in a loop and, on my way down, as I was changing direction towards the sea, my engine became extremely rough and seized up as white glycol fumes poured forth. There was no option but to crash-land the aircraft. I tried to send 'Dogsbody' a hurried message, then blew up the wireless and made a belly landing in a field some 10 miles south of Calais. The Goons, having seen the glycol, were decent enough not to shoot me up as I was landing, but circled about for a time and gave my position away to a German cavalry unit in a wood in a corner of the field. One of the pilots waved to me as he flew overhead, and I waved

back just before setting fire to the aircraft. Due to the petrol
in the cockpit, and because I was carrying a port-fire issued
for this purpose, igniting the aircraft was easy. No sooner had
I done this than a party of shrieking Goons armed with rifles
came chasing over and that was the end of me! What eventually
happened to the lone Spitfire which I went to help out I have
no idea. As the 109s followed me, I assume that he got away
okay, I certainly hope so.

Flight Lieutenant Casson had been the victim of *Hauptmann*
Gerhard Schöpfel, *Gruppenkommandeur* of III/JG 26:

My III *Gruppe* attacked a British bomber formation, after
which my formation was split up. With the British on their
homeward flight, I headed alone for my airfield at Ligescourt,
near Crecy. Suddenly I saw a flight of Spitfires flying westwards.
I attacked them from above and after a short burst of fire the
rear machine nosed over sharply and dived away. Whilst the
other aircraft flew on apparently unaware, I pursued the fleeing
Spitfire as I could see no sign of damage. The British pilot
hugged the ground, dodging trees and houses. I was constantly
in his propwash and so could not aim properly. Because of the
warm air near the ground my radiator flaps opened and so
my speed decreased. It thus took me a long time to get into
a good firing position. Finally I was positioned immediately
behind the Spitfire and it filled my gunsight. I pressed the
firing button for both cannon and machine-guns, but – click!
I had obviously exhausted my ammunition in the earlier air
battles. Of course the British pilot had no way of knowing
this and I still wanted to strike terror in him for so long as he
remained over French soil. I thus remained right behind him,
at high speed. Suddenly I was astonished to see a white plume
of smoke emit from the Spitfire! The smoke grew denser and
the propeller stopped. The pilot made a forced landing in a
field east of Marquise. I circled the aircraft and made a note
of the markings for my victory report, watched the pilot climb
out and waved to him. Just before being captured by German
soldiers, he ignited a built-in explosive charge which destroyed
the centre-section of his aircraft.

I returned to my field and sent my engineering officer to the site to determine the reason for the forced landing. He found, to my amazement, that the Spitfire had taken a single machine-gun round in an engine cylinder during my first attack. Had I not pressed on after running out of ammunition, therefore forcing the pilot to fly at top speed, he would probably have reached England despite the damage. Just a few weeks before, in fact, I myself had made it back across the Channel after two of my engine's connecting rods had been smashed over Dover. On this occasion over France, however, the British pilot, a flight lieutenant, now had to head for prison camp whilst I recorded my thirty-third victory.

Returning to the French coast, Pilot Officer Johnson saw a lone Me 109 below. Suspecting it to be one of the three which had chased him into the cloud just a few minutes previously, Johnnie anxiously searched the sky for the other two: the sky was clear. From astern, Dogsbody Four dropped below the 109 before attacking from its blind spot, below and behind. One burst of cannon shells sent the enemy fighter diving earthwards emitting a plume of black smoke. Pilot Officer Johnson came 'out of France on the deck, low and fast', his Spitfire roaring over waving civilians, just feet above their fields. At the coast, German soldiers ran to their guns, but in a second the fleeting Spitfire was gone. Climbing over the Channel, Dogsbody Four realised that something might have happened to Wing Commander Bader:

> As I was crossing the Channel, Group Captain Woodhall, who obviously knew that there had been a fight from the radar and R/T, repeated 'Douglas, are you receiving?' This came over the air every five minutes or so. I therefore called up and said 'It's Johnnie here, Sir. We've had a stiff fight and I last saw the Wing Commander on the tail of a 109.' He said, 'Thank you. I'll meet you at dispersal.'

The silence from 'Dogsbody' over the R/T clearly meant one of two things, either that his radio was unserviceable, or he had somehow been brought down. Air Marshal Sir Denis Crowley-Milling, then a flight commander in Ken Holden's 610 Squadron, recalled that:

The greatest impression I have is the silence on the R/T. Douglas always maintained a running commentary. Had the worst happened? The colourful language and running commentary had suddenly ceased, leaving us all wondering what had happened. Was he alive or dead? Had his radio failed? I know we were above thick cloud on the way home and asked the Tangmere Controller to provide a homing bearing for us to steer. This was way out in accuracy, however, and unbeknown to us we were flying up the North Sea, just scraping in to Martlesham Heath with hardly any fuel remaining – it was indeed a day to remember!

So confused had been the fighting, so numerous the aircraft in this incredible maelstrom over St-Omer, that only Wing Commander Bader himself had the answers to the questions regarding his present state and whereabouts. After the first downwards charge, 'Dogsbody' found himself alone after flattening out at 24,000 feet. In front of him were six 109s flying in a line-abreast formation of three pairs. Flying alone, Bader knew that he should leave this enemy formation and adhere to the instructions issued to his pilots: get out and get home. He considered these 109s to be 'sitters', however, and, in a split-second, greed won over discipline and good judgement. Alone over France, Wing Commander Bader stalked the middle *Rotte*. He later reported:

I saw some more Me 109s. I arrived amongst these, who were evidently not on the lookout, as I expect they imagined the first formation we attacked to be covering them. I got a very easy shot at one of these which flew quite straight until he went on fire from behind the cockpit – a burst of about three seconds.

As two 109s curved towards him, 'Dogsbody' broke right, violently, although anticipating, with some bravado, that his course would take him between a pair of 109s. Suddenly something hit Spitfiire 'DB'. Due to the close proximity of the enemy aircraft, Bader assumed that he had collided with a 109. The Spitfire went completely out of control, diving earthwards, its control column limp and unresponsive. As he looked behind, Bader's impression was that the entire fuselage aft of the VHF aerial had gone, although he was later to report that it was 'probably just the empennage'.

At 24,000 feet, 'Dogsbody' was unable to consider escape due to the lack of oxygen outside the cockpit at that height. His dilemma, however, was that the doomed fighter was already travelling in excess of 400 mph, so would soon be subjected to forces so great that baling out would become impossible. Yanking the canopy release mechanism, the hood was sucked away, the cockpit immediately being battered by the airflow. Without legs though, would he be able to thrust his body upwards to get out? As he struggled to get his head above the windscreen, he was nearly plucked out of the cockpit, but halfway he became stuck – the rigid foot of his artificial right leg jamming in the cockpit, the grip vice-like. Ever downwards the fighter plunged, the pilot helpless and continuously battered by the rushing wind, half in and half out of his crashing aeroplane. Desperately gripping his parachute's 'D' ring, Douglas Bader struggled furiously to get out. Eventually, at about 6,000 feet, the offending artificial leg's restraining strap broke. Free at last, the pilot was plucked out into mid-air; as the Spitfire continued its dive, he experienced a moment of apparently floating upwards. That terrible buffeting having thankfully ceased, in the silence he was able to think. His hand still gripping the 'D' ring, he pulled. There was a slight delay before the parachute deployed and then he was really was floating, gently to earth beneath the life-saving silk umbrella.

At 4,000 feet Wing Commander Bader floated through a layer of cloud, emerging below to see the ground still far below. Alarmed by the roar of an aero-engine, he saw a Me 109 fly directly towards him, but the bullets he must have half-expected never came as the enemy fighter flashed by just 50 yards away. It may surprise many people to know that such a parachute descent, made due to enemy action or some other mishap while flying actively, was often the first a pilot would actually make, there being no formal parachute training. Consequently, Bader had never before had to consider the practicalities of landing with artificial legs, or indeed one such leg, as he drifted earthwards. Having had some minutes to ponder this matter, suddenly French soil rushed up to meet him and he hit the ground hard, in an orchard near Blaringhem, to the south-east of St-Omer. For Wing Commander Douglas Bader, the air war was over: his personal period of operational service had lasted just eighteen months.

Johnnie recalled the scene back at Westhampnett: 'Group Captain Woodhall was waiting for me on the airfield, and when Dundas, West,

Hepple and the others came back the consensus of opinion was that the Wing Commander had either been shot down or involved in a collision.' In his logbook, Johnnie wrote that on this penetration over France there had been 'more opposition than ever before'. Squadron Leader Burton's logbook recorded, 'Had a bad time with 109s on way out and had to get into cloud.' As the clock ticked on, it became clear from fuel considerations that the two Spitfires reported missing during the radio chatter over France were unlikely to return to Westhampnett. Reasoning that if flying damaged machines the pilots might land at one of the coastal airfields, Tangmere telephoned each in turn, receiving negative responses from all. Douglas Roberts was a Radio Telephone (Direction Finding) Operator at the Tangmere 'Fixer' station which was, perhaps oddly, located on West Malling airfield in Kent:

> We were told that Wing Commander Bader was missing and so listened out for several hours. Our system was basic when compared to modern equipment today, but nevertheless very efficient. The aerial system was a double dipole which, when rotated, would indicate either a true bearing or a reciprocal. Despite our diligence, nothing was heard from 'Dogsbody'.

Had either of the two missing pilots reached mid-Channel, then there was an excellent chance that they would be picked up by air–sea rescue. If their dinghies had drifted closer to the French coast then it was more likely that the Germans would get to them first, unless their positions could be discovered and a protective aerial umbrella established. Consequently Dundas, Johnson, Hepple and West were soon flying back over the Channel, searching. At Le Touquet, Dundas led the section north, parallel to the coast and towards Cap Griz-Nez. Avoiding flak from various enemy vessels, especially near the port of Calais, a steep turn at zero feet returned the Spitfires to Le Touquet. At one point Hepple broke away to machine-gun a surfacing submarine, but otherwise the only item to report was an empty dinghy sighted by Sergeant West. To Johnnie, that empty, life-saving rubber boat was somehow symbolic of their fruitless search. With petrol almost exhausted, the section landed at Hawkinge. No news had yet been received of either missing pilot. Immediately the aircraft were refueled, the 616 Squadron pilots took off, intending to head back across the Channel to France. Shortly after take-off, however, Group Captain Woodhall cancelled the sortie, fearing that a second trip was too risky as the enemy might now be waiting. Swinging round to the west, the Spitfires flew back to Westhampnett. For Hugh Dundas, the thought of Bader dead was 'utterly shattering'. He drove back to Shopwyke House 'alone and utterly dejected'. Back at the Mess, he and Johnnie shared a whole bottle of brandy. Despair had overtaken the inner sanctum.

When the Red Cross had announced that Wing Commander Bader was a prisoner, on 14 August, there was absolute euphoria within Fighter Command, and in particular, of course, at Tangmere. Group Captain Woodhall broadcast the news over the station tannoy. Sir Denis Crowley-Milling remembered:

> The loss of Douglas Bader had left us all stunned. A few of us, including Dundas and Johnson, were with Thelma Bader in their married quarters at Tangmere when the telephone rang. After speaking, Thelma came back to join us and very calmly said, 'Douglas is safe and a prisoner.'

The Germans, however, had been unable to decide for certain which of their pilots had brought down this famous British war hero. Wing Commander Bader's personal view, so shocking was the damage to his Spitfire, was that he had collided with an enemy machine. Indeed, collision, due to the very great number of aircraft engaged, was Johnnie's greatest fear in this action. The reality, however, was quite different, and readers are referred to Flight Lieutenant Casson's account. As we have seen, 'friendly fire' was not uncommon, and aircraft identification in such fast-moving and high-stress combats was often fraught with danger. The enemy lost but one 109 in this fight, the tail of which was not shot off; the only other aircraft downed was Bader's Spitfire. There can be no doubt that in the heat of the moment Flight Lieutenant Casson – an experienced and able fighter pilot – made a perfectly understandable mistake. Buck died, in fact, convinced that he had destroyed a 109 that fateful day – but the evidence confirms that was not the case. So it was, therefore, that the 'Master's' active war against the Germans was not abruptly ended by the shells of a German fighter, but by those from another Spitfire. Johnnie remembered:

When Douglas was shot down it really was his own fault. He was tired, ready for a rest. Leigh-Mallory had asked him to come off Ops, as 'Sailor' Malan, leader of the Biggin Hill Wing, had already done so, having recognised in himself the signs of strain. Douglas wouldn't go, of course, and so the AOC agreed to let him stay on until the end of the season, the end of September when the weather started failing. Flight Lieutenant Peter MacDonald MP, our adjutant, who had served with Douglas since 1940, also recognised in him the signs of strain. He insisted that Douglas and Thelma should join him on a week's golfing at St Andrews. They were, in fact, booked to go on 11 August. Douglas was exhausted. Irritable. And he couldn't see things quickly enough in the air. On the day in question, when Ken Holden sighted the 109s and Bader was unable to see them, he should have let Ken come down and attack as he suggested. In not allowing this he lost us six, maybe even seven, seconds, by which time the high 109s were down on us. But of course Douglas was a bit greedy and would not, therefore, allow this. As he couldn't personally see the enemy, Douglas should have stayed put and covered Ken Holden whilst he attacked. Douglas was greedy, especially towards the end. Someone had seen a 109 down here and Bader would go after it with thirty-six Spitfires bounding after him. It was chaotic.

Indeed, once the Wing Leader's ASI went unserviceable shortly after take-off, he should not simply have allowed Flight Lieutenant Dundas to lead the formation across the Channel in his stead, but should have turned back. After battle had been joined, Wing Commander Bader had swiftly been separated from the rest of his section. At that point he should also have headed home – as per his own instructions. The whole sequence of events represented a catalogue of errors, but the prevailing press-on attitude was so typical of the man. There were also other problems generated by Bader's style of leadership. It was wrong for him to exclusively lead the Wing at the head of 616 Squadron. Johnnie:

> Yes, that was a mistake. I can understand to a degree that Douglas wanted people around him upon whom he knew he could depend, and that by flying with the same pilots in Dogsbody Section we

all got to know the form pretty well, what he required and how
the thing worked, and so on and so forth. What I think he should
have done was perhaps kept the same wingman, but rotated the
squadrons with whom he flew. Whilst we of 616 and 610, based
at Westhampnett obviously saw Douglas daily, and we of 616
had a particularly close relationship with him of course as he
flew with us and operated from our dispersal, those squadrons
based at Merston, firstly Stan Turner's 145, then Gaunce's 41,
never saw him. The other problem was that by always leading
the Wing at the head of 616, Billy Burton never got to lead his
own squadron – and he, a Cranwell Sword of Honour man – was
a very capable leader indeed. Once I heard Burton say, 'Now
Douglas, could you fly with "B" Flight today?' You can imagine
where this is going, can't you? Douglas responded, 'No Billy, I
am not flying with *fucking* "B" Flight today. I want Sergeant
Smith, Cocky and Johnnie with me and that's an *order*!' And
that was that.

Nonetheless, Bader's had left an inspirational and indelible
impression on many of his young pilots – not least Johnnie:

> You can learn ninety per cent of the skills required for leadership,
> man management, being straightforward with your subordinates
> and so on, but that last ten per cent, which wins the hearts and
> minds, is an indefinable gift given to but a few, such as the gift of
> a great artist or writer. Bader had that gift, make no mistake.

The experience gained that summer was, as Air Marshal Sir Denis
Crowley-Milling said, 'unforgettable' and 'stood us in good stead'.
Johnnie: 'Douglas Bader had shown us the true meaning of courage,
spirit, determination, guts. Now that he was gone it was our job to
follow his example and signposts pointing the way ahead.'

Under Wing Commander Bader's leadership and guidance
Johnnie had gained both inspiration and experience. His combat
reports have a common feature: whenever possible he was getting
in as close as possible before opening fire, and attacking from
below and behind – a blind spot and a tactic favoured by Werner
Mölders himself. Johnnie had flown numerous operational sorties
over France, participating in complex operations and frequently

engaging the enemy. His apprenticeship was coming to an end. On his Spitfire, Johnnie had painted 'Bader's Bus Company – Still Running'. And so, with Bader a prisoner, the war continued for Pilot Officer Johnson and the Tangmere Wing.

3

Bader's Bus Company:
Still Running

Inspirational and exciting though the summer of 1941 undoubtedly was for the Tangmere Wing's Spitfire pilots – it was also a deadly one. Air Commodore Sir Archie Winskill was then a flight lieutenant flying Spitfires with 41 Squadron:

> On 14 August 1941 I was shot down near Calais. I baled out and fortunately received help from the French which eventually enabled me to escape over the Pyrenees, returning home via Spain and Gibraltar. Whilst hiding on a farm in the Pas-de-Calais, I was visited by a British agent, Sidney Bowen, who was from an escape organisation based in Marseilles. He asked me why more Spitfires were crashing in France than Me 109s. I had no answer for him.

Bowen was right. The Non-Stop Offensive was not going to plan. German fighters were not being destroyed in droves, as Douglas and Leigh-Mallory intended. In June 1941, for example, Fighter Command claimed 176 enemy aircraft destroyed and 74 probables – the Germans actually only lost 44. Between 14 June and 31 December 1941, the RAF lost 411 fighters. Indeed, by the end of 1941 Fighter Command was losing the day-fighter air war over France by a ratio of two to one. The German invasion of the Soviet Union on 22 June 1941, however, dictated that the offensive had to be maintained, according to the War Cabinet, as a 'disagreeable necessity'. America, of course, had yet to enter the war, and Britain was under pressure to somehow assist the Russians. Geographically this was largely impossible from a perspective of direct military assistance, and a second front was, of course, completely out of the question at that time. So although British and German forces were fighting in the Middle East, on the Channel front Churchill's only option was to bomb the enemy at night and continue with the daytime fighter offensive. Ineffective though the latter was known to be, not least due to ULTRA decrypts, it was crucial to maintain a positive relationship with Stalin. As Wing Commander David Cox remarked, 'What else could we do?' Although Fighter Command's intention was to draw *Luftwaffe* units back to the Channel coast from Russia, this never happened: JG 2 and 26 were not reinforced. Little wonder, then, that the enemy dubbed Douglas and Leigh-Mallory's campaign 'The Non-Sense Offensive'.

On 12 August, Johnnie was transferred from 'A' to 'B' Flight, now commanded by Flight Lieutenant Darling following Buck Casson's capture. Johnnie flew Spitfire W3437 on a Target Support sweep to Gosnay, the Tangmere Wing acting as Cover Wing that afternoon, protecting the withdrawal of Hampdens returning from Le Trait. On 14 August, Johnnie joined 616 Squadron on an 'offensive patrol after bombing operations in Boulogne'. In his logbook he wrote, 'Attacked Me 109F. No result. Poor shooting.' On 19 August, the Tangmere Wing provided Close Escort to Blenheims bombing Longuenesse. This, however, was a Circus with a difference. When he baled out over France, Wing Commander Bader had broken one of his artificial legs. Chivalrously, Adolf Galland and his officers had entertained Bader at their Audembert HQ, on which occasion the former Tangmere Wing Leader requested that the Germans ask, via international communication channels, for his spare legs to be sent over. This was duly done. Indeed, the Germans offered safe passage for a British aircraft to land at St-Omer to deliver them. Woodhall immediately volunteered to fly the sortie, but Churchill vetoed the scheme, angrily emphasising the fact that RAF aircraft did not require safe passage to fly over France. So it was, then, that the 'Leg Operation' took place. On the trip to Longuenesse, an 82 Squadron Blenheim dropped the spare legs by parachute. Johnnie's logbook simply recorded, 'Tin legs dropped by parachute SW of St-Omer'.

The familiar round of operations continued. Johnnie: 'Bader was replaced as Tangmere Wing Leader by a man called Woodhouse, but he wasn't in Bader's league as a leader.' On 21 August, Johnnie claimed an Me 109 probable on a Circus to Béthune. It was a bad day for the Tangmere Wing and 610 Squadron in particular: over Hazebrouck 'A' Flight was bounced by 4/JG 26, four out of six Spitfires being shot down. Among those who failed to return was Flight Lieutenant Crowley-Milling, who also escaped over the Pyrenees back to England. The final day of August was a busy day for Johnnie. His first flight was a 'Wing escort to HM destroyer operating off French coast'. Next the Wing flew a sweep to St-Omer, 'B' Flight attacking 'about twenty Me 109s', but Johnnie made no claim. The final sortie was Close Escort to Blenheims 'attacking Trait-en-La-Seine'. Johnnie also wrote of that sortie in his logbook that 41 Squadron provided top cover but lost another pilot. The 616 Squadron diarist concluded that the month had been

> a disappointing one from the operational point of view, owing to poor weather conditions. Although sixteen offensive sweeps were carried out over France, their effectiveness was in several cases hampered by too much cloud, making it difficult for the Wing to keep together. Wing Commander Bader DSO (and Bar) DFC, and Flight Lieutenant Casson were shot down on 9 August and are now prisoners of war. This was a serious loss to the RAF, the Wing and the Squadron.

Fighter Command had, in fact, lost a total of 108 fighters. The combined losses of JG 2 and 26, however, were just eighteen – a loss ratio of six to one in the enemy's favour.

On 4 September the Tangmere Wing provided cover over the Channel for bombers returning from Mazingarbe. Johnnie and Sergeant West, of 'A' Flight, both attacked the same Me 109E, claiming it as probably destroyed. This enemy fighter was most likely from 5/JG 26, which was still equipped with the older *Emil*, but the unit recorded no losses this day. Johnnie:

> We are talking about the period immediately Bader had been brought down, by which time I had been in the Tangmere Wing for some time, certainly all that spring and summer, and I had shot down at least four enemy aircraft. Soon after Bader disappeared I was awarded the DFC and made up to flight lieutenant on the same day, which I think was one of the highlights of my career, because when the CO told me that I had got the DFC together with a chap called 'Nip' Hepple from Newcastle. Another pilot called Jeff West from New Zealand had got the DFM, and then the Squadron Commander said, 'Oh, and by the way, I'd like you

to take over "B" Flight.' My feet I don't think touched the ground for about two days, a feeling of great elation to have these two things. Winning the DFC and being promoted means that you are at last out of your apprenticeship and were now an experienced flight commander with upwards of 100 offensive sweeps under your belt.

Johnnie's next big fight came on 21 September, while escorting Blenheims to Gosnay. The top cover wings, however, failed to make the rendezvous. Johnnie's combat report described the events that took place at 1515 hours, just inland of and 20,000 feet above Le Touquet:

I was Blue One, leading my Flight … I was flying at 20,000 feet and shortly after crossing the French coast at Le Touquet we were engaged by at least thirty 109s which dived to attack my Section from above and behind. I broke my Section to the left and after manoeuvering for position attacked a 109F with cannon from quarter astern and slightly below, closing from 200 to 70 yards. I observed pieces falling away from the port wing and wing root and then broke to starboard as another 109 was coming down on me. On completing my turn I saw a parachute just opening at approximately the same position in which I had seen the 109. This was also seen by my Number Three, Pilot Officer Smith, and this aircraft is claimed as destroyed. I then lost Pilot Officer Smith and as the Beehive had long since disappeared into France I decided to work my way out as there were several 109s about who seemed anxious to destroy me. I spun and spiralled down to sea level with my pursuers getting in an occasional shot. When about ten miles off Le Touquet at nought feet I saw an E/A come in from astern. And waited until he was almost within range before I carried out a steep climbing turn to the left. He pulled up to attack and I distinctly saw four streams of machine-gun fire and one of cannon, but his aim was unsteady and I wasn't hit. As I straightened out I saw another 109F just ahead of me – I opened fire and closed in from the quarter astern again, firing a long steady burst of cannon, recalculating my deflection as I closed to about fifty yards. E/A climbed steeply, stalled, and as I broke away, I saw him fall on to his back and then into the sea – this engagement taking place between sea level and 1,000 feet. This E/A is claimed as destroyed. There were still two 109s about and although I could out-turn them they seemed to possess a greater speed and caused them to abandon their attack. They eventually gave up the chase when about ten miles South of Dover.

This was great shooting: two 109s definitely destroyed. These kills also made Johnnie's tally six enemy aircraft destroyed (not counting those shared, damaged or probably destroyed), making him officially an 'ace', such status being achieved upon a fighter pilot's fifth victory. On 30 September, the award of Johnnie's DFC was gazetted:

> This officer has participated in forty-six operational sorties over enemy territory and has destroyed at least four hostile aircraft. Flying Officer Johnson has at all times shown great courage.

Back home, Johnnie's brother, Ross, recalled that 'the folks were as proud as punch'.

On 1 October, Squadron Leader Burton was rested after what had been a long spell on operations. He was posted to 11 Group HQ as Squadron Leader Tactics. Early the following year this extremely promising officer no doubt destined for high rank was promoted to wing commander and posted to the Middle East. There he led 329 Wing on tank-busting operations, winning a DSO for 'brilliant leadership' and the French Croix de Guerre for a daring low-level attack on a desert fort, enabling the escape of the famous French General Leclerc. Having spent some time in England on leave, on 3 June 1943 Group Captain Burton was a passenger aboard an unarmed Hudson aircraft returning to the Desert Air Force. Over the Bay of Biscay, the Hudson was destroyed by a Ju 88. There were no survivors. As CO of 616 Squadron, Burton was replaced by a New Zealander, Squadron Leader Colin Falkland Gray DFC. Johnnie:

> Colin was a very able and successful fighter pilot, but he did not have the same qualities of leadership as Billy Burton did. He was rather a rough, aggressive sort of man.

Five days later 616 Squadron's tour at Tangmere concluded. By this time Flight Lieutenant J. E. Johnson DFC had flown 183.40

operational hours and destroyed six enemy aircraft. Moreover, the conclusion of 616 Squadron's tour at Tangmere was the end of a profound experience for Johnnie.

At Kirton, back in 12 Group, Johnnie recalled that 616 Squadron

> settled down to a winter of training new pilots, of convoy patrols off the east coast, a little night-flying over Hull and the industrial cities which were being bombed during that winter, but we couldn't do much from a Spitfire because of its limited vision at night and it was a tricky aeroplane to land at night because of that narrow undercarriage. Our Honorary CO was a man called Lord Titchfield. All auxiliary squadrons had honorary COs, and he had a big estate not far away at Welbeck Woodhouse, which had one of the best pheasant shoots in the country. He knew that some of us were very keen on shooting, so every week or so four or five of us were invited to shoot at Welbeck, which was very enjoyable, and I loved every moment of it myself. As I say, we trained a lot of pilots, we sent a lot of pilots overseas, got a lot of new ones to replace them, and trained them too.

The monotony of training flights was broken on 8 November 1941 when 616 Squadron formed a wing with the Canadian Spitfire Squadrons 411 and 412, operating out of West Malling in 11 Group on Circus 110. This was Fighter Command's last Circus of 1941, but was a disaster. Two targets were attacked, a distillery at St-Pol and the railway repair works at Lille. The sun favoured the *Luftwaffe*, which also hampered the Beehives forming up. The 12 Group Wing flew as the second rear support wing. Incredibly, the formation was led by Wing Commander Douglas Scott AFC, a 33-year-old without any combat experience. His formation reached the French coast in good order but had to orbit over Dunkirk, as it was too early. Heavy flak caused the formation to break up, at which point II/JG 26 fell on the Spitfires. Three Canadians of 412 Squadron were shot down, and the 'Wingco' also failed to return: his last radio message was: 'I guess I'm too old for this, boys.' This ill-fated operation indicated the folly of Fighter Command's strategy throughout 1941: seventeen Spitfires were lost, fourteen pilots being killed. This disaster fortunately marked the end of the 'season'.

Significantly, *Hauptmann* Joachim Müncheberg's II/JG 26, which had taken such a toll of 12 Group Wing fighters on Circus 110, was equipped with a new fighter. After this action, Flying Officer Hepple reported that the enemy fighters engaged were not 109s but had radial engines. All agreed that this new enemy machine was superior to their own Spitfire Mk V in every respect. The new menace in the sky was the Focke-Wulf 190, appropriately known by the Germans as the 'Butcher Bird'. The 190 had, in fact, first appeared in small numbers during September 1941. The radial engine caused confusion, and the possibility of a superior new German fighter was at first dismissed by RAF intelligence, which stated it was more likely to be a Curtis Hawk (some airworthy examples of which had been captured by the Germans in 1940). In October, however, cine-gun camera film definitely confirmed that this was no obsolete Hawk, but was indeed a potent new enemy fighter.

The FW 190 was powered by a 1,700-hp BMW 801D-2 fourteen-cylinder radial engine. This provided a maximum speed of 312 mph at 19,500 feet; with a one-minute override boost it could accelerate to over 400 mph. The 190's operating ceiling was 35,000 feet, and it could climb to 26,000 feet in 12 minutes. Furthermore, it was extremely manoeuvrable. By comparison, the Spitfire Mk VB, with which Fighter Command's squadrons were most commonly equipped at this time, could reach 371 mph at 20,000 feet, but could not operate much above 25,000 feet (359 mph), and took some 25 minutes to reach that height. The Spitfire Mk V was essentially a Mk II airframe coupled with a more powerful Rolls-Royce Merlin 45 engine. Initially, the Mk V was seen merely as a stopgap, to provide a fighter with a better high-altitude performance than the Mk II. By October 1941, over 100 FW 190s had been delivered and began engaging on an increasing basis. Initially, however, the first pilots to fly the new fighter, II/JG 26, were forbidden from operating further than the French coast for fear of being brought down over or close enough to England for a 190 to be captured and examined by the British. The German pilots were impressed with the 190's rate of roll and acceleration, but significantly it was unable to out-turn a Spitfire Mk V.

On 23 December, Flight Lieutenant Dundas was promoted to squadron leader and left 616 Squadron, of which he was the last surviving original member still serving with the unit. Johnnie:

Yes, I missed Cocky, of course. He went off to command 56 Squadron, which was starting to fly the new Hawker Typhoon. Although this later proved an excellent ground-attack aircraft, initially there were a lot of problems caused by carbon monoxide leaking into the cockpit – which led to fatalities. Cocky had to sort all this out, and it couldn't have been an easy job.

On 30 January 1942, 616 Squadron moved from Kirton to Kingscliffe, in Northamptonshire, 12 miles west of Peterborough in Cambridgeshire. Johnnie:

Kingscliffe was a Wittering satellite, and there we were re-equipped with the Spitfire Mk VI, which had extended and pointed wingtips, meant to operate at 40,000 feet, which was very high in those days. In fact, I took one up to 42,000. So there we were at Kingscliffe with these high-altitude aircraft designed to operate in the desert and shoot down those high flying Ju 88s etc., and what do they do – put us on convoy patrols at 500 feet! So that was really a waste of a good aeroplane and not very pleasant because, as they were pressurised to some extent, the hood was locked down and had to be unlocked by the groundcrew, although you could blow it off if there was an emergency. It wasn't such a nice feeling as the old hood, which slid back, so I often took to flying with no hood at all, especially on comparatively low-level convoy patrols over the sea. You still suffered, though, as it was so noisy without the hood that you couldn't hear the R/T very well.

The day after the Squadron moved to Kingscliffe, another old friend from Tangmere days left 616: Flight Lieutenant Hepple DFC was posted to Malta. The air fighting over that all-important Mediterranean island was, some say, of such ferocity that it made the Battle of Britain look 'like child's play'. In those lethal skies Hepple would continue to make a good account in the finest Dogsbody Section tradition. Ten days later Sergeant Jeff West DFM, another 'Dogsbody', followed him. The old team had now completely broken up.

As the weather began to improve, Fighter Command continued with its offensive policy. During April 1942, 616 Squadron participated in seven major sweeps over France. From Kingscliffe,

616 would fly down to West Malling in Kent, forming the 12 Group Wing with 609 and 412 Squadrons. On 12 April, the Wing covered the withdrawal of bombers returning from the Hazebrouck marshalling yards. Engaged by 190s, Johnnie's 'B' Flight lost two pilots, and 412 Squadron lost another. On 15 April, the 12 Group Spitfires flew as Escort Cover Wing to Blenheims and Hurribombers attacking Desvres. Johnnie's combat report detailed events:

> When about 5–7 miles inside the French coast, near Le Touquet, I saw several FW 190s and Me 109s 4,000 feet above the Squadron and manoeuvring for position in the sun. One FW 190 broke away and came down to attack Number Four of my Section so I ordered them to break to port. The 190 fired and pulled away in a fast climb. When straightening the Section out I saw two E/A – a FW 190 and a 109 diving ahead of me. I followed the 190, closing in from the quarter, and gave him a 1–2 second burst with cannon at 200 yards range, and observed strikes on the port wing root. He emitted glycol immediately and a piece of fuselage fell away. This was also observed by Pilot Officer Bowen (Blue Three). I broke off the engagement, as I had lost 4,000 feet and there were many E/A about, and climbed back to re-join the Squadron at 19,000 feet.

The 190 was credited as damaged. 616 Squadron, though, lost another two pilots. Johnnie:

> Yes, the 190 was causing real problems at this time. We could out-turn it, but you couldn't turn all day. As the number of 190s increased, so the depth of our penetrations over France decreased, they drove us back to the coast, really.

On 27 April, 616 Squadron was one of eleven Spitfire squadrons escorting six Bostons attacking Ostend; two bombers were shot down by flak. Flying with the 12 Group Wing was 123 Squadron, an 'Eagle' unit of American volunteers, which lost a Spitfire on this sortie. On 10 May, Johnnie flew Spitfire BR256 on an 'Offensive Patrol' from Martlesham Heath. This sortie involved only two other Spitfires, Sergeant Smithson and the New Zealander Wing Commander Pat Jameson DFC, the Wittering Wing Leader. In his logbook, Johnnie recorded:

The weather gradually lifted until we reached the Dutch coast at
15,000 feet. My engine very rough – boost capsule sticking. No
E/A seen but about fifteen to twenty 'E' boats sighted approaching
Zeebrugge Harbour and reported.

Johnnie recorded the details of an unusual experience on 25 May:

Blue Section (Pilot Officer Brown and Sergeant Welch) and Green
Section (self and Sergeant Smithson) intercepted a Do 217 four
miles north-west of base at 4,000 feet. Closed to 100 yards but
did not engage as E/A had British roundels – E/A opened fire and
was then engaged by Sergeant Smithson, Pilot Officer Brown and
Sergeant Welch. Was seen with glycol streaming from one engine
and therefore claimed as damaged. Pilot Officer Brown wounded
in the eye by return fire but made a successful landing at North
Ruffenham.

This is an odd occurrence. As we have seen, aircraft misidentification
was common, but it is unlikely that four Spitfire pilots, especially
one with Johnnie's experience, would fail to correctly identify
a lone German bomber in a comparatively low-stress situation.
Nonetheless, German aircraft are not known to have carried British
markings as a ruse to escape interception. Also of interest is the
fact that Johnnie could easily have added another victory to his
tally, but instead he allowed the three inexperienced pilots he was
leading to intercept and share the glory. On 3 June, 616 Squadron
once more flew out of West Malling with the Wittering Wing, flying
a sweep over the French coast between Boulogne and Le Touquet.
Johnnie recorded having seen 'a squadron of 190s and 109s', but
there was no engagement. Nonetheless, *Oberfeldwebel* Leibold of
Stab I/JG 26 picked off Pilot Officer Peter Moore of 'A' Flight, who
was reported missing.

The date of 9 June 1942 was significant for Johnnie: he was
awarded a Bar to his DFC. Gazetted on 26 June, the citation read:

Since being awarded the DFC in September 1941, this officer has
participated in many sweeps over enemy territory, during which
he destroyed two Me 109Fs and damaged a FW 190. He has also
carried out a large number of convoy patrols. Flight Lieutenant

Johnson is an exceptional leader and the magnificent example he sets is an inspiration to other pilots.

22 June saw a significant event: *Oberleutnant* Armin Faber of *Stab* III/JG 2 landed by mistake at Pembrey in South Wales – presenting the RAF with an intact 'Butcher Bird'. Rapidly evaluated at Farnborough, the essential data discovered was immediately fed into the Spitfire development programme. Fighter Command's need to get the Spitfire back on top was urgent, and the engineers responded to the call. That month the first Mk IXs began reaching the squadrons. The first were received by 64 Squadron at Hornchurch, followed by 401 and 402 (Canadian) Squadrons in August, and 133 ('Eagle') Squadron in September. Production output increased slowly, however, and so for some time the majority of RAF fighter squadrons had to sally forth with the obsolete Mk V.

On 8 July, 616 Squadron was sent back into the line, joining the Kenley Wing in 11 Group. Johnnie:

It was being whispered at the time that I was going to get command of a squadron. I was getting telephone calls from staff officers asking me how many operational hours I had accumulated, and when did I last have a rest and so on.

Two days after arriving at Kenley, Johnnie was posted to 610 'County of Chester' Squadron, another AAF unit, at Ludham. The posting was as a 'supernumerary' flight lieutenant, but everyone knew that this meant Johnnie was imminently to become a squadron commander. Johnnie:

My 1942 diary says that we had a farewell party in the 'Greyhound' at Croydon with all 'B' Flight pilots and all the groundcrews, including my fitter, old Fred Burton. I had been with the Squadron almost two years and had seen a great many changes amongst the pilots, but the groundcrew had remained constant, and we had become very attached to each other. On the way to Norfolk, I spent the night with Cocky Dundas at Newmarket. He was at a place called Snailwell, commanding the first Typhoon squadron, 56, which was having a lot of teething troubles and killing a lot of pilots. He kept the morale up; he was a very good leader, Cocky.

We then set course for the big Wittering summer party, calling in at 'The Bridge' at Huntingdon, and 'The Haycock' at Wansford. We had lots of beer and spirits, and, oh yes, lobster and crab – we certainly lived well in those days! The following evening, Cocky organised a party to celebrate my promotion with his pilots, and this was attended by, amongst others, John Grandy, who went on to become Chief of the Air Staff, and Paul Richey, author of *Fighter Pilot*. We had a right old session, but the following day it was off to Ludham and 610.

First I went to the Sector Station, Coltishall, where I had an interview with the Station Commander, Group Captain Lees, and met the Wing Commander (Flying), a chap called Prosser Hanks who had flown during the Battle of France with Paul Richey. Ronnie Lees told me that I would be taking over 610 Squadron from a chap called 'Scruffy' Haywood, a regular chap, but he said, 'I don't know whether you'll see him or not because I haven't even seen him for several weeks. So far as I can make out he is shacked up with some society woman in a caravan just outside the airfield!' The 'society woman' was Lady Margaret Strickland, who had been a bit of a beauty in her day and still was, and achieved a certain amount of fame for anti-blood-sports and that sort of thing. Then it was off to Ludham, hard by Hickling Broad, to meet the people of 610 who seemed to be a pretty good bunch. The Squadron had been commanded by Ken Holden when in the Tangmere Wing, so I knew a bit about it. We had eleven pilots in 'A' Flight, and the same in 'B'. These included people from Canada, France, Belgium, Norway, and even a Rhodesian, people from all over the place. That was a big change from pre- and early war days.

That Johnnie, the policeman's son and former grammar schoolboy from Melton Mowbray, should be promoted to command an AAF unit was an equally 'big change'. Johnnie had achieved this through sheer ability alone – not the connections of a privileged socio-educational background.

On 13 July 1942, Johnnie was officially promoted to squadron leader and posted to command 610 Squadron. By this time, his ability as a pilot was officially endorsed as 'Exceptional'. The 27-year-old with a double DFC would now demonstrate that he was an equally exceptional fighter leader.

4

Squadron Commander:
Rhubarbs & JUBILEE

When I got to Ludham [recalled Johnnie] Denis Crowley-Milling, or 'Crow' as we called him, was a flight commander on 610, with whom he had flown during Tangmere Wing days. He was really senior to me, having been commissioned before me and won a DFC before me, and it put me in a bit of an invidious position to suddenly become his Boss. I told the Group Captain, who lived at Coltishall, this when I took over the Squadron, but he told me not to worry as Crow would be getting his own squadron any moment now. In fact he got one of the very first Typhoon squadrons.

One thing that caused Squadron Leader Johnson a certain amount of frustration early on during his time with 610 Squadron was that the 12 Group Wing Leader, Wing Commander Pat 'Jamie' Jameson, insisted that his squadrons flew in the outdated line-astern formation. Given the clear superiority of the Finger Four, it is surprising that this formation had still yet to be universally adopted throughout Fighter Command. It is also indicates that the lack of tactical consistency remained prevalent. Unsurprisingly Johnnie put to Jameson that the Wing should change over to the Finger Four and stated a sound case for doing so:

> The thing was that in line astern it was OK for those up front, but the chap at the back was unprotected. Inevitably he was the first to go down, often unseen by everybody else. Our Finger Four had everybody spread out in line abreast, so everybody had the same chances. Jamie wouldn't agree to it, and insisted that when 610 flew with the Wing, we did so in line astern. Crow agreed that the Finger Four was the best, and so we hatched a plan that 610 would cross the Channel in line astern, but once at our operating height we would switch over to line abreast. We were hoping that Jamie wouldn't notice as we were usually Top Cover.

Johnnie added:

> My diary for 18 July 1942 says that I was lying in bed early
> on listening to the radio when it was announced that Wing
> Commander Paddy Finucane, leader of the Hornchurch Wing,
> had been killed. He had been beating up a machine-gun post
> on the French coast but was hit, turned his Spitfire around but
> with the motor cutting he went straight in. His boys circled the
> spot for some time, but all they saw was a patch of oil on the
> surface. What a bloody end, another great pilot lost on another
> useless Rhubarb – for what? Although he may have shot a line at
> one time, since he had the Wing he had improved tremendously,
> proven by analysis of his combat films.

Later, Johnnie would have an influence on Rhubarbs being
discontinued, but for the time being, for Johnnie's pilots at Ludham,
these senseless operations meant a long two-way flight over the
uninviting North Sea to the Dutch coast. During the month of July,
610 Squadron had been completely re-equipped with the Spitfire
Mk VB, with Merlin 46 engines. These particular machines were
fitted with long-range jettisonable fuel tanks, which extended the
fighter's limited range. On 22 July, for example, Johnnie crossed
the sea with Pilot Officer Collinge on a Rhubarb to Holland. The
Spitfires shot up lock gates and appended machinery, two large
barges on a canal, and a dredger. Had a pilot of Johnnie's calibre
been lost on such a sortie, however, it would have been a poor
exchange. While at Ludham commanding 610, Johnnie would fly
many similar sorties:

> On one occasion, we took off on a Rhubarb at 0500 hours, with
> Yellow Section, that being the Group Captain and one of my
> chaps, turning back after the Groupie's aircraft developed tank
> trouble. The rest of us hit the Dutch coast and when five miles
> inland we broke out of 6/10ths cloud at 600 feet. Murder, wasn't
> it? Of course luckily the place was flat, but we didn't know what
> the pressure was to re-set our altimeters.

Clearly such operations were fraught with all manner of dangers.
By this time, the *Wehrmacht* was rolling ever onwards to the

Russian Caucasus, having annihilated 300,000 Soviet troops at Kharkov and Kiev. The Japanese were overrunning the Far East and even threatening to link up with advancing German forces in Russia. In North Africa, things were also going badly: the British 8th Army was in headlong retreat. In spite of demands made by the Soviet dictator Josef Stalin for the Allies to invade France, such an enormous undertaking was still impossible at this time – even though America had entered the war on the Allies' side after 7 December 1941. Yielding to pressure from Stalin, and because ultimately the Allies' intended to liberate enemy-occupied Europe, it was nonetheless agreed to probe the enemy's coastal defences on 19 August 1942. Operation JUBILEE, the proposed amphibious landing at Dieppe, represented the largest combined-service operation of the war so far.

On 16 August the major part of 610 Squadron, thirteen officers and sixty-four airmen, equipped with eighteen aircraft, moved on attachment to RAF Station West Malling for temporary reinforcement of 11 Group for JUBILEE. Dieppe, a thriving French coastal town, was protected by high cliffs, on which were situated heavy coastal batteries. It was necessary for commandos to destroy these guns prior to a seaborne assault by two brigades of the Canadian 2nd Army and a Canadian tank regiment. Of the 6,000 men involved, in fact, 5,000 were Canadian. The Operation's goal was to ascertain whether the harbour town could be seized and held for a day. While on French soil, Allied troops would also destroy installations and any naval vessels moored in the harbour.

Air Vice-Marshal Leigh-Mallory, still AOC of 11 Group, which would bear the brunt of the Dieppe aerial fighting, saw the Operation as an opportunity to lure the *Luftwaffe* into action on a scale not seen since the Battle of Britain. The fighter force at his disposal comprised fifty-six squadrons, forty-eight of which were Spitfire-equipped. The raid took place on 19 August. For Johnnie's 610 Squadron, according to the unit's diarist, 'Dieppe Day' started early with 'a breakfast of egg and chips in the wee sma' hours'. By 0300 hours, the Squadron was at readiness: 'Pilots were very early astir, but ground crews were before them – busy as bees through this night, fitting long range jettisonable tanks to the Spitfires.' At 0740 hours, Squadron Leader Johnson led 610 off from West Malling in Spitfire VB EP254, DW-B. As a part of the 12 Group Wing, with

411 and 485 Squadrons, 610's brief was to patrol Dieppe as top cover at 10,000 feet. Some three miles off the French coast, Johnnie and his pilots found about fifty enemy fighters, both Me 109Fs and FW190s, flying singly, in pairs, or in fours. From Dieppe, the Spitfire pilots could see a heavy pall of black smoke rising. The 610 Squadron Operations Record Book (ORB) reports that the German fighters 'fought persistently'. A large-scale dogfight was already in progress ahead of 610 Squadron, into which Johnnie and his boys sallied, engaging the enemy at 7,000 feet. Not surprisingly, during the ensuing scrap the Wing, and squadrons, were split up. 610 Squadron's CO reported:

> I saw thirty-forty Me 109s and FW 190s 2,000–3,000 feet above the Squadron and manoeuvring to attack us. I climbed the Squadron fast and when the attacks commenced I broke in towards them. I climbed after a 190 and opened fire from astern, closing from 250–150 yards. The E/A turned to port and I closed in and attacked from the beam with both cannon and machine-gun. The E/A commenced smoking, its wheels dropped and it dived steeply to crash into the sea, as seen by Flight Lieutenant Crowley-Milling DFC, Pilot Officer Hokan and several others. We were then attacked three or four times and had to take violent evasive action.
>
> I then chased an Me 109F and opened fire from astern, closing from some 250–200 yards with cannon and machine-gun. Two other pilots of my Section also fired at this E/A. Pieces flew off as he started to smoke heavily. I closed right in and the E/A half-rolled and dived vertically out of control. Pilot Officer Wright and I saw him crash into the sea. After we attacked, I saw one of my Squadron with glycol pouring from the aircraft but under control and heading for the emergency landing ground east of Dieppe.

This FW 190 was Johnnie's eighth kill and his first of that feared type. The Spitfire seen streaming glycol was flown by an Australian, Flight Sergeant 'South' Creagh, who later reported:

> At approximately 4,000 feet, whilst doing a climbing turn to port I was then attacked from below and behind, receiving hits in the engine and fuselage behind the cockpit. The cockpit became

filled with liquid glycol and smoke. I was temporarily blinded and on recovering found that I was diving at 280 mph. I wiped the windscreen and pulled up, then seeing white smoke issuing from the starboard exhausts I decided to bale out. I eased the stick back to 200 mph, at the same time trying to contact Red One on the R/T. I was then facing Dieppe and with the glycol temperature at 130° I slid back the hood, opened the side cockpit door, took off my helmet, released the Sutton harness and rolled aircraft onto its side. I fell out with ease and after a few seconds pulled the ripcord. I jumped at about 4,000 feet and immediately lost sight of the aircraft. On nearing the water I was trying to blow up my Mae West using CO_2, but this did not function so I concentrated on the landing but could not release the 'chute till I struck the water. Once in the water there was no difficulty so I then blew up the Mae West by mouth. My dinghy came away from the pack and was still attached to the Mae West but I did not bother to blow it up as an MGB was heading my way and just visible. I was picked up six miles to the NE of Dieppe by MGB 317. I was told that my Spitfire had gone in about three miles south of that position.

Meanwhile, Johnnie had regrouped 610 Squadron and turned inland at 20,000 feet. 'Heavy reinforcements' could be seen approaching Dieppe from the south-east. Having informed the Wing Leader, Wing Commander Jameson, Johnnie turned to outflank a 190 flying on his port beam at the same height. With only machine-gun ammunition remaining, Johnnie closed from the starboard beam and let fly. He saw strikes around the cockpit and small pieces flew off. The 190 then began streaming white smoke (which was not glycol, the 190's BMW 801 radial engine being air-cooled). At just fifty yards' range, the Spitfire broke off and rejoined Red Three, Pilot Officer Smith. The latter had also attacked the same 190 before tagging onto four Spitfires of 411 Squadron. An Me 109F then pounced out of the sun, although Smith managed to get on his tail and fire a long shot from 500 yards. The 109 then pulled away back into the sun, too fast for the Spitfire pilot to follow. Flight Lieutenant Crowley-Milling also reported a success:

On climbing up into sun on the left of Colon Leader [Squadron Leader Johnson DFC], I saw an Me 109F and an FW 190 coming

up behind my Number Four, Pilot Officer St Remy. I turned hard
to starboard over the top of Colon Leader and got on the tail of
the Me 109F. I gave it a short burst of cannon and machine-gun
fire, followed by three bursts of machine-gun fire only. As it turned
over onto its back, I saw a small stream of glycol coming from
underneath the E/A. I then had to break hard to port as an FW
190 came up on portside and behind. On doing two complete
turns to evade the 190, I saw a pilot bale out of a 109 about 8,000
feet below me. I also saw two Spitfires going down pouring glycol
about three minutes later.

Pilot Officer 'Hokey' Hokan:

I saw one FW 190 go down belching white smoke and hit the
sea after a short burst by Red One. I attacked an FW 190 flying
at 8,000 feet, firing a two-second burst from port quarter, closing
from 350 to 300 yards. I saw strikes on the tail and claim this
aircraft as damaged. Whilst carrying out this attack, shells from
another 190 hit my Spitfire, severely damaging it. Having lost
sight of my Number Two and being without radio contact I
returned to base alone at sea level.

Alone over Dieppe, Squadron Leader Johnson singled out a 190.
As Johnnie bore down on the German, he yawed his Spitfire to
check the blind spot before attacking. As he did so the enemy
pilot saw him, turned and came hurtling at the Spitfire. Both pilots
broke left into a tight turn, each trying to bring their guns to bear.
Despite the Spitfire Mk Vs reputation at being able to out-turn the
lethal 190, in this case the 190 was gaining. The two fighters had
descended to virtually nought feet and it appeared to Johnnie that
they were 'street fighting in Dieppe itself!' The Spitfire swung out
to sea, roaring over the promenade and beach. Sighting a Royal
Navy destroyer, despite the danger from 'friendly' flak, Johnnie
pushed his throttle through the gate and, with an extra 16 pounds
of boost, skimmed above the waves, hurtling towards the British
ship. Inevitably the destroyer's gunners opened fire, and tracer
flashed dangerously close to Johnnie's cockpit. Hauling back on
the stick to pull up over the destroyer, once clear he broke left,
searching for the 190, of which he was relieved to see no sign.

Either the German had broken off the chase over the coast or had been hit by the destroyer.

At 0920 hours, 610 Squadron landed back at West Malling. Three pilots were posted missing. Two hours later, Colon Leader led 610 off to Dieppe once again. Little opposition was encountered on this sortie, although four 190s were chased inland beyond Dieppe. Unable to catch up, in frustration Johnnie loosed off a burst at 800 yards. Flight Lieutenant Crowley-Milling, however, was able to damage a 109 from 300 yards. At 1256 hours, 610 Squadron returned, intact, to West Malling. At 1400 hours, 610 was off again, but again there was little incident. Johnnie fired ineffectively at two 190s from extreme range, but both half-rolled out of sight. Four other 190s approached but were attacked by Hawker Typhoons. The Squadron was safely home at 1525 hours. 610 Squadron's last sortie of 'Dieppe Day' was flown between 1735 and 1905 hours, when the Spitfires orbited mid-Channel. Four 190s approached but were driven off and headed back towards Dieppe. Johnnie led his Spitfires in hot pursuit, but only closed within range when at nought feet over the French coast. Opening fire at 400 yards without result, Colon Leader broke off the chase. The Spitfires then gave cover to a British rescue vessel patrolling about 5 miles off Dieppe, before heading for home.

The 610 Squadron ORB concluded:

> Not the least memorable activity of the day was the take-off in rapid succession in the early afternoon of six fighter squadrons – three of Spitfires and three of Typhoons. How eagerly was news lapped up when the Squadron's first aircraft returned from the first patrol; as it happened, Squadron Leader Johnson was able to report quick successes for 610 and an altogether terrific party. What hearty congratulations there were when 'Hokey' safely landed his Spitfire with the tail almost shot away; what relief when it was learned in the evening that Flight Sergeant Creagh, who had to bale out during the first patrol, had been picked up safely from the sea. Altogether a stirring day, but one which left among the exaltations regrets over the loss of Flight Lieutenant Pool and Sergeant Leech, both of whom are missing from the first patrol.

'Stirring' and newsworthy though the day had been, by the close of
play the Operation had actually been a disaster for the Allies. The
Germans had reacted swiftly and consequently some 1,096 Allied
soldiers were killed, 1,943 were captured, and 397 were missing.
None of the intended objectives were achieved. The cynical suggest
that this was a deliberate failure intended to prove to Stalin that
the Second Front was not an option at this time. If true, the point
was made at a high cost of young lives, the majority of which were
Canadian. It is interesting to note, however, that when the liberation
of Europe was eventually mounted, no attempt was made to seize a
French port. When the time came, so as to avoid another Dieppe, the
Allies towed a prefabricated harbour in sections across the Channel.
Disastrous though Operation JUBILEE had been, vital lessons had
been learned.

From an aerial perspective, 11 Group believed that it had achieved
considerable success. Nearly 100 enemy aircraft were claimed
destroyed, and 170 probably destroyed or damaged. Actual German
losses were 48 destroyed and 24 damaged. Unpalatable though the
thought may be, RAF losses of 97 to enemy action and 3 more to
flying accidents, with 66 further aircraft damaged, made Dieppe
a victory for the *Jagdfliegern* and German anti-aircraft gunners.
To further confirm the point, the RAF lost 47 fighter pilots, as
opposed to the *Luftwaffe*'s 13. In total, the RAF had flown nearly
3,000 sorties, the enemy 945. The Operation in no way, therefore,
provided the success that was intended. Johnnie:

> Dieppe? It was a bloody tragedy. The Canadians on the ground
> were slaughtered. Someone said afterwards that it was a seaborne
> 'Charge of the Light Brigade'. Even the German gunners felt sorry
> for the Allied soldiers as they pounded them to pieces. Did it
> achieve anything? As usual we had over-claimed, so although LM
> hailed it as a great victory, the truth has since come out. I do recall
> that whilst in combat that day I was rebuked for my swearing over
> the R/T by Pat Jameson! After Dieppe, I went grouse shooting
> with Cocky Dundas, who was related to half the aristocracy of
> north-east England, or so it seemed to me. Anyway, all of them
> seemed to have a bloody great house and a grouse moor! They
> were all his second cousins, the Halifaxes, the Allandales, and
> what have you. He'd write and ask whether he and I could have

a walk on the outskirts, but they would always write back saying 'no, you can't walk the outskirts but you can come and join us in the butts and do it properly', and so on. So that was that. Great week that was, shooting at Lord Allandale's. His son, now the present Lord, was already a prisoner.

On 24 September, Johnnie flew an 'Intruder Patrol' to Holland, shooting up a train North of Schagen. The next day he flew to 12 Group HQ at Hucknall. Johnnie:

> We then expected to be posted back to 11 Group, having been in 12 Group for a while. We were fed up, in fact, with all those long sea crossings on these pointless but extremely hazardous Rhubarbs. Instead we were posted to Castletown, on the northern tip of Scotland – we couldn't have had a posting further from the action! I even went to see the Commander-in-Chief, Air Chief Marshal Sholto Douglas, about it, and consequently got my arse kicked for my trouble, so to Castletown go we would!

On 26 September, Johnnie flew up to Castletown and familiarised himself with that station in readiness for the Squadron's move. There was to be a temporary reprieve, however: the following day, a signal was received postponing the move. On 2 October, therefore, Johnnie led 610 Squadron to Martlesham Heath, joining 485 and 411 Squadrons to provide rear cover to American B-17 Flying Fortresses returning from St-Omer. This was a doubly significant sortie: from a personal perspective it was Johnnie's 100th sweep. Secondly, this was the first occasion of many during which Johnnie participated in operations with American bombers, which were newly arrived in England.

In February 1942, the Americans had sent staff officers, under the command of Brigadier General Ira Eaker, to England where they prepared for the arrival of US combat units. These men and machines of the Eighth Air Force were to be based in England for participation in operations against Hitler's *Festung Europa*. Eaker believed in the concept of strategic bombardment as a war-winning use of air power, and had already spent two years in England studying RAF operations. Although the Eighth Air Force and the RAF were to work alongside each other, there would be a

major difference in their respective operations: while RAF Bomber
Command continued to pound the Third Reich by night, the
Americans intended to do so by day, thus creating 'round-the-clock'
bombing. Having already suffered heavy losses very early on in the
war during daylight bombing operations, the RAF was sceptical
of the Americans' intention to attack without the protective cloak
provided by darkness. Nevertheless, at the Casablanca Conference
on 21 January 1943, the Combined Chiefs of Staff would agree
that a combined RAF Bomber Command/Eighth Air Force strategic
bomber offensive should indeed be mounted, beginning in 1943,
and immediately the weather sufficiently improved. The Combined
Bomber Offensive Directive (CBOD) was therefore intended to be
a strategic preparation for Operation OVERLORD, as the proposed
invasion of enemy-occupied France was codenamed. The Directive
to Allied air force chiefs was clear:

> Your primary objective will be the progressive destruction and
> dislocation of the German military, industrial and economic
> system and the undermining of the morale of the German people
> to a point where their capacity for armed resistance is fatally
> weakened.

Targets were listed in order of priority: U-boat construction yards,
the German aircraft industry, enemy transportation networks, oil
installations and 'other targets' connected with the German war
industry. On 17 April 1942, General Eaker had flown in the lead
aircraft of the second wave of B-17 Flying Fortresses attacking
the railway marshalling yards at Rouen-Sotteville. Visibility was
excellent, and from 23,000 feet Eaker's bombardiers dropped 36,900
pounds of general-purpose bombs. The bombing was reportedly
'reasonably accurate', with half of the bombs falling within the
target area. The mission's success confirmed the Eighth Air Force's
unshakeable faith in high-level precision daylight bombing.

After several postponements (one of which involved a chase to
recall a road party who had started out before the postponement
message was received), on 8 October a considerable part of 610
Squadron moved temporarily to Biggin Hill. This was part of Fighter
Command's contribution to what would be the Allies' biggest
daylight bombing raid of the war so far – which went ahead the

following day. In his logbook, Johnnie wrote: 'Cover Wing to 108 Fortresses returning from Lille'. On that day, the 92nd, 93rd, 97th, 301st and 306th Bomb Groups of the American Eighth Air Force sent a record total of B-17 Flying Fortresses and B-24 Liberators to the Fives-Lille steelworks in Belgium. The 610 Squadron ORB reported that:

> The Squadron helped provide cover for the withdrawal of over 100 Fortresses which bombed Lille by day – an operation that made the headlines as our biggest day bombing raid of the war and one in which sensational successes were scored by the Fortresses against enemy fighters. 610's part was comparatively quiet, however. Only Squadron Leader Johnson fired his guns and he did not make any claim'.

The American bombers claimed fifty-six enemy fighters destroyed, twenty-six probably destroyed and a further twenty damaged. The more experienced British, in the main, treated these claims with scepticism, and rightly so. We now know that the more aircraft that are engaged, then the greater the number of claims. Actual losses are always much lower, because the speed of combat often deceives the human eye. Imagine, then, several hundred American gunners blasting away at fleeting enemy fighters. How many of them simultaneously fired at the same target and genuinely believed that they were personally responsible for the enemy's destruction? It is easy to understand, therefore, why the over-claiming on this day was so high. Nevertheless, it was a great propaganda coup and President Roosevelt himself broadcast the results to his people. Although figures were later revised to twenty-one destroyed, twelve probables and fifteen damaged, it is now believed that the Germans only, in fact, lost two fighters.

Four American bombers were lost, however, and forty-six were damaged. This was the first mission, though, for both the 93rd and 306th, as a result of which bombing was poor. Many bombs fell outside the target area, resulting in civilian casualties. Nevertheless, the raid proved that heavy bombers could penetrate enemy-occupied territory with but moderate losses – in daylight. The Americans therefore reasoned that with experience their results could only improve. It is, however, important to understand that the bombers' operational radius was still dictated by that of their fighter escorts. RAF Bomber Command's early wartime sorties in daylight, without fighter protection, had already proved how essential escorts were, all the way to the target and back. During the Battle of Britain, the *Luftwaffe*'s bombers were protected by Me 109s all the way in and out when attacking targets in southern England. When German bombers attacked the North of England, however, flying from bases in Norway and escorted by the twin-engined Me 110 (which proved inadequate in this role), they were so badly mauled by Spitfires and Hurricanes that such a raid was never again attempted. The answer, of course, was to create a single-engined fighter with the range of a four-engined bomber. But how? Where does the fuel go? How can the balances be achieved between speed, power, manoeuvrability and weight? While the designers struggled to overcome these problems, it fell first to the Spitfires of RAF Fighter Command, despite their limited range (even with long-range jettisonable auxiliary fuel tanks), to provide protection for the Americans. Until this crucial matter of extending the fighters' range was resolved, however, a frustrating time lay ahead.

Having experienced these first American raids, 610 Squadron's move to Castletown was even more frustrating. On 14 October, Johnnie 'and thirty others' were flown in a Harrow transport aircraft from Ludham to Doncaster, then onwards to Castletown. The tempo of operations inevitably proved to be a complete contrast to the Squadron's previous experience in 12 Group. Johnnie:

> But still, we had a good time up there, plenty of game about. We were up there to protect the fleet at Scapa Flow. Not surprising, really, because from what I could make out the buggers rarely left the anchorage!

On 10 November 1942, the 610 Squadron ORB explained that changes were afoot in Johnnie's personal circumstances:

> This day the Squadron had a real excuse for a party. The CO, Squadron Leader JE Johnson DFC & Bar, having decided to take the flip (whence there is no return) into matrimony and the date of take-off (or 'prang' as you like it) being imminent. Officers and senior NCOs, with the Station Commander, Wing Commander

GAW Saunders DFC, and Station Adjutant, Flight Lieutenant Reeves, as guests, chose the Dunnet Hotel as rendezvous. Much signing – and not a little 'partaking of refreshment', as the old saying has it! And so, for Squadron Leader Johnson, the beginning of farewell to bachelordom.

On 14 November, the ORB continued:

Squadron Leader Johnson married at the Registrar's Office, City Hall, Norwich, to Miss Paula Ingate, youngest daughter of Mr & Mrs Sidney Ingate, 73 Park Lane, Norwich. His old friend Wing Commander HSL Dundas DFC was best man. Squadron officers present, who gave the occasion something of an international flavour were Flight Lieutenant WA Laurie DFC, Pilot Officer RW Pearson, Flying Officer GS Malton (Canada) and Lieutenant A Hvinden (Norway).

Other guests included Wing Commander the Hon. Max Aitkin DFC, son of Lord Beaverbrook, and Lord Lovett. Paula Johnson remembered those days:

We met at the Sampson and Hercules Ballroom in Norwich. I was dancing with a schoolfriend of my brother's called 'Ham' when Johnnie, who was then based at Ludham, cut in. He asked my name and I told him. He replied that he had seen the name 'Ingate all over Norfolk!' Our family owned several small businesses in East Anglia, including a marine garage at Bungay, but my mother wanted to move to Norwich, so we moved to the city. We spent a delightful evening together on the occasion of our first meeting, upon conclusion of which Johnnie drove me home. I knew straight away that he was the right man for me, that there could be no other. Not long afterwards Johnnie asked my father for permission to marry me, promising to always take care of me, which he did. After our wedding there was a sit-down wedding breakfast for thirty at the Haymarket, the food provided by local farmers. My sister had been to Woolworths and bought toy Spitfires which were placed on every table – Max Aitkin roared with laughter and exclaimed, 'We don't need to return to base – we have a squadron right here!' Johnnie and his pilots were a real band of brothers, all quite mad, of course! In fact I became known as 'Paula' because of Douglas Bader. My real name is Pauline, but he said, 'We can't have that, the "Perils of Pauline". You must be called "Paula" to go with my wife, Thelma!' I remained in Norwich throughout the war, where I worked for the Fire Service. At the time there was a saying, 'Careless Talk Costs Wives'. Johnnie was very protective and didn't want me on the station.

After his honeymoon, Johnnie returned to Castletown, where 610 Squadron presented their popular CO with an onyx cigarette box to commemorate his marriage. In flying terms it was a bleak period, up in the far north. Severe weather towards the end of November severely curtailed all flying. On 3 December, Johnnie flew Tiger Moth DE626 with Flying Officer Malton occupying the rear seat – toting a 12 bore shotgun! In his logbook Johnnie wrote, 'Two swans/geese destroyed!' Bird strikes, of course, were always a hazard, and Castletown was attracting too many feathered visitors. On 14 December Johnnie and Flight Lieutenant Reeves were up in the Tiger Moth again, getting up to more mischief: flying an 'Army beat up' they fired a Very pistol at the 'Brown Jobs', igniting a haystack! The following day, having previously arranged hind shooting for various pilots, Johnnie 'organised' the gift of a hind carcass for the Squadron. Officers and Senior NCOs had a party at the Dunnet Hotel and, according to the 610 Squadron ORB,

> found the hind very tasty. They also found much to admire in Squadron Leader Johnson's grand manner as he dispensed the portions with the air of a proud father administering to the needs of an outsize family! The beer flowed freely both during and after the meal, and of course there was much singing!

These are the actions of a gifted leader maintaining morale in poor weather and well away from any action.

On 12 January 1943, there was cause for another celebration, as the ORB reported:

> News received of the award of the DFC to Flying Officer PB Wright, the 'Old Man' of the Squadron in point of service with it as pilot. There had to be a party at the Dunnet Hotel, to celebrate

this honour to the Squadron and to a capable, conscientious pilot and officer. The fact that in the end several 'happy' people were a little confused as to just who had won the DFC does not really matter, but we'll record it even if only to prove that the celebration was worthy of the event!

The following day, no doubt nursing a hangover, Johnnie flew to Chedworth to attend No. 1 Fighter Leader Course under Wing Commander Paddy Woodhouse DFC AFC – Wing Commander Bader's successor at Tangmere. After a local flight over the River Severn on 16 January, and aerobatics the next morning, on 18 January Johnnie was recalled to Castletown: the Commander-in-Chief had not forgotten his promise to Johnnie that early in 1943 his Squadron would get a place back in the front line. On 20 January, 610 Squadron relieved 131 Squadron at Westhampnett. Johnnie was home again, back at Tangmere. Coincidentally, on this day, 610 Squadron received a new pilot, Flying Officer Colin Hodgkinson. This would have been unremarkable but for one thing: like Wing Commander Douglas Bader, 'Hoppy' Hodgkinson had no legs, having also become a double amputee as the result of a flying accident. Inspired by Bader's example, however, Colin was also determined to fly again. Like Bader, not only did he simply fly, he likewise flew Spitfires on operations from Westhampnett until he too was captured near St-Omer. By 23 January, all elements of 610 Squadron had arrived at Westhampnett, the move having come much earlier than expected. The 'Old Timers' found Westhampnett much changed since their last stay in 1941. The station had increased in size but facilities were well dispersed, requiring service bicycles to be issued to many personnel. The Wing Leader was Wing Commander Peter Brothers DFC & Bar, a distinguished veteran of the Battle of Britain and an experienced fighter commander. Johnnie:

> Whilst at Castletown we had received a number of replacement pilots, so these chaps were keen to see action, to prove themselves. It was an exciting time for the Squadron, a challenge which 610 was ready for.

On 26 January, Johnnie flew with 485 Squadron on a Wing patrol of Hardelot, covering the withdrawal of bombers. North of Le

Touquet, due to, according to Johnnie, 'Excellent controlling by Appledore', the Tangmere Wing intercepted 2/JG 2. In the short, sharp fight that followed, Wing Commander Brothers and a 165 Squadron pilot both destroyed FW 190s. One of the Germans lost was *Oberleutnant* Christian Eickhoff, an experienced pilot and the *Staffelkapitän*. On this occasion these victories were for no loss. On 3 February, Johnnie led 610 Squadron on a sweep with 485 Squadron between Berck and Le Touquet. The trip was uneventful, although the Northolt and North Weald Wings were heavily engaged. Three days later, 610 suffered its first loss since returning to 11 Group: Sgt H. R. Parker, a New Zealander, was missing from a Rhubarb. The pilot was last heard of about 20 miles north of Cherbourg. Parker was the fourth Westhampnett pilot to be lost in just three days on Rhubarbs; his body was never found, despite an extensive ASR search led by Johnnie. 10 February, however, was, according to the unit's ORB,

> A black day. On bomber escort to Caen, Squadron was jumped by FW 190s. Squadron Leader AE Robinson (supernumerary), Flying Officer LA Smith DFC and Sergeant HR Harris (NZ) all reported missing, whilst Pilot Officer KS Wright managed to stagger home with an aircraft badly shot up about the tail.

Johnnie recorded in his log that the 'Bombers flew at cloud base and thus made it impossible for 610 to give them cover support. Bounced by 190s on the turn.' To lose three pilots on one sortie was a bitter blow indeed. All were married men. Johnnie:

> Yes, that was a particularly bad trip. The problem was that, so as to provide as small a target as possible to the flak gunners, the Ventura leader flew just below cloud, meaning that we had no room to position ourselves above his formation. I therefore placed 610 Squadron at the bombers' rear, as other escorting Spitfires were on each flank. My intention was to sweep the target after the Venturas had bombed, but the 190s carved us up during the turn. About thirty fell on us through a gap in the cloud, so they had the advantage of height, surprise and speed.

In the ensuing combat, the tail was shot off Flying Officer Smith's tail, the pilot being seen to bale out over the sea, about three miles from the French coast. The Polish Sergeant Lisowski's Spitfire was also hit, and was smoking badly, but he ignored Squadron Leader Johnson's order to turn around and crash-land in France, instead staggering back to England and safety. Pilot Officer Wright's Spitfire was hit by a cannon shell and flung upside down, but by some miracle his controls responded sufficiently for him to drop to sea level and head for home, alone. So ferocious was the attack by I/JG 2 that diving for the deck was the only option for Johnnie and his remaining pilots. The CO of 610 Squadron knew that in the past the Germans had shown a marked reluctance to engage at sea level, so it was just above the waves that the Spitfires levelled out. If necessary they would turn tightly, just above the wave tops, enticing the Germans to follow; only the most skilful pilot would survive. As the Spitfires streaked across the waves towards England, Johnnie was too late in shouting a warning to two Spitfires flying ahead. A pair of 190s hit them hard, both Spitfires going down.

The Spitfire flown by Squadron Leader Anthony Robinson, serving as supernumerary with 610, suddenly became enveloped in flame. As the other pilots watched helplessly, Robinson screamed all the way down over the R/T. Seconds after impact, the sea had closed completely over the aircraft, of which there was no trace. Johnnie:

> That incident was awful, and will always remain pretty much etched into my memory. It was shocking. We had never experienced anything like it before. None of us spoke for the rest of the way home. It seemed at the time that there was no solution to the 190 menace. As we have previously said, our radius of operations was reduced to the enemy coastline for some time, and all of this because of one fucking aircraft type! We were losing a lot of chaps, far too many. It got to the stage that we had to avoid combat unless the Controller gave us the perfect bounce. We needed the Spitfire Mk IX – badly. Although some squadrons were flying them, it was frustrating for the rest of us.

On 13 February, Johnnie probably destroyed an FW 190 over Boulogne:

610 Squadron, led by myself, was flying as top cover to 485 Squadron and formation was under Appledore Control. Wing started to climb off Shoreham and crossed French coast just South of Boulogne at 1310 hours with 610 at 21,000 feet and 485 at 17,000 feet. After several vectors during ten to fifteen minutes, about fifteen FW 190s were seen flying West in the Montreuil – Stella Plage area at approximately 10,000 feet. Squadron Leader Grant, leading 485 Squadron, called up saying he was going to attack, and I led the Squadron down, still maintaining height above 485. Before 485 could engage the E/A they ran into approximately twenty more 190s, which were at 13,000 feet south-west of Boulogne, and immediately turned head-on to engage them. 485 Squadron was considerably outnumbered and as Squadron Leader Grant called for assistance I led 610 Squadron into the general melee which was developing. After some time at 12,000 feet, I singled out a 190 which was climbing to the South, above the main engagement, but was out of range and so I did not open fire. The 190 then made 180° left-hand turn and dived down, and I got into position by executing a steep turn, and opened fire from port quarter from above with cannon and machine-gun from 350–400 yards. As I closed gradually, giving several short bursts, I saw a large piece of the E/A fall away. The 190 then dived vertically, streaming black smoke. As I broke away and turned, I saw a crashed aircraft burning to the South of Montreuil woods, just before the Squadron left the French coast. Combat was broken off at 9,000 feet. Several pilots saw this E/A diving down but none can confirm that it was this 190 that crashed, but Sergeant Lisowski, flying at 2,000 feet, saw a 190 pass him at fifty yards in a vertical dive, just before the former crossed the coast on the way back. Cine-gun was exposed and I claim this FW 190 as probably destroyed.

The Tangmere Spitfires had been led into a trap by *Hauptmann* 'Wutz' Galland, *Kommandeur* of II/JG 26 and brother of the legendary Adolf, whose *Gruppe* was operating with 7/JG 2. Galland and two of his pilots destroyed three 485 Squadron Spitfires, while Pilot Officer Skibinski, of Johnnie's 610 Squadron, was picked off by a 7/JG 2 pilot. 485 Squadron claimed two 190s destroyed in response, in addition to Johnnie's probable, but in reality the enemy withdrew unscathed.

Early in March, Wing Commander Brothers was posted away. Before another Wing Leader was appointed, on 8 March the Tangmere Wing was led by Wing Commander Duncan Smith DSO DFC, who was actually Wing Commander (Flying) at North Weald. On this sortie, 610 and 485 Squadrons provided withdrawal cover to Fortresses that had bombed Rennes. There were no combats. On 10 March, Johnnie led the Wing on Rodeo 180. Again, the trip passed without incident. Changes, however, were afoot. Johnnie:

I had been getting an increasing number of calls from a staff officer, asking me how many operational hours I had, how many sweeps had I done, so I told him, and he asked, 'When did you last have a rest?' I said, 'Well, I've just had one. We've been up to Castletown, no operational flying up there whatsoever, shot lots of grouse and downed a fair bit of malt!'

He said, 'Oh, so you count that as a rest, do you?'

I said, 'Yes I do, and the salmon fishing was pretty good too!' Well, it was better than going to be an instructor at some bloody OTU, wasn't it, teaching a lot of ham fisted buggers how to fly!

He said, 'Oh, I'll call you back.' I was concerned that this interest was because they intended to rest me from operations, which was the last thing I wanted. The staff officer called me back and said, 'The Commander-in-Chief (who by that time was Air Marshal Sir Trafford Leigh-Mallory) sends his congratulations; you are to put up your Wing Commander's stripe immediately and take over the Canadian Spitfire Wing at Kenley.

On 19 March, Wing Commander J. E. 'Johnnie' Johnson DFC & Bar left 610 Squadron, which he had successfully commanded for eight months. With his faithful black Labrador, Sally, for company, he set off in his old Morris for Kenley and the Canadians. A whole new era was about to begin.

5

Wing Commander (Flying):
Greycap Leader

By the time of Johnnie's promotion and appointment as Wing Commander (Flying), his personal score of enemy aircraft destroyed was just into double figures. Being a Wing Leader, however, was not about a personal score, but that of the team. Now was the chance for Wing Commander Johnson to demonstrate the depth of his leadership qualities. Johnnie:

> It was a quantum leap from being a squadron leader to becoming a wing commander. The dream of every fighter pilot at that time must surely have been getting a wing in 11 Group, which I had now achieved. To say that I welcomed and looked forward to this new challenge was an understatement! The RAF, in my day, taking my career from sergeant-pilot in the VR to Wing Commander (Flying) in three and a half years, would have been impossible in the army. No one in the Life Guards, for example, could have gone from trooper to lieutenant-colonel in three years. Never. Rank and privilege, and class and breeding was very much to the fore in the army in those days, and in the RN to some extent, but it wasn't by now in the RAF. In the RAF, if a man could do his job and hold his own in the squadron and that sort of thing, then that is all we required of him. He had equal opportunities for promotion whether he had been to the local grammar school or Eton or Harrow. That was the great thing about our service: equal opportunities.

Kenley was a long-established fighter station in Surrey, south of London. The personnel of the Spitfire Wing now based there were Canadian, as Johnnie remembered:

> The Canadians? They had a reputation for lacking discipline, bloody-mindedness and so on and so forth. Stan Turner, for

example – a very prickly pear. Bader could handle him. Bader knew that Stan Turner, when the chips were down, would be there when lesser men had fled because he was such a fucking obstinate bastard, wouldn't give in, but he was ill dressed and wouldn't shave occasionally, and when he was pissed he always had a six-shooter somewhere on him. When he was pissed he used to let this fucking gun off in the Mess or wherever he was! Of course on the old Bader Wing, 145 was taken out of the line and Stan was very pissed off about this, so he went up to Catterick and they'd got an old man commanding Catterick called Beisegal, who was very dyed in the wool, pre-war regular, and old Stan got his six-shooter out and started loosing off, shooting pictures off the wall, and there was talk of a court martial, and Leigh-Mallory himself had to get on the blower and put the thing right! Funny thing was about Turner, later on in life he went out to the Mediterranean, where he was still scruffy, ill dressed, but he finished up in 1944, beginning of 1945 as our Group Captain! He took over 127 Wing and he comes up from the desert in all his khaki, he's still got the fucking gun, and then he became the toughest disciplinarian that you ever met: 'Must Court Martial the bugger, can't have that, put him under close arrest, he's not properly dressed', and *this* from bloody Turner! Talk about the changeover from poacher to gamekeeper! What I am trying to get at is that the Canadians had a reputation, through people like Turner, of being tough and obstinate and difficult to handle. When I got the Canadian Wing, the Group Captain down at Tangmere said, 'Oh Christ, they'll all have six-shooters and they'll be shooting stuff off the wall. They'll never take any notice of you!' But in fact they were the finest bunch of people you ever did meet. They flew well – beautiful discipline in the air; they'd all done a lot of flying hours in Canada, many as instructors, and they could *really* fly.

As Wing Commander Johnson motored to Kenley, many thoughts occupied his mind, but uppermost was that the Kenley Wing was equipped with the new Spitfire Mk IX – the answer to the FW 190 threat:

Really, when I had commanded 610 Squadron, flying the Spitfire Mk V, we were cut to pieces by the 190s. So having the Spitfire

IX, which was a different aeroplane altogether, you've got a chance of getting stuck into these bastards. The IX was far more powerful, the Merlin 61 engine matched the airframe (there was no undue torque or bad flying characteristics like there was later with the Griffon marques). The IX was a very good combination of airframe and engine. The IX was the best Spitfire. When we got the IX, we had the upper hand then, which did for the 190s! We could turn inside him and hack him down, which we did. Those cannon shells were about as thick as your wrist, and when you sent them crashing through his armour, he didn't fucking like it one bit! There were two Spit IX squadrons at Kenley in March 1943, 403 and 416, and two of Spit Vs, 411 and 421, at Redhill. I was supposed to look after the flying of the Redhill squadrons too. Kenley's squadrons were both Spitfire IXs, the Redhill squadrons still being on Spitfire Vs. This did not become a 'Big Wing' affair, however, because, due to the difference in performance, you could not operate Vs and IXs together, and also Kenley could not take any more than two Spitfire squadrons anyway.

Group Captain H. A. 'Jimmy' Fenton, who had commanded 238 Squadron during the Battle of Britain, was the Station Commander: 'Kenley seemed to have everything: comfortable quarters, entertainment including a camp cinema, and an abundant source of girlfriends for the boys!' Hugh Constant Godefroy was then a pilot officer serving with 403 'Wolf' Squadron and remembers Johnnie's arrival:

Charlie Magwood was made CO of 403 Squadron, and we were told that we were getting an RAF Wing Leader, Wing Commander J. E. Johnson DFC & Bar. Group Captain Fenton brought him in at lunchtime, and with Squadron Leader Bud Malloy's help introduced him around. He made a positive first impression. When he spoke, it was firm and decisive. He was a wiry sort of fellow who walked with almost a cocky swagger. There was none of that fishy eye aloofness about him. He looked at the person talking to him as though he was paying attention. His face broke into a smile, which emphasised the chip out of a top tooth. He called the Wing into the Briefing Room for an introductory orientation. Using short crisp sentences and slow, almost Churchillian emphasis, he stated that he expected implicit obedience to his flying orders. Flying discipline was the only discipline he was interested in; he didn't give a tinker's damn what we did on the ground. He favoured the 'fluid four' formation to provide better cross cover. He stated that he expected it would take a little time for us to get used to each other, but that he looked forward to leading a Canadian Wing.

'Any questions?'

There was dead silence.

'OK, chaps,' he said with a broad grin, his eyes twinkling, "give me a chance for a quick squirt, and I'll see you in the bar.'

There was a roar of laughter, and as the gathering broke up, it was evident that he had won the pilots' respect immediately.

On 22 March 1943, Johnnie flew Spitfire Mk IX, EN398, for the first time, a sortie of 50 minutes of 'Local flying'. He also made four landings and immediate take-offs, just to get used to the Mk IX. EN398 became the Wing Leader's regular mount, a Canadian maple leaf painted below the cockpit and the initials 'JE-J' painted on the fuselage. For ease of identification in the air, it had become customary for Wing Leaders to have their initials so painted, although the practice not always found favour with intelligence officers, as Johnnie recalled:

> To see your initials painted on a Spitfire was really something, you really knew then that you had made it, as it were. The 'Spy' suggested, however, that I should not conform for fear of the enemy identifying and singling me out in the air. I told him ... well ... you can imagine what I told him, and 'JE-J' was duly applied!

Johnnie also had to select a radio call sign and chose 'Greycap'. The scene was now set for excellence.

The weather was slowly improving, and with better flying conditions the daylight fighter war was due to increase in both tempo and ferocity. To his dismay, however, Wing Commander Johnson had found that his new Wing still flew the antiquated line-astern formation; he remembered:

Yes, that is true. We had a long talk about it early on and naturally I intended that we should fly in line abreast. Syd Ford of 403 favoured the line astern, and Foss Boulton of 416 couldn't make up his mind. We agreed that for the first few shows I would lead the Wing with 416, which would fly in finger-fours. 403 was to fly top cover, some 3,000 feet above us, in whatever formation Syd chose. I agreed to review the position after a few sorties so that a decision could be made for the whole Wing. Of course I could have insisted that we flew finger-fours from the outset, but that was not really my way. I wanted to win them round by showing them the benefits of the finger-four in action. It was more democratic that way and more likely, I thought, to motivate and encourage. In respect of one matter, however, I did follow Syd Ford. His guns were harmonised on the 'spot' principle, rather than the more usual shotgun type spread pattern. Syd's combat films showed the devastating effect of his particular choice of harmonisation, so I made it mine too.

Until this point, the winter weather had been unfavourable to offensive fighter operations, but was now starting to turn. Action was not far ahead, and the afternoon of 25 March showed promise when Rodeo 194 was ordered. At 1650 hours, the Wing, led by Greycap, took off from Kenley but headed independently through cloud to RV over Dungeness. The Wing swept the area of Boulogne, St-Omer, Sangatte, between 25,000–28,000 feet. As Johnnie led his Canadians over the French coast at Boulogne, they passed the Northolt Wing's Spitfires heading back to England. Visibility was poor, though, and no reaction was forthcoming from the enemy. By 1830 hours, the Kenley Wing was landing back at base. When dawn broke on 28 March the weather was bright and sunny, with only scattered cloud, the wind blowing gustily from the west. Soon the teleprinter clattered away and the Form 'D' came through: the Kenley Wing would fly on Ramrod 48 and provide high cover to American bombers attacking the railway marshalling yards at Rouen. As we have seen, the American bombers' first missions were tentative probes to targets close to the French coast, mainly those connected with the Directive's primary target: the U-boat. The Biscay-based submarines, however, were protected in massive concrete bunkers, built by the Germans using slave labour. Anti-aircraft units also heavily defended them, St-Nazaire soon becoming 'Flak City' to the Americans. Railway marshalling yards were also important targets because through them passed supplies to the U-boat bases. Having already struck at an important marshalling yard in Germany itself, in March 1943, the 'Mighty Eighth' began attacks on such targets in France. The attack against Rouen on 28 March, in which the Kenley Wing was involved, was one of those raids. On that day, Wing Commander Johnson led the Kenley Wing off at 1230 hours, and headed for Beachy Head at 26,000 feet. There the Spitfires met the bombers, eighty B-17s and twenty B-24s, orbited right and set course for Hastings. Johnnie later wrote in his logbook: 'American bombers straggled badly and the 100 covered about twenty miles'. When 20 miles off Dieppe, the bombers were instructed to 'pancake', so Johnnie hauled the Kenley Wing round and swept the Channel behind the bombers. The operation was not, therefore, a success.

The following day was another sunny one, with only scattered cloud and variable wind. Wing Commander Johnson led the Kenley Wing off at 1245 hours on Circus 277, an attack on the marshalling yards at Abbeville. High over Beachy Head the Spitfires met twelve Ventura bombers that immediately began climbing, contrary to plan. For some unrecorded reason, 5 minutes later six of the bombers turned back with the Spitfire Mk V Wing. The remaining box continued on course, bombing the target from 10,000 feet. Abbeville aerodrome was a famous *Luftwaffe* fighter base, from which four FW 190s were seen to scramble, but no engagements took place. The German flak gunners hammered away all the while, however, although there were no hits due to shells exploding at the wrong height. On the way out, Squadron Leader Ford reported the position of a 6-inch heavy gun near Lancheras, and six E-boats were noted in the Somme Estuary as the Beehive passed out over Cayeux. By 1405 hours, the Spitfires were back at Kenley, their guns again unfired.

On 31 March the morning weather was fair but cold, with a gusting westerly wind, the Kenley Wing was detailed to fly Ramrod 47. This time the B-17s were bound for Rotterdam, and the Kenley Spitfires rendezvoused with seventy bombers over Harwich at 1105 hours. Ten minutes later the Wing crossed the French coast at 26,000 feet and swept the area Dunkirk–Le Touquet–St-Omer.

At 31,000 feet over St-Omer, twenty FW 190s were sighted. Later, Johnnie wrote in his logbook, 'Could not engage as Huns going NE and we were short of gravy'. Despite the improvements that the Spitfire Mk IX enjoyed, limited range remained a problem. The Wing returned over Dunkirk and Hawkinge, landing at 1220 hours. Flight Lieutenant Charlie Magwood wrote with frustration in his log that the Germans 'wouldn't stay and play'. Johnnie himself recognised that his Canadians needed action, and soon. He wrote, 'We wanted a full-blooded scrap with the Abbeville boys to weld the Wing together.' The unsettled spring weather, however, continued to make this difficult. On 3 April, 'Ops' were on with Ramrod 49. The plan was for the Hawker Typhoon fighter-bombers of Squadron Leader Denis Crowley-Milling's 181 Squadron to make a low-level attack on the enemy airfield at Abbeville-Drucat. As the 'Bombphoons' turned for home, the Kenley Wing was to sweep the area between Le Touquet and St-Omer, engaging any scrambled German fighters. Such a Ramrod was bound to provoke a lively reaction, and anticipation was high. Kenley was the only fighter wing involved and would be controlled by Squadron Leader Hunter, the Senior Controller of the new radar station at Appledore in Kent (codename 'Grass-seed'). Appledore's radar was of a higher resolution than existing appliances, which were designed for home defence, and could therefore detect bandits over France and beyond. For the first time, Wing Leaders would have the great advantage of advance information in the air regarding the presence, size and direction of enemy aircraft.

At 1445 hours, the Kenley Wing crossed the French coast at Le Touquet, the eight Typhoons being well below and racing home having given the hornets' nest a violent stir. As the Spitfires swept over St-Omer between 24,000 and 26,000 feet, Grass-seed vectored Greycap on to fifteen to twenty FW 190s of II/JG 26. The bandits, having taken off from Vitry, were still climbing and flying west, towards the coast in finger-fours and at staggered heights. In a demonstration of excellent controlling and teamwork between Squadron Leader Hunter and Wing Commander Johnson, the Kenley Wing was soon positioned over Montreuil, 3,000 feet above and up sun of the enemy, in perfect position for a bounce. The only problem was that Grass-seed also reported more bandits behind the Spitfires. Although reportedly some miles away, no one knew how

accurate this information was, given that the radar was operating
at its maximum range. What was Johnnie to do? Upon seeing the
190s below, his mind was made up: it was too good an opportunity
to miss. First, remembering the fate of Wing Commander Bader,
Johnnie satisfied himself that the 190s concerned were not merely
bait, then led 416 down to attack on the port side while 403 dived
on the starboard. Johnnie's combat report subsequently related that
he 'attacked an FW 190 from astern using cannon and machine-
gun. Opened range at 400 yards and closed to 200. I saw cannon
strikes on the wing roots and fuselage of the enemy aircraft that
flicked over and went down smoking and burning.' *Unteroffizier*
Hans Hiess (6/JG26) baled out, but his parachute failed to open.
A veritable melee ensued as the Canadians fell on the unsuspecting
Germans. Flying Officer Fowlow and Flying Officer Cameron, both
of 403, saw a 190 go down, having been attacked by Squadron
Leader Ford, pouring black smoke and flames from the cockpit,
later enveloping the entire machine like a 'ball of fire' (ORB). Flight
Lieutenant Charlie Magwood blasted a 190 from 50 yards. There
was a succession of long flashes and flames from cannon strikes all
round the centre section of the fuselage and wings. Chunks flew off
just before the aircraft disintegrated – completely. Just a black cloud
hung in the air. Flying Officer H. D. MacDonald fired at another
190 from 100 yards, which soon streamed white smoke, dropped
an undercarriage leg and was abandoned by the pilot.

416 Squadron fared not quite so well. Squadron Leader Boulton
claimed a 190 destroyed, Flight Lieutenant R. A. Buckham and Flying
Officer N. A. Keene sharing a probable, and Flying Officer J. A. Rae
one damaged. *Oberfeldwebel* 'Adi' Glunz of 6/JG 26, however, shot
down Flying Officer A. M. Watson, over Le Touquet, this being
the Germans' only victory in this engagement. The pilots of the
two 190s hit by the COs of 403 and 416 Squadron, *Unteroffiziere*
Heinrich Damm and Albert Mayer, were both killed, but the other
three 190s claimed destroyed by the Wing all managed to struggle
back to land safely at Vitry and Merville. Now in a very hostile sky
with more 190s hurrying to the scene, Grass-seed advised Greycap
to withdraw. Johnnie:

> We didn't need telling twice! We got out as quick as we could
> and raced across the Channel. After the combat the Wing had

naturally become fragmented, so we came home in pairs and fours. News of our success had spread rapidly and naturally the pilots were jubilant – this was what we had all been waiting for. It was a great shame that we lost Watson, however, but nevertheless we had gone over there and given the 190s a clobbering. We were all delighted and I telephoned Appledore and thanked Hunter for his excellent controlling.

Both the new British 'Wingco' and the Canadians had shown each other their mettle. Richard Booth was a pilot in 416 Squadron:

Upon conclusion of a Wing operation we would have a re-hash of the day's activities with 'JEJ'. At the end of one of these early sessions he invited suggestions. We complained that we had difficulty understanding him on the R/T, at which point Johnnie volunteered to try and talk more like a Canadian over the ether! At the next de-brief he inquired as to whether he was clearer over the air, but to a man we advised him to go back to normal!

Eileen Steel was a young WAAF working Kenley's Pass Office, situated immediately above the station's main entrance. From that vantage point, Eileen and her colleagues, all 'starry eyed youngsters, often watched Wing Commander Johnnie Johnson coming and going. We hero-worshipped him even then.'

4 April was another fine and sunny day, perfect for Ramrod 51. The Kenley Wing was ordered to provide First Withdrawal cover to the leading box (of seventy) B-17s returning from a raid on the Renault factory at Billancourt, Paris. Greycap led the Wing out over Beachy Head at 24,000 feet, crossing the French coast at 1432 hours over Quiberville. When Johnnie reached the RV, near Rouen, 'FW 190s were attacking bombers heavily when we sighted them'. Major Oesau, *Kommodore* of JG 2, had intercepted the bombers with his I *Gruppe* and the operational squadron of a training unit, JG 105, after they had successfully hit their target. Before the Spitfires arrived, II and III/JG 26 also joined in, charging the B-17s head-on. The 'Forts' were tightly grouped in two large boxes, providing mutual fire support, but one Fortress was seen spiralling downwards; only one parachute emerged. The backdrop was provided by way of a huge pall of smoke rising some 7,000 feet high over Paris, and flak

bursts here and there. Greycap despatched Squadron Leader Ford and 403 Squadron, who were 10 miles away, to attack the 190s and 'sort them out'. From 200 yards, Squadron Leader Ford delivered a long burst at a 190, causing a large explosion and fragments to fly off. The undercarriage soon dangled limply and the front of the aircraft became engulfed in 'solid yellow flame' (ORB). The port wing broke upward and the 190 dropped towards the ground over 20,000 feet below. Flight Lieutenant Magwood thumbed the trigger at a 190 that had hurtled vertically through the bombers, while Pilot Officer E. L. Gimbel DFC, an American, and Flying Officer W. J. Cameron saw a B-17 destroy a 190 before diving themselves onto a 190 a couple of thousand feet below. Gimbel fired and Cameron watched pieces fall off the 190, which rolled and went straight down. As the two Spitfire pilots broke away they were attacked by three 190s, flying in close line astern, from 200 yards astern. Cameron shouted 'Watch out, Ed!' (ORB) and broke sharply right and upwards. Gimbel did not reply but Cameron saw a Spitfire going down 'in a gentle dive streaming black smoke' (ORB).

At 1435 hours, Flight Lieutenant Magwood fired at a 190, which dived away and crashed on the edge of a big wood near Bellencombre. Together with his Blue Two, Sergeant L. J. Deschamps, Magwood climbed to 23,000 feet and got in a short burst at another 190 from 200 yards astern but without result. Deschamps gave chase and hit the 190 around the cockpit area that immediately became enveloped in flame, the stricken enemy fighter plummeting earthwards. A few minutes later Deschamps was bounced by two 190s from out of the sun. Magwood watched helplessly as Blue Two 'skidded off to starboard, streaming glycol' (ORB). Magwood himself then started a running engagement until crossing the coast about St-Valéry where he dived beneath a 190 that he attacked from astern. Delivering a short burst, Magwood saw 'flashes of flame from cannon strikes all around the cockpit and along the starboard wing, chunks flew back, the cockpit was enveloped in flames and he fell off, diving vertically followed by two splashes' (ORB). As the 190s pursued the B-17s across the Channel, Flying Officer MacDonald followed twenty of them, singling one out which he attacked. The 190's starboard wingtip fell off and 'bright scarlet flames' (ORB) were seen in the cockpit. This enemy fighter also crashed into the sea, witnessed by Flying Officer Aitkin, who also saw both splashes.

Although Squadron Leader Boulton exchanged blows with a 190 that attacked him head-on, 416 Squadron, with which Greycap was flying, made no claims. The Wing crossed the English coast 8,000 feet above Shoreham, landing at 1525 hours. Two Spitfires were missing. Ed Gimble had collided with a 190, safely baled out and successfully evaded capture; he was safely back in England by August. Although it was hoped that Leo Deschamps would make a safe forced-landing, he was, in fact, killed. Four B-17s were lost, all before the Spitfires' arrival. Again, this emphasises the extra danger faced by the Americans when they ventured beyond the range of their fighter escort. The need for a long-range escort fighter was becoming ever more pressing.

403 Squadron claimed five FW 190s destroyed and one damaged. From available German records, we know that JG 26 lost Karl Fackler to either Magwood or MacDonald (and two other pilots to the B-17s). *Obergefrieter* Jürgen Birn, of 4/JG 54, was also killed in this battle, but by whom is not known. Five 190s, two each of II and III/JG 26 and one of 4/JG 54, returned to base with combat damage. All of the claims for 190s destroyed by 403 Squadron appear accurate, however, so it is possible that they belonged to I/JG 2 or JG 105. In return, the pilots of JG 26 claimed eight Spitfires destroyed (six of which being confirmed), and I/JG 2 two. Fighter Command actually lost eight Spitfires in total that day, two of 403 and six of the Northolt (Polish) Wing. It is worth reflecting on the sad fact that during the raid on the Renault factory, in support of which the Kenley Wing was flying, 200 Parisian civilians were killed. The death toll of civilians caused by Allied bombing in the occupied lands was high. A heavy price was therefore ultimately paid for the freedom of France, Belgium and Holland in particular. Quite rightly, however, Johnnie and his pilots felt flushed with success. That morning, Squadron Leader Syd Ford had presented the 'Wingco' with Canadian shoulder flashes to be sewn on his battledress. This was a clear indication that Johnnie had already won the Canadians over.

On 5 April, another fine day, the Americans sallied forth to attack the ERLA aircraft factory at Antwerp. Ramrod 52 saw the Kenley Wing flying First Fighter Cover to the first box of a force comprising 104 B-17s and B-24s. In an effort to extend range, Johnnie had first led his Wing down to Manston, near the Kentish coast, and refuelled; just those few extra miles might mean life or death to a bomber crew. Just west of Ostend and 10 minutes early, due to a strong tail wind, the Wing rendezvoused with the bombers, which were outward bound, at 25,000 feet, getting into formation down-sun and above the leading box. The Americans had firstly feinted towards Abbeville before turning towards Antwerp, thus forcing the shadowing FW 90 pilots to waste fuel. Nevertheless, Major 'Pips' Priller led 8/JG 26 and III/JG 26 straight to Antwerp and formed up for head-on attacks, the Germans' favoured method against the heavily armed American bombers. Priller charged almost immediately after Greycap and his Spitfires arrived on the scene. The 'Wingco' and 416 Squadron challenged the 190s and became engaged in a running battle on the bombers' starboard side. Johnnie subsequently claimed three 190s damaged, Squadron Leader Boulton and Flying Officer Rae one each. The 190s did not attack the port side, where 403 Squadron was positioned. Later, 403's pilots were agreed that the 190s' attacks 'were determined and persistent and were mostly from ahead, above and below in singles, fours and sixes'. Priller, of course, was an *Experte* and clearly knew what he was about.

Just north of Ghent, the Spitfires were ordered to return, with fuel states very much in mind, and had to abandon the bombers to their fate. An increasing number of enemy fighter units were scrambled to attack the American 306th Bomb Group, which lost five B-17s. The 306th, based at Thurleigh, claimed the destruction of five enemy fighters, although JG 26 only actually lost one FW 190: *Hauptmann* Fritz Geisshardt, *Kommandeur* of III/JG 26. This was an important loss as Geisshardt was an experienced *Experte* with 102 victories (75 of which had been in Russia). Nevertheless the day was the most successful so far for the *Jagdwaffe*, especially considering that, for the first time, German fighter controllers had managed to co-ordinate the combined forces of three different commands (JG 1, JG 2 and JG 26) throughout the interception.

At midday on 7 April the Wing was released and most of the pilots went up to London. Hugh Godefroy describes one such 'sortie' with the ever-popular 'Wingco':

> In the air, Johnnie Johnson was 'Greycap Leader', cool, commanding, and as aggressive as a bull terrier. But when the sun went down, he didn't mind being called 'Johnnie'. He was one

of us. His responses seemed Canadian, pure and simple. 'What we need is a pissup! I've had my fill of liver and onions. Monty!'

'Sir!'

'Call the Red Lion at Redhill and tell them to kill the bloody fatted calf. We're on our way. Come on lads, fill up the vans and follow me. Hughie, you'd better come in mine. I may need a second pair of eyes on the way home!'

Chuckling with anticipation, everybody grabbed their caps and piled into the vans. As expected, it was a hair-raising ride. What with the masked headlights and my poor night vision, I didn't see obstructions until we were almost upon them.

'Get out of the bloody way, you stupid bastard!' Johnnie would shout, as he suddenly overtook a vehicle.

'Clear the road, the Kenleys are coming!'

'That's original, Hughie, I rather like that.'

'Look out Johnnie, there's a man in the middle of the road!'

'Bloody Canadian, you obviously haven't learned to drive in England yet!'

I was greatly relieved when we pulled in the parking lot of the Red Lion.

'There we are – my kingdom for a pint of Guiness!'

To the amusement of most of the regulars we took over. There was plenty of beer, games of darts and skittles. Johnnie, with the help of Walter Conrad, led a singsong around the piano with old favourites like 'Roll out the Barrel', 'Waltzing Matilda' and the South African Zulu war dance, 'Hey zinga, zumba, zumba, zumba'. There was food for those who wanted it: smoked salmon and excellent steak-and-kidney pie.

When the proprietor shouted:

'Time gentlemen, please!' there was a Chorus of:

'A-w-w-w-w-w-!'

'Time gentlemen, for one more for the road!'

'Right you are,' said Johnnie. 'OK lads, you've 'ad it. Bottoms up! There's work to do in the morning.'

I offered to drive.

'What?' said Johnnie. 'You drive in your present state of public drunkenness? Not bloody likely! What we need is a sober man at the wheel. Look, some stupid clot has boxed me in. I'll show the bastard!'

With a crunch, Johnnie backed the van into the car behind, shunting it a good six feet to the rear.

'That's better. All aboard, chaps!'

When the van was full, we were off in a cloud of dust. But now, with a few pints of ale and a steak-and-kidney pie under my belt, somehow it didn't seem to matter. After a while, in the dim light of our shielded headlights, I saw half-a-dozen women walking on the right side of the road. With a squeal of tyres, Johnnie slammed on the brakes.

'There they are chaps, same level, 12 o'clock, get into them and don't let any of them get away!'

Tittering with laughter, Johnnie led us in pursuit of the women who had now broken into a trot. Johnnie caught the hand of a young lady straggler and as he spun her round she butted her cigarette in his left ear.

'O-w-w-w,' he said. 'You nasty little bitch!'

The ladies in front stopped, and from their midst we hears a querulous voice say, 'Nobody calls my daughter a "nasty little bitch". I say, what's all this in aid of?'

'They've got us outnumbered, return to base!'

To the sound of Johnnie's giggling laughter, we all piled back in the truck again and took off. It was a happy light-hearted evening, full of harmless fun, and in the Johnson tradition punctuated with the unexpected. There wasn't a man who didn't waken refreshed and ready to follow him in the morning.

Such was the mark of a great leader. Johnnie:

Personalities at Kenley? Ford I was very impressed with. He got a DFC & Bar. He had flown a lot up at Digby. We had some good flight commanders, but the rank and file had not a lot of experience. When I got there they had not done a lot of flying over France. Of course you can't in the winter months because of the weather. Buck McNair had a bit of the Stan Turner in him. I remember going into the Mess one night, we hadn't done much flying then, he was promoted about May time and he had a few beers. I went into the bar after dinner and he shouts out, 'Hey Wingco, when are we going to do some flying? The fucking guns are rusting up!' So all eyes switched to the 'Wingco' wondering

'How's he going to handle this one?' So I said, 'Get me a pint, Buck, and we'll talk about it.' It was the only way to deal with it, he was a bit aggressive was Buck. Fortunately, I got there at the right time: we had the Spitfire IX, the weather was getting better all the time and these guys could fly very well; they knew how to handle their Spitfires and don't forget that Kenley was in a built-up area – very difficult to find in murky weather. 'Batchy' Atcherley, who had been the Station Commander sometime before, had erected a series of tents around the circuit and painted them white. If you saw the tents you just kept turning inwards and the runway appeared! It was one of the first landing aids that I ever came across. The impressions were that the Canadians were actually a very well-disciplined outfit, both in the air and on the ground, except, of course, when they got pissed. Then some pissed pilot officer would come and clobber a squadron leader or something and it all went pear-shaped! Fortunately they mostly got pissed in the Mess, so it was all kept in house, and the following morning there would be an apology or whatever. There was still a leavening of peacetime guys, who had been through Kingston, the Canadian equivalent of Cranwell, 'Iron Bill' MacBrian, for example, who took over as Station Commander from Jimmy Fenton, he had been to Kingston, and he was a very nice chap.

Johnnie was making progress with fighter formations:

By now I had the Wing flying finger-fours. To me, the two-squadron wing was ideal, being far more manoeuvrable than a wing of three or more squadrons. In the air, there would be 50 yards, say, between my number two and me, 100 yards then the other pair, then about a quarter of a mile the other four and so on. Then stepped up, down sun so that they could see, two or three thousand feet higher, would be the other squadron. We covered a lot of sky, a mile or so.

There was still no standard formation operating procedure within Fighter Command, however. The Kenley Wing became noticeable in the air, and Johnnie's formation became known as the 'Wolfpack'. Johnnie:

The climb out of Kenley would depend on what the job was. If it was a fighter sweep then we would keep low level until we could see the Dutch or French coast, then climb as hard as we could to cross it at a reasonable height to get above the flak, say 12,000–14,000 feet, or 24,000–25,000 feet, which was our best height. If we were escorting Fortresses then we would climb high from base, because the higher you were the greater the range. The fighting height was between 24,000 and 26,000 feet. The Germans always seemed to have a little bit of height on us due to the fuel injection.

More clear and bright weather on 15 April saw Greycap leading the Kenley Wing on Rodeo 204. The Wing crossed the French coast at 25,000 feet over Berck-sur-Mer and swept to port. Vectored by Appledore to St-Omer, the Wing manoeuvred to attack various forces of enemy aircraft but without sighting any of them. As Johnnie wrote in his logbook, 'They were under 9/10ths cloud at 20,000 feet and we were over.'

By now, American fighters were entering the arena. By the first week in April, three P-47 Republic Thunderbolt Fighter Groups, 4, 56 and 78, were ready for operations. The P-47 was a huge, radial-engined beast of an aircraft. At 15,000 lbs gross, the P-47 was twice the weight of a Spitfire and soon nicknamed the 'Juggernaut', or more commonly the 'Jug'. In comparison trials against the RAF's captured FW 190, the P-47 appeared capable at 20,000 feet and above, but was found wanting below. To its advantage, the P-47 was armed with eight .05-calibre machine-guns, the standard American aircraft weapon of the Second World War. This packed a heavier punch than the RAF's .303-calibre 'pea-shooters' and would serve the Americans well. The P-47s made their first, uneventful sweep, from Debden in Essex, on 10 March 1943. Technical problems delayed the next incursion until 8 April, when the 'Jugs' sallied forth over the Pas-de-Calais. During these early trips the P-47s were escorted by Spitfires, as was the case on 15 April when all three P-47s groups swept Ostend and clashed with II/JG 1. The soon-to-be 'ace' Don Blakeslee shot down a 190, and two other 190s were also claimed as destroyed by the P-47 pilots. One 'Jug' was shot down, however, and two more failed to return due to engine failures. Later, the 'Jug' would earn an enviable reputation as both a long-range bomber-escort fighter, as was intended, and a low-level ground-attack fighter-bomber in support of the Allied armies. To start with, however, the P-47's range was similar to that of the Spitfire, some 170 miles, so the immediate difficulty of finding a long-range offensive escort fighter remained unresolved.

The entry of another new American fighter, the P-38 Lockheed Lightning, was delayed firstly due to it being difficult and slow to build. The Lightning, featuring an unorthodox design, was, however, brilliant in concept and promising in performance. When the P-38-equipped 78th Fighter Group arrived in England during 1942, and took over Goxhill, the situation in North Africa dictated them being redirected to that theatre. Further supplies of P-38s were subsequently sent not to England but to North Africa and the south-west Pacific. It would not be until the autumn of 1943 that the Eighth Air Force would receive the Lightning for operations in the European Theatre. As things turned out, the twin-engined P-38, like the Me 110, proved no match for single-engine fighters. American bomber losses, however, indicated that if they were to continue their task then increased protection from the German fighters was *essential*. The *Luftwaffe* had 800 fighters in the West, and the energetic *General der Jagdflieger*, Adolf Galland, was doing his level best to increase that figure. As things stood, the Germans were still able to carefully co-ordinate and time their interceptions to coincide with that point in time when the bombers' 'Little Friends' had to turn back due to the constraints of fuel.

On the morning of 17 April, Wing Commander Johnson flew over to West Malling to examine two FW 190s that had landed there by mistake during the early hours. By 1417 hours, Greycap was back at Kenley and taking the Wing up on Circus 285, providing escort to twelve Venturas attacking the marshalling yards at Abbeville. The RV was at zero feet over Beachy Head, the bombers being 4 minutes late. While the Beehive proceeded to the French coast, a Defiant and a Mosquito were observed shadowing the raiders. Wing Commander Johnson broke radio silence and sent a section to investigate what transpired to be 'friendlies'. At 1453 hours the formation crossed the French coast at Cayeux with the Spitfire Mk Vs of 411 Squadron flying as close escort to the Venturas at 13,000 feet. The target was duly 'pranged', and Greycap wrote in his log, 'Excellent bombing'. He had positioned his fighters to the east of the bombers, providing

such an effective screen that *Hauptmann* Wutz Galland was heard
by the British Y-Service ordering his 190s to remain in formation
as there were 'too many Spitfires'. While 411 Squadron and the
bombers re-crossed the French coast, homeward bound, between
Le Treport and Cayeux, Johnnie led his Mk IX squadrons back
around at 24,000 feet towards Abbeville – spoiling for a fight. As the
Kenley Spitfires continued to climb inland, Greycap was informed
by Appledore that the Hornchurch Wing was engaged. When the
Kenley Wing was up sun and at 33,000 feet, Flight Lieutenant
Godefroy, Yellow Leader, asked Greycap's permission to take his
Section down to attack three 190s that he could see climbing out to
sea some 10,000 feet below. The 'Wingco' agreed, and Godefroy's
finger-four peeled off to attack. Yellow Leader fired at the right-
hand 190, with cannons and machine-guns, causing the port cannon
magazine to explode and flashes of flame along the fuselage in front
of the pilot. The 190 pilot was unable to recover his aircraft from a
spin and baled out; both pilot and aircraft ended up in the Channel.
Meanwhile, Yellow Two, Pilot Officer P. K. Gray, opened fire from
200 yards astern on the port 190. The German pilot half-rolled,
was hit by Gray again, and entered a spiral dive pouring white
smoke. This pilot also baled out, his 190 likewise crashing into the
sea. The rest of the Wing made no claims, but Johnnie recorded in
his logbook that the 'Wing was involved in a general dogfight over
the French coast'.

Having landed back at Kenley by 1552 hours, there was more
action ahead for the 'Kenleys'. At 1745 hours, Greycap and his
Spitfires were off on Circus 286. The Spitfire pilots' task was
firstly to provide Target Support for twelve Venturas bombing
the marshalling yards at Caen, and then sweep the general area.
The Beehive crossed out at less than 500 feet above Brighton,
climbing to 21,000 feet and crossing the French coast at Dives
and turning south for Caen. The bombing was accurate once more,
but the flak was equally on target and intense over the target. The
Spitfires then flew at 22,000–25,000 feet to 25 miles north-west of
Fecamp. Appledore then informed Greycap of a gaggle of bandits
apparently engaged on an ASR operation near Dieppe, so Johnnie
led the Wing down to 2,000 feet. Coming along the coast were
four FW 190s and four Me 109s, which were attacked by the
whole Wing!

Flight Lieutenant Magwood had just given lead of 403 Squadron
to Flight Lieutenant Godefroy on account of his R/T suddenly
becoming unserviceable. Godefroy, having 'Tally Ho'd', led the
charge of Yellow and Red Sections, being followed by Magwood
with Blue Section which engaged a single 109 from another enemy
formation before also attacking the 190s. One of the 'Butcher Birds'
actually pulled up vertically and went through the surprised Spitfires,
breaking sharply right and racing towards France. Magwood reacted
swiftly and half-rolled onto the 190 which did likewise but, being
too low, crashed into the sea while 'trying to aileron out of it' (ORB);
Magwood had not fired a shot! As Godefroy was about to fire at
a 190 he suddenly had to break to avoid colliding with several
Spitfires that cut across in front of him. Having recovered, he noticed
two splashes in the sea, one of which being Magwood's 190, the
other, smaller, probably being a pilot. Flying Officer Fowlow then
fired at a 109 that pulled up in front of him, but it then dived away
with no results being observed. Pilot Officer Dean Dover saw a 109
climbing into the sun and fired at it, but likewise would make no
claim. As the Canadian turned away from France he suddenly found
himself head to head with a 190. Dover immediately thumbed the
trigger and Sergeant Brown, flying behind, saw the 190 dive into
the sea. According to the Squadron ORB:

> On the evidence available it appeared that various sections of the
> Squadron were all involved with the same FW 190, with no one
> pilot appearing to have accounted for it in clear-cut or definite
> style. For that reason the *whole squadron* shared the credit for
> destroying one FW 190.

Squadron Leader Foss Boulton, leading 416 Squadron, had fired
a long burst of cannon at an Me 109F, which was confirmed as
destroyed following an analysis of Boulton's combat film. All of the
'Kenleys' returned safely to base and were all down by 1930. By the
close of play on what was a busy day, the Germans had lost a total of
eight FW 190s, offset against just three Spitfires. To the great credit
of their escorts, remarkably not one Ventura was lost.

On 20 April a complete change in the weather brought clear, still
and sunny skies. The day's first operation was Rodeo 209. The Wing
swept the Le Touquet and Abbeville area, coming out at Dieppe.

Appledore recalled the Wing, however, when 'Seventy-five plus E/A were reported in the vicinity of our Wing all alone' (ORB, 403 Squadron). Johnnie, as we have heard, insisted on iron discipline in the air, for obvious reasons, and this included the matter of radio silence. In his logbook, however, he wrote, 'Rodeo 209 with the Polish Wing jabbering Russian over the R/T!' Next came Ramrod 67, Target Support to eight Typhoons bombing Tricqueville aerodrome, which was successfully attacked. Afterwards, the Spitfires were taken over by Appledore Control and vectored to a formation of twenty-one-plus bandits at 29,000 feet over Dieppe. Six 190s subsequently made a head-on attack against 416 Squadron, but Boulton and his men reacted swiftly, the CO himself destroying one, Pilot Officer R. D. Phillip damaging another, all for no loss. Appledore then informed Greycap that fifteen FW 190s were closing from behind to attack. Low on fuel, Johnnie ordered the Wing out, this command being 'smartly obeyed' (ORB, 403 Squadron).

On 1 May, a cloudy May Day that threatened rain, Wing Commander Johnson led the Kenley Wing down to Portreath in 10 Group, from which airfield the Spitfires were to provide Top Fighter Cover for Circus 28. Again, the movement to operate from a forward airfield was to extend the Spitfires' range. The B-17s of the 306th Bomb Group were to bomb the U-boat installations at Lorient, an important target given that the Commander-in-Chief of the *U-bootwaffe*, Admiral Karl Dönitz, had his headquarters nearby at Kernaval. The Lorient boats were among the most successful operating from the Biscay coast, and therefore anything to impede or prevent their operations was vital. Greycap's Spitfires rendezvoused with the Portreath and Exeter Spitfire Wings on time before flying first to Ushant, thence to north of Brest at 26,000 feet. The German-occupied French port put up a protective screen of intense light flak as the Spitfires passed overhead and swept the area inland. Just before the Spits re-crossed the coast on the way home, five FW 190s were seen above and about two miles behind. The Kenley Wing turned about to engage but the 190s' leader sensibly chose to make off to fight another day when the odds were more favourable. The Germans half-rolled and dived away. Although this was the only incident of note so far as the Kenley Wing was concerned, sadly it was a different story for the American bomber crews. As always, *Jagdfliegerführer* (*Jafu*) Brittany waited until the Spitfires had turned back before unleashing his fighters, which rapidly fell on the B-17s. Of the seventy-five participating in this attack, seven were destroyed and two more were damaged.

On 4 May, Flying Officer J. Danforth 'Danny' Browne joined 403 Squadron. Although serving in a Canadian fighter squadron, Dan was in fact an American:

> I signed up in the RCAF in 1940, I was called up to the Commonwealth Air Training Plan in the February of 1941, and then I got my 'wings' in late August of 1941, and went home on a month's leave in New Jersey, said 'goodbye' to my mother. We were in Halifax at the time of Pearl Harbor, and sailed a few days later. I was on a ship called the *Letitia*. I think that Atlantic crossing was some of the most terrifying experiences of my life! We ran into 108 knot winds off Iceland, my God those waves were huge and so they decided to really hunker everything down. We had the *Normandie* lose all its lifeboats during the storm, and several destroyers literally went straight through those huge waves, which was amazing. It was very frightening, especially when I climbed up the mast to watch proceedings. I would look down and see the green Atlantic, look the other way and just see froth! Eventually we got to Bournemouth, from where I thought that we would go to Singapore, which is why I thought we were on the High Seas. As we left Gibraltar we were attacked by FW Condors. We were picked up by the Condor two days out, and attacked by submarines on the third. We lost a couple of ships out of the convoy, although my ship, the old P&O liner *The Viceroy of India* was safe. We went into Cape Town, picked up the Vichy French in Madagascar. Then we heard that Singapore had fallen to the Japanese, which was frustrating as I wanted to get into combat, which is why I, an American, had volunteered before my own country came into the war. It was an exasperating time, as they then posted me to fly Gloster Gladiators in Iran, in defence of certain oil refineries. We were then shipped back, going all the way round Africa without anything exciting taking place. Back in the UK, I was then posted to the OTU at Rednal in Shropshire, near Wales. Got through the course and then had good fortune to be posted to the Canadian Spitfire Wing at Kenley in 11 Group. This was better than Gladiators, to say the least! So, with no

operational combat experience I joined the Kenley Wing, which turned out to be one of the happiest events of my life. I later had the opportunity to transfer from Kenley to the American air force, but I stayed where I was. My mother was Canadian and I enjoyed their company. One thing, we had some fine Canadians at Kenley. Some had been miners and lumberjacks, just roughnecks all their lives, so it was a weird combination. It was perhaps a stroke of genius to put Johnnie in command, although he was an Englishman. I was delighted to find Spit IXs at Kenley, which had a two-stage, two-speed engine. When you got up to about 19,000 feet, that second stage kicked in, at which point it was *your* air and no longer the Germans' air. Also, being 'green', it was an incredible experience to go on your first operational sortie with Wing Commander Johnnie Johnson, who was definitely headed for great things.

7 May dawned fine and no time was lost in the planning of operations. In the morning, 416 Squadron carried out various local flights, searchlight co-operation exercises, and convoy patrols. Johnnie flew his usual Spitfire, EN398, on a test flight to jettison an auxiliary fuel tank. This was probably a flush-fitting 'slipper' tank, fitted beneath the cockpit section and containing either 45 or 90 gallons of extra fuel, which designers had found to be the best option. The idea was that, with the 90-gallon tank, the pilot would take off and for the first hour and twenty minutes draw fuel from the auxiliary tank. When the enemy was sighted, the 'slipper' was jettisoned, flying characteristics thus resuming normal. Using the 45-gallon tank, the Spitfire Mk IX's radius of action was 240 miles, 270 miles with the 90-gallon tank. Johnnie:

Owing to the lack of foresight by the fucking Chief of the Air Staff, Portal, the Spitfire could have had the same range as the Mustang, but he told Churchill that it would impede its performance as a defensive fighter, which of course is quite wrong. So the Spitfire never really had the range, and we should have done, simple as that. What pissed us all off so much is that we still had the same range in a Spitfire as we had in 1940, although Churchill himself is on the record writing a minute to Portal saying 'Cannot the range of the Spitfire be improved?', and Portal writes back saying 'Not without detriment to its performance as an interceptor', which was absolute rubbish. That really needs highlighting. We did have auxiliary tanks, the largest being of 90 gallons, but that meant that there was more fuel outside the aircraft than in given that the Spitfire normally carried 85 gallons. Sometimes the bloody tank wouldn't come off, so they devised a little plunger in the cockpit which, if the tank got stuck, you kicked down. The Americans also fitted tanks to their Thunderbolts and Lightnings, but although it sounds fine in theory, doubling the range and so on, in practice it was not the answer. Dolfo Galland could attack our fighters as they were on the way in, making the pilots jettison their tanks, in which fuel was still plentiful, thus defeating the whole object of the exercise. No, it wasn't the answer, but the lack of range comes back to the English way of thinking, which is all about defence. Our lack of range was a big concern, and as the summer of 1943 progressed, so too did our frustration.

On 9 May, Flying Officer Bob Middlemiss joined 403 Squadron on what was his second tour of operations:

> From soon after my arrival, whenever Johnnie Johnson led the Kenley Wing it was often with me flying as his Number Two. He was a great leader and had the knack of knowing where the Huns were, and was always there, personally, leading the squadron in for kills. Flying with him was great and of course as Number Two your job was to ensure that the Wing Leader was not attacked by the 'dreaded Hun'.

11 May was sunny and warm with a light southerly wind. First thing, Wing Commander Johnson flew another tank-jettisoning test, a sortie of 40 minutes in his usual Spitfire, EN398, and 416 Squadron practised deck landings at Dunsfold. Then came the briefing for the day's operation: Circus 295, in which the Kenley Wing would provide 'second fighter echelon' (ORB, 403 Squadron) to a formation of B-25 Mitchells bombing the port of Boulogne. At 1210 hours, Greycap led the Wing to North Foreland at 500 feet before making a wide orbit off Dunkirk at 14,000–16,000 feet. The Spitfires, however, were recalled by 'Wytex' (Codename for Kenley, ORB, 416 Squadron) and then vectored under Appledore to cross the

enemy-occupied coast at Mardyck, there being, as Johnnie recorded in his log, 'Huns about' inland. Having orbited St-Omer, by which time the other aircraft involved in the Circus had withdrawn, as Greycap prepared to leave France via Gravelines a gaggle of bandits was 'Tally Ho'd', as Johnnie's combat report relates:

> FW 190s were sighted above when the Wing was over Gravelines, so we turned to engage in order to avoid an enemy bounce. Eight 190s flying in fours line abreast passed under my section, followed by a further three 190s in line astern. I turned after these three E/A and attacked number three from 10° starboard astern, with cannon and machine-gun – range 300 yards. I saw a piece of E/A fall off near the perspex hood, and E/A climbed steeply for 200–300 feet and then fell over and dived vertically. I broke away and immediately afterwards searched below in order to locate this aircraft. I saw an aircraft go into the sea about two miles off Gravelines'

Greycap's wingman, Flying Officer R. Wozniak, confirmed the victory, adding that 'I saw a splash in the sea in the area of Wing Commander Johnson's combat immediately after he had fired.'

Red Section of 403 Squadron was also engaged, attacking eleven 190s that were sighted beneath the Canadian Spitfires. As a high-speed running fight developed, Squadron Leader 'Foss' Boulton of 416 Squadron managed a long burst at a 190, but made no subsequent claim. As quickly as it had began the engagement was over, and the Wing returned safely to Kenley at 1335 hours. For Johnnie, the day's flying was not over. In his log he recorded a local familiarisation flight of 20 minutes in a Spitfire Mk XII (serial number not given). This is interesting, given that this flight was his first in a Griffon-powered Spitfire. Although the Rolls-Royce Merlin was extremely successful, having proved capable of development, there were nevertheless limits to the power that could be obtained from a 27-litre engine. This had, in fact, been recognised very early on in the Spitfire's development programme and work had begun on a new engine shortly after the outbreak of war. The new engine was another of twelve cylinders, called the Griffon, but the capacity was more: 36.7 litres. The resulting output was a potent 1,700 horsepower. Pilots would find the main handling difference from the Merlin being that the Griffon rotated in the opposite direction, so instead of swinging to the left on take-off, the Griffon variants swung to the right.

After more poor weather, on 13 May it was sunny and warm with a light southerly wind. The Kenley Wing's first task of the day was to provide 'second fighter echelon' (ORB, 403 Squadron) on Circus 296. Greycap led the Spitfires out over North Foreland at 5,000 feet, crossing the French coastline over Dunkirk at 22,000 feet. Heading east towards Cassel, control passed to Appledore and the Spitfires climbed towards St-Omer, which was reached at 27,000 feet. Given that in total fifteen Spitfire squadrons were active over France, escorting just six B-25s to Boulogne, the Germans wisely refused to engage *en masse*. Nevertheless, the Kenley Wing was attacked by some twenty FW 190s from both above and below. Another running battle ensued. 403 Squadron's CO, Squadron Leader Charlie Magwood DFC, leading Yellow Section, was attacked by a *Schwarm* of 190s from 4,000 feet below. The Canadian half-rolled out of the sun, forcing all but one of the one-time 'Butcher Birds' to take evasive action. With Magwood 350 yards astern and closing, that 190 broke to port, but it was too late: Yellow One opened fire with cannon and machine-guns. The 190's hood and bits of wing flew off as the missiles found their mark; it then rolled over and spun down with 'smoke and flames billowing from the cockpit' (ORB, 403 Squadron). The outcome was in no doubt, and Magwood later claimed this 190 as destroyed. On the way out, he engaged and hit another FW 190, which was claimed as damaged. 416 Squadron also enjoyed success, 190s being claimed destroyed by Squadron Leader Boulton, Flying Officer R. H. Walker and Flying Officer J. A. Rae; Boulton also claimed another as damaged. Although there were no personnel casualties, three 416 Squadron Spitfires landed back at Kenley having sustained varying degrees of damage.

The next offensive sortie for the Kenley Spitfires was Ramrod 71, the AOC-in-C Fighter Command, Air Marshal Sir Trafford Leigh-Mallory, sitting in on the pilots' briefing. He gave a short address, complimenting the Canadians on their good morning's work and explained a little of the current strategy of aerial warfare as it affected all fronts. In this afternoon sortie, Johnnie's Kenley Spitfires were to meet B-17s of the Eighth Air Force's 1st Bomb Wing attacking the Potez repair facility at Meulte. Covered by three P-47 fighter groups, the B-17s of the 4th Bomb Wing made a diversionary attack on the already pockmarked airfield at St-Omer. The *Luftwaffe* did not react, however, watching closely the progress of the larger 1st Bomb Wing force which, after zig-zagging northwards up the English Channel, finally turned for France. Over Berck, the Kenley Wing joined the last boxes of Fortresses, watching 'nibbling' (ORB, 403 Squadron) attacks by enemy fighters on the lead bombers before the force reached Amiens. On the way in, one B-17 was seen to go down 15 miles inland of Berck. Between the target and the approaching Fortresses was now a strong force of JG 26 190s led by Major 'Pips' Priller. The 91st Bomb Group soon lost two Flying Fortresses to Major Priller and *Leutnant* Hoppe, while another went to flak. Among eleven B-17s damaged during these attacks was one hit by a bomb dropped by a 190, so determined were the Germans to defeat the Americans by whatever means available. Nonetheless, the B-17s' target was soon wreathed in brown smoke and completely hidden to the aircrew fighting for their lives high above. For one American crew, violent death came suddenly when their B-17 exploded and disintegrated over Meulte.

By now, the Kenley Wing was heavily engaged, fighting off attacks as best the Spitfire pilots were able between burning Meulte and the Channel at Le Touquet. Red Section of 403 Squadron was bounced by a *Schwarm* of 190s, one of the assailants attempted a head-on attack against Red Two, Flying Officer R. D. 'Trapper' Bowen, but Red Four, Pilot Officer H. J. Dowding, responded in like fashion, opening fire at 200 yards and closing *rapidly*. Hits were seen around the 190's cockpit, and it was soon going down. As Fortresses approached the French coast on their homeward journey, Greycap saw a *Schwarm* of 190s approaching and clearly bent on attacking the bombers from the starboard side:

> I closed in on the leader and gave him several short bursts from the starboard beam, closing to starboard quarter, strikes being seen near his wing root. The enemy aircraft turned left and flicked right over. He dived and I followed for three or four thousand feet. E/A flicked over twice more and I gave him a short burst although at this stage I was almost out of range. I then broke away and rejoined the bombers but my Number Three (F/O Foster of 416) followed the aircraft down and saw the pilot bale out.

After their respective combats, Flying Officer Bowen and Pilot Officer Dowding, of 403 Squadron, then formed up with Greycap and Flying Officer Foster, who were heading home. Minutes later, the four Spitfires were attacked by two 190s when halfway back across the Channel. One of these the Spitfires isolated and 'chased into the sea' (ORB, 403 Squadron). Red Three, Pilot Officer W. T. Lane, dived on two other 190s, giving several bursts of cannons and machine-guns, strikes being witnessed by Greycap. Flight Lieutenant H. D. MacDonald, Blue Three, attacked the last of two Me 109s at 23,000 feet, striking the target with his second burst of cannon and machine-gun fire. A lone Me 109 flew below Yellow Section, positioning himself down sun, attacking above and to port. Flight Lieutenant H. C. Godefroy, Yellow One, fired at the 109 and saw hits on the tail and rear fuselage. Back at Kenley, the pilots of 403 Squadron excitedly made out their combat reports, but three Spitfires were missing: Sergeant W. G. Uttley of 403, who had last been seen over Doullen (and was possibly the Spitfire reportedly seen going down over that location (ORB, 403), and both Squadron Leader Foss Boulton and Sergeant C. W. McKim of 416. The latter had been heard to shout over the R/T that he had been badly hit and was seen to ditch his Spitfire in the Channel, 20 miles west of Le Touquet, but of Boulton nothing had been heard or seen. Immediately their Spitfires could be turned around, Greycap led a number of his pilots to sweep back over the Channel, searching for their missing comrades. An 'oil patch, pieces of aircraft wreckage and a barrel or unexploded torpedo with red and white circle at one end' were seen, but no trace of the three missing Kenley pilots. Sadly, Uttley and McKim, both twenty-one, were both dead. The 416 Squadron CO, however, was more fortunate: having baled out at 26,000 feet in spite of head, back and arm wounds, Squadron Leader Boulton was captured. The likelihood is that all these three Kenley Spitfire pilots were those victories claimed by Major Priller, *Hauptmann* Naumann, the *Staffelkapitän* of 6/JG 26, and *Leutnant* Leuschal, *Staffelkapitän* of 10/JG 26.

On 14 May, the Kenley Wing was not to be among those able to afford the luxury of enjoying this 'hot and very lovely day' (ORB, 403 Squadron), the morning's Form 'D' having provided all necessary details for Ramrod 73. The Canadian Spitfires were to escort forty B-17s of the 4th Bomb Wing attacking the base of III/JG 26, the airfield at Wevelgem, just across the French border into Belgium, near Courtrai. Greycap's Spitfires rendezvoused with the bombers at 8,000 feet over South Foreland, and set course for France. Another Beehive could be seen, this being the 1st Bomb Wing and a B-24 group bound for the shipyards at Kiel. Some enemy aircraft were sighted shortly after the Courtrai force crossed the French coast over Dunkirk, and when 15 miles inland a B-17 turned back, although not due to enemy action. As the bombers approached the target, Me 109s and FW 190s began harassing the formation but, in the main, were driven off by the Spitfires. Flight Lieutenant Buckham of 416 Squadron shot down a 190, which became a fireball, and Greycap nailed another. Some 10 miles west of Courtrai on the homeward run, Flight Lieutenant Godefroy of 403 Squadron pressed home an attack on a 190, and watched with satisfaction 'the cannon mounting and perspex hood come off and then a big ball of black smoke enveloped the E/A, as though it were disintegrating' (ORB, 403 Squadron). Flight Lieutenant MacDonald, also of 403, dived onto an Me 109 that was flying with two FW 190s, fired and noted strikes on the cockpit and wing roots as chunks of debris span into the air. Flying Officer Bowen saw this 190 spin into the sea.

In spite of the Spitfire pilots' best efforts, two Fortresses were shot down. *Oberleutnant* Hans Naumann, *Staffelkapitän* of 6/JG 26 claimed one of these, having fired at a 351st Bomb Group B-17 near Wevelgem with his last twenty rounds. The crew baled out, however, and these may have been the American parachutes later reported by 403 Squadron. Wevelgem had nonetheless been hit hard. Enemy aircraft had been destroyed and damaged, and a number of personnel, including both pilots and ground staff, were killed or wounded. The airfield was also badly cratered. A newcomer to the western front, *Oberleutnant* Erwin Leykauf, *Staffelkapitän* of 12/JG 54, actually tried to get up in his 109 during the attack, but the aircraft's undercarriage legs were sheered off by a bomb crater. So badly damaged was Wevelgem, in fact, that III/JG 26 was forced to move temporarily to the smaller field at Lille-Nord. It was the first, but not the last, time that a JG 26 airfield was rendered unserviceable by Allied bombing. The Americans had also made another first this day by putting a total of 200 bombers in the air. After their earlier losses, an ever-increasing quantity of replacement aircrew and aircraft, including fighters and both heavy and medium bombers, had been arriving in England from America, despite the U-boats' best efforts. The process was even afoot to convert certain B-17s and B-24s into heavily armoured and armed 'destroyer escorts'. At the time, given the limited range of the single-engined fighters available and considering that auxiliary fuel tank tests had yet to be finalised, this was really the only realistic short-term option to afford the bombers greater protection all the way to the target and back. All of this indicates the resolve of the Eighth Air Force to succeed and see the job through. As Johnnie said, 'You couldn't help but admire them, could you?'

On the morning of 15 May, Greycap flew a Spitfire V, 'DN-O', across to Horsham St Faith, where he liaised with the P-47 Thunderbolt-equipped 56th Fighter Group. At this stage of the game it was vital for the Americans to listen to the experiences of RAF pilots like Wing Commander Johnson who had been 'at it' for a long time before Pearl Harbor. These liaisons were also important for morale and developing a spirit of mutual co-operation. Johnnie remained with the 56th Fighter Group for two days, leaving on the morning of 17 May for Bassingbourne, where he lectured fighter tactics to the 91st Bomb Group, a B-17 unit.

In his logbook on 23 May, Johnnie wrote simply 'Awarded DSO'. The citation for this Distinguished Service Order was more descriptive, and in part read:

> Acting Wing Commander Johnson has led a Wing on a large number of occasions and has displayed outstanding skill and gallantry. During an operation one morning in May 1943, his formation was heavily engaged by a large force of enemy fighters. In the ensuing combats four enemy aircraft were destroyed without loss. The same afternoon he took part in a similar sortie and three enemy fighters were destroyed, one of them by Wing Commander Johnson. The next day, this officer took part in another successful sortie. By his skilful and courageous leadership, Wing Commander Johnson contributed materially to the success achieved. He has personally destroyed at least thirteen enemy aircraft.

In addition to his flying prowess having been recognised by the award of a double DFC, Johnnie's contribution as a leader had also now been rewarded. Dan Browne added his view regarding the successful combination of Johnnie and the Canadians:

> We had some fine Canadians at Kenley. Some had been miners and lumberjacks, just roughnecks all their lives, so it was a weird combination. It was a stroke of genius in itself to put Johnnie in command, although he was an Englishman, and they gave us these Spit IXBs, and I suspect that there was some politics behind that to keep us colonials quiet. Johnnie got along with them beautifully; he'd go out and shoot crap with them. Johnnie has the most extraordinary vocabulary of evil songs, drinking all night long you know. We'd draw off that oxygen bottle in the morning – it just revived you! Johnnie's leadership was not about iron discipline; it was just that everybody wanted to do things the way that he wanted them done, because they were so proud of being in that Wing. All Johnnie had to do was ring London and say, 'I want this pilot off my Wing.' No questions would be asked and when the guy landed he would just be ordered to report to some obscure duty in the middle of nowhere! Johnnie would shoot crap with us on the ground, and everybody would call him 'Wingco'.

Hugh Godefroy: 'As a leader, Johnnie Johnson was like the Pied Piper. We found ourselves bounding out of bed repeating his catchy phrases like "OK chaps, get into 'em!"' Johnnie: 'Yes, it was quite something to get the DSO, especially on the same day as a chap like Al Deere, who I admired and respected enormously because he had been at it for such a very long time.' Air Marshal Sir Trafford Leigh-Mallory wrote a letter of congratulation to Johnnie on the occasion of his first DSO, stating that he 'was very much impressed by what I saw of your work during my short visit to Kenley the other day, and I am satisfied that the high standard of the Kenley Wing is very largely due to your high qualities of leadership'. Another letter arrived from Air Vice-Marshal 'Dingbat' Saunders, the AOC 11 Group: 'My heartiest congratulations on your well-earned DSO. The Kenley Wing has done marvellous work recently under your leadership, and I am quite sure will continue its good work. Good luck and good hunting!'

On the night of 23 May the 'Kenleys' headed for London to celebrate their Wing Leader's DSO. The Biggin Hill Wing Commander

(Flying), the New Zealander Al Deere, had also been awarded the DSO and arrangements were made for a joint celebration at the Kimmul Club in Burleigh Street. A popular venue with aircrews, the club was run by a former RFC Captain, Bobbie Page, and the DSO party was soon in full swing. Also present that night, with a crowd of 'Bomber Boys', was Wing Commander Guy Gibson DSO & Bar, DFC & Bar, who had led the highly publicised 'Dambusters' raid only the previous week. Five days after that night in the Kimmul Club, when he bought Johnnie a pint on account of his DSO, Guy Gibson's Victoria Cross was gazetted.

The daily grind of bomber-escort sorties continued without respite. On the afternoon of 31 May, for example, Johnnie led the Wing on Circus 309, at 1655 hours. The Kenley Wing was to mount the second wave of a fighter sweep while twelve Venturas bombed Zeebrugge from 12,000 feet. The Spitfires crossed out over Deal at 100 feet, climbing to 18,000 feet and crossing the French coast at Nieuport. Sweeping towards Bruges and Ostend, at 21,000 feet, twenty-five FW 190s of II/JG 26 were seen by Greycap, some 500 feet below and diving on the port side. Followed by two 403 Squadron Spitfires, Johnnie headed for the 190s. 421 Squadron came down to cover 403 but also became engaged. Five of the Squadron's pilots fired their guns, damaging two 190s. One minute after the combat began, Greycap saw a 190 dive vertically past him, its pilot apparently trapped in the cockpit, and watched it crash into the sea. Flying Officer N. R. Fowlow then shouted at Sergeant G. R. Brown, of 403 Squadron, to 'break hard port' on account of their Section being attacked by two 190s. The first overshot, but the second, *Oberleutnant* Sternberg, *Staffelkapitän* of 5/JG 26, hit Brown who skidded to port, his Spitfire pouring black smoke. With relief, Fowlow saw a white parachute blossom at 8,000 feet, off Nieuport. According to the 403 Squadron report, 'Three other pilots of the Squadron heard someone say 'Goodbye' in a debonair manner', which was presumed to be Sergeant Brown. Three splashes were seen in the sea, all so large that crashing aircraft could be the only possible cause. One was Brown's Spitfire, the other two 190s, one of which had been seen by Greycap. The latter was later credited to Flying Officer Fowlow, who had seen a 190 'go straight down' after he had hit it from 200 yards. The second 190 was associated with a brown parachute seen later in the combat and was shared by Pilot Officer Isbister and Horten of 421 and Sergeant Small of 403. These claims were perfectly accurate given that II/JG 26 lost two 190s, both of which went into the sea, their pilots being killed (*Leutnant* Georg Mondry, 5 *Staffel*, and *Feldwebel* Hans Danneburg, 4 *Staffel*). Squadron Leader Hall and Flight Lieutenant Quint, both of 421, also claimed one damaged 190 each. The Spitfire pilots experienced heavy flak over Ostend, with moderate heavy flak at Bruges and Nieuport. This was 'exceptionally accurate', and one shell exploded between Johnnie and his Number Two, Flying Officer R. D. Bowen. Hugh Godefroy remembers:

> A shell went off behind and to port of Greycap, blowing him almost over on his back. There was a pregnant silence as we all watched him come back straight and level. For a second his aircraft dodged around a little bit like a bird that had experienced a near miss. Finally he came on the R/T: 'Makes you bloody think, dunnit?'

On 1 June the weather was 7/10ths cloud, perfect for the search and destroy mission, Rodeo 225, that the Kenley Wing found itself flying at 1130 hours. The Wing was the second wave of a fighter sweep of Hardelot–Doullens–St-Pol, controlled by Appledore. *Jafü* 2 scrambled I/JG 27 from Poix, and all available JG 26 fighters, to intercept, attempting to sandwich the Spitfires between the two German formations. Greycap's pilots, however, saw some thirty-plus bandits climbing from a direction of Albert, so 421 Squadron provided cover while 403 went down to attack. The enemy broke right, and a huge dogfight began involving some eighty aircraft. Warrant Officer A. V. Hargreaves, of 403, damaged one of a pair of 190s flying in close line astern at 10,000 feet. Flight Lieutenant Harry MacDonald saw 'a FW firing at an Me 109 from close range astern. This was seen by Blue One to go into a moderate steep dive and explode between St-Pol–Hesdin. It was claimed as destroyed by the Squadron because the Squadron's attack led to the FW mistaking the 109 for a Spitfire and attacking it' (ORB, 403 Squadron). On the way back, Greycap personally scored again:

> After engaging thirty-plus enemy aircraft in the Doullens–St-Pol area, the Wing reformed and we headed towards the French coast

on the outward journey flying at 23,000 feet. When four to five miles inland of Berck-sur-Mer I saw about eight Me 109s behind 403 Squadron. We turned to engage and all enemy aircraft dived away except two 109s which went into a shallow dive towards Le Crotoy. Enemy aircraft were flying line abreast and I opened fire with cannon and machine-gun on the starboard aircraft from 500 closing to 300 yards. I saw several cannon strikes on the rear portion of the fuselage and on the tail plane. At 9,000 feet I broke off the attack as E/A was now diving vertically; he did not recover and I saw him crash on to the north bank of the Somme. My Number Two, Flying Officer Bowen DFC, also fired at this enemy aircraft and I claim it as destroyed, shared with him.

In total, I/JG 27 lost three Me 109s, including the *Kommandeur*, *Hauptmann* Erich Hohagen, who baled out wounded, but it is impossible to ascertain who shot down whom.

On 11 June an early ground haze cleared and the sun came out. At 1605 hours, Wing Commander Johnson led the Wing on Rodeo 229, at the head of 421 Squadron. In this operation the Kenley Wing was to be the second wave of a fighter sweep between Abbeville and Poix. At 25,000 feet over the latter, fifteen-plus bandits, mainly Me 109s, were seen flying from a direction of Abbeville and 1,000 feet below. Greycap turned his Spitfires to starboard and engaged with 421 Squadron, the fighters whirling around between 26,000 down to 7,000 feet. Squadron Leader Hall shot the tail unit completely off a 109, and damaged another, but although other pilots of 421 Squadron fired their guns there were no other claims. As the Squadron's ORB states, it was a 'good show'.

On 13 June, the Kenley Wing's pilots were given a talk about the new 'Tactical Air Force in Great Britain' by an Army officer. The pilots concluded that this was 'very interesting' (ORB, 421 Squadron). Fighter Command had originally been created as a defensive force, but when the long-awaited invasion of enemy-occupied France eventually came, there would clearly be a change of role. Then, RAF fighter pilots would not be defending their homeland, as in 1940, but on the contrary providing tactical support to the advancing British and Canadian armies (the American Ninth Air Force would similarly support American troops). The Allied fighters would also have to ensure aerial supremacy over the battlefield, and become mobile units able to keep up with the advancing armies. The idea was, therefore, to create a composite, tactical force of fighters, bombers, fighter-bombers and army co-operation aircraft, independent of existing Commands. This tactical air force would exist exclusively for deployment in support of the Allied Expeditionary Force, which was being formed to undertake the proposed invasion. On 1 June 1943, this new aerial entity officially became the 2nd Tactical Air Force (TAF), comprising largely units formerly of No. 2 Group Bomber Command (the RAF's light bomber force) and various squadrons from Fighter Command. Soon, Fighter Command itself would, in fact, cease to exist altogether, the responsibility for home defence becoming that of 'Air Defence Great Britain'.

On 14 June, Wing Commander Johnson analysed his operational flying on this tour, which had started on 13 July 1942, and wrote the result in his logbook:

Operational Flying Times this Tour	120.30
Circuses	37
Ramrods	16
Rodeos	20
Roadsteads	NIL
Rhubarbs	2

At the other end of the spectrum, at this time, was Flying Officer Danny Brown, who had only recently started flying on operations with 403 Squadron. Of that early period he remembered:

Getting into the combat experience, you were first treated like a mother treats a chick, get your feet under you and then start to think up there in the air. I remember telling Johnnie, the first time that I flew in combat, which was with him, that if someone had asked me what my name was I was not sure that I could have remembered it! He bounced a 109, and my job was to stay with him and cover him. I saw this plane right in front of us, right close, and all of a sudden I saw little tiny puffs of something, all the while thinking in nano-seconds, all the while thinking 'Well, I wonder what in the world that is?', when I realised, idiot, that he was shooting a plane down! We watched it take on fire and smoke and watched it crash into the Somme delta. With that, you steadily gained more experience, but when you first start, you just don't get the opportunities. Remember that the German Air Force was not to be sneezed at. One of the great things about war is that you have to learn to get along with and be trusted by your fellow pilots. If you're not accepted then you might as well go home.

Although it was a showery day with a good deal of low cloud, on 15 June the Kenley Wing flew Ramrod 95. The Canadians provided the second wave of high cover to elements of a force of forty B-17s bombing Bernay aerodrome. Due to adverse weather, however, the bombers aborted before reaching the RV over Fecamp, so Greycap was given permission to proceed inland at his own discretion. Climbing towards Rouen, Appledore informed Johnnie of bandits nearby. Going down to 24,000 feet, the Spitfire pilots saw fifteen FW 190s of I/JG 2 flying in line abreast. Johnnie:

> I flew at 24,000 feet in order to avoid making smoke trails ... I ordered 421 to remain top guard and led 403 to attack. I myself attacked the starboard 190 with cannon and machine-gun, closing to 200 yards. I registered several cannon strikes on this E/A, which pulled violently upwards, almost to a stall. The hood was jettisoned and I saw the pilot drop out but did not see his parachute open. This E/A is claimed as destroyed. I then saw a further fifteen FW 190s on my port side and they had gone into line astern – all turning port very slowly and covering about two miles. I closed in on the last E/A and attacked him with cannon and machine-guns from five to ten degrees port astern, closing to good range. I registered several cannon strikes and pieces flew off this E/A. As he went into a slow spin the magazine in his starboard wing exploded, blowing off huge pieces of the wing and fuselage. He was soon completely enveloped in black smoke and this E/A is also claimed as destroyed.

This was remarkable shooting. Unsurprisingly the propaganda process later made much of the fact that Wing Commander Johnnie Johnson, the fighter ace from Melton Mowbray, had got 'two Huns before breakfast', his Wing described as 'one of the busiest in Fighter Command'.

The next noteworthy operation took place on 17 June. From dawn until 0830 hours, 421 Squadron was at readiness, but there was no scramble. The Squadron's CO, Squadron Leader Hall, was posted on rest to 58 OTU, the ORB recording, 'All sorry to lose our chief who was a good fellow and well liked by all personnel'. His place was taken by Squadron Leader Philip Leslie Irving Archer DFC, who had reported to 421 Squadron as a supernumerary squadron leader just two days previously. Archer had flown with the highly successful 92 Squadron from Biggin Hill during 1941, thence 416 Squadron the following year. He had now returned to operations after a rest with five enemy aircraft destroyed and one damaged to his credit. His last claim was a Do 217 on 18 July 1942, and all his previous victories were Me 109s; he had not yet scored against the FW 190s.

The weather was reportedly 5/10ths cloud and very windy, but nevertheless the Kenley Wing received orders to fly Rodeo 231. In this operation, the Wing was to provide the third wave of a fighter sweep of the Pas-de-Calais. Greycap led the Spitfires out over Dover at 15,000 feet, crossing into France at 24,000 feet over Gravelines. Operations informed Greycap of the presence of some thirty plus 190s climbing from Ypres towards Dunkirk. Earlier in the day, a dozen Bostons had attacked Vlissingen, and elements of JG 26 had engaged the Spitfires providing rear cover off Zeebrugge. When the first wave of the afternoon Rodeo swept in, *Jafü* 2 expected bombers to follow, but when this did not happen two *Gruppen* of JG 26 were vectored towards the last wave of Spitfires – the Kenley Wing. The Spitfires slowly orbited until the bandits were sighted climbing towards the French coast, strung out in line abreast, and some 10,000 feet below. This was the *Geschwadergruppe*, acting as bait, while *Hauptmann* Wutz Galland, *Kommandeur* of II/JG 26, climbed his 190s with the intention of bouncing the Spitfires as the latter took the bait. As predicted, the Spitfires pounced. Wing Commander Johnson led 421 Squadron down and attacked the last *Schwarm* of 190s:

> I attacked number two on the starboard side, and as I commenced fire with cannon and machine-guns he turned slowly to starboard. I closed in to 150 yards range and saw cannon strikes on the cockpit and wing roots. As I was overshooting, I gave him a final burst and pulled steeply upwards, the enemy aircraft caught fire and started to burn, spiralling slowly down.

Johnnie had hit *Unteroffizier* Günther Freitag, of 8/JG 26, who crashed and was killed at Steenvorde in Flanders. A confused fight followed, involving 80 to 100 FW 190s and some 24 Spitfires.

By this time, Galland was diving into the Spitfires' rear, so the two Kenley squadrons turned to face the attack. Flying Officer K. P. Marshall, Yellow Three of 403 Squadron, saw Squadron Leader Archer of 421 Squadron flying alongside him at about 21,000 feet. Marshall saw two 190s closing in on Archer, and was about to yell 'Break!' when his own aircraft was hit. He broke upwards and to port but did not see 421 Squadron's new CO again. Flight Sergeant G. M. Shouldice, Yellow Four, fired a long burst of cannon and machine-gun at Yellow Three's assailant, but had to break due to being attacked himself. Shouldice's kill was confirmed by Pilot Officer Bullick of 421, who saw a '190 with bits flying off and streaming black smoke, going straight down' (ORB, 403 Squadron). Having disengaged, Blue Section of 403 Squadron came out over France at 16,000 feet, while Red and Yellow Sections turned back inland over France to allow Marshall and Shouldice time to catch up. The former's aircraft was damaged, but the young Canadian managed to land safely at Redhill. Squadron Leader Archer of 421 was credited with having destroyed a 190, but sadly the new CO failed to return. Flying Officer McNamara of the same squadron was awarded a 190 'damaged', but he too was missing. The 27-year-old Squadron Leader Archer was buried at Longuenesse Souvenir Cemetery, St-Omer, but Flying Officer James Emmett McNamara was never found.

Oberleutnant Horst Sternberg, *Staffelkapitän* of 5/JG 26, was awarded a Spitfire destroyed, 5 kilometres south-west of Hazebrouck, and *Unteroffizier* Paul Schwarz, of 6/JG 26, made his first 'kill' 10 kilometres south-west of St-Omer. Both German kills were made in roughly the same area, therefore, which makes sense given that both of the Kenley Wing's casualties were from the same squadron. It is therefore impossible to say which German shot down which Spitfire pilot. Sternberg's kill was timed at 1545, and at the same time he later reported having collided with a Spitfire, forcing him to bale out, wounded. As none of the Kenley pilots reported having witnessed such a collision, the probability is that Sternberg collided with the crashing Spitfire of either Archer or McNamara. Back at Kenley, the Wing claimed three FW 190s destroyed and one damaged. The Germans had, in fact, lost two: Freitag to Johnnie and Sternberg to an alleged collision. The following day, the British press reported:

A Canadian Spitfire Wing added three more FW 190s to its score during a sweep over Belgium yesterday afternoon, bringing the day's score of our fighters up to a total of nine enemy aircraft destroyed. The Canadians' three victims were destroyed in a series of combats between Ypres and the coast at heights varying from 22,000 feet to 26,000 feet. The Wing was led by Wing Commander J. E. Johnson DSO DFC & bar, who himself shot down a FW 190, bringing his score to seventeen. The Spitfires first encountered a formation of about 30 enemy aircraft. Shortly after a dogfight with them about twenty more enemy fighters were seen. The Spitfires immediately dived in amongst the FW 190s and scattered the formation. Two of our Spitfires are missing.

The following day, Kenley's popular Station Commander, Group Captain Jimmy Fenton, left for pastures new. He considered that:

As Wing Leader, Johnnie Johnson was undoubtedly type-cast for the role, being outstandingly successful both as a fighter pilot and leader. As we were the most successful Sector in the Group, some reflected glory came my way, of which I was always happy to be the recipient! We were in a well-organised and well-led Group with Air Vice-Marshal 'Dingbat' Saunders as AOC. Morale was at its highest. It was the lead up to the invasion, still a year ahead, and the phase was vitally important in providing the disciplined and experienced fighter force that we were, in the event, lucky to have.

At 0500 hours on 22 June, the 'Wingco' briefed his pilots on Ramrod 99, in which the Kenley Spitfires were to meet and escort a formation of B-17s returning from attacking industrial targets in Germany's Ruhr Valley. By now, the Americans had accepted that if the daylight offensive was to continue, especially in the absence of a long-range offensive escort fighter, priority must be given to targets connected with the *Luftwaffe*. These included not only enemy airfields but also targets connected with the German aviation industry, such as aircraft factories and other associated depots. The target on that day, for 235 Flying Fortresses of the 381st and 384th Bomb Groups, was the synthetic-rubber plant at Hüls. As Germany was cut off from supplies of natural rubber, this *Chemische Werke* was of vital importance to the aircraft manufacturing industry given that it produced 30 per cent of the nation's total output of synthetic rubber. This trip to the Ruhr was the deepest penetration so far attempted by the Americans. The Ruhr flak belt, as RAF Bomber Command knew only too well, was lethal, however, and this time the bombers also had to run the gauntlet of *Jafü* Holland-Ruhr.

At 0540 hours, the Kenley Wing took off, 'pancaking', at Manston, at 0615. At 0930, the Spitfires were up again, bound for the Dutch coast. Greycap set course for Schouwen Island, which was reached at 20,000 feet, and from there inland to Sleidrecht, over which the Spitfires arrived at 24,000 feet. Six boxes of B-17s were seen coming out over the Dutch coast, escorted by 'Little Friends', crossing out over Schouwen between 24,000 and 27,000 feet. The Kenley Wing remained over the exit point until the last box of bombers had left. Although some twenty Me 109s and FW 190s were seen, no substantial attacks were made and the Canadian Spitfires were not engaged. The bombers had hit the target accurately. Just under a quarter of the total tonnage of bombs dropped had fallen within the factory itself, the damage arising rendering the factory completely useless for a month, and normal production was not resumed for a further six. Sixteen bombers were lost and 170 more B-17s were damaged. Over the North Sea, about 40 miles west of Schouwen, the Kenley pilots saw a Fortress at 5,000 feet, covered by eight Spitfires. Later, a large flash was seen mid-Channel, and when the Spitfires arrived over the area shortly afterwards, large patches of oil marked the last resting place of more brave American airmen.

Another show was planned for the afternoon, the Wing being led off by Greycap at 1554 hours on Circus 341. Together with the Hornchurch Wing, the Canadians were to support twelve Venturas withdrawing after bombing Abbeville aerodrome. While the Spitfires were in the Abbeville area, an aircraft was seen going down in flames, and a large fire was seen near Dieppe. Seven enemy aircraft were seen, but these were too far east and could not, therefore, be engaged. The sortie was otherwise without incident and Johnnie's Spitfires were back at Kenley by 1728. As the 421 Squadron ORB commented, it had been a 'long day'. Of interest is that the Kenley Wing operated in conjunction with the Hornchurch Spitfires, led by the New Zealand ace Wing Commander W. V. Crawford-Compton DFC & Bar. The Spitfires often seemed outnumbered over France, so Johnnie thought it worth increasing numbers. Air Vice-Marshal Saunders agreed to an experiment, and arranged that the Kenley and Hornchurch Wings would operate together. This represented a four-squadron force of Spitfire Mk IXs, some forty-eight aircraft in total. Johnnie: 'It was just that the Huns always had greater numbers, which didn't seem to cause them problems from a defensive viewpoint, which is perhaps worth studying, so we just thought that it was worth a go.' First thing in the morning of 22 June, Johnnie flew up to Hornchurch and worked out the finer points with Wing Commander Crawford-Compton, then returned to Kenley, all ready for Ramrod 100. Over Beachy Head, the Kenley and Hornchurch Wings met and rendezvoused with seventeen Flying Fortresses bound for Bernay aerodrome. After a penetration of 10 miles into hostile airspace, the bombers turned back, however, due to unfavourable weather conditions. The entire Allied force returned without incident via St-Valery.

24 June was a clear, warm and still day. This would be the Kenley Wing's busiest day so far this year. After an early briefing, Greycap led his Spitfires up from Kenley at 0705 hours, on Ramrod 102, a sortie not including the Hornchurch Wing. The Spitfires roared over Deal at zero feet, climbing to 18,000 feet en route to Flushing docks, which was being bombed by twelve 2 Group Bostons. The Spitfires swept over the target, which was smoking, at 25,000 feet, and experienced some accurate and heavy flak. After sweeping Nieuport and Ostend, the Kenley Wing returned via Deal, having seen not one enemy aircraft. The next sortie was Ramrod 103, in which the Kenley Wing was to fly the second wave of a fighter sweep over the Le Touquet, Fruges and St-Omer areas, in support of more Bostons attacking railway facilities at St-Omer. Greycap climbed the Spitfires hard immediately after take-off, at 1125 hours, crossing out over Rye. When 10 miles off Hardelot, Appledore informed Johnnie that there were bandits off Cap Gris Nez at 25,000 feet. After several orbits, during which the Spitfires clawed for more height, the French coast was crossed at 24,000 feet over Le Touquet. Appledore then vectored Greycap north-east of Hazebrouck, where

Flight Lieutenant H. D. MacDonald, Red Three of 403 Squadron, sighted what appeared to be three Me 109s below at 14,000 feet. Together with Red Four, Sergeant D. Small, Red Three was despatched to engage the enemy, but the Germans dived away and escaped. Red Three and Four then rejoined Red Section, Red One being Greycap, and Red Two Flying Officer N. J. Ogilvie. The Wing then proceeded to St-Omer.

While the Spitfires cruised at 25,000 feet, fifteen FW 190s, in several small formations, were reported at 18,000 feet, so Greycap, leaving 421 Squadron as top cover, ordered Yellow Section of 403 Squadron down to engage while he led Red Section towards some other bandits. Again, however, the Germans half-rolled away and refused to engage. While Red Three followed Red One and Two down, however, a Spitfire suddenly cut between him and the leading pair. To avoid a collision, MacDonald immediately broke to starboard and upon straightening out at 20,000 feet saw two formations of enemy aircraft being chased by Spitfires. A third gaggle of bandits broke starboard and went into a defensive circle. These six FW 190s soon straightened out, in pairs. Red Three dived out of a steep turn onto the port aircraft of the last pair and delivered a short burst of cannon and machine-gun fire from 150 yards. The Canadian noted strikes on his target's port wing, then, upon breaking away, saw the 190 doing a series of lazy downward rolls. At 6,000 feet a parachute opened adjacent to this 190, making MacDonald believe that he had destroyed it. What had, in fact, happened, however, was that Red Four, Sergeant Small, had been attacked and shot down by *Unteroffizier* Gomann, of 5/JG 26, and it was he who MacDonald had seen bale out. The latter had hit and wounded *Oberfeldwebel* Alfred Günther, also of 5 *Staffel*, but the German managed to land his damaged 190 safely at Vitry. After Yellow Section's unsuccessful attack, the Spitfires were shadowed to the coast by some ten FW 190s, but no interception took place. Having left France over Cap Gris Nez at 27,000 feet, heavy flak had tracked the Wing from St-Omer to the coast. Throughout the entire proceedings, 421 Squadron had maintained top cover, but four pilots came home very short of fuel: Pilot Officer Linton forced landed at Dungeness, and three others landed at Redhill. By 1315 hours, the Wing was all accounted for, excepting Sergeant Small who had been captured by the enemy.

Ramrod 106 was the next show that day, Greycap leading the Wing off from Kenley at 1645 hours. The Spitfires were Forward Target Support Wing, sweeping the Rouen area, while twelve Venturas bombed Yainville power station. The English coast was crossed at zero feet over Newhaven, the Wing then climbing until offshore at St-Valery-en-Caux, where an orbit was made. Heading inland at 14,000 feet, Greycap received reports of forty enemy aircraft climbing up from Rouen towards Le Havre. Although the Germans had the tactical advantage, the Kenley Wing engaged in an effort to prevent them from molesting the bombers. The brief clash was inconclusive, so the Spitfires re-formed and attempted to engage three FW 190s, flying from Rouen towards Fecamp, but again unsuccessfully. Two more 190s were then sighted shadowing the Wing and apparently intending to catch the odd straggler, as Johnnie noted:

> They were about two miles behind the Wing and I climbed both squadrons steeply into sun and carried out one orbit to port. The FW 190s, which were then down sun of us, appeared to lose sight of the Wing and flew beneath us, representing an excellent target. They were seen 1,000 feet below my Section and a mile ahead. I ordered my Number Two, Squadron Leader McNair, to engage these aircraft with me. The remainder of the Squadron (421) were told to keep high in order not to scare the Huns. I closed in on number two E/A from line astern and opened fire from 300, closing to 150 yards. Cannon strikes were seen on the fuselage and tail plane of this E/A and a large piece fell away from the starboard half of his tail unit. The E/A spun down and was seen to crash at Valmont.

Squadron Leader McNair destroyed the leading 190, these two enemy fighters probably being from *Jafü* 3's I/JG 2. The two successful Spitfire pilots then rejoined the Wing, returning home via Eletot and Beachy Head. Two pilots of 421 Squadron had to put down at the coastal airfield of Friston, out of fuel. By close of play, it had been another long, hot day.

On 27 June, cloud was 7/10ths, but the day was otherwise bright. At 1015 hours, Greycap led the Wing on Rodeo 235, a freelance sweep of the St-Omer area in conjunction with the Hornchurch

Wing, and controlled by Appledore. The Hornchurch Spitfires were
positioned to the port-side of the Canadians. Johnnie:

> [After] making rendezvous at Dungeness, I set course for Berck.
> When halfway across the Channel, Appledore gave me a vector of
> 90° but I had to swing to starboard to avoid Boulogne. Appledore
> then warned me of bandits approaching and instructed me to steer
> 70°. Shortly afterwards in the St-Omer area I saw approximately
> thirty FW 190s approaching from the port bow at 25,000
> feet with a high cover of twenty Me 109s to port and above
> them. Kenley bottom Squadron was then at 23,000 feet. I asked
> Hornchurch to engage and 403 also turned into the high cover.
> I climbed 421 steeply under the 190s, which split up and carried
> out a moderate turn to port. Six 190s, however, straightened out
> and flew in line abreast heading in the Nieuport/Ostend direction.
> I instructed my Section to engage these six enemy aircraft but just
> as I was within range they all dived steeply. I followed my aircraft
> and opened fire from 250 yards with cannon and machine-guns.
> Several strikes were seen on his fuselage, wing roots and tail unit
> and he commenced to emit thick black smoke, as I broke away I
> saw at least one half of a wing break off.

After the brief combat, the Spitfires re-formed over Gravelines
before going home independently. When mid-Channel, the Kenley
Wing was informed of bandits in the Dover area, so Greycap took
the Spitfires down to sea level, sweeping towards Boulogne, but no
enemy aircraft were seen. By 1114 hours, the Spitfires were safely
back at base.

In his logbook, Johnnie recorded that his total number of enemy
aircraft destroyed to date was eighteen and two-thirds. It was an
impressive score. Johnnie:

> My life as a Wing Leader was fantastic. It just revolved around
> fighter pilots, Spitfires, flying and fighting. The Wing Commander
> Flying appointment was excellent, not least because previously
> the senior squadron commander would lead, but then there was
> always argy-bargy about who was the senior! Being a Wing Leader
> was the best job in Fighter Command. You had no administrative
> duties whatsoever, apart to recommend chaps for a gong. I don't

think I put pen to paper at Kenley for any other reason. All you had to do was look after your pilots and aeroplanes with a very simple chain of command. It was a marvellous job. The Station Commander was usually a Group Captain, who had to do the food and the clothing, the general well-being of the Station with perhaps 2,000 personnel. Occasionally, like Jimmy Fenton, he would fly with us, just to keep his hand in, but he had to fly a desk most of the time! So the whole command structure was simply Fighter Command C-in-C, the Group AOC, the Station Commander, then the Wing Commander Flying. A very short, sharp chain of command. A very good one too, and a very good relationship between the guys at the top. I remember on one occasion we had come back from escorting some Fortresses and we had got into some rather stiff fighting, although we had done well, and I got back in my office about five o'clock in the evening and some staff officer from Fighter Command HQ rang up and said, 'Hello, is that Wing Commander Johnson?'

I said, 'It is.'

He said, 'Well just a moment, the Commander-in-Chief would like a word.'

All the Boss said was 'I thought that I would call you up Johnnie and say how very well you have done today, thank you very much, goodnight.'

Marvellous, wasn't it? Leadership, *real* leadership. We held conferences at Uxbridge with the AOC 11 Group, Air Vice-Marshal 'Dingbat' Saunders, or we'd go up to Bentley Priory when Leigh-Mallory called one. Mind you, these chaps, Leigh-Mallory and so on, were all the while coming down to see us. LM was very good at keeping a good liaison, he didn't fly much himself but he'd get flown down in some old Proctor or something about once a month. He'd always come down if you got a gong; he was very much a father figure who wanted to help all the time. What did used to happen was that if there was a good show, the chaps at Fighter Command would produce a document containing extracts of the relevant reports and circulate this amongst the Wings. They were very good at disseminating information this way and had really got it together by 1943. By mid-1943, Al Deere and I were the 'Old Boys', so they had to listen to what we had to say. Old LM would say 'So tell me, Johnnie, what did you

do then', and so on, 'Can we improve that? Is there anything I
can do? Do you want another squadron, perhaps? Do you want
to lead more squadrons?' So we always had this backing. I held
Leigh-Mallory in high regard. He could be a little bit pompous
but he had a heart of gold, super chap, and we were all very sad
when he was later killed.

Due to his increasing number of aerial victories, Johnnie was starting
to attract significant publicity:

It wasn't until early May time, when we started to escort the
Fortresses and hack a few Huns down, that I got a bit of
publicity. They used to produce a Fighter Command score sheet,
of which Sailor Malan was at the top, and it also showed you
who was deceased! The public relations chaps used to push
the score sheet out to the newspapers. Of course there wasn't
much good news at the time, lots of disasters in the Middle
and Far East, so the air fighters became a bit of news, 'glamour
boys'!

Clearly it was a time for heroes, and Wing Commander Johnnie
Johnson was now among the foremost 'knights of the air'. Dan
Browne:

We did these missions called the 'Milk Run' and the 'Mail Run',
one of which was to Abbeville. We'd all cross over on the deck,
with propellers no higher than an office desk above the water, to
avoid radar detection. Of course there was rigid radio silence. The
bombers would then climb up, and we'd climb up and get above
them. As you know, Abbeville was a very active fighter field so
pretty soon the bombers would drop their bombs, the target being
just eighteen miles from the coast. The bombers would then turn,
dive back out and go home. We would be still climbing up, going
inland towards Germany, and soon start getting reports: 'There
are 200 plus coming up over Cambrai', 'There's 200 plus coming
up over Lille' and so on. There were only twenty-four of us! We
would keep climbing until we got to a safe altitude, then we'd
turn around and head back. Of course we had superior altitude
in the Spit IX, so as the 190s couldn't reach us they'd pull up

vertical and fire at us from some way below. The trick was to
stall and spin out.

After Ramrod 117 on 1 July, Wing Commander Johnson was sent
off on a fortnight's well-earned leave. Upon conclusion, Johnnie
flew from Rearsby (in Leicestershire) to Kenley in an Auster, his
co-pilot being a Squadron Leader Edwards. Bob Middlemiss, of
403 Squadron, had also spent some of that leave with Johnnie in
Melton Mowbray:

> Johnnie organised a trip in the latest Auster IV at Rearsby, with
> the Chief Test Pilot, a Mr Waite. The latter was taking up a new
> Auster, MT454, and went along on the test flight. He taxied out to
> the runway in use and said that he would demonstrate a short field
> take-off. He applied the brakes, opened full throttle, got tail up into
> flying position, then let go of the brakes and after a very short run
> indeed we were up and flying. On completion of the air test he said
> 'I will now demonstrate the very short field landing capabilities of
> this aircraft.' After touchdown he applied full brakes – needless to
> say we stopped after a very short run, and no doubt was left in my
> mind of the aircraft's short take-off and landing capabilities!

Back at Kenley on 15 July, Johnnie re-familiarised himself with
Spitfire 'JE-J', EN398, in which he undertook an hour of local flying.
Greycap's first flight was a cannon test of 15 minutes. On this day
of scattered cloud and good visibility, the Kenley Wing was not
up on operations until 1613 hours. The sortie was Rodeo 245, a
sweep of Hardelot, Abbeville and Poix, controlled by Appledore.
The Wing began climbing soon after take-off, crossing out over
Rye at 5,000 feet before making landfall over Hardelot at 20,000.
From Boulogne, accurate and intense flak was sent up, after which
Greycap was vectored to the Poix area, just south of Abbeville.
Bostons of 2 Group's 107 Squadron had just bombed Poix airfield,
escorted by Typhoons and Spitfires. Combat had been joined with
losses resulting for both sides, the fight having just finished when
the Canadians arrived on the scene. Appledore warned Greycap of
bandits ahead, however, and he immediately saw two *Schwärme* of
Me 109s directly ahead and at the same height. Johnnie's combat
report described what happened next:

I turned slightly starboard to get advantage of the Hun but all E/A except two Me 109s climbed and were not seen again. These two Me 109s flew head-on towards the Wing and when not more than 1,000 yards away turned to port and away from the Wing. I lead my Section to attack and when almost within range E/A started to climb steeply. We had the advantage of speed, after one dive, and so experienced no difficulty in overtaking the E/A. I instructed my Number Two to take the highest Me 109, and I opened fire on the lowest with cannon and machine-guns from dead astern, range 300 yards. I gave him a four-second burst, strikes being seen on the port Wing root, engine cowling and fuselage. E/A at once started to pour thick glycol vapour and went down in a wide spiral. His course was easy to follow as he left a strong trail of white glycol in the air. He was seen to crash in the Bangy–Senarpont area and continued to burn and smoke for some minutes. This E/A is claimed as destroyed.

As usual there was no doubt regarding the accuracy of Johnnie's claim. The other Me 109 was attacked three times by Flight Lieutenant MacDonald, Red Three of 403 Squadron, with which Section Greycap was leading the Wing. On Red Three's second pass, the 109 half-rolled to port and dived, and on the third attack strikes were seen on its port wingtip, fuselage and cockpit. From 12,000 feet, the 109 dived straight in. Three FW 190s were then sighted near Le Treport, but these quickly dived away and escaped when a section of 403 Squadron Spitfires gave chase. The Wing then re-formed and left France via Berck, crossing back in at 5,000 feet over Dungeness. By 1750, the Wing was safely down with two more confirmed victories to add to a growing tally.

At 1945 hours, the Kenley Wing was up again, on Rodeo 246, sweeping Hardelot and Poix, again under Appledore. When offshore at Hardelot, Greycap was vectored south and found six FW 190s flying south at 12,000 feet over Le Touquet. 421 Squadron dived after them but were unable to close the gap, the 190s having half-rolled and dived inland. After the unsuccessful chase, Greycap re-formed his Spitfires and headed home, landing at 2015. He wrote in his logbook, 'Six FW 190s intercepted but E/A ducked as we were just opening fire!'

A dull and wet morning cleared by noon on 16 July, the weather improving steadily throughout the afternoon. The Wing was up at 1915 hours, Greycap leading on Ramrod 144, a sweep with Hornchurch of Dieppe, Grandvilliers, Abbeville and the Somme Estuary, in support of Marauders bombing Abbeville marshalling yards. The Spitfires crossed out over Beachy Head, then climbed steadily, making landfall just west of Dieppe at 22,000 feet. The Wings then flew to Grandvilliers and were given a vector: bandits below at Angels Twelve. The Spitfire Mk IXs dived and intercepted the 'enemy', which proved to be the Tangmere Wing's Spitfire Mk XIIs! The IXs then re-formed and climbed to 23,000 feet, the Hornchurch Wing slightly above and up sun of Abbeville. At this point, twenty FW 190s were seen coming head on, so Greycap manoeuvred to give Hornchurch the advantage. Although the Germans were bounced by Wing Commander Crawford-Compton and his men, no claims were subsequently made. The Kenley Spitfires then left France over the Somme Estuary at 20,000 feet, flying north to Berck before setting course for Rye. By 2050 hours the Wing was safely down. In his personal log, Johnnie wrote, 'Hornchurch rather missed a good opportunity.'

Times were changing. On 20 July the 421 Squadron ORB recorded, 'Everybody preparing for move to 127 Airfield in 83 Group. Practically all Squadron personnel, except pilots, are already posted to 127 Airfield, which is forming here at Kenley.' This was all preparation, of course, for the proposed Allied liberation of enemy-occupied Europe. It was clear that air power would play a decisive role on the battlefield, fighter-bombers and medium bombers flying in support of ground forces. To achieve that end the fighter-bomber units would lead a nomadic existence, able to operate from temporary airfields and move at short notice. The whole process was now being geared up to achieving that aim.

On 25 July, according to the 421 Squadron ORB, there was a 'big improvement in the weather', which perfectly suited the Allied air forces' purposes. In the morning, 100 B-17s bombed Hamburg, following up the RAF's nocturnal raid. To prevent the enemy fighters of *Jafü* Holland-Ruhr engaging the Americans, the RAF's No. 2 Group despatched a dozen B-25 Mitchells to bomb the Fokker aircraft factory at Amsterdam, and Eighth Air Force B-26

Marauders bombed the coke ovens at Ghent. First off, the Kenley Wing flew across to Coltishall, to operate from there on another escort sortie, Ramrod 158, this time providing Target Support to the Bostons attacking Amsterdam. At the Norfolk aerodrome, the pilots were briefed while their Spitfires were refuelled before take-off at 1415. The Spitfires crossed the Dutch coast at 24,000 feet over the target area and sighted the bombers. The Wing then skirted north of Amsterdam and followed the Bostons out over the Dutch coast. Greycap then led his pilots on a sweep along the Dutch coast to Noordwijk but no enemy aircraft were encountered. By 1555, the Spitfires were back at Coltishall, being 'turned around'.

At 1915 hours, the Kenley Wing was up again, this time on Ramrod 158, providing Forward Target Support to twelve Bostons bombing Schipol aerodrome. Crossing the Dutch coast at 22,000 feet between Noordwijk and Zandveert, the Spitfires then flew to Schipol, which was reached on time. Johnnie:

> At 1957 hours I was flying on the East side of Schipol at 22,000 feet, when I saw an Me 109G, with under-slung guns in wings, flying in the same direction about three miles ahead of the Wing. Enemy aircraft turned to port and was obviously positioning himself to attack the beehive, which was then crossing the coast. I instructed the Wing to remain at their height and took my Section down to attack this E/A. I closed in on E/A, then at 12,000 feet, and opened fire with cannon and machine-guns closing to 170 yards. The 109 was flying directly into the sun and owing to this fact I could not see the result of my fire, but as I broke away he turned to port with glycol streaming from his starboard radiator. I saw him go down to about 6,000 feet and my Number Two saw him after this, diving vertically towards the ground. As I climbed away I saw an aircraft burning on the ground to the west of Schipol. As there were no Wing losses in the combat area I claim this Me 109 as destroyed on this evidence.

The Wing Leader was supported by Pilot Officer Isbister, flying Black Two:

> Wing Leader opened fire, firing several bursts closing to point blank range. The enemy aircraft was pouring white smoke and

AIRFIX-72 SCALE
SPITFIRE IX

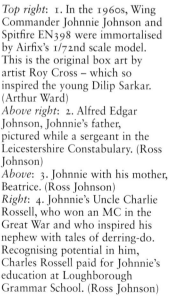

Top right: 1. In the 1960s, Wing Commander Johnnie Johnson and Spitfire EN398 were immortalised by Airfix's 1/72nd scale model. This is the original box art by artist Roy Cross – which so inspired the young Dilip Sarkar. (Arthur Ward)

Above right: 2. Alfred Edgar Johnson, Johnnie's father, pictured while a sergeant in the Leicestershire Constabulary. (Ross Johnson)

Above: 3. Johnnie with his mother, Beatrice. (Ross Johnson)

Right: 4. Johnnie's Uncle Charlie Rossell, who won an MC in the Great War and who inspired his nephew with tales of derring-do. Recognising potential in him, Charles Rossell paid for Johnnie's education at Loughborough Grammar School. (Ross Johnson)

Top left: 5. Johnnie, for once following behind, and brother Ross on a family outing. (Ross Johnson)
Above: 6. Johnnie, centre, while playing rugby at Loughborough Grammar. (Ross Johnson)
Left: 7. Johnnie, extreme left, with other aircrew aspirants at ITW in late 1939. Also pictured are Sergeants Peter Fox (third from left), who flew Hurricanes with 56 Squadron during the Battle of Britain, and Bob Poulton (third right) who flew Spitfires with 74.
Below left: 8. Off to war: 18 December 1939. Sergeant J. E. Johnson of the RAFVR reports to 22 EFTS, Cambridge.

No 78 Course.
1 S. F.T.S.
SEALAND.

Top left: 9. A still 'wingless'
Sergeant Johnson (middle row,
third from left) at EFTS.
Top right: 10. Johnnie (centre)
with other trainee pilots during
early 1940. He loved the
camaraderie of the service.
Above left: 11. A class photograph
from SFTS, although curiously
Johnnie does not appear in it. The
crosses indicate those who did not
survive the process.
Above right: 12. Johnnie (left)
with two unknown pilots, wearing
Sidcot flying overalls, at SFTS. A
Fairey Battle light bomber stands
behind them.
Right: 13. In September 1940,
Pilot Officer Johnson was posted
to fly Spitfires with 616 Squadron,
commanded by Squadron Leader
Billy Burton DFC – pictured here at
Tangmere the following summer.

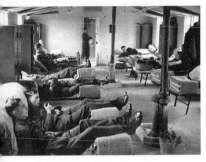

Top left: 14. 616 Squadron pilots' room at Kirton, late 1940.

Above: 15. Johnnie, arm in sling, recuperates with friends in Leicestershire after surgery to his shoulder, which saved his flying career in 1940.

Left: 16. Pilot Officer Ken Holden of 616 Squadron. Upon return to the Squadron, Johnnie's only ambition was to 'live and fight' with such veterans.

Below left: 17. A lifelong friend of Johnnie's, Pilot Officer (later Group Captain Sir) Hugh 'Cocky' Dundas. The pair met on 616 Squadron in 1940, and shared Johnnie's first kill, a Do 17 on 15 January 1941.

Top left: 18. Johnnie with 616 Squadron's
Intelligence Officer, Flt Lt E. P. Gibbs, at
Kirton during the winter of 1940/41.
Top right: 19. Johnnie (right) with two
other future fighter aces at Kirton during
the winter of 1941: 'Nip' Hepple (left) and
Roy Marples (centre).
Above left: 20. Pilot Officer Phillip 'Nip'
Hepple of 616 Squadron.
Above right: 21. Pilot Officer Johnnie
Johnson of 616 Squadron – his Spitfire
proudly sporting one and a half swastikas,
indicating his combat claims to date.
Right: 22. Wing Commander Douglas
Bader, Leader of the Tangmere Wing in
1941. Bader was a massive influence on the
young Pilot Officer Johnson. The pair were
lifelong friends.

Above right: 23. Sergeant (now Sir) Alan Smith, Wing Commander Bader's usual Number Two in Dogsbody Section.
Above left: 24. Group Captain A. B. 'Woody' Woodhall, who had been Station Commander and 'Boss Controller' at Duxford in 1940, controlling the 12 Group Wing led by Squadron Leader Douglas Bader. In 1941 Woodhall performed the same function at Tangmere, by which time Bader was the first Wing Commander (Flying) there.
Left: 25. Johnnie with one of his many Labradors, 'The Pusher'.
Below left: 26. Johnnie with Cocky Dundas and Pusher at Tangmere, summer 1941.

Top right: 27. Johnnie (left) with Flight Lieutenant Ken Holden (centre) and Cocky Dundas (sporting cricket pullover) at Tangmere, summer 1941.

Above: 28. Wing Commander Bader always led his Wing with 616 Squadron, and based himself with that unit at Westhampnett. 'Dogsbody' is pictured here with Johnnie (extreme right) and other 616 Squadron pilots Flight Lieutenant Colin MacFie (centre), Flying Officer Hugh Dundas (second left), and Squadron Leader Billy Burton (extreme left).

Right: 29. Johnnie's groundcrew at Tangmere.

Below right: 30. 'A' Flight of 616 Squadron at Tangmere, summer 1941. Seated, from left: Flying Officer Cocky Dundas, Pilot Officer Nip Hepple, Sergeant Alan Smith. Standing, from left: Pilot Officer Johnson, Sergeants Mabbett, Scott and McCairns. Mabbett would be shot down and killed over St-Omer, while flying as Johnnie's Number Two, 21 July 1941.

31. Group Captain Woodhall (front row, centre), with Wing Commander Bader (with pipe, at Woodhall's right) and pilots from 610 and 616 Squadrons, Westhampnett, summer 1941. These include: front row, extreme left: Pilot Officer (later Air Marshal Sir) Denis Crowley-Milling (610); third left: Squadron Leader Ken Holden (CO, 610); third from right: Squadron Leader Billy Burton (CO, 616); second right: Flight Lieutenant Lionel 'Buck' Casson; third right: Pilot Officer Roy Marples. Middle row: extreme right: Sergeant Jeff West (616); third right: Pilot Officer Johnnie Johnson (616); and fourth right: Pilot Officer Nip Hepple.

Left: 32. 'A' Flight of 616 Squadron, Westhampnett, 1941. From left: Flight Lieutenant Colin MacFie, Flying Officer Cocky Dundas, Pilot Officers Nip Hepple and Johnnie Johnson.

Below: 33. High summer at Tangmere, 1941: a section of Spitfires takes off from Westhampnett for an offensive operation over enemy-occupied France.

Above left: 34. The legless Wing Commander Douglas Bader back at Tangmere after a sweep, summer 1941. He failed to return from Circus 68 on 9 August 1941. Accidentally shot down by another Spitfire pilot, 'Dogsbody' became a prisoner of war.

Above right: 35. 'Dogsbody' – Wing Commander Bader – with Squadron Leader Burton (CO, 616, extreme left) and pilots of 616 Squadron who flew in the Wing Leader's famous 'Dogsbody Section': Pilot Officer Johnnie Johnson, Flight Lieutenant Cocky Dundas, and Sergeant Alan Smith.

Right: 36. The New Zealander Sergeant Jeff West of 616 Squadron, who often flew as a wingman in 'Dogsbody Section', at the head of which Wing Commander Bader led the Tangmere Wing.

Below right: 37. Johnnie's 616 Squadron Spitfire being rearmed at Kingscliffe, late 1941. This is a presentation aircraft, paid for by public subscription under the auspices of the Spitfire Fund.

Above right: 38. A shot of
Johnnie's Spitfire Mk VB at
Kingscliffe. The steamroller
is tamping down the runway
– on the construction of which
worked Johnnie's brother,
Ross, also a surveyor. By
chance, therefore, the Johnson
brothers – both of whom
served their country, but in
very different ways – enjoyed
each other's company at
Kingscliffe that particular
winter.

Above left: 39. 616 Squadron's
groundcrew at Kirton, late
1941.

Left: 40. Flight Lieutenant
Johnnie Johnson and the
Squadron 'Spy' ponder which
direction to take: was there a
choice?

Below left: 41. Johnnie, by
now a flight commander, with
his faithful groundcrew at
Kirton: Rigger Arthur Radcliffe
(left) and Fitter Fred Burton.

Above left: 42. Flight
Lieutenant Johnnie
Johnson DFC, standing
in cockpit, with his flight
at Kirton. Once more the
Squadron was absorbing
and training replacement
pilots prior to resuming
operations as a front-line
fighter squadron in 11
Group.
Above right: 43. Flight
Lieutenant Johnson
returns to Kingscliffe and
a news interview.
Right: 44. Johnnie gives
his report on camera
– one wonders what
happened to this film.
Below: 45. The
groundcrew 'turning
around' Johnnie's Spitfire
at Kirton.

Top: 46. Flight Lieutenant Johnson (third left) with Squadron Leader Colin Grey DFC (in greatcoat), a New Zealander and Battle of Britain ace, who commanded 616 Squadron at Kingscliffe in 1942.

Centre: 47. Squadron Leader Johnnie Johnson, seated centre, with his first command: 610 'County of Chester' Squadron of the AAF in 1942.

Bottom: 48. One of Johnnie's flight commanders in 610 was Flight Lieutenant Denis Crowley-Milling DFC, with whom he had flown in the Tangmere Wing. Another member of Douglas Bader's inner sanctum, 'Crow' was shortly given command of one of the first Hawker Typhoon squadrons.

Above left: 49. On 14 November 1942, Squadron Leader Johnnie Johnson DFC married Pauline Ingate at Norwich. The best man was Squadron Leader Cocky Dundas DFC, who would later be godfather to the couple's second son, Christopher, born in 1946.
Above right: 50. 'Plumbers' rearming Johnnie's ever-hungry guns.
Right: 51. Squadron Leader Johnnie Johnson DFC, drawn by the famous war and portrait artist Cuthbert Orde in 1943.
Below: 52. Greycap Leader: Wing Commander Johnnie Johnson poses with his personal mount at Kenley, Spitfire Mk IX EN398 – the most successful combat Spitfire of the Second World War.

"JOHNNY"

S/L. J.E. JOHNSON. D.S.O.   610 SQUADRON.

Above left: 53. Squadron Leader 'Bud' Molloy DFC, CO of 401 Squadron.
Above right: 54. Johnnie's great friend, the American J. D. 'Danny' Browne, who won his spurs flying with Johnnie's Canadian Wing in 1943.

55. Squadron Leader Hugh Godefroy DFC, who succeeded Johnnie as Kenley's Wing Leader.

56. Squadron Leader Foss Boulton DFC, CO of 416 Squadron.

Above left: 57. Flight
Lieutenant Dean MacDonald
DFC of 403 Squadron.
Above right: 58. Wing
Commander Johnson with the
Kenley Station Commander,
Group Captain Harry Fenton
(extreme left), and Canadian
Squadron Leaders Foss
Boulton and Syd Ford.
Right: 59. Wing Commander
Johnson back from a sweep
over France, 1943.
Below right: 60. Squadron
Leader Syd Ford and Flight
Lieutenant Charlie Magwood.

Above left: 61. Pilots of 421 Squadron after a sortie – a posed shot for the Canadian press.
Above right: 62. Wing Commander Johnson (extreme right), with, from left, Flight Lieutenants Dean MacDonald and 'Trapper' Bowen, Hugh Godefroy and Walter Conrad.
Left: 63. 'With Sally at Kenley, 1943'.
Below left: 64. Greycap Leader: Kenley, 1943.

Above left: 65. Wing Commander Johnson – a born leader able to relate and inspire all under his command, regardless of their status. Johnnie always paid tribute to the essential work carried out by his units' ground staff.

Above right: 66. 'One of our Spitfires is missing'; from left: Flight Lieutenant Norman Fowlow, Wing Commander Johnnie Johnson and Flight Lieutenant Dagwood Phillips. The 'Canada' flashes on Johnnie's battledress were presented to him by his Canadian pilots.

67. One Spitfire that failed to return to Kenley was this one: LZ996, of 421 Squadron, which was shot down over Flanders on 17 June 1943.

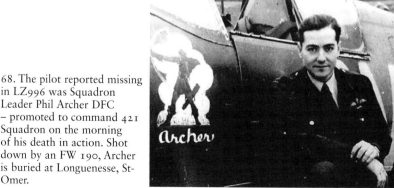

68. The pilot reported missing in LZ996 was Squadron Leader Phil Archer DFC – promoted to command 421 Squadron on the morning of his death in action. Shot down by an FW 190, Archer is buried at Longuenesse, St-Omer.

Above: 69. Johnnie leads 127 Wing off from Lashenden in his clipped-wing Spitfire LF Mk IX.

Left: 70. In 1996, Dilip Sarkar led an expedition to France and recovered LZ996 from its crash site at Blaringhem, near St-Omer.

Below left: 71. The Kenley Wing ultimately became 127 Wing of the 2nd TAF. With the invasion approaching, the fighter squadrons were required to fly in a tactical role, supporting the army and keeping on the move. Consequently 127 Wing moved from the brick-built comforts of Kenley to begin a nomadic existence, starting at Lashenden in Kent, living under canvas.

Bottom left: 72. The armour plate, compressed air and oxygen bottles of Squadron Leader Archer's Spitfire LZ996.

Above left: 73. On 23 August 1943, Johnnie shot down and killed Oberfeldwebel Erich Borounik of 10/JG 26. This is that enemy pilot's FW 190A-5, 'Black 12', taking hits from Johnnie's guns over Artois.

Above right: 74. Before taking command of the Kenley Wing, Johnnie served as Squadron Leader Tactics at Uxbridge. There his masters were Group Captain Jamie Jameson, another fighter ace from New Zealand (right), and Air Commodore Harry Broadhurst (left). Johnnie would later become closely associated with 'Broady' in both the 2nd TAF and post-war RAF.

Right: 75. Wing Commander Johnnie Johnson DSO DFC, Wing Commander (Flying), Kenley, 1943. Note that Johnnie's top button is undone – the sign of a fighter pilot.

Below right: 76. Wing Commander Johnnie Johnson DSO** DFC*, leader of 144 Wing, 1944.

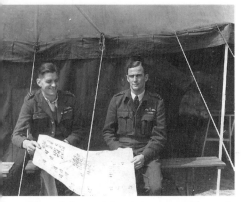

Above left: 77. Johnnie in 1944 with another Wing Leader, Wing Commander 'Hawkeye' Wells.
Above right: 78. Group Captain 'Iron Bill' MacBrien, Johnnie's boss in 144 Wing.

Below: 79. Another FW 190 taking hits from Greycap.
Left: 80. Squadron Leader Danny Browne DFC and groundcrew.

81. 144 Wing just before D-Day, 'Somewhere in England', in June 1944. That these men faced an uncertain future is indicated by the fates in brackets of those who did not survive the next eleven months of war. Back row, from left: F/O Horrel (KIA), F/O Pichie (KIA), F/O Munro (POW), F/L Hunter, F/O Costello, F/O Young DFC (POW), P/O Curtis, F/O Dunning, F/O Cochand, F/O Irwin, F/O Plummer, P/O Blair, F/O Cashman, F/L Robillard DFM, F/O Graham, F/L Wilson DFC, P/O Campbell, F/O MacDonald, F/O Kimball, P/O Hill (KIA), P/O Fleming. Middle row, from left: F/L Johnstone, F/O Saunders, F/O Henderson, F/O Foster, F/O Williams, W/O Urquhart, F/O Ockenden DFC, F/O Fairfield, F/O Hodgins DFC, F/O Clarke, F/L Troke DFC, F/O Gilbert, F/O Aziz, F/L Scarlett, F/O Caldwell, F/O Fergusson, F/O Gamey (KIA), F/O Mackintosh (KIA), P/O West, P/O Trott. Front row, from left: F/L Mott DFC, F/L Shenk (KIA), F/L Russell, S/L Dowdy DFC, S/L Brannagan DFC (POW), F/L MacLennan DFM (POW), S/L Browne DFC, S/L McLeod DFC (KIA), W/C Johnson DSO**** DFC*, S/L Russell DSO DFC, F/L Keltie DFC, F/L Moore, unknown, F/O Walz, F/L Draper, F/L Stovel, F/L Wright DFC, F/L Roseland (KIA).

Above left: 82. Air Marshal Coningham, Commander of the 2nd TAF, addresses a gathering of Allied troops in England before D-Day, 24 May 1944.
Above right: 83. Johnnie and Broady at a pre-invasion dinner with 'Ike' and 'LM', Officers' Mess, RAF Tangmere.
Right: 84. Air Vice-Marshal Harry Broadhurst, AOC 83 Group, 2nd TAF, and a guest enjoy the pre-invasion high life.

Above left: 85. Wing Commander Johnnie Johnson in Normandy with Sally, 1944.
Above right: 86. St-Croix-sur-Mer, just inland of the invasion beaches and where Johnnie's Spitfires were the first to land in France after D-Day.

Above: 87. Johnnie, fifth from left, in that familiar arms-crossed pose. Note that sidearms have been issued. St-Croix: D-Day plus three, 144 Wing, first Spitfires to land and refuel in France following the Allied landings on 6 June 1944.
Left: 88. A welcome smoke after yet another sortie: Johnnie and pilots at St-Croix.

Top left: 89. 144 Wing's first party on French soil.
Top right: 90. Johnnie and Sally at St-Croix – as Paula said, 'Always Labradors!'
Above right: 91. Shooting game in Normandy with an American paratrooper's carbine.
Above left: 92. Six-shooter! Johnnie looking the part in Normandy.

Top left: 93. Johnnie in his Operations Transport, Normandy 1944.
Top right: 94. Group Captain McBrien looks on while Johnnie and other officers of 144 Wing meet Churchill in Normandy.
Above left: 95. A pensive Greycap at St-Croix.
Above right: 96. High jinks on Sword Beach.
Left: 97. St-Croix, from left: Wing Commander Johnnie Johnson, Group Captain Jimmy Fenton, Squadron Leaders Dal Russell and Wally McLeod.

Above left: 98. Motley crew: a bare-chested Johnnie and 144 Wing pilots, Normandy, summer of 1944.
Above right: 99. Johnnie, centre, and Squadron Leader Danny Browne, left, during the 'Long Trek'.

100. New Year's Day, 1945, Eindhoven. The result of Operation Bodenplatte.

101. Eindhoven, 1 January 1945.

102. Johnnie and pilots during the 'Long Trek', winter 1944/45.

Left: 103. Wing Commander Johnson, left, with Group Captain Stan Turner at an ALG during the 'Long Trek'. Note the PSP temporary runway surface.
Below: 104. Johnnie's 125 Wing Spitfire Mk XIV in 1945.

Above left: 105. Johnnie and Sally on the 'Long Trek'.
Above right: 106. Just after the war, Group Captain Johnson was stationed near Copenhagen and organised an air show to benefit local children. He is pictured here at that event with the Danish Queen.

107. Group Captain Johnson, centre, with Air Chief Marshal Sir Sholto Douglas.

108. Group Captain Johnson with General 'Boy' Browning.

Above left: 109. Group Captain Johnson with the 'Father of the Royal Air Force', 'Boom' Trenchard himself.
Above right: 110. Group Captain Johnson shakes hands with Field Marshal Montgomery.

111. Johnnie, left, escorts Air Marshal Coningham.

112. Group Captain Johnnie Johnson in Germany, 1945.

Above left: 113. A formal photograph of Group Captain Johnnie Johnson, the top-scoring RAF fighter pilot of the Second World War.
Above right: 114. The only known photograph of Johnnie, second left, while serving in Korea with the USAF.

115. Group Captain Johnson inspecting an unknown ATC unit post-war.

116. Johnnie (second right) and Broady (third left) with the British Prime Minister Harold MacMillan (sixth from left) during the Cold War.

Above left: 117. Johnnie, centre, and Broady, right, after a V-Bomber flight at Cottesmore in the Cold War.

Above right: 118. A Handley-Page Victor landing at Cottesmore, in Leicestershire, while Johnnie was Station Commander.

Above left: 119. Group Captain Johnson and Air Vice-Marshal Broadhurst escort Princess Margaret on Her Royal Highness's visit to 10 Squadron at RAF Cottesmore, October 1958.

Above right: 120. Family man: Johnnie with sons Chris (left) and Michael, and wife Paula, on a post-war fishing trip.

Above left: 121. Dad plays with his boys: 'He was a father first and foremost', remembered Chris.
Above right: 122. Johnnie, technical advisor on the film *Reach for the Sky*, discusses a point of detail with actor Kenneth Moore, who starred as Douglas Bader.

123. Group Captain Johnson at an air show, while still a serving officer, with Group Captain Douglas Bader (centre) and Supermarine Chief Test Pilot on the Spitfire programme, Jeffrey Quill.

124. Air Vice-Marshal Johnnie Johnson – a crowd-pulling air show guest – recreates the iconic photograph taken at St-Croix, albeit minus Sally. Spitfire Jubilee Airshow, IWM Duxford, 1996.

Above left: 125. Johnnie with the author, Dilip Sarkar, pictured at the Air Vice-Marshal's Derbyshire home in 1998. The tankard Johnnie holds was presented to him to celebrate the destruction of 'Kenley's 99th Hun' in 1943.
Above right: 126. In 1996, Dilip Sarkar was able to show Squadron Leader Danny Browne and Johnnie some of the artefacts recovered from LZ996's crash site. Here Danny is pictured with Johnnie, holding a shrapnel-holed compressed air bottle. Tragically, Danny was killed while flying a light aircraft in America on 29 December 2001.

127. Johnnie trout fishing. The only memorial to this great man, so distinguished in both war and peace, is a bench at his favourite fishing spot. It is simply inscribed 'In Memory of a Fisherman'.

taking no evasive action except medium turns. He then broke up and the last I saw of the E/A it was diving towards the ground at a very steep angle at 6,000–8,000 feet, pouring white smoke.

Flying Officer L. Foster added:

After the Wing Leader broke off his attack, I attempted to watch the E/A crash. I was able to see it still diving at about 3,000 feet but lost sight of it due to the thick ground haze. Shortly after I saw what could have been the E/A burning in the area I last saw said E/A diving.

The Me 109 concerned was probably from III/JG 54, based at Schipol, the pilot of which was killed.

After this combat, the Spitfires re-formed and headed for the Dutch coast. When south of Ijmuiden, at 15,000–16,000 feet, eight P-47 Thunderbolts were seen above and behind the Wing, flying the same course. The Americans misidentified the Spitfires and consequently one P-47 dived at Flying Officer Zary, White Four of 421 Squadron. At 200 yards, the American pilot opened fire, but fortunately for Zary his marksmanship was poor and White Four was unscathed. The Thunderbolts were last seen heading towards Horsham. As the Kenley Wing Form 'F' later reported, 'Had this Section not been bounced by the Thunderbolts, they would probably have been able to engage two FW 190s which were seen below and to port.' Without further incident, the Kenley Wing landed back at Coltishall at 2055, returning to Kenley after the Spitfires had been refuelled. Four aircraft of 421 Squadron had been forced to return early from this sortie, having been unable to jettison their auxiliary fuel tanks. Red One of 403 Squadron, Squadron Leader Godefroy, had also returned early with a technical problem. By 2220 hours, the Wing was safely back at Kenley, however, and as the 421 Squadron ORB reported, 'It was a long day.'

Although the weather remained slightly uncertain, 28 July would see the Americans mount their heaviest attack yet against the German aircraft industry. The 1st Bomber Wing's 182 B-17s crossed the North Sea and bombed the Fieseler works at Kassell-Bettenhausen, while the 4th Wing's 120 were to make the deepest penetration into

Germany so far: the AGO fighter assembly plant at Ascherleben, near Magdeburg. Both works produced the FW 190 and were therefore top priority aircraft industry targets. The lead force of the latter Wing was the 94th Group based at Bury St Edmunds, led personally in the air by the Commanding Officer, Colonel Fred Castle, who anticipated it being a 'hot' one. First the B-17s feinted towards Hamburg before turning south-east towards Oschersleben. Over the Continent, however, bad weather again caused problems, dispersing the Fortresses. Over the Dutch coast, JG 1's FW 190s engaged the bombers, some of these fighters using, for the first time, aerial rockets. These were actually 21-cm mortars adapted to be underslung on both wings. Also, Me 109s of the Jever based II/JG 11, dropped 500-lb bombs onto the Fortress formations! This was a new concept, only practical against tight formations, but devastating when successful. These new and perhaps somewhat desperate measures indicate the resolve with which the Germans defied the Allied CBO. It also emphasises just how increasingly vulnerable the bombers were becoming without complete fighter support. As the Americans battled onwards and further into Germany, through a gap in the cloud Castle's bombardier in *Sour Puss* recognised a landmark, from which he was able to accurately calculate time from target. The majority of other B-17s in this formation followed suit. When reconnaissance photographs were later taken, a large concentration of bombs was found to have been dropped within the target area, this causing sufficient damage to write off a whole month's production: fifty FW 190s.

To extend range, the Kenley Wing operated from Manston on Ramrod 165. Greycap's brief had been to meet the homeward bound B-17s three miles north of The Hague, but the rendezvous was changed, in the air, to eight miles south of Rotterdam. By then the B-17s were protected by a gaggle of Allied fighters, so the Kenley Wing did a couple of orbits before sweeping south-west along the Dutch and Belgian coast at 20,000 feet. A lone Fortress was seen coming out between Dunkirk and Nieuport, its crew no doubt being grateful for the escort provided by a couple of dozen Canadian Spitfires! For Squadron Leader Buck McNair of 421 Squadron it was to be a trip of high drama. At 1226 hours, over the inhospitable North Sea just off Knocke, McNair's Spitfire developed engine trouble. Unable to keep up, he dropped behind the Wing, covered by Pilot Officer Parks. Slowly losing height from 20,000 to 10,000 feet, when 12 miles off Dunkirk and over the Channel, McNair's engine caught fire. Traumatically, the pilot lost control of his aircraft, which plunged seawards. At 5,000 feet, Squadron Leader McNair managed to break free of his doomed Spitfire. At 2,000 feet Pilot Officer Parks saw with relief his chief's parachute open. McNair splashed into the Channel, Parks immediately taking a fix and transmitting a Mayday signal. The young pilot then orbited McNair's position for an hour and a half, until relieved by 411 Squadron. As the 421 Squadron ORB says of Park's effort, it was a 'good show'.

Immediately 421 Squadron landed at Manston and heard of their CO's predicament, the Spitfires were refuelled, the pilots taking off to participate in the ASR operation to rescue Squadron Leader McNair. A little while later, 421 Squadron watched a Walrus pick up McNair, the Spitfires then providing escort back to Hawkinge for the curious-looking but life-saving seaplane flown by Squadron Leader Grove. As Greycap's log relates, the ASR sortie had lasted an hour and ten minutes, and McNair's ordeal in the water had lasted two hours. He was one of the lucky ones, as the 421 ORB reports: The Chief was burned about the face and had a real close call, but is now resting satisfactorily in hospital and should be back in a few days.' During this mission, the Eighth Air Force lost a total of twenty-two B-17s lost (and some 198 men, therefore), and four more so badly damaged that they only just reached England. It was hardly surprising that this period became known by the Americans as the 'Bloody Summer of 1943'.

29 July was a bright and virtually cloudless day, perfect conditions for the Eighth Air Force's purposes. The target for that day was the Arado plant at Warnemünde, another works producing the FW 190. For the RAF's 2 Group, the task of providing diversionary attacks continued. The Kenley Wing was first to fly Ramrod 112, providing Top Cover to American B-26 Marauders attacking Schipol aerodrome. The complexity of planning such an operation is evident from the details of 12 Group's Order No. 12G/6:

Bombers: 18 Marauders of No. 3 Wing, No 323 Group USAAF
Fighters: Close Escort Cover   402 Sqn (LR Spitfires) (Digby)

	416 Sqn (LR Spitfires) (Digby)
	611 Sqn (LR Spitfires) (Coltishall)
	118 Sqn (LR Spitfires) (Coltishall)
Escort Cover	302 Sqn (LR Spitfires) (Portreath)
	317 Sqn (LR Spitfires) (Portreath)
Top Cover	303 Sqn (Spitfires IX) (Northolt)
	316 Sqn (Spitfires IX) (Northolt)
	403 Sqn (Spitfires IX) (Kenley)
	421 Sqn (Spitfires IX) (Kenley)

The Close Escort Spitfires took off from Ludham and Matlask at 0935 hours, and rendezvoused with the Marauders 14 miles north of Southwold at 11,000 feet. The bombers, however, set off for the target a minute early and their formation became scattered. Some 20 miles off Ijmuiden, the Marauders turned south and flew parallel to the Dutch coast until reaching the Hook of Holland. Bombs were then jettisoned, after which the Americans turned west and headed home. The two Wing Leaders of the close cover escort Wings, Digby and Coltishall, were perplexed, however, as no enemy aircraft were in sight and visibility was unlimited, but tried in vain to contact the bombers over the R/T. The bombers had aborted due to a navigational error, having made landfall 18 miles further north than intended. The Kenley Wing, however, continued to the target, crossing the Dutch coast at 22,000 feet over Zandvoort and sweeping between Ijmuiden and Schipol. Johnnie:

Enemy aircraft were seen below and I instructed various Sections of 421 Squadron to engage, leaving 403 Squadron as High Cover. I attacked the last aircraft of a pair of Me 109G with cannon and machine-gun from 450–200 yards range, firing several short bursts from astern. Enemy aircraft gave off stream of black smoke and two de Wilde strikes were seen on the cockpit. As there were other enemy aircraft about I broke off this combat and last saw the 109 diving slowly down to 10,000 feet with a steady stream of black smoke coming away from the aircraft.

Johnnie had fired 134 rounds of 20 mm, and 270 of .303. The 109 was claimed as damaged. His wingman, however, was more successful. Pilot Officer K. R. Linton:

I was flying Black Two on 12 Group Ramrod Twenty-two, behind
Wing Commander Johnson. After crossing the Dutch coast I saw
an Me 109 which Wing Commander Johnson immediately turned
in and attacked. He could not get close enough, so pulled up
and soon after this we saw one FW 190 chasing two 109s. Wing
Commander Johnson's ammunition was getting low, so he told
me to attack it whilst he covered me. It was 2,000 feet below and
at two o'clock to me. I dived on him and when within 250 yards I
gave several short squirts from dead astern. The top of his rudder
was shot away and I could see strikes on the fuselage and wings,
then he turned slightly to port and I got in a three second burst
from 20 degrees. The whole of the FW 190 seemed to burst into
flames and he half-rolled and dived straight into the deck just SW
of Schipol aerodrome. At least four other pilots saw this. I claim
this FW 190 as destroyed.

While 403 Squadron provided Top Cover, 421 Squadron got stuck in,
as the pilots' combat reports testify. Flying Officer W. E. Harten:

On 12 Group Ramrod 22 I was flying Green One. About 1035
hours I was about ten to twelve miles west of Schipol when three
Me 109s flew about 500–600 feet below me going north-east.
They were turning to starboard, I followed them around and
when we were about 500 yards away the centre one and the
extreme starboard one half-rolled and went straight down. The
third one continued on. I closed in and fired from about 250–300
yards, 30° off. He then turned slightly to port which brought
me in line astern. I fired from 100–50 yards, observing strikes
on cockpit and starboard wing. He turned over to left and went
straight down, smoking. I circled the area then returned home.

Flying Officer L. R. Thorne:

I was flying Green Two to F/O Harten. About ten miles west of
Schipol we sighted three Me 109s. F/O Harten led the Section
around, closing in on them. Two of them half-rolled straight down
but a third continued straight on and seemed to be turning slightly
to starboard. F/O Harten fired and the a/c streamed white smoke.
F/O Harten then pulled away and I was in a position to see the

enemy aircraft burst into flames on the starboard side. He (E/A) turned to the left and went straight down. I saw him fall 2–3,000 feet then we did a turn to starboard and on looking back I saw him burning on the ground, south of the lake just north of Leiden, about five miles. The E/A fired at by F/O Harten is definitely destroyed.

Flight Lieutenant N. R. Fowlow:

I was flying White One at 15,000 feet south-west of Amsterdam when I saw two Me 109s flying west in echelon port, 5,000 feet below. I turned and dived down to attack the Number One in the formation, followed by my Number Two who attacked the port aircraft in the formation. The aircraft I attacked took violent evasive action, doing a quarter roll to starboard. I followed firing intermittingly and closing from 300 yards to 200 yards. The aircraft rolled on its back at about 5,000 feet with smoke pouring from it and I saw it dive straight down into the deck. I claim this Me 109 as destroyed.

Sergeant N. B. Dixon:

I was flying as White Two to F/Lt Fowlow. When south of Amsterdam he sighted 2 Me 109s crossing to port at 18,000 feet. Turning sharply port he cut in behind as one Me 109 rolled over. He chased it down steeply and as the other Me turned starboard down after him, I gave him 3 squirts ranging from 300–50 yards, from 60° down to dead astern and above. With no reflector sight I hosepiped him and saw hits on the starboard wing. When he dived away he was turning and going down fast at a 70° angle. I pulled up and headed home, chased by one Me 109. I observed three fires caused by burning aircraft south of Amsterdam. Near a lake I saw another small fire caused by burning aircraft.

On this sortie, Pilot Officer J. E. Abbotts and Flight Lieutenant Golberg of 403 Squadron were flying White Three and Four respectively with 421 Squadron. South-west of Amsterdam, White Section was bounced and Abbotts simply disappeared. Fortunately the young pilot survived being shot down, but became a prisoner of war. 403 Squadron was about to attack three enemy fighters that appeared below, but then sighted a whole gaggle of bandits above. Upon climbing to investigate, Squadron Leader Godefroy confirmed these aircraft to be Spitfires before turning home. The Wing, fragmented after 421 Squadron's hectic and successful combat, crossed out over Noorwijerhout at various heights and times, pancaking back at Coltishall at 1115.

The 421 Squadron claims were as follows:

- Wing Commander Johnson: one Me 109 damaged
- Pilot Officer Linton: one FW 190 destroyed
- Flying Officer Harten: one Me 109 destroyed
- Flight Lieutenant Fowlow: one Me 109 destroyed
- Sergeant Dixon: one Me 109 damaged

For one missing Spitfire pilot, it was an excellent result. Among the German losses was at least one experienced fighter pilot and leader, *Hauptmann* Karl Anton Waldemar, the *Staffelkapitän* of 7/ JG 54 *Grun Herz*. The III *Gruppe* of this famous *Jagdgeschwader* had been brought to the west from Russia, and was now based at Oldenburg and Nordholtz on Heligoland Bight. JG 3 *Udet* was also moved from Russia to the west, and JG 26 was pulled away from the Channel coast to operate on a daily basis from bases on the lower Rhine and Holland, right on the American approach routes. The Me 109s of 2/JG 27 were withdrawn from North Africa, these augmenting the strength of JG 11, at Jever, which had been formed in April 1943 out of JG 1. Hitler, however, had yet to consider that the Reich defence force was top priority, and still sent the bulk of fighters to both the Eastern and Mediterranean fronts. In the first eight months of 1943, in fact, the output of Me 109s and FW 190s soared to 7,477, but those available to the home defence force rose but slowly: 162 in May, 255 in June, and 300 in July.

After 421 Squadron's successful fight, Greycap led his Spitfires from Coltishall back to Kenley. At 1748 hours, the Wing was up again, on Ramrod 171, a sweep of Dieppe, Neufchatel and the Somme Estuary in support of No. 2 Group bombers attacking the airfield at Yanville. The sortie passed without incident, however, and the Spitfires were safely home by 1920 hours. The day did not end there, however, as after refuelling the Kenley Wing flew back to Coltishall, where the pilots again stayed overnight, this being necessary for another early start.

On 30 July, 186 B-17s struck out and again attacked Kassel. The resulting interception by German fighters signified the fiercest clash so far between the 'Mighty Eighth' and the *Luftwaffe*: seventeen Fortresses were lost, eighty-two more damaged, and two Thunderbolts also failed to return. After this trip, the Eighth Air Force were really in no position to fly another major mission to Germany without first making good losses in both men and machines. At the start of 'Blitz Week', the Americans had 330 aircraft and crews ready to go. Within a week that figure had been reduced to around 170. Over 100 B-17s had been lost, and around 90 crews were either missing, killed or wounded. As Johnnie said, 'They took some hard knocks.'

At Coltishall, the Kenley Wing's Canadians were among a number of fighter pilots briefed for 12 Group Ramrod 23, a raid by thirteen Bostons, of 2 Group's 107 Squadron, on Schipol aerodrome. Close Escort Cover was to be provided by the Digby and Coltishall Wings, Top Cover by the Kenley Mk IXs, and Rear Cover by 609 Squadron's Typhoons (based at Coltishall). The Kenley Wing was up at 1005 hours, Greycap leading. Rendezvous was made with the Beehive over Coltishall at 1009 hours, and a direct course was set for the target. At 1036 hours, the Kenley Wing started to climb and crossed in over Ijmuiden with squadrons stepped up to 23,000 feet. The Beehive thence proceeded inland to Schipol, the Bostons dropping their bombs on target. As the bombers crossed out over Noordwijerhoot, two aircraft were seen 6,000 feet below and about 7 miles behind. Suspecting the presence of more bandits, Wing Commander Johnson took the whole of 403 Squadron down, leaving 421 as Top Cover. Johnnie:

> There were some six E/A in this area, and I attacked the starboard 109 of the original pair. I opened fire from 400 yards with cannon and machine-guns, but E/A turned to port and dived down. As he dived away, I gave him a burst from 450 yards. I watched E/A and was surprised to see him pull out and climb steeply up. I closed in and saw that both wheels were down. I gave him another burst but did not observe any results. The 109 was then stalling and I broke away to see Flying Officer Lambert destroy the second 109.

I orbited and saw a parachute descending from the combat area. This enemy aircraft is claimed as destroyed, shared with Flight Sergeant Shouldice (403 Squadron).

Flight Sergeant G. M. Shouldice was Greycap's wingman, Red Two:

Red One led our Section down to attack in a very steep dive from approximately out of the sun. When we were about 600 yards from these two E/As the port a/c veered off to port while the starboard one turned and dived to the right. Red One attacked the E/A which turned to starboard and I followed Red One. Red One took a squirt at the E/A and his wheels dropped down, and some black smoke was emitted. I took a short burst at about 400 yards after Red One broke off his attack. In the course of the scrap I had about four short bursts at the E/A but cannot definitely say that I saw strikes. At about 7,000 feet I took one short burst when the E/A had wheels and flaps down and was almost stalled – no results observed. After this Red 1 observed the pilot in his parachute from this aircraft. Since it is not clear whose fire caused this, we claim one Me 109 destroyed (shared).

Flying Officer J. F. Lambert was Red Three in Greycap's Section:

Red One and Red Two dived on the starboard E/A whilst I led Red Four on the other which climbed inland to starboard. As I went after it, it dived steeply and rolled and then straightened out again. I was closing on it. At about 7,000 feet and at very high speed, it began to pull out. I shot a two–three second burst at about ten to fifteen degrees deflection at about 500 yards range and then since I was very low I pulled back hard out of the dive. Levelling out at about 2,000 feet I then climbed back up to the Squadron. I last saw the enemy aircraft at about 5,000 feet, diving away very steeply and at high speed, but I did not see the result of my shooting since I had to pull out very quickly. Because of what Wing Commander saw, however, I claim this aircraft as destroyed.

Flight Lieutenant H. J. Southwood was Yellow Two of 403 Squadron:

I was following Yellow One down when at about 12,000 feet the windscreen fluid tank discharged nearly all its contents over the cockpit and myself. At first, I presumed there was an engine glycol leak and by the time I had organised myself and cleaned off my windscreen I had somehow managed to lose the rest of my Section. My height was about 10,000 feet and I was flying north when I recognised an Me 109 coming towards me, slightly below and about 500 yards ahead. The enemy aircraft turned in on my starboard and I turned in towards and dived straight down on him, at the same time taking a very short vertical burst at about 300–400 yards but there were no results. The enemy then turned starboard and I got astern of him. He then continued diving at 300–400 mph. I took a long burst at about 300 yards, then a much longer one closing to about 50 yards. I used up the cannon first and ended up using machine-guns. After the first long burst from astern the wheels fell down, and I saw black smoke over the tailplane but due to the fact that I was firing into the sun and the haze, I am not sure of seeing any strikes. My windscreen was still clouded up from the windscreen tank blowing up. I broke off my attack at about 4,000 feet, last seeing the E/A spiralling down to starboard with his wheels down and black smoke trailing. I claim this 109 as damaged.

After the combat, 403 Squadron re-formed and rejoined 421 Squadron. The Kenley Wing left Holland via Zandvoort, where two FW 190s were seen but were out of range. The Wing was safely back at Coltishall by 1140 hours, refuelled and returned to Kenley at 1320 hours. It had been another successful day for the Canadians, 403 Squadron's score being as follows:

- Wing Commander Johnson and Flight Sergeant Shouldice: one Me 109 destroyed
- Flying Officer Lambert: one Me 109 destroyed
- Flight Lieutenant Southwood: one Me 109 damaged

By now, Johnnie was attracting an increasing amount of publicity, being hailed as 'Finucane's successor'. The following article appeared in the *Yorkshire Post*, headlined 'Hunts Huns in Foxes' Head Scarf':

Wing Commander J. E. Johnson DSO DFC & bar, the Melton Mowbray fighter ace, now has 19 German planes to his credit.

I met Johnson a year ago when he was a Flight Lieutenant at a fighter station on the East Coast. In private life he was an assistant in the office of the Borough Surveyor at Melton Mowbray.

And appropriately enough for a man from hunting country, he never flies without a yellow scarf dotted with brown foxes' heads round his neck.

At that time he had shot down about seven Germans, and the Air Ministry would not then pass his name for publication. Today he has reached the amazing total of 19. It is amazing because nowadays fighter pilots have to go out and chase Huns. That is why sweeps are organised. In the Battle of Britain the Germans came here.

When I met Johnson he spoke confidently.

On the door of his little office was painted the words 'Flight Lieutenant Johnson and Pusher'. Pusher was the most peculiar looking mongrel I have ever seen. He waved a long tail and looked like a spaniel with a setter's legs. He was a strange puce colour. But he adored his master, and 'Johnnie', as the riggers of his Spitfire called him amongst themselves, seemed to return the worship.

When he went out to his plane to take part in a sweep over France that sunny April morning, Pusher followed.

Some six months later I met him again. He looked older and harder. He had a bar on his DFC. We talked about the previous meeting. Pusher was dead, he said, killed by a lorry. He changed the conversation.

On 31 July, although the Eighth Air Force's bombers were stood down, the B-26 Marauders of Eighth Air Service Command were still active, and it was in support of twenty-one such bombers that the Kenley Wing took off at 1045 hours (Ramrod 179). The target was the aerodrome at Merville, and the Canadian Spitfires provided cover as the Marauders withdrew amid the black puffballs of a heavy flak barrage. South of Bergues, a dozen Me 109s were seen orbiting 6,000 feet below, so Greycap took 421 Squadron down to attack. Although Johnnie later wrote in his logbook 'Me 109s bounced but E/A ducked!' Pilot Officer Linton fired at a 109, on which strikes were seen around the cockpit area. The enemy fighter was last seen trailing a plume of black smoke, at 3,000 feet. After this inconclusive combat (in respect of which Linton was awarded one Me 109 damaged), the Wing flew to Guines and Montreuil, between 22,000 and 29,000 feet. The remainder of the sortie was uneventful, however, and by 1225 hours the Wing was back at Kenley. The day's second operation was Ramrod 181, Forward Target Support to Marauders bombing Abbeville. The mission went according to plan but no enemy aircraft were seen, the sortie therefore passing without incident. At the end of the month, the score of the Kenley Wing squadrons was as follows:

403 'Wolf' Squadron:	One FW 190 destroyed
	Six and a half Me 109s destroyed
	One Me 109 damaged
421 'Red Indian' Squadron:	Four Me 109s destroyed
	Four Me 109s damaged
	One Me 109 probably destroyed
	One FW 190 destroyed
	One FW 190 damaged

In total, the Kenley Wing had flown an impressive 935.53 hours on operations; as Dan Browne says, 'We were a keen bunch.'

On 4 August, Squadron Leader Godefroy briefed the pilots on the impending move to 126 Airfield at Lashenden, near Headcorn. Needless to say, Johnnie organised one last 'glorious thrash' in the Mess at Kenley, before the Wing moved into tented accommodation in Kent. Invitations were sent to all the Wing Leaders, the 'top brass' at RCAF HQ, and 2nd TAF. Suffice to say, the 'Big Wing Ding' was a huge success! Fortunately there was no flying the following day, which was spent drawing tents and other equipment in preparation for the imminent move to Lashenden. In the afternoon, the groundcrews erected their tents around the airfield perimeter. These were later taken down and all slept in the crew rooms and at dispersal, ready to go early in the morning. At 1000 hours the next morning, pilots not flying aircraft joined groundcrews and left Kenley in a motor convoy for Lashenden. The groundcrews were, in fact, formally posted to '127 Airfield HQ', only the aircrew being assigned to 403 and 421 Squadrons. The convoy reached its destination at 1430, at which time tents had to be erected and the whole Wing unpacked.

At 1000 hours on 7 August 1943, Wing Commander Johnson led his Spitfires off from Kenley for the last time, bound for 127 Airfield. It was the end of another highly successful era. As the Canadians landed at Lashenden just 15 minutes later, a new and even more exciting time began.

6

127 Wing:
Tactical Air Force

The whole Allied effort in the West, following success at last in the desert, was now gearing up to the liberation of Europe. American materiel continued to arrive apace, in spite of the U-boats' best efforts. The question was not 'if' but 'when' would the invasion take place. The tactical necessity for aerial supremacy over the battlefield meant that the Allied fighters would become fighter-bombers, attacking enemy ground targets and harrying troop and vehicle movement whenever and wherever possible. Fighter squadrons could therefore expect a nomadic existence in tented accommodation, keeping on the move with the advancing Allied front. In recognition of this forthcoming change, RAF Fighter Command was reorganised into Air Defence Great Britain (ADGB) and the 2nd Tactical Air Force (TAF). It was the groups of 2nd TAF, each of which included fighters, fighter-bombers and medium bombers that would support the invasion troops.

The commander of this new tactical air force, responsible for supporting the Second British Army, was Air Marshal 'Maori' Coningham who had previously been the Western Desert Air Force's first chief. When he arrived in North Africa during 1941, there was little co-ordination between the air force and army in respect of combined operations. Coningham therefore pioneered tactical air power, understanding the army's requirements for reconnaissance and air support. Proof of Coningham's success was provided by *Feldmarschal* Rommel himself, who wrote of the second, decisive, Battle of El Alamein: 'British air superiority threw to the winds all our tactical rules ... the strength of the Anglo-American Air Force was the deciding factor.' After this victory, Coningham was promoted and given command of the new North-West African Air Force, while Air Vice-Marshal Harry Broadhurst became chief of the Western Desert Air Force. At thirty-seven, 'Broady' was the youngest high commander in the RAF; unlike his peers, however, he had actually fought operationally in this conflict. There was another significant difference between Coningham and Broadhurst: the former always considered himself the army commander's equal, while the latter appreciated that as the army occupied the ground and undertook the bulk of the fighting, the soldier was the senior partner while the air chief's job was to provide the best possible air support. Moreover, Coningham ultimately resented that when victory came in North Africa, Montgomery took credit that was due not to the army but to the air force. This ultimately led to strained relations between them in the years ahead.

So it was, in readiness for the 'Great Adventure', that Johnnie's Kenley Wing ceased to exist. The Canadians would now operate out of temporary accommodation at 127 Airfield, an 'Advanced Landing Ground' (ALG) at Lashenden, under the command of 83 Group, 2nd TAF. The Group Commander was Harry Broadhurst. The entire Allied Expeditionary Air Force (AEAF) was commanded by Air Chief Marshal Sir Trafford Leigh-Mallory. Strategic control of the Allied air forces was exercised by the Deputy Supreme Commander at Supreme Headquarters Allied Expeditionary Force (SHAEF), Air Chief Marshal Sir Arthur Tedder, who had served in the desert with Coningham and Broadhurst. The new mobile wings had to learn how to pack, move and unpack in the minimum amount of time and in the most efficient manner possible. Again, the ALG was another legacy of North Africa, where the tactical air force had to keep short-range fighter-bombers close to Allied troops engaged at the front. To facilitate this, Servicing Commando Units (SCU) were formed to support Airfield Construction Groups (ACG). Servicing Commandos (SC) were trained infantrymen whose task was to reach the proposed ALGs with all necessary supplies, including defensive weapons. In addition to their ability to provide tactical defence, the SCs were also trained to service a wide variety of aircraft types. The ACG personnel were Royal Engineers (RE) trained to construct fully serviceable albeit temporary airfields. Before the invasion, however, 2nd TAF clearly had to practise these techniques in preparation for the real thing.

At 1400 hours on 7 August 1943, a pilots' briefing was held at Lashenden: the Wing was now 17 Wing of 127 Airfield of 83 Group, 2nd TAF. Soon it would become simply '127 Wing', and for the purposes of clarity and continuity this reference is used hereafter. No longer did the Canadians enjoy the luxury of brick-built accommodation. Bob Middlemiss:

> We had left the luxuries of batmen, soft beds, hot showers, good food, nice bar and lounge, and a short ride by electric train to the lights and excitement of London. We traded all this for tents, canvas beds, canvas wash basins, cold water for shaving, damp, cool nights and the general mud and lack of amenities that we had become accustomed to. The 'Mess Hall' was a large tent, for example, where we ate off tin plates and sat at great wooden tables. The idea was to prepare and train us for the eventual landing in France and the mobile aerial and ground warfare that an eastward Allied advance would dictate. These primitive living and operating conditions were not exactly what we had bargained for, however! The airmen, under our 'Chiefie', Flight Sergeant Champion, fared no better than we officers, in fact they were able to improve their lot by building stoves from half forty-five gallon drums and having a trickle of oil dripping down for constant fire. They were able to heat and cook on these ingenious contraptions. Of course working conditions were far from ideal. The fuel was delivered in forty-five gallon drums and the aircraft re-fuelled by pumping fuel from the drum through a chamois to trap any water or condensation that may have accumulated in the drums. The daily maintenance and repairs had to be carried out in the open and under varying weather conditions, not the easiest way of maintaining the aircraft. The airfield had two runways of Pierced Steel Planking (PSP), and a tent for our Operations Room, the telephones manned by LACs Batty and Bennett. The Spitfires were dispersed around the airfield. The main farmhouse, owned by the Palmer Family, is where Group Captain MacBrien and Wing Commander Johnson bunked. It was also the Wing Operations Centre.

Having rested after the maximum effort of 'Blitz Week', the Eighth Air Force was once more ready to go. During that fortnight, staff officers had planned the greatest raid so far. The greatest priority was still destroying the enemy's capacity to produce fighter aircraft. The main production centres for Me 109s, and indeed nearly 50 per cent of all German fighters, were at Regensburg and Wiener

Neustadt, a long, long way from the American bases in East Anglia. If the bombers flew to those targets and returned to England, the enemy would literally have a field day. It was agreed, therefore, that instead, the bombers would fly out from England, bomb the target, but then fly on and land at Allied bases in North Africa. Such a route would undoubtedly confuse the enemy, in the process reducing casualties. Later it was decided that, as not all 1 Wing B-17s were fitted with long-range 'Tokyo' fuel tanks, Wiener Neustadt should not be attacked by the Eighth Air Force in England, but by the two B-24 Liberator Groups of the Ninth, based in North Africa, and those three of the Eighth currently on detachment in Libya. To cause maximum confusion, however, both targets were to be hit on the same day: 7 August. In the event, bad weather prevented this, dictating that the plan be changed to permit each force to attack its specified target as and when improved weather conditions allowed. While the Eighth Air Force planners anxiously awaited the opportunity to put their ambitious plans into action, the pressure was maintained on other targets. On 12 August, therefore, 330 B-17s attacked industrial targets in the Ruhr valley. Cloud caused problems over Germany, however, preventing the American bombardiers getting a clear sight of their targets. Consequently, only two Bomb Groups bombed their objectives, the remainder seeking targets of opportunity. The Germans concentrated their fighters inland, beyond reach of the outward bound escorting P-47s. The result was devastating: at least 25 bombers were destroyed, with over 100 sustaining damage. It was a tattered and badly beaten up force, therefore, that droned back towards England, anxiously awaiting the arrival of 'Little Friends'.

To extend range, and thereby the protection provided to the American bombers, The Canadians began operating from the coastal airfield of Bradwell Bay. On 12 August, the early morning was very cold with thick fog. The Wing was tasked with Ramrod 194, providing escort to the B-17s returning from Germany. The fog, however, delayed the Spitfires' take-off from Bradwell by 30 minutes. Bob Middlemiss:

> A fine example of Johnnie's leadership concerns the events of this day. We were briefed for the trip, to escort B-17s withdrawing from Germany, but the fog was so thick that we thought the

operation would be cancelled. The Wing Commander informed us of the desperate need for escorting the Forts because of the pounding they had taken both on the way in to the target and equally out on return. He had us start up and taxi into position at the end of the runway. He finally said that he personally would take-off and test the weather, and if found suitable then the rest of the Wing was to follow. Johnnie took off, and was soon giving us the word to follow on and join him. We took off in absolutely zero weather, wingmen hanging on to their leader's wings, the latter having taken off blind, on instruments alone. Thankfully the fog was not actually too thick, and the Wing came through with flying colours. Johnnie could easily have aborted this mission because of the bad weather conditions, but, knowing of the bombers' need for our help, he made the decision of a true leader.

Once airborne and formated on their leader, the Spitfire pilots headed for the Belgian coast, which was crossed at 22,000 feet. Shortly afterwards, the Hornchurch Wing was sighted to the North, covering a number of withdrawing Fortresses. Greycap led his Wing to the Rotterdam area, making an orbit there before turning south. More bombers were then seen, escorted by Thunderbolts. Another box followed, without escort, with a single B-17 straggling some distance behind. Eight Me 109s, operating either singly or in pairs, were attacking these unprotected bombers. Kenley Control asked Greycap to protect this last box. Johnnie:

As I attacked a Me 109, who was nibbling at a straggling Fortress, I instructed my Number Two, Flight Lieutenant Conrad, to engage another Me 109 in this vicinity. I opened fire on this E/A from 300–100 yards, firing several short bursts. Cannon strikes were seen on his wing roots and the E/A fell away in an exaggerated 'falling leaf', skidding and stalling from side to side. An aircraft was seen to crash by Flying Officer Browne (Yellow Three) and owing to the proximity of Flight Lieutenant Conrad's attack, one of these two E/A was undoubtedly destroyed. Pending examination of cine film, these two E/A are claimed as one destroyed and one damaged, shared by Flight Lieutenant Conrad and myself.

Flight Lieutenant Phillip of 421 Squadron broke off to engage an
Me 109, chasing and slightly damaging it. The Wing then re-formed
and stayed with the bombers as the formation ponderously made its
way back across the North Sea. When 15 miles off the Dutch coast,
an Me 109 stalked 421 from astern. Flight Lieutenant Phillip and
White Section crossed over to investigate, and when within range he
opened fire, seriously damaging the German. It was the last combat
during this trip, which saw the B-17s safely back to England. It had
been a long flight for the Spitfire pilots. 127 Wing had taken off from
Bradwell Bay at 0925 hours, but had not landed, at various forward
airfields, until 1130. Johnnie:

> With regard to operating procedures when protecting the Forts,
> you didn't get too close to them for a start because they fired
> at everybody! Consequently I never got nearer than a thousand
> yards, unless we were chasing somebody. I remember chasing
> some 190s making a head-on attack, which half-rolled. I was
> underneath them, and the Forts were firing at every fucker – every
> fucking gun was blazing away! So you never got within a thousand
> yards! In fairness, despite all their knocks, they kept going, and
> they did get knocked about a bit of course. We had liaison, of
> course. I used to go and lecture them regarding enemy fighter
> tactics and that sort of thing. I went to the Eighth Air Force HQ,
> where they got all their squadron commanders together on the
> outskirts of London. Sometimes I would go off to Bassingbourne
> and go to their debriefings. The great thing in war, remember, is
> to have an objective and stick to it, through thick and thin. This
> the Americans did regarding daylight bombing, and all credit to
> them for it.

In spite of bad weather during the first half of August, Operation
STARKEY went ahead. This was aimed at deceiving the Germans,
through increased aerial activity, that Allied landings in France were
imminent. This was to prevent the reinforcement of enemy units in
Italy and Russia. After various offensive operational sorties, on 16
August came Ramrod 205, in which Johnnie's Spitfires provided
Forward Target Support to Marauders bombing the JG 2 airfield
at Beaumont-le-Roger. Notification of this operation was only
given at 1600 hours, there then being 'quite some panic' (ORB, 403

Squadron) to get the Wing off by 1620. Nevertheless, the sweep went according to plan, although south of Rouen a gaggle of FW 190s were sighted. These, according to Johnnie's personal log, rapidly 'ducked as usual', however, and were not therefore engaged. Back at Lashenden, there was 'another panic for a while as all aircraft had to go to Bradwell Bay for an early morning sweep' (ORB, 403 Squadron). Even a couple of spare Spitfires were flown down to Bradwell, where the Canadians again stayed overnight to be ready for an early morning operation. It would be the big one.

17 August was the day that the Americans had been waiting for. With favourable weather over both Europe and the Mediterranean, the decision was made to go ahead with the Regensburg mission. The 4th Bomb Wing, equipped with Tokyo tanks, was to attack the famous Messerschmitt factory, then, instead of returning to England, fly on to and land in North Africa. The 1st Wing was to concurrently attack the Schweinfurt ball-bearing factory and then return to East Anglia. The weather over England itself was still not that good, however, especially over East Anglia where the B-17s found themselves fog-bound. As so often in war, the best laid of plans became subject to hasty changes. As the 4th Bomb Wing needed to land at the unfamiliar North African airfields in daylight, take-off could only be delayed for an hour. The 1st Bomb Wing, however, had to wait three and a half hours before take-off for the Regensburg fighter escorts to return and refuel. Fighter leaders were apparently not consulted regarding this change of plan which, however necessary, gave their groundcrews one hour less to turn their aircraft around. This meant that fighter cover would be significantly reduced. Circumstances, over which the planners had no control or influence, were beginning to suggest that the mission would become a compromise.

Wing Commander Johnson's pilots' first task in connection with the day's major operations was Ramrod 206 Part I. 127 Wing was to be among the Allied fighters escorting the outward-bound Regensburg force of 146 Fortresses. Having taken off at 1315 hours, Greycap rendezvoused with the B-17s as planned, just north of Walcheren Island. The Spitfires then escorted the Fortresses to Antwerp, the limit of their radius of action, where they were relieved by Thunderbolts of the 353rd Fighter Group. By this time, I and III/JG 26 were up, but although their FW 190s could be seen some way off, the Spitfires were unable to engage. Reluctantly, Greycap turned his Wing about and returned to Bradwell Bay, landing at 1457. Soon the Thunderbolts would also have to return, leaving the bombers to the mercy of the intercepting German fighters. Then, I/JG 1, I and II/JG 3 relieved I and III/JG 26, and were able to attack the B-17s unhindered. Johnnie:

> After leaving the Regensburg Forts, we went back to Bradwell Bay and had a wad and a cuppa, and so on whilst the aircraft were turned around. About an hour and a half later the Controller rang me and said, 'Can you get off quickly, the Forts are in trouble.'

The Spitfires were up again immediately, on Ramrod 206 Part II, at 1608 hours, making haste to Antwerp. Crossing over the Belgian coast near Blankenburg, the B-17s were met at 24,000 feet over St-Nicolas at 1647. Johnnie:

> It was a devastating sight. This proud formation that we had escorted out was now very knocked about. There were great holes in the formation, and stragglers lagged well behind the main boxes. It was obvious that things had not gone well, as we anticipated would happen. I thought then and I still think now just how inexcusable it was that we had not been given the required range in the first place. Deplorable, wasn't it?

The 127 Wing Combat Report describes events:

> Dogfight seen in Antwerp area and one E/A seen to disintegrate. Three-four Me 109s seen in Antwerp area and six-seven Me 109s seen in Hüls area, following the bombers, but the Wing was unable to engage. Me 110 seen stooging around north of Ghent and attacked by 403 Squadron. W/C Johnson (Red One), F/Lt Dover (Blue Two), F/O Foster (Blue Three), and F/O Preston (Blue Two), all making attacks and seeing strikes on E/A which resulted in silencing rear gunner and setting port engine on fire. This E/A was seen to go down in flames and crash, and is claimed as destroyed. F/Lt Southwood (Yellow Two) attacked an Me 109G in this area without observing results. 421 Squadron escorted bombers to English coast, 403 Squadron leaving the bombers in Bruges area

to investigate a/c that proved to be friendly. A lone FW 190 was seen near Bergues, and Yellow Section went down to investigate. Squadron Leader Conrad, Red Three, and his wingman, Flight Sergeant Shouldice, Red Four, cut over the top of Yellow section, so keen were they both to attack. The 190 was subsequently hit by a veritable storm of shot and shell, and was last believed seen, by Flying Officer Dan Browne, Yellow Three, breaking up before piling straight in.

Disaster then struck Conrad and Shouldice, whose Spitfires collided. The former's tail unit and an aileron were seen to break off. Conrad's Spitfire was last seen tumbling earthwards from 3,000–4,000 feet over Bergues. The right aileron and wingtip of Shouldice's Spitfire was also damaged. Johnnie:

> That was a terrible shame as young Shouldice was a good pilot. He told me what happened over the R/T and I told him to climb up to 10,000 feet and bale out. The problem was that his hood had also been damaged during the collision, and was jammed. The only option was to try and get him back across the Channel, so I called up Kenley and got the controller to organise ASR. Having given Shouldice a course for Dover, we went looking and found him just off the French coast. It didn't look good. The aircraft kept trying to yaw to the right, and every time Shouldice had to struggle with the control column to pull the aircraft on course. We were halfway home, with just ten miles to go, when he lost the struggle. The Spitfire yawed right over, wings vertical. I could see Shouldice struggling with the hood, but he just couldn't open it and went straight in. There was a great splash and that was that.

Johnnie called up and fixed the position where the Spitfire had crashed, but nothing was ever seen again of Flight Sergeant Shouldice.

Having landed and refuelled at Bradwell Bay, by 1750 hours the Wing was back at Lashenden. There two now poignant items of news awaited the pilots' return: Walter Conrad had been promoted to Acting Squadron Leader and appointed to command 403 Squadron, and Flight Sergeant Shouldice had been commissioned.

Walter Conrad was, however, more fortunate than his wingman, given that he managed to safely bale out. Landing in the Pas-de-Calais, assisted by the French Underground he successfully evaded capture and trekked over the Pyrenees into Spain. From there, passage to England was arranged, the fortunate young pilot arriving on 10 October.

At Regensburg, the Americans had bombed the target from 17,000–19,000 feet with great accuracy. Major damage was caused to two-thirds of the workshops. Included in that destruction were the fuselage jigs of the secret Me 262 jet fighter, which now faced a serious production delay. The cost, however, was high: twenty-four B-17s were missing, of which five had ditched in the Mediterranean due to fuel exhaustion and engine failure. Schweinfurt had also been successfully pranged, but thirty-six B-17s and over 370 airmen failed to return from that target. Furthermore, many other American fliers had returned either dead or wounded in damaged bombers. The dramatic events of this day represented the most awesome air battle that the world had seen so far in this global conflict. Although the Germans were confused, as intended, by the Regensburg force's southern turn over Italy and onward flight to North Africa, the German controllers undoubtedly managed their forces extremely well. For JG 26, for example, the balance sheet represented one of the unit's most successful days of the whole war. Even so, it was not without cost. Among the *Geschwader*'s five dead pilots was the popular Major Wilhelm-Ferdinand 'Wutz' Galland, *Kommandeur* of II/JG 26 and brother of General Adolf Galland.

On 20 August, 127 Airfield moved from Lashenden to nearby Headcorn, bound for which location sixteen Spitfires took off at 0755 hours, pancaking 20 minutes later. The Wing's communications aircraft, a Tiger Moth, followed at 0815, the remainder of personnel moving by transport 45 minutes later. At Headcorn, the pilots busied themselves erecting tents and dispersal marquees. According to the 403 Squadron ORB, 'Everybody was busy all day loading and unloading trucks, and then a sweep came off in the afternoon in the middle of the panic!' At 1450 hours the Wing took off on Ramrod 211, Forward Target Support, but no enemy opposition was encountered. By evening, 'everyone was pretty well settled' (ORB, 403 Squadron). Johnnie, however, had not flown on Ramrod

211 (contrary to the 403 Squadron ORB). Instead he had taken off in a Spitfire Mk V, 'WH-M', bound for Bolt Head, but for some unknown reason had to put down at Warmwell. From there he flew to the Sector Station at Middle Wallop, lunching with the Station Commander, Group Captain Stephen Hardy, an old friend from Kirton days. Later, Greycap flew up to Rearsby, in Leicestershire, and started a 48-hour leave. Of course there was great interest in his career back home, Meltonians in particular following Johnnie's exploits with great pride. Johnnie's brother, Ross, recalled that

> when he came home Johnnie just enjoyed having a quiet pint like anyone else. He did used to talk to me, though, about his flying. In fact I was also a surveyor and was building runways for a time at Kingscliffe whilst Johnnie was stationed there, so I got to see first-hand what went on.

Johnnie's wife, Paula, recalled that 'When he came home on leave he would be mobbed by youngsters, imploring Johnnie to tell them what it was like flying Spitfires. "Well," he would say, "it's a bit hairy, actually!"' The following article was published in a county newspaper and was entitled 'Melton Ace in Over 200 Air Operations':

> When the Melton Mowbray air ace, Wing Commander Johnnie Johnson DSO DFC & bar, leader of Fighter Command's top scoring Canadian Wing, leads his men into battle, he wears on the shoulders on his flying tunic the 'Canada' name flash. The badge does not appear on his other tunics. He wears it as a token of fellowship and admiration for the Canadians with whom he has flown and fought for the past six months. Under his leadership this Wing has destroyed more than seventy enemy aircraft and probably destroyed or damaged many more. His own score is 23 enemy aircraft destroyed, the latest on Monday, which makes him next to Group Captain 'Sailor' Malan, the highest-scoring pilot still in service with Fighter Command. He has taken part in more than 200 daylight operations. Fourteen of his victories have been won in the same Spitfire, and though in it he led the Canadian Wing on more than 90 sweeps over enemy territory, it was never once touched by bullets or AA fire, states the Air Ministry News

Service. Some of his victories were won while flying as No. 2 to Wing Commander Douglas Bader, the legless fighter ace now a prisoner of war. He was with Bader on his last flight. Johnson was born at Loughborough in 1915, and his home is now in Melton Mowbray.

Another reporter wrote that:

Yesterday an RAF Spitfire pilot told me: 'We reckon Johnnie is the "find" of the year. In six months he has proved himself a great leader'. Like Malan, Johnson fights unselfishly, thinking always of the rawest youngster in his Wing, nursing his men, giving them a chance to destroy planes while he manoeuvres them to do it. But this did not stop him in one period of five days in May (1943) shooting down himself three FW 190s and sharing in the destruction of a fourth. So Johnson's twenty-three victories have come almost in spite of himself. He is in no race to gather victims any more than other brilliant newcomers among the top rankers, including Wing Commander Bill Compton and Squadron Leader J. M. Checketts.

It was clear to all that here was an exceptional fighter pilot and, more importantly, gifted leader.

In the evening of 21 August, Wing Commander Johnson rejoined his Wing at Headcorn. Two days later Greycap scored again. The cloud covering on 23 August had thinned to 3/10ths. At 0800 hours, Greycap led the Wing off from Headcorn on Ramrod 214, Target Cover to Marauders bombing Gosnay. 403 Squadron was led by Flight Lieutenant Dean Dover, and 421 by Squadron Leader McNair. Halfway over the Channel, however, the bombers were recalled, but the Wing swept on. Johnnie:

Appledore took over and after two vectors I sighted Huns in the Bethune area. There was fifteen plus E/A with an up-sun cover of a further three E/A. I instructed one Section to shadow these three E/A until the remaining aircraft were in a position to attack the main force, but unfortunately both Section Leaders misinterpreted this order and as a result only four aircraft were left to deal with the fifteen plus (421 Squadron top guard). E/A turned to port and climbed steeply. I selected a FW 190 in the middle of the gaggle and opened fire from 300–180 yards, with cannon and machine-gun – angle off 5°. Towards the end of the burst, several strikes were seen in the cockpit and wing roots and E/A caught fire and spun down enveloped in flame. This FW 190 is claimed as destroyed.

Most Wing pilots saw Greycap's victim to go down in flames, pouring heavy black smoke. Flying Officer Bob Middlemiss was flying as Greycap's Number Two:

I fired a burst at the E/A flying on the starboard side of Red One (Wing Commander Johnson). The first burst I under-deflected and saw no results. I gave it another burst with less deflection and saw strikes on the port side about the wing roots. My attention was distracted by a large sheet of flame on my port side, which was evidently Wing Commander Johnson's one. I therefore saw no further results on the E/A which I had fired at, and so I claim one FW 190 as damaged.

The Spitfires had clashed with 10/JG 26, and had, in fact, destroyed both FW 190s engaged: *Oberfeldwebel* Erich Borounick and *Gefrieter* Helmuth Ullman were both killed, their aircraft crashing in Artois. 127 Wing all landed safely at 0900 hours. Interestingly, in his log, Johnnie recorded the victory as an 'Me 109', emphasising once more the difficulties of aircraft identification.

On 26 August, Johnnie received a visitor: Squadron Leader Nip Hepple DFC, a former 616 Squadron and Tangmere Wing comrade, now a successful fighter pilot having scored well over Malta. In the morning, Johnnie and Nip flew up to Kenley in a Proctor, enjoying lunch in the Officers' Mess. The pair then returned to Headcorn, Squadron Leader Hepple waving his friend off at 1805 hours on Ramrod S5. 127 Wing was to be the fourth wave of a fighter sweep over Tricqueville, Rouen and Caen. Over France, a gaggle of fifteen-plus Me 109s and FW 190s were engaged in a running battle fought in and out of cloud from 12,000 to 5,000 feet. Several combats took place at close range but were inconclusive due to the cloud cover. Wing Commander Johnson, however, flying as Red One of 403 Squadron, destroyed a FW 190 over Caen. According to the

421 ORB, another 190 was 'frightened by Green Section into firing at and destroying an Me 109. This E/A is claimed as destroyed by P/O Cook. All of our aircraft returned safely and were home by 1940 hours.'

For the next few days, poor weather curtailed operations. On 29 August, Johnnie flew his Spitfire, EN398, on a 30-minute air test following a 240-hour engine change and 'general check at Hamble'. The following day, he flew over to 122 Airfield at Funtingdon, in Sussex, home of 19, 65 and 122 Squadrons. Flying Officer Peter Taylor was a young pilot with 65 Squadron at the time:

> I remember that. Johnnie Johnson came over to talk to us as his Wing was having more success than we were at lower altitude. He related to us his experience then returned to Headcorn for yet another operation.

That sortie was Ramrod S14, Target Support to a bombing raid on St-Omer airfield. 127 Wing swept the Armentieres area, covering the bombers. As the Pas-de-Calais was covered by scattered cloud, the bombers' results could not be seen. By 1958 hours, the Canadians were back at Headcorn, ready to celebrate: their highly popular and successful leader had been awarded a Bar to the DSO. The citation read:

> Since being awarded the DSO this officer has destroyed a further seven enemy aircraft and shared in the destruction of another. He is a relentless fighter whose brilliant leadership and outstanding skill have inspired all with whom he has flown. Within a period of two months, Wing Commander Johnson led large formations of aircraft on very many sorties during which twenty-seven hostile aircraft were shot down and a large number were damaged.

The Wing continued flying operations over France on a daily basis. On the afternoon of 4 September, Ramrod S31 was laid on, in which 127 Wing was to provide High Cover to 36 Marauders bombing Lille. In the target area, nine FW 190s of the *Geschwaderstab*, 8 and 10/JG 26, were seen approaching the bombers, so Wing Commander Johnson took a Section of 403 Squadron down to engage. The 'Wingco' fired at and hit *Oberfeldwebel* Walter Grünlinger, who

made off to the west before crashing in flames. Squadron Leader
Grant, the new CO of 403, then shot down *Unteroffizier* Horst
Schühl (8/JG 26); although the German baled out, his injuries were
so horrendous that the Canadians could see blood on his parachute.
Grant's own luck then ran out, however, and he was shot down
himself, probably by *Oberleutnant* Leuschel, *Staffelkapitän* of 10/JG
26. The target had been successfully hit, many fires and explosions
being seen a few minutes after the attack. Having safely escorted
the bombers home, 127 Wing returned to Headcorn, landing at
1845 hours. Of the kills claimed by Wing Commander Johnson
and Squadron Leader Grant, the ORB of 421 Squadron had this
to say:

> Formed in November 1942, the Canadian Kenley Wing, which
> is now partly on 126 and the remainder on 127 Airfield, today
> scored their 99th and 100th successes ... A raffle had been held
> and the sum of £100 went to an airman in the Maintenance
> Section. Officers from 126 Airfield visited this airfield in the
> evening'

To mark this auspicious achievement, engraved silver tankards
had been commissioned, one of which was presented to Wing
Commander Johnson. Sadly, Squadron Leader Grant would never
receive his: the 28-year-old, from Brockville, Ontario, was dead.

The morning of 5 September was sunny with scattered cloud. At
0748 hours, Greycap led 127 Wing up on Ramrod S33 Part I, High
Cover to seventy-two Marauders bombing Mairelbeke, another
Operation STARKEY mission. In the Beynze area, five Me 109s were
sighted trailing the bombers. Greycap and 421 Squadron's leading
Section engaged four of these bandits. Two 109s were damaged, one
by the 'Wingco', the other by Squadron Leader McNair. South of
Gravelines, two FW 190s appeared and attacked 421 from 1,000
yards, but were 'soon chased off. Over Mardyk, three aircraft were
seen on the aerodrome. Flak was experienced by our Wing from
Dunkirk, Ostend, Ghent and the target' (ORB, 403 Squadron). The
Spitfires were all safely down by 0926 hours. Back at Headcorn,
one flight of 403 Squadron was released, the other remaining at
readiness until dusk. The ORB of 421 Squadron observed that 'It is
now practically a month since this Squadron went under canvas for

the first time. The personnel have adapted themselves to this new life and seem quite at home in it.'

The weather on 6 September remained bright and sunny, with a near cloudless sky. At 0700 hours, Greycap and 127 Wing were up on Ramrod S35 Part V, Second Fighter Sweep to seventy-two Marauders bombing Rouen. One of the bombers was seen to crash in flames between Lydd and New Romney, but there was no reaction from the enemy. The operation was carried out according to plan, and the Spitfires were down by 0840. Greycap then flew home to Leicestershire, landing his now famous Spitfire at Rearsby, for a 24-hour leave with Paula. Significantly, on this day the 403 Squadron ORB makes first mention of a legendary Canadian fighter pilot: Flying Officer George 'Screwball' Beurling DSO DFC DFM & Bar. Having started his career in 403 as a Sergeant Pilot, the maverick Beurling was now back from Malta, where he had enjoyed phenomenal success, his score now being twenty-nine enemy aircraft destroyed with many others damaged. Bob Middlemiss:

One day, having had lunch in the Mess Tent at Headcorn, I was lying down on the ground sunning myself when I felt a kick at the bottom of my boot. I looked up and standing there as large as life was George Beurling, having just re-joined our Squadron. He looked fit, full of vim, vigour and vitality, and, if I knew 'Screwball', was ready to take on the whole *Luftwaffe*. When he had been with us previously, he would often fly the Tiger Moth locally, doing aerobatics and spins, disappearing below the treetops. On a number of occasions we thought he would crash, but he was a superb pilot and had full control of his aircraft, whether a Spitfire or a Tiger Moth. At times he would land in some field and talk the farmer into selling him some fresh eggs. Upon his return, we all then had a good feed in the Mess, courtesy of Screwball.

Johnnie had this to say:

Beurling? I just couldn't do anything with him. I remember MacBrien coming to see me and saying, 'Canada House has been on and wants to put Screwball Beurling into the Wing, what do you think?' Of course Beurling had a reputation, he had got a DSO and a DFC, and a DFM & Bar or something. He had more

fucking gongs than I'd got at that time, but he also had this
reputation of being very difficult to handle. Beurling came down,
he didn't wear a tie, he was unshaven, and he had an old battered
hat on. To all the youngsters he was God, you see, but he was
a very, very bad example to them. He flew one show with me,
towards the end of my tour, and suddenly we were at 25,000 feet
when he half-rolled and disappeared down towards the ground.
We got back and I sent for him. He said, 'Well I saw a train,
Wingco, so I thought that I'd go and give it a squirt.'

I said, "Well nobody squirts anything unless I detach them to
do so.'

He said, 'Goddam it, Wingco, you've got to take a pot at these
fucking Krauts.'

I said, 'Well you do it once more and you're out, do you
understand that? I don't know what you did in Malta or wherever
but here we fly as a disciplined team, nobody breaks away unless
I tell them to or unless we are bounced, and I just won't put up
with this sort of stuff.'

One day Beurling went off shooting, just took my gun and my
dog, wearing his scruffy battledress, no tie, no hat, and he shot
two of the rarest waterfowl on the fucking moat of Leeds Castle,
great crested grebes or something! Not surprisingly the owner,
some titled gent, went absolutely fucking barmy, and came down
to see me, complaining bitterly!

There was a positive side, however. In an effort to make him a
part of the team, Johnnie made Beurling the Wing Gunnery Officer,
hoping that he could pass on some of his deflection shooting genius
to the other pilots. Bob Middlemiss considered that 'Screwball did
very well in helping many of the pilots improve their shooting
capabilities'.

Back at base after operations on 8 September, it was clear that
something big was brewing. Group Captain 'Iron Bill' MacBrien,
Officer Commanding 17 Wing, 'talked to everyone tonight at
muster parade regarding an operation taking place tomorrow, an
attempt to aid in the destruction of the German air force' (ORB, 403
Squadron). The following day was to be the climax of Operation
STARKEY. Landing craft and other shipping were positioned in the
Channel, and Allied air operations over the French coast and Pas-

de-Calais were intensive. The intention was to deceive the Germans into believing that the invasion was actually being launched, and therefore provoke the enemy fighters into a massive reaction on the scale of the previous year's air battle over Dieppe. For 127 Wing, the day's first sortie was 'Beach Patrol No. 1', Wing Commander Johnson leading the Spitfires off at 0715 hours. The Spitfires patrolled over Cap Gris Nez, then south to Boulogne, but the enemy made no reaction. By 0830, the deflated Spitfire pilots were back at Headcorn. Next was 'Beach Patrol No. 2', a duplicate of the first sortie and with the same frustrating result. Ramrod S43 Part II was then laid on, in which 127 Wing flew Top Cover to eighteen Mitchells bombing Bryas Sud airfield. The only enemy fighters seen were two FW 190s diving away over Bethune. This trip was led not by Greycap but by Squadron Leader Hugh Godefroy, formerly CO of 403 Squadron. The Wing's last show was at 1720, when Wing Commander Johnson led his Spitfires on Ramrod S44, High Cover to twelve Bostons bombing Courtrai aerodrome. However, when the Wing reached the English coast, poor weather over France dictated that the mission be aborted. The Spitfires returned to Headcorn, landing at 1750. Given that the Germans had not reacted to what was supposedly an invasion attempt, Operation STARKEY was not, therefore, a success. Flying Officer Ken Wilkinson flew with 165 Squadron throughout that day, and many years later commented that 'What was supposed to be the greatest air battle of all time was actually a damp squib.'

The end of Operation STARKEY also marked a significant event at Headcorn: it was the end of Wing Commander Johnnie Johnson's first operational tour as a Wing Leader. Johnnie:

> Yes, it was the right time to end that tour. Of course I had been on operations for three years, during which time I had flown, in total, 332 operational sorties, 127 or so with the Canadians, and my personal score was twenty-four. I was very tired, and I knew that. Things like flak were giving me more concern than previously, and instead of sending down appropriate Sections to attack, I had started going down myself which was wrong.

Operational fatigue was something not to either overlook or take lightly. Wing Commander Douglas Bader, for example, had put so much energy and enthusiasm into leading the Tangmere Wing during 1941, but his press-on personality had not allowed him to admit that he was exhausted. The consequence was four years as a prisoner of war. Other Wing Leaders were even less fortunate: they were dead. Johnnie:

> Anyway, that was it. 'Iron Bill' MacBrien came over to Headcorn and told me that my tour was over. I had no objections, I knew that the time was right, and I also knew that Hugh Godefroy would succeed me, in whom I had every faith and confidence. There was nothing to be gained by staying on, but everything to be gained from having a rest. Also, we all suspected that the invasion would come off the following year, so I thought the likelihood was, given the timing, that if I went and rested now, I would be back for that long-awaited event. It made sense.

On 11 September, Wing Commander J. E. Johnson, DSO & Bar, DFC & Bar, left for his new job, flying a desk on 11 Group's Operational Planning Staff at Uxbridge. One week, 127 Wing held a dinner, the guest of honour being Wing Commander Johnson. Bob Middlemiss:

> That afternoon, George Beurling and a number of us were outside our tent, Screwball with shotgun in hand, when a low-flying Auster passed overhead. Beurling said casually 'I will now demonstrate deflection shooting by giving the Auster a ring and a half'. He fired. Unbeknown to us, flying in the Auster was Air Vice-Marshal Dickson, our 83 Group AOC, who was attending the Wing Commander's farewell party. The Auster landed with buckshot in the elevator, and the AOC was naturally extremely irate. Questions were asked, of course no one knew anything about a shooting, we all said that it must have been a local farmer!

The dinner was served in the Headcorn Mess Tent, starting at 1930 hours, and was followed by after-dinner speeches by Air Vice-Marshal Dickson and Group Captain MacBrien. Several senior officers from the Kenley Sector were also present, the occasion being a 'most enjoyable affair' (ORB, 421 Squadron). Bob Middlemiss:

We gave Johnnie a very expensive gold watch as a token of our esteem for him as our Wing Leader. The Group Commander decided that because of the very late night and our condition, the Wing would be stood down next day!

Thereafter, Wing Commander Hugh Constance Godefroy DFC replaced 'Greycap' as 'Darkwood Leader'. He had big shoes to fill. Hugh Godefroy:

Before leaving the Wing, Johnnie decided that he needed a new car. After some dickering, I offered him £35 for his Morris Minor, on the understanding that he replaced the two back tyres. It was only after taking and accepting delivery I discovered that both 'new' replacement tyres had come off a 127 Wing starter battery cart, and the car had a very temperamental engine ...

7

Staff Appointment:
'My Closest Shave of the War'

Having bid 127 Wing a fond farewell, Johnnie was able to spend two weeks leave with Paula in Norfolk. During a shooting trip, he experienced his 'closest shave of the war', however, when Mrs Johnson accidentally discharged a shotgun, peppering the fighter ace and his dog with 'earth and bits of sugar beet'. The incident, in fact, marked Paula's 'last appearance on the shooting field'! His leave over, Wing Commander Johnson drove to 11 Group HQ at Uxbridge, where he found his new boss to be his old Wing Leader, Group Captain Pat Jameson. Johnnie joined a small team whose job it was to plan the daily operations of both the 11 and 83 Group Wings. It was mainly a question of co-ordinating escort and support wings for the four bomber organisations of RAF Bomber Command, the American 8th and 9th Air Forces, and 2 Group, 2nd TAF.

RAF Bomber Command, however, still droned over enemy-occupied Europe on a nightly basis. In July, the Battle of Hamburg had started with 1,500 German civilian casualties. Three nights later, a high ambient temperature coupled with low humidity led to the Hamburg firestorm. Even now it is only possible to estimate the numbers of dead on that terrible night: 40,000. Other German cities suffered too, as Air Marshal 'Bomber' Harris complied with the Combined Bomber Offensive Directive. Although the *Luftwaffe* night-fighter and flak crews fought back bravely, the losses they inflicted were insufficient to halt the nightly oncoming tide of *Terrorflieger*. Hitler, and his staff at *Oberkommando der Wehrmacht* (OKW), pinned their hopes now not on air defence but on *Vergeltungwaffe*, or reprisal weapons. Allied agents reported that a test range had been created on the Baltic coast at Peenemünde, and new hidden concrete structures at Watten and Wizernes in the Pas-de-Calais. Similar constructions were also observed in the Cherbourg peninsula, but the first problem faced by Allied intelligence officers was to make sense of all this unusual information, which included reference to experiments with various types of rocket weapons. Needless to say, RAF Bomber Command lost no time in attacking these sites, but ultimately Hitler's 'V' weapons, although too late to affect the war's outcome, would fly, and indeed cause significant damage and loss of life.

While Johnnie was at Uxbridge, raids against the rocket targets, codenamed 'No Ball', were ongoing. In addition, the 'Mossies' of No. 2 Group were most active. Presenting fleeting, low-level targets, the Germans were usually unable to oppose the 'Wooden Wonders' with fighters, but the flak was often intense. Johnnie was not completely isolated from the front line, however:

> Once a month I used to get a light aircraft and fly to Tangmere, Hornchurch or Kenley, and then fly a Spitfire on ops with the various wings. On reflection that was a mistake, really. There was I, a very experienced chap, and they would say, 'You can fly with Flying Officer so and so, and stay out on the flank.' I therefore had no control over what was happening, which was frustrating and looking back I shouldn't have done it; it was foolish, but I wanted to keep my hand in and keep a good relationship with the various wing leaders, men like Ray Harries who got the first Griffon-engine Spits.

The introduction of this new Spitfire, the Mk XII, with an even more powerful and new Rolls-Royce engine, changed tactics, as Johnnie discovered:

> We always thought that he who had height controlled the battle, but Harries, in the new Spitfire, used to fly at 12,000 feet. That was the XII's best operating height, and Ray's plan was to lure them down to that height and hack the fuckers down. It always seemed a bit dicey to me, though, flying underneath the Huns, a bloody hard way to earn a living I always thought! But to be fair, by then we were getting on top, and the German fighter pilot wasn't, by beginning of 1944, the same aggressive, experienced and skilful animal that he had been between 1940–43.

While at Uxbridge there was one area of tactics that Johnnie desperately wanted to influence: Rhubarbs. Johnnie was not alone

in considering Rhubarbs 'bloody murder' and put his view to the
AOC 11 Group, Air Vice-Marshal 'Dingbat' Saunders. In this
he was supported by Group Captain Jameson, with the proviso
that Rhubarbs may still be of value if continued on a reduced
scale over Holland, where the flak was lighter than in France.
The AOC agreed that Rhubarbs would no longer be flown as a
matter of course, but only as a 'special operation', i.e. if the target
was sufficiently important to justify the means. This action of
being principally responsible for the cancellations of Rhubarbs
is to Johnnie's great credit, and the number of young pilots'
lives that were saved as a result must not be underestimated.
Here was an officer who really understood air fighting, and was
not afraid to be outspoken to his senior officers when the need
arose.

On 18 January 1944, Johnnie was awarded the American DFC
for his efforts escorting Eighth Air Force bombers. This was well
deserved, especially because there is a tendency to assume that
American bombers were largely escorted by their own fighters. That
is simply not so. Purpose-built long-range American escort fighters
were unavailable in the early days of the daylight bombing offensive,
which is why it fell to Spitfire pilots, inadequate though their machine
was for this unintended role and without even auxiliary fuel tanks
at that time. It was heart-rending for the Spitfire boys to have to
leave the bombers only a short distance within enemy-occupied
territory on their inward-bound flight – leaving them to the mercy
of German fighters until reaching the same point while outward
bound. The ill-fated Regensburg raid was a prime case in point,
evidencing the folly of bombers operating without adequate fighter
protection. So Johnnie and others like him had done their best in
difficult circumstances – and the Americans were clearly grateful.

By early 1944, in fact, there were developments afoot. Johnnie:

> I was getting a bit itchy by then as it were, anyway, so I was
> delighted when the Canadian Paul Davoud came to see me. He
> had exciting news: two new Canadian fighter wings, one Spitfire,
> one Typhoon equipped, were soon to be formed, both of which
> would be in our 83 Group. Paul wanted a Wing Leader for the
> Spitfire Wing, and the Canadian authorities were agreeable when
> he suggested me.

Johnnie's AOC, Air Vice-Marshal Saunders, agreed to let him go in
March 1944, by which time he would have served the obligatory
six months at HQ. Johnnie:

> Yes, I was delighted of course. As I have said before we knew that
> the invasion was coming, and of course I wanted to be leading
> a Spitfire Wing when it happened. Although we obviously didn't
> know when the invasion would happen, but the climate dictated
> that it would be in the summer. This new Canadian Wing consisted
> of pilots fresh out of training school, but I thought that if I went in
> March, there would still be time to be sorted out Bristol fashion
> for the invasion. Immediately I knew that I had command I
> also started organising a few pilots from my original 127 Wing,
> so there would be a degree of combat experience. I knew that
> 144 Wing would eventually move across the Channel after the
> invasion, which we all felt must come during the forthcoming
> summer. When I was with 616 Squadron Cocky and I enjoyed
> the services of an excellent batman called Fred Varley. I knew
> that his services would come in very handy when we would soon
> be keeping on the move across France. Varley was a first rate
> character and excellent at his job, so I persuaded the CO of 616
> to let him join me at Digby, where I was off to after my leave to
> take command of 144 Wing.

Fred Varley reported to Wing Commander Johnson at Uxbridge,
and together with the Wingco's ever-present Labrador, they set off in
Johnnie's Lagonda. Their first destination was Nottingham, where
Varley spent the weekend with his family, Johnnie doing likewise
at Melton Mowbray. On Monday the pair continued onwards to
Digby and new adventures. Yet another era was about to begin
– this one decisive.

8

144 Wing:
Shot & Shell

At the beginning of March 1944, Wing Commander Johnson DFC & Bar, DSO & Bar arrived at RAF Digby, in Lincolnshire, and became Wing Commander (Flying), 144 (RCAF) Wing. His logbook provides some impressive statistics recorded at this point:

Ramrods, Rodeos, Rhubarbs & Circuses:	232
Operational Flying Hours:	441
Total Flying Hours:	1,451.25
Enemy aircraft destroyed:	24

It was with impeccable credentials and an inspirational reputation, therefore, that Johnnie joined the Canadians at Digby.

Upon arrival Johnnie sought out the Station Commander, Group Captain Paul Davoud DSO, his new boss then introducing him to 144 Wing's squadron commanders: Squadron Leaders George Urquhart Hill DFC & 2 Bars bars of 441 'Silver Fox', 'Brad' Walker DFC of 442 'Caribou', and Henry Wallace 'Wally' McLeod DFC of 443 'Hornet'. As indicated by their impressive gallantry decorations, these three men were experienced and successful fighter pilots all. Their squadrons had been formed at Digby on 8 February 1944, their pilots, who the new Wing Leader soon met, all fit, capable and eager for action. The squadron commanders aside, however, the Wing's pilots lacked actual combat experience. Consequently and not unnaturally therefore, Johnnie arranged the transfer of certain competent individuals known to him from 127 Wing days, among them Flight Lieutenant G. C. Draper and Flying Officers J. A. Brannagan, C. A. Graham and P. A. McLachlan, all to 441, while Flight Lieutenants R. G. Middlemiss and I. G. Keltie DFC became 'unofficial' flight commanders in 442.

While working up, the squadrons of 144 Wing were equipped with the Spitfire Mk VB, but poor weather conditions coupled with inexperience on type led to several flying accidents: on 1 March Spitfire AD249 'pranged' and two days later EE617 'turned turtle' on the snow-covered runway, although fortunately both pilots were unhurt (144 Wing ORB). The station itself was a hive of activity, as everyone prepared for the mobile operations and invasion that all knew lay ahead. New trucks arrived which had to be fitted out as mobile work shops, while other personnel practised tent erection and convoy procedures. Preparing for the forthcoming invasion of enemy-occupied Europe, of course, remained the essential backdrop to this period in time. As early as December 1943, the American General Dwight D. Eisenhower, known commonly as 'Ike', was appointed by President Roosevelt as Supreme Commander, Allied Expeditionary Force. Of course during the Battle of Britain, RAF Fighter Command had maintained Great Britain's integrity and security, without which base the proposed landings in France would not have been possible. After America was eventually forced into the war by the Japanese surprise attack on Pearl Harbour, however, enormous resources began pouring into Britain and without which Operation OVERLORD would likewise have been impossible. Given the investment of men and machines by the USA, it was obviously going to be an American Supreme Commander. Eisenhower's appointment was made public in January 1944, as was the identity of the Deputy Supreme Commander at Supreme Headquarters Allied Expeditionary Force (SHAEF): the British Air Chief Marshal Sir Arthur Tedder. The following month, the Combined Chiefs of Staff issued Eisenhower with a clear directive:

> You will enter the Continent of Europe and, in conjunction with the other United Nations, undertake operations aimed at the heart of Germany and the destruction of her armed forces.

Allied land forces were commanded by a Briton, General Sir Bernard Law Montgomery, the hero of El Alamein whose 'Desert Rats' had defeated Rommel's *Afrika Korps* in the Western Desert. It was Montgomery who actually formulated the plan for the proposed Normandy landings. As the Combined Chiefs of Staff had decreed that OVERLORD should take place in May 1944, from January onwards all Allied efforts were concentrated on training and preparing for D-Day.

Across the Channel the Germans, of course, knew that the invasion was coming, but did not know when or where. The Western Front was 600 miles long as the crow flies and, the enemy knew, could not be held with the forces available which, especially after the disaster at Stalingrad, had been drained by the Eastern Front. *Oberst* Bodo Zimmerman, a staff officer at Western HQ (*Oberbefelshaber West*), later described the German defences in 1943 as 'A mere patchwork. Commanders, troops and equipment were second rate.' To conceal this deficiency, Hitler ordered the construction of substantial concrete fortifications along the Channel coast: the so-called 'Atlantic Wall'. It was also OKW policy to rotate exhausted and depleted units from East to West, so although on paper mighty divisions appeared present in France, the reality was that they were shadows of their former selves. Immediately back to strength, however, these formations were returned to the Russian meat-grinder. During the late summer of 1943, Hitler, in *Führerweisung* 51 (*Führer* Directive No. 51) decreed that from that point onwards the Channel coast would become the main defence area, in support of which policy the bulk of new heavy weapons production and necessary munitions would be sent to that theatre. Operational instructions were clear: the enemy must not be allowed to maintain a foothold on the coast, but must be thrown back into the sea at once. The coast must be held at all costs and any withdrawal was forbidden. The German commander in the West, however, that old architect of previous victories *Generalfeldmarschall* Gerd von Runstedt, responded, pointing out the reality:

1. Most German soldiers in the West were too old and unfit.
2. Most units were insufficiently mobile and therefore of limited tactical value.
3. There was a severe shortage of heavy weapons, especially tanks.
4. Precious few parachute and *Panzer* divisions were actually fit for operations.
5. There was no strategic reserve in the west (for decisive intervention once the invasion had been launched).
6. The *Luftwaffe* was too weak to contain the Allied air forces.

7. The *Kriegsmarine* was virtually non-existent and the Channel was too shallow for effective submarine operations.

Although Hitler promised suitable reinforcements, these either arrived in too small numbers or were absorbed by the Eastern Front as one crisis after another overwhelmed the German forces engaged there. Regarding the *Luftwaffe*, Hitler promised Von Runstedt that immediately the invasion began, all available fighters would be transferred west. Towards the end of 1943, Hitler appointed *Generalfeldmarschall* Erwin Rommel, Montgomery's famous adversary in North Africa, to inspect the Western coastal defences. Not only did the 'Desert Fox' possess initiative, experience and a sound technical knowledge, but his very personal presence was hoped to be morale boosting. At a meeting in Paris, however, Von Runstedt described the situation to Rommel, concluding that 'It all looks very black to me.'

Over the Christmas period of 1943, Rommel reported to Hitler his belief that the Allied invasion would be made between Boulogne and the Somme, and either side of Calais. There were sound reasons for this, but Hitler maintained that the landings would be made in Normandy. All along the Atlantic coast in January 1944, however, the construction of foreshore obstacles commenced. According to Rommel, the object of these underwater obstructions was 'not only to halt the enemy's approach which will be made in hundreds of landing boats and ships, in amphibious vehicles and in waterproof and underwater tanks, all under cover of darkness or artificial fog – but also to destroy his landing equipment and troops'. Within three months, Rommel had immeasurably improved the defences; had he started three months earlier, the success of D-Day would definitely have been in grave doubt. As things stood, however, Rommel himself was far from satisfied with the military situation in France.

At Digby, on 4 March, the Canadians appointed their own Wing Leader, to shadow Johnnie: Wing Commander James Elmslie Walker DFC & 2 Bars. Walker was a 25-year-old from Alberta who had seen extensive action. In 1941 he had gone to Russia with 151 Wing, flown the usual round of Fighter Command operational flights upon returning to the UK in November, and in 1942 went out to North Africa, where he became CO of 243 Squadron. He

was successful in all theatres but found himself back in the UK and
leading first 127 then 126 Wings before returning to Canada on
leave. Before his appointment at 144 Wing in March 1944, for the
previous six months he had been a student at the RAF Staff College,
indicating the ability and potential of this bright and capable young
officer. The weather during early March remained poor, however.
The opportunity was therefore taken to take photographs of all
pilots wearing civilian gear, for escape purposes, and to issue camp
and emergency first-aid kits. All pilots were lectured on cine-gun
cameras, aircraft recognition, AFV recognition, dinghy drill and the
geography of France as it would concern forthcoming operations.
On the evening of 9 March, the weather cleared sufficiently for Wing
Commander Johnson to lead two squadrons of his new Wing on a
formation practice flight lasting over an hour. According to the 442
Squadron ORB, the Wing Leader considered the exercise 'a really
good show'. Johnnie:

> They were very keen, these chaps, and I wanted to get into the
> air and have a look at them. I could see ahead a time when we
> were going to change our tactics. Big wings of thirty-six Spitfires
> were OK for pre-planned offensive operations, but this would
> have to change once we got to France. The time factor would not
> allow for such a large number of aircraft to take off and form up,
> and if the Germans struck at low level then there would be no
> warning whatsoever. Also, we knew that after the invasion our
> main task would be to fly in support of our advancing armies.
> That meant a fundamental change as our role would become
> that of a fighter-bomber, rather than bomber escort or offensive
> fighter. It meant that we would have to respond quickly to calls
> for help from the army, and the only way to do this would be to
> operate smaller formations at a tactical level, such as a flight or
> squadron, as opposed to an entire wing. Nevertheless I needed
> to get these chaps into the air to have a look at them, and I was
> suitably impressed with their standard of flying, enthusiasm and
> potential. It was good to be back at the helm, especially with
> another outfit of Canadians.

A few days after Johnnie's arrival his new Wing's first Spitfire Mk
IXs arrived, replacing their obsolete Mk Vs and which 442 Squadron

concluded were 'really quite nice to look at and everyone seems anxious to get in them and see what they are like' (442 Squadron ORB). Flying Spitfire Mk IX MK394, Johnnie led the Wing on a further formation practice flight, and then spent a few days selecting his personal mount. On 13 March, he air-tested both MK443 and MK504, flying the latter aircraft to and from Tangmere the following day. Back at Digby it was for some reason necessary for Johnnie to give MK504 a 20-minute air test, which was the last time he flew that particular machine. Greycap then air-tested another Spitfire, MK392, with which he was sufficiently satisfied to have his initials and wing commander's pennant painted thereon. As Johnnie later said, 'As before with EN398, which I had flown when leading the Kenley Wing, I never had occasion to regret the choice.'

On 8 March, 83 Group HQ had sent a signal ordering 144 Wing from Digby to Holmsley South, near Bournemouth. The move was to take place on 15 March and entailed packing up all personnel and equipment for conveyance by rail, road and air. The amount of work involved in such a move must not be overlooked, however, and the Wing ORB records that 'The theory of making us mobile quickly is all very well, but in conjunction with the training programme and inexperience of the bulk of personnel, it presents a hectic problem. However, we'll manage.' Preparations had started immediately, and on the appointed date the main road party of seventy-nine vehicles set off as planned. The advance party had already erected canvas accommodation before digging slit trenches around the perimeter of their new but already well-dispersed airfield. While many of the Wing's ground personnel were engaged on the move, the pilots remained at Digby until appropriate facilities had been established at Holmsley.

On 15 March, Johnnie led all three squadrons of 144 Wing, for the first time, in MK392, and put that Spitfire through its paces the following day with 30 minutes of aerobatics. On 17 March, Johnnie flew down to Holmsley, inspected preparations to date, and returned to Digby. Next day, 144 Wing left its Spitfire Mk Vs at Digby, flying in a formation of fifty Spitfire Mk IXs to Holmsley South. Johnnie:

> Although the Spitfire Mk IX was my favourite, we still suffered from the same fucking problem: lack of range. The tanks went

some way to helping, but it was really not good enough that the fucking Air Ministry had not the foresight to provide the specification for and order a long-range offensive fighter. The Spitfire was, of course, intended as a defensive fighter, in which role it excelled, and it is to R. J. Mitchell's great credit that we were able to adapt and modify his creation for roles never originally envisaged. What we needed was a purpose-built long-range offensive fighter. By now the North American Mustang had arrived, which had fuel stuffed into just about every spare square inch of airframe, or so it seemed to us at the time, and the range of which was exactly what we had always needed. The Mustang's range was such that it could stay with the bombers much further, and was the first fighter able to go all the way to the target and back. So whilst we looked forward to the invasion it was with the knowledge that our role had largely changed from pure air fighting in an escort role to being fighter-bombers.

144 Wing was, in fact, officially classified as a fighter-bomber unit, indicating that the main tactical function would be to attack enemy vehicles and troops by strafing or dive-bombing attacks. Once Allied superiority had been established over the invasion beaches and subsequent bridgehead, many RAF units would find themselves pressed into this ground attack role. The addition of bombs, however, caused a drawback in the quest for range: the Spitfire's wings were just not strong enough to take 1,000 pounds of bombs *and* extra fuel. This restricted auxiliary fuel to just one tank, situated beneath the pilot's cockpit and between the inboard wheel wells. Rather than bombs, most Spitfire pilots would have preferred to see the weight involved used for fuel, to extend range and thus increase the prospect of some proper air fighting over Germany itself.

The typically poor March weather, however, was working against Wing Commander Johnson, who was anxious to pitch his new command into battle. On 28 March the opportunity came when the grey cloud over Northern France cleared at last.

442 Squadron ORB:

Wing Commander Johnson mentioned that there might be a show on today, which caused great excitement among the pilots. Pilots were briefed at 1230 and at 1300 we set course for Tangmere where additional gen was picked up. The Squadron took off from Tangmere at 1355 and set course for France. Light flak off the coast, no enemy aircraft encountered. Our aircraft made a supporting sweep in connection with attacks on airfields in Northern France by escorted Fortresses of the USA 8th Bomber Command.

441 Squadron's CO, Squadron Leader Hill, was forced to miss the operation due to illness. His place at the head of 441 was therefore taken by another notable, Wing Commander 'Hawkeye' Wells, a New Zealander. When 441 and 442 Squadrons were halfway across the Channel, Greycap climbed the formation to 10,000 feet. Johnnie's radio then went u/s so he handed over lead to Hawkeye. The Spitfires subsequently crossed the French coast at St-Valery, changing course over St-Clair for Chartres. At Dreux airfield, some twenty to thirty mixed enemy aircraft were seen parked around the perimeter. Wells ordered 442 Squadron to remain at 10,000 feet as a decoy and top cover, while personally leading 441 Squadron to attack the airfield from up sun and at zero feet. Johnnie:

We crossed the southern boundary of the aerodrome at 400 mph, each pilot selecting his target on the western side. I attacked a twin-engined aircraft (probably a Ju 88) with cannon and machine-gun in a five second burst. Many hits were registered on the E/A and after crossing the northern boundary of the aerodrome I climbed steeply to 7,000 feet in order to see the results of 'B' Flight's attack and to see the second flight, 'A' Flight, make their attack. During this climb I was fired at continually by intense light flak, but the gunners were under deflecting, probably due to very high speed and rate of climb. I saw three twin-engined aircraft burning and a fourth, single-engine aircraft, had its back broken and was smoking badly. 'A' Flight carried out their attack but unfortunately they too attacked the western dispersal instead of the eastern dispersal where there were several more E/A including two Me 109s taxiing on the perimeter track. 'A' Flight continued at ground level and the Wing re-formed several miles to the North, returning to Tangmere uneventfully.

Wing Commander Wells:

> When approaching Dreux airfield at about 9,000 feet, between
> twenty–thirty twin-engined and a few single-engined aircraft
> could plainly be seen on the airfield. It was such a very
> concentrated target and being so well inland, I decided that an
> attack by one squadron out of the sun and at very high speed
> would give profitable results. Accordingly, having 442 Squadron
> above (8,000 feet) as both a decoy and top cover, I turned 441
> Squadron into the sun and echeloned them starboard. Then we
> dived very fast to ground level on the South side of the A/F
> and made an extremely fast run across it. I fired first at a flying
> control building which was in my line of flight and then at an
> Me 410, on which I saw strikes.
>
> We continued low and fast for a couple of miles and then pulled
> up fast and re-formed without any trouble.

Flying Officer Brannagan (White Five):

> I attacked the West side of the field, going from South to North.
> I fired at an army vehicle outside the field but was behind and
> short. I approached the airfield at 400 mph, right on the tree
> tops. A gun was firing from my right and so I had a squirt. Next
> I fired at a flak tower on the left and straightened out and saw
> a second E/A on the left. I had a short burst then had to pull
> up the nose to avoid the trees. I had noticed a twin-engined a/c
> sitting in the front of the hangar at the north-west end of the
> field. I came into the clear, pushed the nose down and fired, then
> had to pull up to avoid the hangars.

Wing Commander Johnson confirmed that Brannagan had
destroyed both an Me 410 and a single-engined aircraft. Flying
Officer MacLachlan:

> I was flying as White Two to Wing Commander Johnson. On the
> attack I echeloned starboard, opening fire slightly after the Wing
> Commander. The front part of the aircraft, which I believe was
> a Ju 88, was obscured with dust and smoke from the cannon
> strikes of the Wing Commander's attack. I continued firing at

this aircraft until forced to break off, seeing strikes all over the front of the aircraft.

144 Wing combat report:

> A flak tower was also attacked and damaged by F/O Graham & F/O Fleming, a control tower attacked and damaged by F/O McKenzie and a HQ building attacked and damaged by F/O Casham. Wing re-formed and returned to Tangmere via Evreux and Cabourg. Moderate heavy flak was encountered at Dieppe, at Evreux and Le Havre. Intense light flak encountered at Dreux A/D. Transport was seen travelling north-west on the Paris Rouen road and also in and around the town of Lisieux. Two fairly large boats were seen in Le Havre harbour. W/C Johnson saw a special target site East of St Clair which was reported to Tangmere. Re-fuelled and returned to base pancaking at 1750 hours.

The 144 Wing ORB added that 'A high feeling of elation was apparent throughout the camp and a very definite uplift in morale was noticed.'

In his logbook, Johnnie recorded the Wing's score:

W/Cdr EP Wells:	1 Me 410 destroyed.
F/O Brannagan:	1 Me 410 destroyed.
F/O McLachlan:	1 unidentified single engine aircraft destroyed.
Self:	1 unidentified twin engine aircraft destroyed – shared.
F/Lt Moone:	1 He 111 damaged & ⅓ Me 410 probably destroyed.
F/O Lake:	⅓ Me 410 probably destroyed & 1 unidentified twin engine aircraft damaged – shared.
F/Lt Hart:	⅓ Me 410 probably destroyed.
P/O Kimball:	1 Ju 88 damaged.

Johnnie reported his impressions of why this attack, against 'this heavily-defended target' was successful:

1. The enemy probably did not anticipate a front-gun attack by s/e fighters on a base so far inland.
2. The gunners were probably at a relaxed state, as three combat wings of Fortresses had just passed to the West of the A/D on their withdrawal.
3. The light flak gunners were probably watching the decoy squadron orbiting at 8–9,000 feet.
4. The attacking fighters attacked from the sun, at a very high speed (400 mph) and presented a very difficult target to the ground defences.

The following day the weather resumed its previous form, cold and damp. The last draft of the operational order was completed regarding 144 Wing's latest move: Westhampnett. Again, the whole airfield was alive with activity as packing got underway. On the last day of March, Johnnie had 441 and 442 Squadrons up over France again, hoping to repeat the success of Dreux, himself leading 442. Greycap led the Spitfires low over the Channel's waves, but although enemy aircraft were reported west of Caen, the sweep was uneventful. On 1 April, described by the 442 Squadron diarist as a 'dull, dreary day with slight rain and low overcast', the main party left South Holmsley for Westhampnett. Interestingly, very heavy traffic was encountered, 144 Wing HQ suspecting this to be the result of a 'general moving day' involving many units. By 1900 hours, however, 144 Wing was sufficiently settled at Westhampnett to serve a hot dinner of spinach, roast beef and potatoes to all personnel. Enough tents had already been erected to accommodate all personnel and sanitary facilities had been installed. These achievements indicate that moving was becoming easier and more efficient with practice.

The weather throughout early April remained 'duff'. On 9 April, fed up with the lack of flying, all pilots were released and 'swept' the nearby town of Chichester. After last orders, the Officers' Mess at RAF Tangmere was 'invaded' and 'operations continued there until closing time!' (442 Squadron ORB). Clearly Wing Commander Johnson was keeping alive and well the Kenley Wing's traditions! On 11 April, though, Johnnie led 441 and 442 Squadrons off to Manston at 0650 hours. There the pilots enjoyed a second breakfast and were briefed to fly a sortie in support of seventy-two B-26 Marauders. The Spitfires took off at 1005 hours and met the

Marauders over the Channel, 441 flying top cover and 442 close
escort. 442 Squadron ORB:

> Marauders did a thorough job of plastering marshalling yards at
> Charlerois in Belgium. No Huns seen and no flak. A Spitfire was
> seen to spin in near our coast but the pilot baled out safely and
> ASR was seen to approach him. Landed at Manston, re-fuelled
> and arrived back at Westhampnett at 1345 hours.

Such attacks against the enemy rail network were part of the 'Railway
Plan'. The War Cabinet knew that for the proposed invasion to be
successful, it was necessary to prevent, or at least delay, German
reinforcements reaching the front. In pursuance of this objective it
was decreed that all eighty-five railway centres concerned would
be attacked. It was recognised, though, that this could cost some
10,000 civilian lives, a figure considered acceptable given that if
successful the invasion, Operation OVERLORD, would actually
save the lives of millions. The Railway Plan also included measures
to attack and disrupt road movement and air transport, but actual
roads, it was agreed, were not to be damaged until D-Day. From
that point onwards, attacks were to be made on bridges over the
River Orne to create 'Choke Points' through the towns of Lisieux,
Caen, Bayeux, St-Lô, Coutances and Valognes. It had already
been discovered that bridges could be accurately and more easily
destroyed by dive-bombers, as opposed to light or medium bombers,
so it was that, as had already been the case during the campaigns
in Sicily and Italy, Spitfires were adapted to carry a 500-lb bomb
beneath each wing. Johnnie:

> When bombing you had to put the Spitfire into a steep dive, aim it
> at the target and release the bombs as you pulled out. Allowances
> had to be made for wind strengths etc. because the bomb had
> not the same flying characteristics as a Spitfire. As there was no
> dedicated sight for this kind of work, it was a case of developing
> our own technique of how to time the bomb release so that the
> target was hit.

After lunch on 11 April, Johnnie lectured the pilots on various
subjects, including a training operation, 'Exercise Trousers',

which the Wing was to participate in with the Army next day.
There was some excitement during the evening, however, when a
badly shot up US P-47 Thunderbolt belly landed on the airfield.
Although the pilot was uninjured, all agreed that his machine had
been 'brought in on a wing and a prayer' (144 Wing ORB). On
12 April, five brigades made a seaborne landing at Stack Bay, the
Spitfires patrolling over the 'beachhead'. Johnnie flew MK392
fitted with an experimental 90-gallon auxiliary fuel tank, and was
consequently airborne for 2 hours and 10 minutes. That day also
saw the attendance of Canadian publicity people at Westhampnett
who took photos of the pilots for newspapers back home. News
was also received that yet another move was in the offing, this
time to nearby Funtingdon, another coastal airfield. A reasonable
morning's weather on 13 April saw 442 and 443 Squadrons
escorting Bostons and Marauders to the Dieppe area. 442 Squadron
ORB:

> Two of the bombers were seen to go down from the heavy flak
> barrage. A section of four aircraft led by Wing Commander
> Johnson went in low south of Paris and strafed lorries, flak towers
> etc.

Johnnie had broken off to lead six Spitfires of 442 Squadron on a
'low level Ranger of Chateau Dun – Chartres'. Flight Lieutenant
Keltie's Spitfire was slightly damaged by flak, 'whilst taking evasive
action' (ORB) but the sortie was otherwise uneventful and all pilots
returned safely.

At Westhampnett, the move to Funtingdon was deferred, and
news was received that General Dwight Eisenhower, the Supreme
Allied Commander, was to visit the airfield on 21 April. Improved
weather on 19 April saw Spitfires of both 442 and 443 Squadrons
fly to and operate from Manson, in Kent, engaged on 'Ramrod
753', close escort to seventy-four Marauders bombing Malines in
Belgium. According to the 443 Squadron ORB, the target area was
'completely covered with bombs'. Johnnie, however, together with
two Spitfires of 442 and three of 443, took off from Manston just
after the main formation, which Greycap followed to the enemy
coastline. There the six Spitfires dived for the deck. Near Brussells,
Squadron Leader Wally McLeod encountered a Do 217, which

he attacked and destroyed at tree-top height. Both engines caught fire and the enemy machine pulled up steeply before crashing near the back gardens of a row of cottages. The Spitfire pilots later reported having seen some of the hapless crew trying to bale out, but the aircraft was too low and none of their parachutes opened. Johnnie:

> Brussels was on our right and Louvain to our left. We were in a dangerous area because the German airfields near Brussels were all heavily defended, and for that reason we flew towards Louvain. My Red Two was Wally McCleod, who reported a Do 217 at 12 o'clock, also at low level. I gave him permission to attack, and what followed was an example of fine shooting by a master of the craft'

Although no mention of it is made in any other official records, Johnnie wrote in his flying logbook on that day, 'Self: One goods engine unofficially destroyed'. Several German staff cars and transports were also left ablaze at the roadside.

Johnnie would find 21 April particularly memorable:

> Two days later we tried the same tactics but nearly came to grief. The tactical bombers were operating in the Paris area and I led a section of Spitfires back down to the deck to sweep the numerous airfields scattered around the French capital. After twenty minutes at low level I was lost, although I knew we were a few miles south of Paris. I put away the map and concentrated on flying the various courses I had worked out before leaving base. About another five minutes of this leg and then a turn to the west to avoid getting too close to Paris. Our horizon was limited to about three miles over level country but was considerably reduced when we dipped into a valley. We crossed a complicated mass of railway lines which indicated that we were close to Paris. We sped across a wide river and ahead of us was a heavily wooded slope, perhaps rising 200 feet from the river. We raced up this slope, only a few feet above the topmost branches, and found ourselves looking straight across a large grass airfield with several large hangars on the far side. The German gunners were ready and waiting. Shot and shell came from all angles, for some of the gun positions

were on the hangar roofs and they fired *down* at us! I had never before seen the like of this barrage! It would have been folly to have turned back and made for the shelter of the wooden slope, for the turn would have exposed the vulnerable bellies of our Spitfires. Enemy aircraft were parked here and there, but our only thought was to get clear of this inferno. There was no time for radio orders. It was every man for himself, and each pilot knew that he would only get clear by staying at the very lowest height. It seemed that our exits were sealed with a concentrated criss-cross pattern of fire from a hundred guns. My only hope of a getaway lay in the small gap between two hangars. I pointed the Spitfire at this gap, hurtled through it and caught a glimpse of the multiple barrels of a light flak gun swinging on to me from one of the parapets. Beyond lay a long, straight road with tall poplars on either side, and I belted the Spitfire down the road with the trees forming some sort of screen. Tracer was still bursting over the cockpit, but with luck I should soon be out of range and I held down the Spitfire so that she was only a few feet above the cobbled roadway. Half a dozen cyclists were making their way up the road towards the airfield. They flung themselves from their bicycles in all directions. If you're Frenchmen, I thought, I'm sorry, but I've had a bigger fright than you! I pulled up above the light flak and called the other pilots. Miraculously, they had all come through the barrage, and when the last one answered I pulled the Spitfire into a climbing roll with the sheer joy of being alive.

Johnnie's splendid account provides a vivid glimpse of war through the armoured windscreen of a Spitfire. In his logbook, Johnnie wrote, 'Spitfire below poplar trees! Very accurate flak from Brétigney!!!' Friday 21 April 1944 was also the date of General Eisenhower's morale-boosting visit. Johnnie:

We landed at Tangmere, and never has a cigarette tasted so delicious. Even the usual lukewarm, dark brown NAAFI tea was welcome on this occasion. As we stood in front of our Spitfires talking of our various experiences of but half an hour ago, a few staff cars, full of VIPs, swung along the perimeter track and stopped alongside us. Eisenhower got out of the first car, followed by Leigh-Mallory, now chief of the recently formed Allied

Expeditionary Force. They were accompanied by our new group commander, Harry Broadhurst, who gained great distinction as a fighter pilot in the early years of the war. 83 Group was not his first big command for he had recently led the highly successful Desert Air Force. Broadhurst saw from our dress that we had just returned from a show. He said to the general:

'Come and talk to these chaps, sir, they've just landed.'

Eisenhower was immediately interested and said to me:

'Did you have any luck over there?'

I thought quickly, for we had not fired a shot, and what words could describe our desperate encounter with the flak?

'No, sir,' I answered. 'Our trip was uneventful.'

The General's visit lasted 40 minutes, after which 144 Wing's drivers were briefed regarding the move to Funtingdon. At 2300 hours, 'A' Party moved off, but all sixty-one vehicles soon became lost after the leader took a wrong turn! Unfortunately that road proved to be a dead end, as a result of which the rest of the night was spent turning the convoy around. The vehicles eventually reached Funtingdon at 0730 hours, 5 hours late.

22 April was noteworthy not just because of the move, but equally because the Wing made its deepest penetration into Germany. In the morning an uneventful Ramrod was flown in support of Marauders attacking 'No Ball' targets, the codename for flying bomb installations under the auspices of Operation CROSSBOW, in the St-Omer area. Allied aerial reconnaissance sorties had located such sites, in various stages of completion, all along the French coast, from the Pas-de-Calais to the Cherbourg Peninsula. As the 84 Group ORB records: 'There could be no doubt of the menace they represented, nor of the constant attacks that must be made against them. One site, it is known, was completed and destroyed no fewer than nine times.' In the afternoon Johnnie led 442 and 443 Squadrons to Manston, from where the Spitfires undertook a sweep, again in support of bombers attacking No Ball targets, across Belgium and into Germany as far as Coblenz, on the Rhine. The Wing was briefed to take on enemy fighters, but no enemy aircraft were sighted. Instead the Spitfires were mistakenly bounced by American Thunderbolts and Mustangs, although fortunately no losses were sustained, and flak was heavy. Greycap led his Spitfires

back to their new base at Funtingdon; it had been a long flight: 2 hours and 55 minutes. The 442 Squadron diarist recorded proudly that 'our squadron shared with 443 the distinction of being the first Spitfires to ever make such a deep penetration', adding that although hopes had been high for action with enemy aircraft, 'none were seen and all pilots returned safely in a completely "browned off" condition and with sore bottoms'.

The 144 Wing ORB noted on 24 April that: 'Word was received through Wing that Spits, Mustang III and Typhoons may now attack enemy aircraft on the ground.' The importance of these operations against the *Luftwaffe* in northern France must not be overlooked. A crucial factor in achieving Allied aerial supremacy over the proposed Normandy beaches was that *Luftwaffe* bases had to be pushed so far east that German aircraft would not be able to make a rapid response to any landing. An area was defined, nearly as far south-west as St-Nazaire on the Biscay coast, south as far as Tours, south-east to Paris, and east to, but not including, the Pas-de-Calais. From herein in, the pressure on the *Luftwaffe*, both in the air and on the ground, wherever and whenever it could be found, was set to both increase and remain applied. The improving weather also saw an increase in the tempo of operations, and on 25 April, 144 Wing enjoyed its first proper aerial scrap with the Germans.

It was into a clear and cloudless early morning sky that Greycap led the Spitfires of 441 and 443 Squadrons, to sweep the Paris area 15 minutes in advance of three combat wings of American B-24 Liberator bombers. Johnnie:

> I was leading 144 Airfield on Ramrod 792. We were flying on 120° in the Laon area when Blue 1 reported aircraft at eight o'clock. I told him to turn towards them and sometime afterwards saw six aircraft flying east. We closed gradually and I identified the aircraft as 190s flying in line abreast. I ordered Blue Section to attack the port E/A and led Red Section to attack starboard E/A. I attacked the leader in order to place the rest of my section. As I attacked, he half-rolled so I did too, continuing my fire from 300 yards. I myself did not see any results but two pilots saw large pieces fly away and the E/A went straight down and crashed. After this combat I followed another 190 down to ground level. He flew straight and level at 360 IAS. I was able to follow him at

1,000 yards range and after 15–20 miles at ground-level he eased up to 300 IAS. I closed to 250 yards and gave him several short bursts. Strikes were seen and E/A turned to port, climbed steeply to 700 feet and then fell to the ground in a straight dive. I claim two 190s destroyed, one on the evidence of Pilot Officer Gomez and Flying Officer Stephens and the other witnessed by myself. As I broke off from attacking the first E/A I saw two Spitfires destroy one FW 190, which on interrogation could only have been Squadron Leader Hill and his Number Two, Pilot Officer Sparling. I also saw one FW 190 crash as a result of an attack by Flight Lieutenant Walz.

In support of Johnnie's claim, Pilot Officer Gomez reported that:

I was leading the port side of Blue Section (Three and Four) as the Wingco ordered to jettison tanks, didn't work on mine so when the attack started I had to drop back in formation and dived straight down after the Wingco had attacked the first 190. I saw black smoke and it didn't recover from dive. Finally crashed in the middle of a bush and blew up.

Flight Lieutenant D. M. Walz:

I was leading Blue Flight (of 443 Squadron) on Ramrod 792, when in the area South of Compiegne I sighted E/A at ten o'clock, same level. I reported these to W/C J. E. Johnson, who was leading Red Flight. We immediately started climbing and working into position for attack. As we closed up, we could see six aircraft flying in a line abreast formation, climbing into sun. W/C Johnson led Red Flight into position on starboard side of E/A, which were recognized as FW 190s, while I led Blue Flight up into position on port side. When in position the W/C gave instructions to drop tanks. I had instructions to take my Flight down on the three on port side, the W/C attacking the three on starboard side. W/C Johnson gave the word to attack and I led my Flight down, attacking from 1,000 feet above and slightly behind and to port of enemy E/A. I singled out the third from the end, getting into position dead line astern 300 yards behind E/A. I opened fire with cannon and machine-gun at 275 yards. Firing steady I closed to seventy-five yards, breaking to port. The enemy a/c was climbing dead into sun and did not break. I did not see my results as I was firing into sun and had to break. I claim one FW 190 destroyed, which was seen to crash by W/C Johnson.

Johnnie reported that:

These Huns were obviously climbing up in order to intercept three combat wings of Liberators who were penetrating on a similar course to the Wing but fifteen minutes later. They (the 190s) were climbing the whole time and I should imagine that shortly after the engagement they had intended to swing round on their reciprocal course in order to intercept the Liberators. I recommend that when other operations permit we be employed in a similar manner (i.e. sweeping fifteen–twenty minutes ahead of the main bomber force). Radius of action with ninety gallon tanks – 265 miles'

Due to having been unable to jettison drop tanks, however, several pilots had been unable to engage, and afterwards those who had found themselves scattered. Three Spitfires of 443 Squadron were able to return safely to base, four landed at Exeter, while two others forced-landed out of petrol. One of the latter pilots, Pilot Officer Brockman, crash-landed near Warmwell and was 'injured about the head and back' (443 Squadron ORB). Although Squadron Leader Hill and Flying Officer Sparling of 441 Squadron were credited with having shared the destruction of a 190, neither pilot returned to base. Hill, the CO, was forced to land his Spitfire near Lâon due to a technical problem, and was seen to safely leave the aircraft and make off into a nearby wood. Although he initially evaded safely, Hill was later captured by the Germans and roughly treated by the *Gestapo*, who suspected that he had knowledge of Allied invasion plans. Flying Officer Sparling was even less fortunate. On the return flight, he notified another pilot that his radio was u/s, and continued on course until 10 miles off Portland Bill. There Richard Sparling was seen to change course towards Bournemouth, but has never been seen since; although Flight Lieutenant Moore led a section of Spitfires on 'extensive searches for Flying Officer Sparling, no trace was found of found of him or his aircraft' (441 Squadron ORB).

25 April was also marred with another tragedy for 144 Wing: Wing Commander James Elmslie Walker, Johnnie's Canadian counterpart, was killed in a flying accident.

During the day on 26 April, 443 and 441 Squadrons were released from operations to facilitate practice bombing at the Selsey Bill range. This was actually in compliance with a new policy that released the Wing for training every third day. In the evening, however, Johnnie led 441 and 443 Squadrons on the Wing's first operational dive-bombing attack, with 500-pounders, against a No Ball target near Dieppe. In his logbook, Greycap wrote, 'Undershot badly. Lots of light and heavy flak.' The 443 Squadron ORB elaborates: 'Bombs fell in the general vicinity of the target but results were not all that could have been hoped for. Flak was very intense but no one was hit.'

According to the 144 Wing ORB, 27 April was 'another beautiful day'. Wing Commander Walker, it was learned, would be replaced by Wing Commander A. D. Nesbitt DFC, and Squadron Leader Hill's place at the head of 441 Squadron was to be taken by an American volunteer, Squadron Leader J. Danforth 'Dan' Browne, who had previously flown with Johnnie, often as Greycap's wingman, during the Kenley Wing days of 1943. There was another important change at 442 Squadron: Squadron Leader Brad Walker DFC was tour expired and was replaced by Squadron Leader Blair Dalzell Russell DFC. 'Dal' Russell had become an 'ace' during the Battle of Britain, flying Hurricanes out of Northolt with 1 (RCAF) Squadron. His appointment was an interesting one. Johnnie:

Dal was reaching the end of his spell as a staff officer at 83 Group, and heard that I was looking to replace Brad Walker. Dal and I had both led Canadian Wings in 1943, and had flown together many times. He came to see me and asked if he could take over Brad's outfit, which surprised me because he was a Wing Commander! I told him to wait for a new Wing, but Dal was concerned that he might miss the impending 'Big Show'. Reverting to squadron commander was a small price to pay, he said, and so there was no contest. I was delighted to have Dal on board and, indeed, to have three squadron commanders, Browne, Russell and McLeod, of such high calibre.

On 4 May, Johnnie's logbook records that he flew to Northolt 'to see the King', and returned later that day, no doubt to receive his latest DSO. That day also saw the late Wing Commander Walker's replacement, Wing Commander Nesbitt, chair a meeting with section heads to discuss organisation of the airfield during the forthcoming invasion. According to the 144 Wing ORB, 'Several interesting points arose, and many queries were answered, to the mutual benefit of all. Meetings such as these are of inestimable value.' The following day, Johnnie led the Wing on Ramrod 831. 442 Squadron ORB:

> Cool with 15 mph winds. W/C Johnson led the three squadrons on a Rodeo to Lille, France, with take-off at 0655 hours. Fourteen started from 442 Squadron, F/O Robillard returned a few minutes later with boost trouble. The OC touched down at 0905 hours, with eight others, the remaining four and the Wing Commander, flying on a Ranger, were back twenty-five minutes later. The Greycap added his twenty-eighth destroyed and Squadron Leader McLeod, CO of 443 Squadron, his fifteenth. Two more went to the Wing for a total of four enemy aircraft destroyed before breakfast.

Johnnie:

> When over Douai I saw six FW 190s flying over the town at ground level. I detached 443 Squadron (S/L McLeod) to go down and search for these E/A. About five minutes afterwards I saw a FW 190 flying west at 2,000 feet. I closed from his port side and opened fire from 300 yards, closing from 20° angle to 5° angle off. After one second burst E/A jettisoned hood and tank and pieces were seen to fly off. I continued to fire and the pilot baled out at 400 feet, and, unfortunately, landed safely by parachute. E/A crashed in a field three miles East of Douai. Claimed as destroyed.

The 190s belonged to II/JG 26, operating out of Cambrai-Süd aerodrome, and had been scrambled to intercept Allied bombers attacking a No Ball target. As the Spitfires searched for the bandits, the 190s whipped round and attacked their pursuers head on. Pilot Officer F. A. W. J. Wilson (441 Squadron):

Saw approximately five E/A in a vic below, off to starboard, so pulled down with my Number Two. E/A saw leading aircraft attack so broke to port and singly were turning on the deck. Singled one out and attacked him in turn, range 200–150 yards. Angle approximately 15°, height 100 feet, fired short burst and saw hits on wing and tail unit. Whilst attacking I saw E/A coming in on myself and Number Two, so broke off engagement and broke up in towards him but lost him in cloud at 700 feet.

Although Wilson himself was unable to see the result of his attack, Squadron Leader McLeod watched the 190 as it 'rolled on back and went straight in, exploding and burned. I returned to scene fifteen minutes later and E/A was still burning. Only thing recognisable was the tail plane. A crowd had gathered but most of them ran like hell when I returned!' Pilot Officer T. C. Gamey, also of 441 Squadron:

Singling one out I came in astern. E/A turned sharply to starboard at zero height, leaving thick wingtip vapour trails. As E/A came out of turn I gave him two–three second burst, height 100 feet, range 250–150 yards, angle 20°–10°. Strikes were observed on starboard side of E/A and while manoeuvring to continue attack, E/A crashed into a ploughed field at a slight angle. After impact, whilst still in motion, port wing broke off upwards and back, starboard wing doing the same. E/A immediately broke into flame. While turning to starboard to view further results, E/A exploded, depositing flaming wreckage at edge of field, across a ditch and along twenty–thirty yards of asphalt road, running at right angle to direction of crash.

Squadron Leader H. W. McLeod:

We bounced from line astern but the E/A saw us and broke sharply to port. A general mêlée ensued. I observed one FW 190 shot down by a Spitfire [Wilson's kill] in a turn, aircraft crashed. I selected a FW 190 which left the gaggle. I chased him due east for ten minutes at tree top height. He finally pulled up to 1,000 feet, broke to port. I cut the corner, firing a two second burst from 150 yards, 30° – 1½ rings. Strikes were observed on cowling and cockpit. Smoke and fire observed, E/A rolled on its back and started in. I fired another short burst (1½ seconds) from line astern, 175 yards – E/A burst completely into flames and crashed, exploding. I circled and took a cine camera shot of the wreck and proceeded to base.

Johnnie's logbook records that McLeod's victory was accompanied by a shout over the R/T of 'Take that, you bastard!' German records indicate that only two FW 190s were actually lost by JG 26 on this day, *Feldwebel* Horst Schwentick and *Unteroffizier* Manfred Talkenberg, who were both apparently killed.

On the morning of 14 May, 144 Wing prepared to move Ford, the airfield to travel in the order of 'A', 'B' and 'C' Echelons, and Air Lift Party, as a practice for the forthcoming move overseas. 122 Wing was scheduled to move from Ford to Funtingdon on the same day. Interestingly, a 'Casualty Air Evacuation' took place in the afternoon, when a DC-3 'Dakota' landed with a number of 'casualties' who were unloaded in stretchers by medical orderlies. The 'casualties' were then put back on the aircraft, which then took off. By evening, however, rain brought an end to 'weeks of sunny weather which has been a joy to all ranks, who are looking tanned and fit'. The move was completed both efficiently and without undue mishap, and by evening the new base was well organised, already boasting electricity, telephones and hot water. The Wing ORB commented that:

> The new camp lies on the Western side of RAF Station Ford, partly in fields, and partly around some of the static buildings. The immediately surrounding country is very flat, the Station being situated on the coastal plain, two miles north of the sea. To the North is a pleasing view of the South Downs, pleasantly wooded here, with the massive pile of Arundel Castle standing guard on the Southward slopes. The surrounding farm lands are well treed, and the ubiquitous English hedge and winding road make our outlook an attractive one.

Heavy rain prevented further operational flying over the next few days, but there was no rest: every morning the Wing's personnel were engaged in 3-mile route marches, carrying full kit. On 18 May, the Wing's officers practised firing small arms – Brens, Stens and revolvers – on the range in Arundel Park, adjacent, commented the Wing ORB, 'to the gate through which William the Conquerer rode with his men on surrender of the castle in 1066'. Wing Commanders Nesbitt and Johnson also lectured the Wing's pilots on 'Invasion Tactics'. On 19 May, all personnel were issued with ammunition and ordered henceforth to carry their arms, equipment and anti-gas equipment to and from work, and for it to be at hand both day and night. The Education Officer gave a demonstration of linguaphone records in speaking French and German; all excess baggage was packed up for storage at a depository in London: there could be no doubt now that with all of this preparation, in respect of even the finest detail, the long-awaited invasion was getting very close. At 1920 hours, Johnnie led his Spitfires to dive-bomb a bridge near the French coast at Le Treport, a sortie conducted without incident.

21 May saw 441 Squadron dive-bomb targets in the Loan area, but bad weather saw strafing trips, planned for both 442 and 443 Squadrons, cancelled. On the morning of 22 May, Johnnie flew MK 392 on an 'Aileron test' prior to leading 442 Squadron to bomb a 'No Ball' target near Abbeville. Although no enemy aircraft were encountered, flak was accurate: Flying Officer Gimball returned with a jagged hole from a shell which fractured an oil line. 441 Squadron's ORB records that 'Very good results were obtained from dive-bombing Ailly-le-Haut', but 443 Squadron's sweep was uneventful. Johnnie:

> By this time the whole area around Southampton and Portsmouth was under arms. Vast amounts of trucks, tanks and other armoured fighting vehicles, not to mention huge supplies of ammunition, had poured into the area and dispersed around the surrounding countryside. Ford Airfield was home to three Spitfire wings and several night-fighter squadrons. The main problem, as I recall, was that with so many servicemen in the area beer was in short supply!

24 May dawned foggy but high drama soon unfolded: a B-17 Flying Fortress crash-landed at Ford but burst into flames. The Wing ORB records that the '144 Airfield crash crew played an outstanding part,

in the midst of exploding ammunition, and burning petrol, and were first on the scene ... Good show'. That evening, 443 Squadron spontaneously organised a 'sweep' into Worthing, where nineteen steak dinners were enjoyed at the Ship Hotel. Johnnie was the Squadron's guest, and all later agreed that it was the most successful 'outing' yet.

The next morning, Johnnie led 144 Wing to operate from Manston, from where the Spitfires flew to and dive-bombed the Sempes marshalling yards near Mons. In his logbook, Greycap later wrote with satisfaction, 'Best bombing to date. Four large fires started in adjacent factories. Yards & rails hit.' Once more, however, there was no flak and nor were enemy aircraft sighted. Of course the *Luftwaffe* was under very heavy pressure, and had to conserve all resources. At night the RAF bombed German cities and industrial installations, and the Americans by day. The priority, therefore, was the Defence of the Reich itself, and fuel, due to the Allied attacks against the enemy synthetic oil industry, was at a premium. Indeed, it was these raids against petrol supply installations that General Adolf Galland later considered to be the most important of all the combined factors that ultimately brought about the defeat of Germany. Nevertheless, *Luftwaffe* fighter forces were sufficiently engaged throughout May 1944 to lose 276 pilots and 487 aircraft.

On 26 May, pilots from all over the south coast were assembled at Tangmere Sector Station where they were addressed by Air Chief Marshal Sir Trafford Leigh-Mallory, commander of the Allied Expeditionary Air Force. No operational flying was carried out by 144 Wing, although the 144 Wing ORB notes, regarding 'Other Ranks', that 'There are indications of "beach twitch" amongst some of them, though what will happen when the pressure really comes on remains to be seen.' The daily round of sweeps and dive-bombing sorties were still being carried out, but largely without incident. On 28 May, Johnnie swept the Paris area with 441 Squadron; both FW 190s and Me 410s were seen but could not be engaged. The weather was extremely hot, 83° F being reported over the Dover Straits. After bombing up at Lympne the next day, 144 Wing's pilots enjoyed a swim before taking off and attacking another target in France 'through heavy flak' (442 Squadron ORB). 30 May saw the Canadian Spitfires dive-bombing and strafing a German radar station near Abbeville. On the last day of May 1944, the AOC 83 Group,

Air Vice-Marshal Harry Broadhurst, addressed all Wing Leaders, Wing Commanding Officers, Senior Administration Officers and Staff Officers at Tangmere. According to the 144 Wing ORB:

> A general outline of our part was given, and in his talk he pointed out that even ordinary comforts, like cooked meals, would probably have to go by the board in the early stages. The programme was to be work and more work, and when you became exhausted you carried on anyway. He emphasised the fact to keep the men away from the slit trench complex on the dispersal sites and runways, otherwise nothing would be done. He also emphasised the need to improvise by all means, and to use any method to get the job done. He pointed out the absolute necessity of keeping runways and perimeter tracks clear, and of employing anyone to assist in doing so, regardless of rank or trade.

Johnnie:

> We were naturally very confident and this feeling increased the closer we got to D-Day. General Eisenhower, the Supreme Allied Commander, was our guest for dinner in the Officers' Mess at Tangmere, and of course it was all inspiring stuff, the prospect of this 'Great Crusade', as I think 'Ike' called it that night, to rid Europe of tyranny. It made me think about my personal journey, which from an operational perspective really began in earnest at Tangmere in 1941, and I thought about Douglas Bader, a prisoner since August 1941, but whose shining example was always before us.

At 1030 hours on 2 June, Johnnie called all of 144 Wing's pilots together in the briefing room for a lecture on dive-bombing and tactics generally in respect of the invasion. Before this was completed, however, four pilots of 442 Squadron were scrambled, recalled, immediately re-briefed and away on a shipping reconnaissance during which nothing was sighted. Wing Commander Nesbitt then addressed all personnel. The 144 Wing ORB records that Nesbitt

> outlined to them the part it had been our good fortune to be assigned in the coming invasion. He pointed out that on us depended largely

the success of the operation, in view of the fact that we were the first airfield to go into the battle as such. The CO has received his route instructions. He will be departing on 5 June. Advice has also been received that 'B' Echelon is to be at readiness from 0600 hours, 4 June.

Johnnie: 'It was clear to everybody that this great thing was going to happen literally any minute. After all these years of war, and all this preparation, we were anxious to get over the Channel and get the job done.'

On 3 June, things really started to happen. 144 Wing received notification from the Movement Control Officer that the airfield was to move into the concentration area, ready for imminent embarkation, at 0700 hours the following day. The 443 Squadron ORB described the busy scene:

> Orders received that Squadron to leave 144 Wing for static station, RAF Ford, at 0900 hours today. This meant moving from tents into temporary quarters (Nissen huts) on the Aircrew site, Ford. All camp equipment and the greater part of officers' personal baggage has been packed in the one three ton lorry assigned to the Squadron for any movements. Aircraft servicing being done by static personnel and those members of the servicing echelon who are on the air-lift party. Pilots of the Squadron are keeping only as much kit as can be carried in a Spitfire aircraft when the Squadron eventually moves overseas ... A start has been made on the painting of white stripes on Squadron aircraft in accordance with TAF instructions on aircraft markings.

Meanwhile, the Wing's Spitfires were prowling over France. 441 Squadron swept the St-Juste area, destroying two military transports north-west of Montdidier and another at Bretevil. 442 Squadron ran into some heavy flak, three Spitfires being damaged. Johnnie himself led 443 Squadron, strafing in the Courtrai area. A total of eleven enemy military vehicles were destroyed by 144 Wing this day. Later, Greycap flew MK392 to Rearsby, in his home county of Leicestershire, visiting his family overnight before returning to Ford on 4 June.

Most of the camp had worked all night to meet the 0700 hours movement deadline on 4 June. Wing Commander Nesbitt himself, however, roused those who had managed a few hours 'kip' with a bugle! The 144 Wing convoy subsequently arrived at Old Sarum on time; the scene there is recounted by the Wing ORB:

> The concentration area is marvellously organised and food is excellent. The bulk of personnel immediately turned in, and played sheet music for the next 14 hours, as most of them had had approximately 2 hours rest in 48. Vehicles were immediately sent to 'snug' where waterproofing commenced. We were informed that our vehicles were in the best shape of any so far to reach the area. It speaks volumes of our MT Officer.

When 5 June dawned after a night of very heavy rain, 441 Squadron was tasked with covering Allied shipping assembling between Selsey Bill to St Catherine's Point. The engine of Spitfire MK465 failed over the sea, however, but Flight Sergeant V. A. G. Brochu safely baled out off Selsey. He would be at sea for 42 hours in a dinghy before being rescued off the French coast! 442 and 443 Squadron's pilots were similarly employed. 442 ORB: 'London dailies reported that Rome had fallen, a false invasion report was broadcast in the USA and rumours here say that today was D-Day but Channel too rough.' Escape equipment was issued to all relevant personnel, and there was a final opportunity to draw pay. All maps were turned in, and the operation's next phase was explained to 144 Wing personnel. That evening the non-flying officers and NCOs held a combined 'thrash' and 'a good time was had by all'.

Having already been postponed due to bad weather in May, the next combination of favourable moon, tide and sunrise necessary for the attack was 5–7 June inclusive. Bad weather would again prevent the invasion going ahead on 5 June, but by evening on 4 June it was predicted that the weather would be acceptable on 6 June. A crucial meeting was held at SHAEF in Portsmouth, the decision being Eisenhower's, and his alone. With incredible coolness, Ike said simply, 'OK, Let's go.'

Between 2100 and 2200 hours on 5 June, Johnnie briefed all 144 Wing pilots in the Intelligence Office regarding the invasion, air operations in support of which were to start at 0001 hours the following morning. Johnnie:

A vital thing to remember about this is that we were all keen to get across the Channel and operate from France itself. No longer would we be faced with the two-way Channel crossing that we had made day after day, year after year. We had lost too many pilots in the drink during that time, so this really was a huge factor to us.

We can only imagine how highly charged the atmosphere must have been at that particular briefing; the 'Day of Days' was now just hours away. Already, though, it was the 'Night of Nights': at 2315 hours, 144 Wing personnel were treated to the awesome spectacle of 240 troop transports passing overhead. Soon these Allied airborne troops would be engaged on French soil, their objectives being to capture key strategic and tactical locations, destroy enemy gun emplacements and establish flare paths to guide glider-towing aircraft. 255 Dakotas and Albermarles dropped 4,310 paratroopers; only seven transport aircraft were lost. Seventy-four gliders were safely released, fifty-seven of which, carrying 493 troops, landed on or near their designated Landing Zones. It was, in fact, British glider troops who would fight D-Day's first action: a company of the Oxfordshire & Buckinghamshire Light Infantry, led by Major John Howard, an experienced and decorated airborne officer, seized and held the bridge across the Orne River and canal between Benouville and Ranville. This small but inspired force took and held the crucial 'Pegasus Bridge' for 24 hours.

The night sky was filled with the roar of Allied aircraft, but Mosquito intruder pilots, patrolling over France and seeking German night-fighters, reported a quiet night with little or no sign of the enemy. Over 1,000 Lancasters, Halifaxes and Mosquitoes bombed ten coastal gun batteries in the invasion area, eight of which were covered with cloud and therefore indicated by Oboe sky markers. An incredible 5,000 tons of bombs were dropped, the greatest tonnage in one night so far throughout the entire war; just three aircraft were lost. Naturally it was necessary to deceive and confuse the enemy as to where the landings would be made, and so a number of complex operations were flown with this objective. Operation TAXABLE involved sixteen Lancasters of the famous 617 Squadron dropping 'Window', in conjunction with a Royal Navy deception operation, thus simulating an invasion force approaching the French coast near

Cap d'Antifer. Operation GLIMMER saw six Stirlings also dropping Window, giving the impression of the Allies approaching Boulogne, in the Pas-de-Calais. Perhaps the most imaginative, however, was Operation TITANIC, in which dummy parachutists, together with two SAS teams, were dropped away from the actual invasion area, near the base of the Cotentin Peninsula, east of the River Dives and to the south-west of Caen. Over the Somme, Lancasters and B-17s established an 'Air-Borne Cigar' (ABC) ground-to-air radio jamming and Window barrage to distract enemy night-fighters away from the transport aircraft inserting Allied airborne troops. Radar Counter Measures (RCM) were also the focus of Stirlings and B-24 Liberators over Littlehampton, which established a Mandrel radar jamming screen between there and Portland Bill, thus hiding the real invasion fleet from German early warning radar. The Mosquito Mk VIs of 21 Squadron, based at Hunsdon, patrolled behind enemy lines that night, attacking trains and transport, and, indeed, anything else that moved. Finally, shortly before 0630 hours, Allied aircraft dropped leaflets over France, telling French civilians that the long-awaited hour of liberation was now at hand, and urging those who lived near the coast to move inland or seek safety in open countryside. Indeed, as the 144 Wing diary recorded: 'It looks like the real thing at last.'

9

D-Day:
'Looking Down into Hell'

It was fitting that the naval component of OVERLORD, Operation
NEPTUNE, was commanded by Admiral Sir Bertram Ramsay, the
sailor who had overseen the evacuation of the BEF from Dunkirk
in 1940. Four years later, almost to the day, Ramsay was back off
the French coast, but this time with the greatest amphibious assault
force ever assembled: 6,483 vessels including 9 battleships, 23
cruisers, 104 destroyers and 71 corvettes. No less than 4,000 landing
craft of all shapes and sizes would carry the troops and apparel of
war ashore. This huge armada was divided into the Eastern Task
Force, under Rear Admiral Sir Phillip Vian, and the Western Task
Force commanded by the American Rear Admiral Kirk. Vian's
fleet left Southampton, Portsmouth, Newhaven, Shoreham, Solent
and Spithead, and conveyed British and Canadian troops across
the Channel to their destination – the beaches stretching 24 miles
westward from Ouistreham to Port-en-Bessin. These scenic stretches
of Normandy sand were codenamed Gold, Juno and Sword. Kirk's
Western Task Force carried American soldiers to their beaches –
Omaha and Utah – west of Port-en-Bessin to Quiselle. The intention
was for the Americans, British and Canadians to establish and
maintain a bridgehead before linking up; the British 50th Infantry
Division was then to push south and capture Bayeux.

Incredibly, given the vast enormity of the undertaking, Operation
NEPTUNE achieved complete tactical surprise, the Eastern Task
Force anchoring some 7–8 eight miles off shore, where troops were
disgorged into landing craft. At 0515 hours, Bombarding Force 'D',
obscured by smoke laid by aircraft, arrived on the eastern flank.
Soon the 15-inch guns of HMS *Ramilles* and HMS *Warspite*, each
capable of lobbing a shell weighing 1,938 pounds over 18 miles,
would open fire on *Festung Europa*. Before dawn, the bombardment
started, the roar of gunfire rolling across the sea, the Normandy
coast illuminated by flares and explosions. H-Hour came first for the

Americans storming Omaha and Utah beaches. Unfortunately, the preceding heavy aerial bombardment of the enemy coastal defences had caused little damage to those in the American sector, which had been covered by cloud. Consequently the 'Yanks' were met by an absolutely withering hail of machine-gun fire, artillery and mortar fire. The British and Canadians encountered less resistance, but fighting was still fierce. As H-Hour had been slightly delayed for the Canadians, at Juno the tide was slightly higher than planned, meaning that the mined beach defences took a significant toll on the landing craft. The obstacle-clearing parties were under heavy fire from enemy troops just 100 yards away, and the seafront was formidably defended by dun emplacements and determined infantry. Unfortunately the prevailing conditions at sea had prevented the launching of amphibious tanks, and so the Canadian infantry hit the beach unsupported by armour. In spite of heavy losses to both mines and crossfire, the Canadians somehow not only got up the beach but by nightfall were 7 miles inland. At Sword the British faced similar problems to the Canadians, but just enough tanks supported the infantry and made the landing successful. Heavy fighting took place, however, in the built-up area beyond the beach where vicious house-to-house fighting lasted until midday. British commandos then linked up as planned with British airborne troops, and by nightfall 3rd Infantry Division was 6 miles inland. A battalion of infantry, supported by just a squadron of Sherman tanks, penetrated just 2 miles short of Caen before dusk, but, lacking appropriate heavy support, was forced back.

From the air, the invasion was undoubtedly a spectacle of infinite proportions. A Spitfire pilot, Flight Lieutenant Bob Beardsley DFC, later told the press that:

> The sky over the target was absolutely packed with aircraft. Fighters and bombers seemed to fill the air, wingtip to wingtip. From above [we fighter pilots] could see the bombs go down. The whole target area was a mass of flames. It was both an impressive and terrifying sight, and I for one was glad that I was not a German soldier.

A Norwegian Wing Leader graphically added how 'Looking down on the target area was like looking down into hell.'

For 144 Wing, the 'Day of Days' had started early. Johnnie:

We were called well before dawn, and driving across the darkened
airfield to the Ford Mess for an early breakfast we heard the
roar of powerful engines as the first formations of day fighters
made their way to Normandy to relieve the night patrols. After
a hurried meal we strapped ourselves into the cockpits of our
Spitfires. I took three squadrons across the Channel, over a
choppy grey sea, to patrol the line of beaches being assaulted
by British and Canadian troops ... The *Luftwaffe* possessed
plenty of airfields within striking distance of the assault area.
They had always been a flexible organisation and capable of rapid
reinforcement. Perhaps the scale of fighting would be similar to
the stirring air battles fought over Dieppe. Tense and eager in
our cockpits, anticipating bitter opposition, we made an accurate
landfall on the Normandy coast. From the pilot's viewpoint, flying
conditions were quite reasonable – better than we expected after
the gloomy forecasts of the previous two or three days. The cloud
base was at about 2000 feet and the visibility between five and six
miles. Calling the Wing Leader of the formation we were about
to relieve, I told him that we were already on our appointed
patrol line. Had he seen anything of enemy fighters? 'Not a bloody
thing,' he replied, 'although the flak is pretty hot if you fly a few
hundred yards inland.' Amongst the mass of shipping below us
was a fighter direction ship. I called the RAF controller on my
radio and asked if he had any plots of enemy formations on his
table. The controller came back with the guarded reply that for
the moment he had no positive information for me.

We swept parallel to the coast beneath a leaden grey sky, and I
positioned the Wing two or three hundred yards offshore so that
we should not present easy targets to the enemy gunners. Our
patrol line ended over the fishing village of Port-en-Bessin, while
further to the West, beyond our area of responsibility, lay the two
American assault beaches, Omaha and Utah. When we carried
out a wide, easy turn to retrace our flight path, a wing of American
Thunderbolts harried our progress and for a few uneasy moments
we circled warily round each other. Formations of different types
of Allied aircraft had attacked each other during the preceding
months, but in this instance recognition was soon effected and

we continued our flight to the South of the Orne. For the present there was little doubt that we were the undisputed masters of this little portion of Normandy sky, so for the first time that morning I was able to turn some of my attention to the scene below.

Offshore the sea was littered with ships of all sizes and descriptions, and small landing craft ploughed their way through the breakers to discharge their contents at the water's edge. We could see a fair number of capsized vessels ... Further out in the bay, cruisers and destroyers manoeuvred to lie broadside on to the assault beaches: we could see the flashes from their guns as they engaged the enemy defences well inland. As I watched the naval bombardment I realised that we flew constantly in an air space between the naval gunners and their targets. No doubt the shells were well above our height of 2000 feet, but I made quite certain that we did not exceed this altitude.

Swimming tanks, a recent innovation, were launched from their parent ships well out to sea. From the air it seemed as if these amphibious tanks had a fairly long and rough sea journey before they reached the beaches. During the last lap of their journey the tanks opened fire against adjacent enemy positions, and this must have come as a considerable surprise to the defenders. Here and there the enemy appeared to be putting up a stiff-resistance: we saw frequent bursts of mortar and machine-gun fire directed against our troops and equipment on the beaches. Small parties of men could be seen making their way to the beach huts and houses on the sea front, many of which were on fire. But the greatest danger to us pilots lay from the mass of Allied aircraft which roamed relentlessly to and fro over the assault areas. Medium bombers, light bombers, fighter-bombers, fighters, reconnaissance, artillery and naval aircraft swamped the limited air space below the cloud, and on two occasions we had to swerve violently to avoid head-on collisions. Towards the end of our allotted patrol time the controller asked me to investigate bogey aircraft flying down the Orne from Caen, but these turned out to be a formation of Typhoons, so we resumed our cruise above the beaches.

144 Wing ORB:

On a recording on the BBC a briefing of some of the pilots taking

part was broadcast as part of the news commentary. Although no
names were mentioned, the voice was unmistakable: W/Cdr J. E.
Johnson DSO DFC, Wing Commander Flying of 144 Wing.

Johnnie: 'Four times that day we made our way across the Channel,
and never a sign of the *Luftwaffe*!' The *Luftwaffe*'s inadequate reaction
was due to the prevalent misconception in Berlin that the Normandy
landings were merely a diversion. Consequently the *Luftlotte Reich*
fighters were not ordered west until afternoon, and did not reach their
new airfields until dusk. None of these reinforcements were therefore
able to engage on D-Day, which, as Rommel knew and history has
since proved, was the crucial period. Johnnie:

> At Dieppe the *Luftwaffe* had reacted swiftly and ferociously to
> what was clearly an isolated landing, but this time the stakes were
> infinitely higher – the German commanders could not react in
> strength until sure that Normandy was not a feint. Don't forget
> that part of the deception plan involved 'secret' maps falling into
> enemy hands, 'confirming' that the main landings would be near
> Calais. The high commanders therefore remained convinced that
> Normandy was a diversion, so reserves of armour and aircraft,
> both vital to repulsing the Allied landing, were not committed
> until it was too late for them to have a decisive impact.

Hitler himself, however, always believed that the Allies would land
in Normandy and ensured that reserves could only be committed
with his personal approval. These reserves comprised 1st SS *Panzer*
Division *Leibstandarte* (Adolf Hitler Bodyguard), 12th SS *Panzer*
Division *Hitler Jugend* (Hitler Youth), 17th SS *Panzergrenadier*
Division *Götz von Berlichingen* and *Panzer Lehr* Division. As it
happened, *Hitler Jugend* was already in Normandy, and had been
since April 1944. The 'Baby Division' had received Codeword
Blucher – invasion alert – at 0230 hours on 6 June. Although
brought to a state of immediate readiness, like every other German
formation in the area, however, *Hitler Jugend* became frustrated by
indecision. The *Panzerspähkompanie* (armoured car company) of
the *Aufklärungsabteilung* (reconnaissance unit) were sent forward
at 0400 hours to establish the actual situation. *Obersturmführer*
Peter Hansmann later remembered that:

We reached the heights of Magny-en-Bessin and a farm with a barn and trees, from where we had a view across the Bay of Arromanches. The armoured cars remained on the rear slope, looking like big bushes due to the excellent camouflage attached by Hans Krapf and Heinz Dahmann. Concealed in this way we could observe the unknown, the improbable, the really unimaginable spectacle. What was this large grey mass spreading out in front of us? I had to make sure once more: there to the west was the steep shore of the Bay of Arromanches. The heaviest artillery fire was concentrated there. Columns of dirt, as big as a house, rose into the air before collapsing. To the east stretched an endless dark-grey mass, the sea. Even the horizon seemed endless, just a little lighter than the ocean. I was looking through my binoculars, now recognising the individual outlines of ships. Next to each other, behind, right to the horizon were ships – ships' masts, ships' bridges. At irregular intervals flashes were constantly coming from various spots. Ship's artillery! A dark-grey sea stretched between the beach and the armada of ships out there. White lines were racing at us through these dark masses of water from the endless line of ships deployed from the steep shores of Arromanches to the horizon east of the mouth of the Orne. These were fast boats with high, white, foamy bow waves, landing craft which then spat out brown clumps of soldiers at the beach.

I could see white columns of water rising in the landing area, probably caused by our coastal batteries. Then I could clearly hear the muzzle fire of MG 42s. At least our coastal defences had not been completely overrun. *Unterscharführer* Dahmann drew my attention to the brown figures slowly moving through the dunes. They were wearing flat steel helmets so were Brits. In groups, platoon strength, even whole companies were advancing slowly through the dunes towards us, seemingly without finding any resistance. They were still about 3,000 metres away and could only be seen with binoculars.

Some houses were burning in Arromanches, the smoke drifting across us and sometimes obscuring our view. Then I spotted tanks, a whole pack, strange forms. They came out of the bay, drove up the coastal road towards us then swung east and zig-zagged through the dunes without stopping to fire. They were probably crushing some individual pockets of resistance. Then

I could clearly make out the large scoops on the tanks' fronts. Did they want to build a coastal road immediately or dig out mines? Without pause, more and more tanks appeared directly from the sea. Was this possible? First we could occasionally see their cupolas, then they rose from the waves like dinosaurs. And no one seemed to interfere with them. Was there no 88 mm flak? Well, no. The fighter-bombers were attacking the back slopes of the steep coast unhindered. They dropped their rocket bombs into the concrete walls of fortifications. I took another look at our lightly armoured reconnaissance vehicles. Were they sufficiently camouflaged? Even our Tigers were helpless against these 'Meat Flies'.

Throughout the day, German troops and transport began moving towards the Allied threat, but were considerably delayed by more 'Meat Flies'. Overwhelming Allied aerial supremacy had effectively isolated Normandy from the rest of enemy-occupied France, and without *Luftwaffe* intervention the enemy ground forces were at the mercy of Allied fighter-bombers. It would not be until evening that *Hitler Jugend*, for example, reached and took up defensive positions in the historic and vitally important city of Caen. Those first hours of confusion and indecision, coupled with the 'Meat Flies', had undoubtedly cost Germany the day. Johnnie:

> We arrived back at Ford from our last, uneventful, patrol as dusk was falling. We had to wait a few minutes for the night-fighters to take off and maintain a vigil over the beach-head. Tired and drained, I drove to the Mess for the evening meal. All my pilots were there. All had flown on this day and some had participated in all the missions. They were very quiet: it was apparent that they were bitterly disappointed with the *Luftwaffe*'s failure to put in an appearance on this day, which was amongst the most momentous in our long history of war. We had gathered ourselves for a day of intense air fighting but the actual result had been something of an anti-climax. I could not let them go to bed in this mood of antipathy and frustration, so I gathered them together for a short pep talk. Although we had still not succeeded in bringing the enemy to combat, I said, it was still a brilliant triumph for the Allied Air Forces as it marked our complete dominance over

the *Luftwaffe* – an ideal we had striven to attain for more than three years. I glanced at my audience. Lounging in chairs, propped up against the walls, rather dirty and many of them unshaven, they received this somewhat pompous statement with the cool indifference it merited. I tried another approach: 'We know that the *Luftwaffe* squadrons in this area are not very strong. In fact the latest order of battle estimates that they have only about 200 fighters and less than 100 fighter-bombers. But they still possess many crack squadrons of fighters based in Germany. You can bet your last dollar that some of these outfits will move into Normandy immediately, if they haven't already done so. You'll have all the fighting you want within the next few weeks, and perhaps more! Don't forget that we shall soon have our own airfield in Normandy and then we shall be ready for them. And now we'll force a beer down before we turn in.'

After just one welcome glass of beer, Johnnie led his pilots off to bed. By that time some 175,000 Allied troops had been landed in Normandy, around 10,000 having made the ultimate sacrifice. According to official US statistics, 3,881 were Americans lost on one beach: Omaha. Although the day had been won, and actually at less a cost in human lives than anticipated, not all Allied objectives had been achieved. The Americans at Omaha had yet to link up with the British on Gold, and it was feared that a German armoured thrust, by 21st *Panzer* Division, might prevent this happening. Neither had it proved possible to take Caen on that first day; indeed that city, contested by the young Nazi fanatics of *Hitler Jugend*, would take over a month to fall at a high price. The Americans would take three weeks to clear the Contentin and take the port of Cherbourg. Quality German reinforcements, like 2nd SS *Panzer* Division *Das Reich*, would eventually reach the battlefield, launching determined counter-attacks with great aggression and verve. The *bocage* terrain of woods, sunken lanes and high hedgerows, extending 50 miles inland, was actually unsuited to advancing armour but entirely favourable to small, mobile anti-tank units. These crucial factors would to some degree negate the Allies' enormous advantages in resources and aerial supremacy, leading to the ferocious Battle for Normandy lasting three long, blood-stained months.

10

Normandy:
Overtaking the Sailor

Clearly the confused German reaction would not last, and, as the battle progressed, Allied commanders rightly expected an increase in the tempo of combat, both on land and in the air. Due to having achieved complete surprise, the fighting had so far gone entirely in the Allies' favour, but wise generals know that campaigns can and often do lose momentum. Hidden by the cloak of darkness, enemy troops had been able to move freely, but every dawn brought death from above. From first light the fighter-bombers of 2nd TAF ranged far and wide across Normandy, attacking enemy strong points and vehicles. The effectiveness of tactical air power is indicated by the fact that SS *Standartenführer* Kurt Meyer's *Hitler Jugend* took 10 hours to travel 40 miles to the Division's start line near Caen. *Sturmann* Helmut Pock:

> As we drive through a small town I see soldiers on vehicles ahead of us suddenly start jumping off and seeking cover. Just as I go to ask what is happening I can see for myself: enemy fighter-bombers are attacking. As we had been taught I take my carbine, load it and follow the daring flight of the fighters from beneath my cover. They disappear in the sun and become invisible. But then, with engines howling and at high speed, the first ones come racing at us. 'Brrrrt, drrrt, brrrrt', the salvo bangs into the road. Low level attack! Just as we had been drilled, I lead the aircraft with my carbine and fire. In the meantime my comrades have also opened fire on the attacking fighters. 'These damned dogs don't notice anything at all!' one of them near me curses. He is right! Despite our fire being fairly accurate, we do not shoot down even one, not even a trail of smoke to be seen. We conclude that we are fairly harmless to enemy aircraft with our K-98 carbines. This realisation creates no joy as we are used to seeing positive results from our actions, and this we have come to expect. In a small

village another halt is ordered. The fighter-bombers are again raking the roads. We are fairly well covered and camouflaged behind houses. We wait under an archway until the fireworks are over. Some vehicles have been caught outside the village by aircraft which dive constantly, and badly aimed salvos slap into the walls and street next to us.

The *Jabos* (*Jagdbomber* – fighter-bomber) did not have it all their own way, however. On 7 June, thirteen were lost to flak. German armour actually included a wide variety of anti-aircraft weapons mounted on tank and half-track chassis. The *Ostwind*, for example, featured a 3.7-cm gun on a *Panzer* Mk IV chassis, while the *Wirbelwind*, also based on the Mk IV, was armed with a quadruple 2-cm weapon. Experience would teach the Germans to ambush the troublesome 'Meat Flies' with *Jabofalle* – groups of highly camouflaged *Flakpanzer* creating concentrated fire.

2nd TAF's Spitfires, however, were still largely employed in providing air cover over the actual beaches. German fighters and fighter-bombers were now starting to use low cloud cover to make hit and run attacks on the beachhead. 144 Wing flew four patrols over the Eastern Assault Area (Gold, Juno and Sword) on 7 June, Johnnie leading two of them. The Canadians of 126 Wing, led by Wing Commander George Keefer, enjoyed success that day, however, intercepting a dozen Ju 88s between the beaches and Caen, subsequently claiming eight destroyed. Their patrol having been uneventful, Johnnie and his pilots had to endure hearing Keefer's pilots' cries of jubilation over the R/T. Wing Commander Bill Crawford-Compton, at the head of 145 Wing's 340 Squadron, destroyed another Ju 88, and five Spitfires of 134 Wing's 312 Squadron drove off sixteen FW 190s attacking British troops near Caen. The large number of Spitfires involved in providing this aerial umbrella over the beaches, however, meant that every patrol had to be flown within very tight parameters of both time and geography. Moreover, under no circumstances could the fighters be drawn off, perhaps intercepting a diversion, leaving the invasion fleet unprotected. Freelance tactics were out of the question, therefore, so those lucky Spitfire pilots who did successfully engage in aerial combat were simply in the right place at the right time.

On 144 Wing's last patrol of 7 June, the Controller sent Johnnie
and a section of his Spitfires on a reconnaissance a few miles inland
to ascertain the strength of any German reinforcements moving
towards the beachhead. Low cloud prevented accurate observation,
however, so after just a few minutes Greycap prepared to rejoin
the Wing. A mile or so inland, however, Johnnie noticed action in
a cornfield below:

> Six or eight British tanks were manoeuvring for an attack against
> a similar number of Tiger tanks which crouched, squat and
> sinister, on the edge of a small orchard. The British were moving
> quite slowly; from the air it seemed that they halted to fire and
> then pressed on against the enemy positions. The Germans, on
> the other hand, fired rapidly from their static positions and their
> superior 88 mm guns scored some hits on the British armour.
> One of our tanks was already ablaze. Fascinated, we watched the
> drama below and I was immediately struck by the great contrast
> between the speed and pattern of our intricate air battles and this
> cumbersome, unwieldy but equally deadly affair on the ground.
> The British continued to receive the worst of the exchange, and
> although our cannons would have little effect against the tough
> armour of the Tigers I manoeuvred my formation for a flank
> attack against the enemy targets. Our support was unnecessary,
> however, since four Typhoons appeared on the scene and without
> further ado proceeded to launch a rocket attack against the Tigers.
> The enemy tanks were soon hidden from our view by the debris
> thrown into the air from the impact of rockets.

Although the exact location of this battle appears unrecorded,
research suggests that the 'Tigers' were actually *Panzer* Mk IVs
belonging to 21st *Panzer* Division's *Panzer* Regiment 22. Protected
by an extra skirt of armour around the turret, the Mk IV (actually
armed with a 75-mm gun) was easily mistaken for the mighty and
much feared Tiger (*Panzer* Mk VI). 21st *Panzer* had previously found
fame in Rommel's *Afrika Korps*, but was virtually destroyed in
Tunisia during 1943. Re-formed in Brittany, by D-Day the Division
had been re-equipped with the Mk IV and was located near Caen.
On that day, 21st Panzer achieved the only significant counter-attack
when *Panzergrenadier* Regiment 902 reached Lion-sur-Mer. The

Mk IVs, however, were hit by anti-tank guns in front of Biéville and Périers, causing them to dig in, hull down. In spite of losing sixteen tanks, there they repulsed the British 27th Brigade, and on 7 June caused consternation among the British 3rd Infantry Division when the Mk IVs were mistakenly identified as Tigers. It seems likely that these 21st *Panzer* Mk IVs were the tanks seen by Johnnie and his pilots that day. In fact, there were no Tigers engaged that early during the Battle for Normandy: *Schwere SS-Panzer Abteilung* 101 was the first Tiger-equipped unit to arrive, on 10 June.

10 June proved to be a red letter day not only for 144 Wing but also for the Allied air forces in general. In the morning, Johnnie's Wing flew a number of mundane shipping patrols south of Beachy Head before receiving exciting news: a strip, 'B3', had been created at St-Croix-sur-Mer, just inland of the British and Canadian beaches and from where 144 Wing could operate. At 0730 hours Greycap despatched Squadron Leader Dal Russell and three other 442 Squadron pilots to land at B3 and ensure all was well. So it was that those four Spitfires became the first Allied fighters to land in France for four years, just four days after the invasion had begun. The feedback was that all was well at St-Croix, and at 1130 hours Johnnie briefed his pilots: this time the entire Wing was landing at B3 to refuel and rearm before sweeping further south. Johnnie:

We took off at 1155 hours and I was very pleased with this new development. Not only would we have the honour of being the first Spitfires to land in and operate from Normandy, but this would give us the extra range needed to sweep South of the River Loire, where we knew concentrations of enemy aircraft were based. We first made a low pass over St-Croix-sur-Mer, familiarising ourselves with the location, and then made a tight circuit to avoid the barrage balloons protecting the beach-head. Bear in mind that this was a strange experience, landing in what had been enemy territory from which we had previously had thrown at us every description of hostile shot and shell. We touched down and left RAF servicing commandos attending to our Spitfires. As we pilots gathered together, the Airfield Commander came over and told us not to stray too far due to minefields and snipers. The airfield control system had been established in an adjacent orchard where we were soon approached by a delegation from St-

Croix. The villagers brought with them gifts of fruit, flowers and wine. Whilst we and the French rejoiced, dead German soldiers still lay all around.

Throughout the twenty minutes that Johnnie and his pilots spent on the ground at St-Croix, an uninterrupted stream of Allied vehicles rolled past the strip, travelling east. Johnnie:

> Had a similar scene been enacted in enemy territory, the column would have been gutted immediately by our fighter-bombers which ranged to and fro over Normandy seeking such a target. In fact, we could always tell which side of the lines we were on by noting the remarkable contrast in the activity and spacing of road traffic.

The subsequent sweep, however, was an anti-climax due to low cloud reducing visibility. Nevertheless, the excited Spitfire pilots returned to Ford at 1800 hours, 'Mud on their shoes and German souvenirs in their pockets' (442 Squadron ORB). Inevitably the press arrived, and Flight Lieutenants Dover and Robillard made recordings for the Canadian Broadcasting Company (CBC) about the milestone operational landing in Normandy. At 1900 hours, all three squadrons were up again for yet another uneventful beach patrol.

A day later the Wing ORB mentioned a pertinent concern:

> It is hoped that Caen is captured shortly, or else 144 is going to have one hell of a job to get going, as at the moment the site of our airfield is right in the fighting zone and still under shell fire.

The besieged city of Caen was still being determinedly and steadfastly defended by '*Panzer*' Meyer's *Hitler Jugend*. Many more lives would be lost on both sides before the ancient city would fall. The overall military situation in Normandy, however, remained favourable to the Allies. The beaches were now linked and the beachhead was now 8–12 miles deep. The British I Corps was preparing to attack Caen from the north-east, and XXX Corps was engaged along the line La Belle Epine–Tilly-sur-Seulles–Bronay, where the defenders enjoyed the benefits of prepared positions and armoured support. The British

7th Armoured Division was poised to assault Villers-Bocage, the key to high ground between the rivers Odon and Orne. The American 4th Division still made good progress along the Contentin peninsula, preventing German reinforcements reaching the besieged garrison of Cherbourg, and the 101st Airborne Division still held Carentan. By having destroyed road and railway networks, Allied air power had achieved the objective of isolating the Normandy battlefield and preventing the Germans from bringing up reinforcements in such numbers as to permit a major counter offensive. Instead the enemy could only react at local level to Allied thrusts, meaning that the initiative remained Montgomery's. It must, however, be said that the Germans were excellent at lashing together small composite battle groups, often out of fragmented units, which fought most effectively. Incredibly, however, the entire German 15th *Armee* still remained in positions around Calais, awaiting the supposed main attack in that area!

Rocket-firing Typhoons were unleashed against the stubborn teenage SS defenders of Caen, on 12 June, but losses to flak were high: seven 'Tiffies' failed to return. On that day the *Luftwaffe* responded in real strength for the first time during the campaign. By the close of play, the Germans had lost fifty aircraft, the Allies forty-three. It was now just a matter of time until 144 Wing found itself in the right place at the right time. During the evening, the fifty-four operational V-1 (flying bomb) sites, between the Pas-de-Calais and the Seine, of *Flakregiment* 155, prepared to bombard England for the first time. That night four V-1s hit south-east England, significant damage being caused to the railway bridge at Bethnal Green; six people were killed, including a twelve-year-old boy and an eight-month-old baby.

The situation on the ground in Normandy remained both extremely violent and noisy, the Allied foothold being constantly bombed and strafed. At St-Croix, Johnnie was happily reunited with his batman, Fred Varley, and Labrador Sally. The Wing Leader lived in a caravan, located in an orchard and adjacent to the other vehicles comprising 144 Wing's nerve-centre, which was a hive of activity. Two army liaison officers had joined the Wing and were busy marking a large-scale map with the disposition of opposing forces. Intelligence Officers were analysing information and confirmed to Wing Commander Johnson that the long-awaited *Luftwaffe* reinforcements had arrived: some 300 fighters based to the south and south-east. The Signals Section had established ground-to-air communications with 83 Group, which would control the Spitfires once airborne. Everything was perfectly co-ordinated, so the past year of intense practice had definitely been worthwhile.

144 Wing was the first to actually remain in and operate from Normandy. Until that point Spitfires had remained based in England, hopping over the Channel to rearm and refuel at the temporary Normandy strips but always returning home across the Channel at the end of each day. Johnnie's pilots would now enjoy the benefits of an increased radius of operation, a distinct advantage over the squadrons still in England. The plan was very simple: if the enemy continued to refuse battle in the air, now that his bases were within range, 144 Wing would destroy the opposition on the ground. Johnnie:

> Yes, that was it: search and destroy. Range was everything, of course, and if the buggers were within range then we were going to get them. On that first day in Normandy, Fred Varley, who had already spent several nights in Normandy, warned me that the evening barrage would be both dangerous and noisy. I rejected his offer to make up my bed in a slit trench. Soon after turning in I was rudely awakened by a Bofors gun constantly banging away just twenty yards from my caravan! It was impossible to sleep so I eventually got dressed and went outside to have a look. Large fires lit the south-east, but enemy aircraft still attacked our shipping in spite of a terrific defensive barrage by the RN. There were thousands of anti-aircraft guns concentrated in what was a relatively small area, so the din was absolutely unbearable. Hot shrapnel fell on my caravan, searchlights swept the night-sky and the ground reverberated. Unable to find Varley, I struggled into my sleeping bag beneath the rear axle of my caravan. Harassing raids continued well into the night, so sleep was quite impossible. By dawn I was very cold and miserable, so crawled from my sleeping bag and went off in search of a hot drink.

Johnnie's squadron commanders, however, had all fared much better: Danny Browne, Wally McLeod and Dal Russell had all bedded down in a substantial German underground bunker, where they enjoyed a deep and peaceful sleep. Needless to say, the Wing Leader joined them the following night! Over the beachhead that night, ADGB Mosquitoes accounted for a Ju 88 destroyed and two others damaged elsewhere; one 'Mossie' failed to return. The Germans also began the main V-1 attack on England, launching 50 'Doodlebugs' at Southampton and 244 at London. A total of 26 V-1s were shot down, but the loss of life, which achieved absolutely nothing, was an indication of things to come.

For 144 Wing, in spite of a sleepless night, 16 June saw the action craved by Johnnie and his Canadians. That morning *Jagdkorps* II ordered all five *Jagdgeschwader* and one *Schlachtgruppe* of *Jafü* 5 to attack the British beachhead from dawn onwards. Bad weather throughout the first sortie, however, dictated that only one pilot of JG 26 would contact the enemy. *Feldwebel* Erhard Tippe, of 11/JG 26, was permanent wingman to his *Staffelkapitän*, Major Mietusch, but took off alone as his Me 109G-6 was not ready. A substitute was found, but although Tippe hastened after his comrades, he actually joined a formation of Me 109s from an unidentified unit. These inadvertently emerged from cloud above the Allied fleet and consequently broke in all directions as the Royal Navy opened fire. Tippe climbed vertically into cloud, but above it found himself among six 442 and 443 Squadron Spitfires! The Canadians attacked immediately, Tippe breaking right and turning tightly. The German was eventually shot down over Le Havre, by Flight Lieutenant Don Walz, and baled out. The German pilot was captured and later wrote of the kindness shown to him by Canadian troops. At 0605 hours, 442 Squadron's Flight Lieutenants Keltie and Wright were making a circuit of St-Croix after take-off when a lone FW 190 bounced them, strafing the airfield before streaking away unscathed. Fortunately neither Spitfire was damaged so they continued their patrol, during which both pilots had a 'squirt' (442 Squadron ORB) at Tippe before his 109 was destroyed by Don Walz.

At 1630 hours, Johnnie briefed his pilots on scramble procedures from St-Croix, which, due to the speed and surprise with which the enemy could still clearly pounce, was going to involve being at cockpit readiness. During the evening, Johnnie, Squadron Leader McLeod and ten pilots of 443 Squadron all sat in their cockpits, fully kitted up, plugged in and ready to go. After 30 minutes, at 2035 hours, the Spitfires responded to a red Very light fired from

Operations and roared into the sky. Just minutes later, battle formation had been assumed and the fighters were vectored by Kenway Control to intercept bandits 5 miles South of Caen. The enemy was reported at low level, nothing definite but below 5,000 feet. Two miles South of Caen, Squadron Leader McLeod Tally Ho'd a mixed gaggle of FW 190s and Me 109s, approaching the Spitfires but well below (at 2,000 feet) and down sun. Leaving McLeod's Section as top cover, Johnnie led his pilots down to attack. Before the bounce was achieved, however, the sharp-eyed Germans broke and faced the threat, which suggested that their leader was a veteran. McLeod's Section immediately joined the fray, twenty-four fighters now 'mixing it'. Johnnie:

> I was on patrol two miles South of Caen when I saw four FW 190s flying south-west at ground level. I dived and opened fire on the starboard E/A, which was slightly behind the other three. Opened fire at 150 yards with a three second burst of cannon and machine-gun fire from dead astern and slightly above. Strikes were seen on the engine cowling and cockpit of the E/A, which dived into the ground and disintegrated. I then broke away and climbed into cloud as I was being engaged by intense and accurate light flak.

Squadron Leader McLeod also scored, destroying an Me 109, which increased his score to seventeen.

Johnnie's victory that day, which was recorded by his cine-gun camera, brought his personal score to twenty-eight, and was 144 Wing's first success out of St-Croix-sur-Mer. There was, however, a bitter pill: an entire section of 443 Squadron Spitfires was missing. Back at St-Croix the Canadians waited in vain for the four pilots' return and no news whatsoever was forthcoming from any source; the Spitfires had, to all intents and purposes, simply disappeared. In fact, Squadron Leader J. D. Hall, Flight Lieutenants Don 'Wally' Walz and H. Russell, and Flying Officer Luis Perez-Gomez had the misfortune to run into a superior force of fighters belonging to JG 53. All four Spitfires were shot down, only Walz escaping with his life – although his petrol tank exploded, he safely baled out and, assisted by French civilians, later returned to Allied lines. Sadly, the Flight Lieutenant Russell killed on this sortie was the younger brother of Squadron Leader Dal Russell, CO of 442 Squadron. This incident was a salutary reminder that the *Jagdfliegern* would still engage whenever the tactical situation was favourable to them, and in such circumstances remained a capable adversary.

In his log on 16 June, Johnnie wrote, 'Matoni and his 190s about'. Johnnie later recalled:

> Yes, the Matoni thing was quite interesting. We had noticed this distinctive long-nosed FW 190, leading ordinary 190s, and our 'spies' confirmed the pilot to be an ace, Walter Matoni.

Matoni was indeed an old hand. During the Battle of Britain he had flown with 9/JG 27, scoring one victory before adding three more over Russia in 1941. Later that year he joined 7/JG 26 on the *Kanalfront* before transferring to JG 2, with which unit he was badly wounded. After a lengthy convalescence, which included a period of instructing, Matoni returned to active operations with II/JG 26 in February 1943. On 17 June he became an ace, destroying a Spitfire to record his fifth aerial success. Shot down and wounded by B-17s in August, Matoni was back in action by December. On 24 February 1944, he shot down an unescorted B-24 near Frankfurt, in the process recording not only his thirteenth kill but JG 26's 2,000th victory. Shortly afterwards Matoni was promoted to *Staffelkapitän* of 5/JG 26, and on 10 May was awarded the German Cross in Gold for twenty victories. Included in this total were eleven four-engine bombers, and all but three kills had been made over the Western Front. Johnnie:

> It was clear to us that Matoni was an experienced chap because although we often saw him in the air he could only be brought to battle if the circumstances were entirely favourable to him. His presence therefore became something of a challenge and I formed the habit of always calling up Kenway and asking if Matoni was about. Some of the boys would belch over the R/T whenever Matoni's name was mentioned, in the hope of winding up the German listening service, but we never did manage to engage him.

Perhaps inevitably, the press got wind of this scenario and soon exaggerated the whole thing into Johnnie personally challenging

Matoni to a duel, in the style of chivalrous knights of the air. Johnnie tried to explain that such a circumstance was impossible, given the current nature of air fighting, but, needless to say, when published the story remained suitably embellished. Johnnie:

> Challenging Matoni to a personal duel was, of course, rubbish. The subsequent newspaper reports put me in the firing line for not only a lot of ribbing by the boys, but also an unexpected written bollocking from Paula who reckoned I was taking unnecessary risks!

Walter Matoni was, of course, exactly the kind of experienced fighter pilot and leader that the *Luftwaffe* so badly needed in Normandy, not least because there was a great disparity in the quality of German fighter pilots, who were either seasoned veterans, like Matoni, or new replacement pilots with comparatively little experience of either flying or fighting. In the autumn of 1944, Matoni succeeded *Hauptmann* Erich Hohagen as *Gruppenkommandeur* of I/JG 1, but on 5 December he was so badly injured in a crash that his flying days were brought to a close. He survived the war, however, after which the German contacted Johnnie, expressing regret at having been unable to accept the 'challenge'. Typically, Johnnie immediately invited his former adversary to dinner, although they were not to actually meet until 8 May 1985. On that day, the fiftieth anniversary of the war's end in Europe, Herr Matoni was a guest at the Thames Television programme *This Is Your Life*, celebrating the life and times of Air Vice-Marshal Johnnie Johnson.

17 June 1944, was a special day for Johnnie personally as he was awarded a second bar to his DSO. There could be no greater recognition or confirmation of his inspirational leadership abilities. This is the only time in history that one individual has been awarded three DSOs. The citation, published in the London Gazette on 4 July 1944, read:

> Since being awarded a Bar to the DSO, this officer has lead large formations of aircraft in many and varied sorties. During these operations thirty-four enemy aircraft have been destroyed, several of them by Wing Commander Johnson. He is a magnificent leader, whose unsurpassed skill and personal courage has inspired all.

Wing Commander Johnson has destroyed at least 28 hostile aircraft.

News was also received that 443 Squadron's Flight Lieutenant F. A. W. J. Wilson had also been decorated, with a DFC, so 144 Wing had much to celebrate that night.

Leadership manifests itself in many ways; Johnnie:

By this time we were also getting pretty fed up with our monotonous rations, so I contacted Arthur King, landlord of the Unicorn in Chichester, who arranged for fresh vegetables, bread, and even lobsters, to be flown out to us in a communications aircraft from Tangmere. Funny thing was that he later got a bollocking from Customs & Excise who told him that he needed an export licence! How fucking ridiculous! We also had Spitfires adapted to carry beer kegs instead of bombs, so we ended up being pretty well catered for!

Bad weather, however, had restricted flying for some days. It broke on 22 June, on which day massive air strikes preceded the American assault on Cherbourg. Montgomery's advance from the Eastern Assault Area was now bogged down in the *bocage*, where fighting was incredibly fierce. Using cheap, mass-produced anti-tank weapons like the one-shot, disposable *Panzerfaust* and the bazooka-like *Panzershreck*, the German infantry was fighting skilfully against the Shermans, Churchills and Cromwells. By noon the sun was shining. 442 Squadron was brought to readiness at 1300 hours, and 30 minutes later Johnnie, the Squadron CO, and a flight commander replaced three pilots scheduled to fly when information from Kenway 'looked interesting'. 441 and 442 Squadrons were scrambled at 1409 hours, Johnnie leading, but three pilots soon returned to base, one only able to get two pounds of boost, the others with R/T failure. Greycap, however, was leading his Spitfires into their biggest scrap over Normandy so far. South of Caen, at 1400 hours, III/JG 26, on a *Geschwader*-strength sweep, had engaged a similar number of P-47s from the American 365 Fighter Group. As the aerial melee progressed southwards, a 368 Fighter Group P-47 unit also engaged, as did enemy fighters from both JG 2 and further elements of JG 26. Soon 144 Wing joined the fray. Johnnie:

North of Argentan at 6,000 feet, Yellow Three (Squadron Leader Russell) reported eight E/A on the deck, flying South. We turned in and after a four minute stern chase E/A broke into the attack. I attacked an Me 109 from port quarter, climbing steeply, ASI 120 mph, angle off 30°. Many strikes were seen in the belly of the E/A and beneath cockpit. E/A commenced burning and went straight into ground about seven miles West of Argentan. Cine gun used.

For no loss, six enemy fighters had been destroyed by 144 Wing. In total, the enemy lost twenty fighters against four Allied machines, all of which were P-47s. Interestingly, among the German casualties was the *Kommandeur* of III/JG 2, Major Josef 'Sepp' Wurmheller, a 102-victory *Experte* and holder of the *Ritterkreuz mit Eichenlaub* (Knight's Cross with Oak Leaves), who collided with his wingman. Missing out on this combat, however, 443 Squadron was engaged on a dive-bombing attack against a suspected ammunition dump in the Bois de Homme, near Gaumont. Several hits were recorded but no large explosions resulted. At 1700 hours 442 Squadron was scrambled again but was unable to find the German convoy it sought. At 2155 hours the Squadron was again up, seeking ground targets. Flak was heavy and Flight Lieutenant Trott's Spitfire was holed. In response he 'destroyed an oil truck and strafed sundry MTs' (443 Squadron ORB). 22 June was actually extremely significant, as on that day the Red Army opened its summer offensive in the east. Along a 300-mile front 146 infantry divisions and 43 armoured brigades attacked Hitler's Army Group Centre. Nazi Germany was now simultaneously engaged in pivotal defensive campaigns against both the Western Allies and the Soviets. The Russian Front was a staggering 1,500 miles long, so the *Luftwaffe* had to divide its attention between there, the Mediterranean, Normandy, and the defence of Germany itself. Fighters were sent east in droves, from Italy and even Normandy.

At 2110 hours the next evening, 442 and 443 Squadrons swept over the Alençon area, led by Greycap. 443 Squadron was soon engaged. Squadron Leader H. J. 'Wally' McLeod:

I was leading Mushroom Blue Section, following Red Section, led by W/C. W/C spotted five E/A below, heading East. He went

down to attack. Blue Section came down behind and on port side
W/C went above cloud. I was to chase them above. Port 3 E/A
broke port and up through cloud. I followed up through, fired at
seventy-five yards at a FW 190. Strikes observed. He went down
through cloud. I followed, firing another short burst. Port wing
came off, aircraft crashed half a mile north of Alençon. This was
observed by W/C. Next observed 190 below cloud, I followed,
a/c rolled on back and went straight in, a quarter mile from first
190. This observed by F/L Prest. Cine camera used, 52 rounds of
cannon, no machine guns used. I claim two FW 190s destroyed.

Some confusion, however, arises from the written record in respect
of how many rounds Squadron Leader McLeod actually fired. The
443 Squadron ORB clearly states that 'the CO used only twenty-six
rounds of 20mm ammunition in the entire engagement', this being
confirmed by Johnnie in *Wing Leader*. McLeod's combat report,
though, is interesting because the number '26' has been crossed out,
apparently in the pilot's hand, and overwritten with '52'. So, did
Wally McLeod use 13 or 26 rounds per cannon? Each gun carried
120 rounds, so whichever is correct this was clearly an example of
superb marksmanship – one Johnnie believed was never equalled.

The *Jagdwaffe* was now most active over the Normandy combat
zone, and the 2nd TAF's aim was to engage the enemy as far
southwards as possible. The *Luftwaffe* formations were small and
flexible, dictating that wings of thirty-six, or even twenty-four,
Spitfires were no longer appropriate. Such formations would have
been conspicuous and unwieldy in the fast cut and thrust of the
engagements in progress. Wing's therefore adopted the operating
procedure of using single squadrons, or even flights and sometimes
sections, on both sweeps and scrambles. To some degree this made
the traditional and intended role of Wing Commander (Flying)
obsolete. Johnnie:

Yes, I suppose that is true, the time had passed for 'Balbos'. But
the Wing Leader remained the focal point who decided tactics,
etc. Instead of leading an entire wing, I would instead fly with a
squadron, and, so as to remain familiar with each unit, and they
with me, I rotated which one I flew with.

The Germans flew in smaller formations for very sound reasons: firstly to reduce the number of aircraft operating from and concentrated at any one airfield, and secondly because the greater speeds and altitudes of their latest fighters dictated wider turning circles and therefore less manoeuvrability. Large formations were still used against the American daylight bombers but the close and swift skirmishes over Normandy made it impossible for a leader to handle any more than a dozen fighters. Also, these low-flying and small German formations often escaped radar detection, but their radio discipline was sometimes so poor that they were heard by Allied listening people, who reported where the enemy could be found. Because the German fighters were so outnumbered and outclassed, they tried to strafe and bomb the beachhead by night but, as the Germans were unable to wait for the benefits brought to night operations of a full moon, they were to find that this kind of combat flying requires great skill, experience and much training. So this tactic was unsuccessful and again German casualties were high.

On 24 June, Johnnie and other 144 Wing officers attended a meeting at 83 Group HQ, where the Wing's commitments over the next few days were outlined. In essence these revolved around Operation EPSOM, a determined attempt to envelop Caen by the entire British VIII Corps, which would do battle along a 4-mile front, stretching from Carpiquet and Rauray, towards the river Odon. The German defenders, however, now included not only the 12th SS *Panzer* Division *Hitler Jugend* and 21st *Panzer* Division, but also 1st SS *Panzer* Division *Leibstandarte*, 2nd SS *Panzer* Division *Das Reich*, 9th SS *Panzer* Division *Hohenstaufen*, 10th SS *Panzer* Division *Frundsberg*, and *Panzer Lehr*. By this time the dreaded Tiger had also made its presence felt on the battlefield, and Allied units could expect to pitch three or four Shermans against just one of these heavily armoured tanks. Opposed by well-armed and highly motivated SS units, Operation EPSOM was always destined to be a bloody battle for VIII Corps. 144 Wing was briefed to the effect that the airfield would host a fourth squadron for Operation EPSOM, this to be serviced by 3207 SC and all squadrons would be flying at least four sorties a day. As recorded in the 144 Wing ORB, 'clearly someone is going to catch hell'. Operation EPSOM, Montgomery's third attempt to seize Caen, was scheduled to start on 26 June.

In advance of Montgomery's troops leaving their start line, a barrage started on the evening of 25 June, lasting all night and continuing into the morning. Unfortunately for Montgomery, the weather was unsettled, limiting air operations. All day long aircraft were coming and going from St-Croix, whether Spitfires of ADGB squadrons landing to refuel after beachhead patrols, or 144 Wing fighter-bombers on operations. Johnnie first flew with 441 Squadron on an 'armed recco' of Argentan, the Spitfires attacking a convoy of German transports, leaving two in flames, three smoking and six more damaged. Greycap then flew a similar sortie with 442 Squadron, resulting in 'two flamers, three smokers' (442 Squadron ORB). Worsening weather, however, was preventing ADGB squadrons from crossing the Channel, and so the 2nd TAF also had to provide beachhead patrols. Heavy rain throughout the afternoon saw both the perimeter track and runways in such a poor state that St-Croix's Airfield Commanding Officer had no option but to declare the airfield as unserviceable. This intervention by the weather, preventing the 'Meat Flies' from wreaking havoc on their enemies, did not bode well for Operation EPSOM.

Fortunately by 0900 hours on 27 June the weather had cleared sufficiently for operations to resume from St-Croix. On patrol east of Falaise, 441 Squadron, led by Johnnie, sighted seven FW 190s at 9,000 feet but were unable to close the gap. By 28 June the weather had improved further still, thus increasing the chances of aerial combat, for which Johnnie and his pilots remained eager. On the ground, though, VIII Corps was paying a high price for every metre of ground. A substantial German counter-attack had been stopped by 11th Armoured Division the previous day, and British tanks continued forward across the river Odon, subsequently engaging the enemy in a truly bitter struggle for the crucial high ground of Hill 112. Naturally the *Luftwaffe* concentrated on Montgomery's new offensive, but suffered heavy losses in the process: 2nd TAF fighters claimed twenty-five Me 109s and FW 190s destroyed that day – every single one by Canadians. At 1106 hours, Greycap led 442 Squadron off from St-Croix towards Caen. Johnnie:

> I was leading 442 Squadron on an armed recco when informed that bandits were SW of Caen. I gained height and saw seven Me 109s at 14,000 feet, flying east, ourselves being at 15,000 feet. E/A

were flying in a four a/c line astern and a three aircraft line astern, all carrying a single bomb. I instructed Green Section to attack the three E/A and myself led Yellow Section into the four E/A. I was about to open fire on 'tail-end Charlie' when I saw strikes all over him and he went down in flames (F/O Robillard DFM). I took number three and opened fire from 300 yards, 15° off, climbing. E/A commenced to smoke and then burn. He went down and crashed SW of Caen, seen by my Number Two, Flight Lieutenant Marriott. I then followed another E/A down to ground level, firing short bursts from 400 yards as I could not close. At ground level I closed to 300 yards and gave him another burst. I saw one single strike on the cockpit and E/A crashed into the ground, SE of Caen. I claim two Me 109s destroyed, cine gun used.

It was great shooting – yet again. At noon Johnnie was up with 441 Squadron on another armed recco. Eight German trucks were destroyed or damaged, three of them left in flames, but no enemy aircraft were seen. By the end of the day, however, 144 Wing had scored many victories – for no loss – and the other 2nd TAF casualties amounted to just six Spitfires against the twenty-five German fighters claimed destroyed.

On the ground, though, XXX Corps had lost Bretteville to the 2nd SS *Panzer* Division *Das Reich*, and VIII Corps had found the German defences across the Odon so formidable that by nightfall the Allied armour had been forced back into the bridgehead. The weather was poor again on 29 June, making the German fighters difficult to find and engage. Throughout the day, all of 144 Wing's squadrons prowled over the Thury Harcourt and Falaise area, battering enemy vehicles. In their wake, after every sortie, German armour and transport was left blazing and smoking. SS *Obergruppenführer* Paul 'Papa' Hausser, commander of the II SS *Panzer Korps*, flung both 9th and 10th SS *Panzer* Divisions, *Hohenstaufen* and *Frundsberg*, at the British, pushing 11th Armoured Division back across the Odon. The *Hitler Jugend* still fought on determinedly and showed no signs of giving up Caen. After just three days Operation EPSOM had failed.

By 30 June, the changeable weather had settled but, still being cloudy, remained far from perfect. This day, however, would see the *Luftwaffe*'s greatest effort to date over Normandy: V *Jagddivision* dispatched eight individual missions, each being a combined effort by up to twelve *Jagdgruppen*. In total the *Jagdflieger* would make over 500 sorties. There was much action. Johnnie:

> I was leading a flight of 441 Squadron on a front line patrol (1250 hours), when Control informed me that bandits were about, South of Caen. When in the Gace area I saw a general dog-fight well underway at 4,000–5,000 feet. There was a thin layer of cloud at 4,000 feet and E/A were avoiding combat by diving in and pulling out well beyond the combat area. I saw a 109 at nine 'o' clock, some 1,000 feet below and so I turned steeply into attack. I opened fire from 300 yards, angle off 40°. E/A flew through my area of fire and as I broke away I saw him going down, pouring black smoke. E/A crashed in a field and I claim one Me 109 destroyed – confirmed by my Number Two, Flight Lieutenant Draper.

Squadron Leader Browne destroyed a 190, Flight Lieutenant Mott a 109, while Flight Lieutenant Johnstone destroyed a 109 and damaged another. 442 Squadron were also in action, destroying three 109s and thereby becoming 144 Wing's top-scoring squadron.

That night there was plenty to celebrate. 442 Squadron's CO, Squadron Leader Russell, invited the Squadron's officers to his tent where he complimented the pilots, being particularly pleased that the kills were spread among so many pilots. The Wing Leader then played host in the Officers' Mess to another thrash – this because the kill he made that day was Johnnie's thirty-third, meaning that he was now the RAF's top-scoring fighter pilot. In achieving this status he had exceeded the score of none other than Group Captain Adolph Gysbert Malan, the Sailor himself. Johnnie:

> Within an hour or so of me landing the news had spread and a clutch of press and radio correspondents arrived on the scene. Of course they made a big thing of it all and just couldn't seem to grasp what I was so anxious they should, that Malan had fought when the odds were enormously stacked against him. Sailor had fought a defensive battle over southern England when the 109s enjoyed the tactical advantages of height and sun. He had continued the fight until rested in 1941, and his massive

experience was then used for the benefit of others. I, on the other hand, had done comparatively little or nothing of this kind of defensive fighting as I had always flown offensively. After 1941 I had a squadron, wing or even two wings behind me. Unlike Sailor, I had, therefore, the opportunity to choose when to strike, to stalk and kill our opponents. The only real disadvantage I had to contend with was invariably operating over enemy territory, meaning that a single bullet in a vulnerable part of the Spitfire could mean, at best, a prison camp.

Nonetheless, Johnnie's story and picture were soon splashed across the pages of newspapers throughout the free world. He had by now become, in fact, a household name.

Johnnie's logbook concludes the historic month of June 1944 with some interesting figures:

Operational hours for June 1944:	47.45
Total operational hours this tour:	95.05
E/A destroyed this tour:	8 ½

The last day of June had also seen another development when 250 Allied heavy bombers, escorted by eight squadrons of Spitfires, dropped 176 tons of high explosive on the town of Villers-Bocage. Afterwards the town resembled little more than a pile of rubble within which could be found the carcasses of wrecked German Tigers. The raid was actually an experiment, the prelude to the still controversial bombing of Caen. By now, however, with Cherbourg in American hands, political pressure was increasing on Montgomery to end the perceived stalemate in the east, capture Caen and break out of Normandy.

11

Normandy:
Top-Scoring Fighter Wing

1 July dawned fair and 144 Wing's morale was further uplifted by the delivery of thirty-five most welcome bags of mail. Johnnie visited 128 Airfield and lectured Mustang pilots on tactics against FW 190s, while his friend, the American Dan Browne, packed up his kit and started the long journey back to New Jersey and a well-earned rest. On 2 July, after several uneventful patrols by 144 Wing's squadrons, shortly after noon 441 Squadron took off, in sections of four, to patrol the Eastern, Western and Easy Areas of the beachhead. Battle was joined at 1310 hours, 3 miles west of Lisieux. Five 109s were destroyed. At 1245 hours, Johnnie led twelve Spitfires of 442 Squadron over Caen, diving on six Me 109s. One of the enemy fighters was already damaged from a previous combat and was destroyed by Flight Lieutenant Roseland. Flight Lieutenant Trott's tail plane was damaged by flak but the pilot returned safely to St-Croix. That same lunchtime, 443 Squadron was up on an armed recco of Villers-Bocage–Vire–Domfront–Flers–Caen. In the Spitfires' wake five enemy transports were left in flames, two more smoking. The day represented a familiar routine. At 1430 hours, Johnnie took the opportunity to review the statistics of June's fighting and share them with his pilots. Although 144 Wing was leading, and 442 Squadron ranked second of the new squadrons in respect of enemy aircraft destroyed, the Wing Leader nevertheless urged his men to 'smarten up their eyesight so that more opportunities would be afforded the Wing' (442 Squadron ORB).

Frustratingly poor weather once more slowed up the aerial offensive. According to the Wing ORB:

> As a result 144 has broken the static record. We have now been three weeks and one day in one place. The longest previous stop, prior to the formation stage, which was six weeks, was twenty-one days.

Slightly improved weather on 5 July saw 442 Squadron fly thirty-six uneventful patrols over the Eastern Assault Area. It would, however, transpire to be a red letter day for 144 Wing, and 441 Squadron in particular. Johnnie:

> Before D-Day, my squadron commanders and I had made a bet with our opposite numbers in 127 Wing that we would shoot down the most enemy aircraft between D-Day – D+30. With just one day to go, we only led by the rather narrow margin of one victory. So, on the wager's last day I was determined to increase our score. Flying with Tommy Brannagan and 441 Squadron, our first patrol was uneventful, but I later decided to take the Squadron on the prowl over Alençon, with 443 Squadron as top cover. That town was, we knew, the supply centre for Von Kluge's 7th *Armee* and was provided air cover by the *Luftwaffe*.

Greycap's hunch proved correct, and an exciting combat ensued:

> We sighted twelve (plus) FW 190s flying beneath cloud. I led the Squadron into attack and a general dogfight ensued. I got on the tail of a 190 which was hitting F/L Copeland's aircraft; opened fire from 250 yards, closing to 100 yards, climbing steeply, angle of 25°. Strikes were seen on cockpit and engine cowling and E/A burst into flames and crashed. At this time I saw another FW 190 spiral down and crash in the area SE of Alençon. I then chased another FW 190 at ground level and after a twenty mile chase at sixteen pounds boost I came within range (350 yards) and touched him on the fuselage with a few cannon shells. E/A broke to starboard and climbed steeply and I had no difficulty in getting on his tail. Then followed a series of aileron turns, half-rolls, dives and zooms, but my aircraft was superior in every respect and I continued to get in the occasional burst. I saw several strikes in the cockpit and E/A went straight in from 4,000 feet.

Flight Lieutenant Roseland, recently arrived in Normandy having previously served as a flying instructor, was a lucky man: when Johnnie hacked down the 190 on his tail, Roseland's left aileron had already been completely shot away. Needless to say, the Wing Leader was not slow in suggesting that he might be owed a drink for the favour! The 190s involved belonged to I/JG 11, and in addition to the two enemy fighters destroyed by Johnnie, other 441 Squadron pilots were also successful. For the loss of one Spitfire, 441 Squadron destroyed eight enemy fighters and damaged four more. 442 Squadron, however, was denied an afternoon victory when a quartet of Spitfires chased but lost an Me 109 in cloud. Johnnie:

> Fortunately 127 Wing had not enjoyed such success that day, the last of our wager, and so immediately we were released I was on the phone, suggesting that they should attend our Mess without delay, bringing our booty, which included a case of champagne. The invitation was accepted and we all celebrated our win with a tremendous party.

Once again, the press pounced on the news, with much being naturally being made in Canada of the fact that 144 Wing was the top-scoring formation in Normandy. Unfortunately celebrations at St-Croix were dampened by sobering news delivered by Group Captain Bill MacBrien: 144 Wing was soon to be disbanded. The existing organisation meant that the Group Captain was responsible for three Canadian Spitfire wings, but given the changing nature of aerial warfare such a formation had proved too cumbersome in practice. Instead, it had been decided that a group captain would be responsible for one wing of three or four squadrons, with a wing commander as operational leader. 144 Wing was the junior formation and therefore had to go. 441 Squadron was to join the RAF 125 Wing, 442 the RCAF 126, and 443 the RCAF 127. Johnnie was to go with 443 and join 127 Wing, which he had previously led in England. Johnnie:

> We of 144 Wing received this news in stunned silence, for although we had not served together a very long time we had fought some exciting battles and had achieved a fine *espirit de corps*. We had started from scratch in March and yet had destroyed more enemy aircraft than the longer established 127 Wing. Nevertheless, the decision, we could see, was sound and made sense.

On the evening of 7 July, the controversial attack by 450 'heavies' of RAF Bomber Command was unleashed against Caen, ground forces having failed to take the essential city. Personnel at St-Croix were among hundreds of thousands of Allied personnel who watched this bombardment in absolute awe. Johnnie:

> Yes, that certainly was an impressive sight, the bombing took place between 3,000–8,000 feet, by Lancasters and Halifaxes, and we could see both the in and outgoing processions quite clearly. We had been called upon to cover the bomber stream, but in the event the *Luftwaffe* failed to react and so we were not required. Positioning my Spitfire to the west of Caen I was able to watch the attack from down-sun. We had been briefed that the targets were all within an area two miles long and a mile deep, but it was clear that many bombs had fallen outside this box. The destruction being wrought on this French city was terrible. We all knew that Caen had to be taken before Montgomery could break out into the open countryside beyond, but couldn't help but wonder whether this objective could only be achieved by what was, essentially, the wholesale destruction of Caen and the death of a great number of its inhabitants. However, flying low on the fringe of the attack I distinctly saw a German tank thrown into the air, like a child's toy, turning over and over before it fell back to earth. After dropping its load, we saw one Lancaster dive on the enemy held territory south of the city, from which a great deal of flak could be expected. We assumed that the Lanc's controls had been hit, but suddenly the big bomber levelled out, flying just a few feet above the main Caen-Falaise road, strafing the buggers as it went! Unbelievable! We clearly saw German drivers and crews abandon their vehicles and take cover in the hedgerows. As this Lancaster eventually climbed away, another repeated the performance. I couldn't resist pulling up alongside the first bomber and giving the crew a cheery wave. Long afterwards I learned that the pilot was a former bricklayer from Scotland called Jock Straw, who won a DFC and bar, and later served as my Adjutant.

Although the inhabitants of Caen had been urged to leave their city for many weeks, some had stubbornly remained and some 400 paid the price with their lives. In an hour the French city had taken the same amount of bombs that were dropped on Hamburg, which had a population twenty times greater, in the infamous firestorm raids of

1943. Survivors still argue bitterly that Operation CHARNWOOD failed to achieve any military advantage, only serving to choke the streets with rubble and hinder the subsequent Allied advance. Once the bombers had finished their work late on that July evening, the artillery of VIII Corps opened fire on roads leading to Caen from the south and south-west, to prevent reinforcements reaching the beleaguered city. At 2300 hours, I Corps' artillery began shelling the villages of La Folie, St-Contest, St-Germain and Authie, this barrage continuing throughout the night. At 0420 hours on 8 July, supported by a huge barrage from the big guns, British and Canadian troops (59th and 3rd British Divisions, 3rd Canadian Division) crossed their start lines and advanced on Caen. The fighting over the next two days was often at the point of bayonet, as Caen was taken literally room by room.

On 8 July, ten 441 Squadron Spitfires were up early on a reconnaissance of the Caen, Thury Harcourt and Falaise areas. Three pilots returned early due to engine and R/T failure, the remainder sighting only scattered enemy vehicles, one of which was attacked and left smoking. The day started early for 442 Squadron, which was at dawn readiness and mounted patrols of four Spitfires from 0450 hours onwards. At 0750, Flight Lieutenant Dover led Flying Officer McDuff, and Pilot Officers Costello and Young up on a coastal patrol. Near the mouth of the Orne, the pilots saw five enemy midget submarines: one half a mile off Cabourg, three more three miles offshore, heading for Bernierville, and another six miles west of Le Havre. Four were subsequently sunk, only one survivor being seen. On the 0840 patrol, Flight Lieutenant Wright, and Pilot Officers Weeks, Burns and O'Sullivan caught more submarines, destroying one and damaging another. When attacked, the latter vessel rolled over slowly and sank. At 1130 hours yet another midget submarine was sighted by 442 Squadron, which orbited the target before making a dummy attack from bow to beam. The submarine did not dive but continued on course. When cannon fire raked the submarine from bow to beam, pieces of orange-coloured wood were subsequently seen in the resulting debris.

The following evening, the Allies announced that Caen was now in their possession. From the Spitfire pilots' perspective, the fall of Caen represented one less area of dangerous and concentrated flak. Johnnie:

We drove into Caen that day to see first-hand and at close-quarters the result of that massive aerial bombardment. The streets were so choked with rubble that we had difficulty in making progress, even in our jeep. Bulldozers were clearing the road, but eventually we had to stop and proceed on foot. Fires still blazed and French civilians were still searching the rubble for the missing. Those to whom we spoke assured us that few Germans were killed as there were no enemy positions in the bombed area. We had all seen the bomb damage to British cities, like London and Coventry, but that was insignificant when compared to the enormity of this destruction. We really did feel that the French had been made to suffer unnecessarily and the whole thing was really just too depressing for words. We cut short our visit and made our way to the nearby beach, where we lay in the sunshine and swam in the sea, hoping to forget those terrible scenes.

With Caen in Allied hands at last, however, the pressure on Montgomery to break out would not decrease but actually increase. The American press was becoming vociferous against him, Churchill was haunted by the spectre of a Great War-style stagnation, and Tedder divided his criticism between Monty and Leigh-Mallory. The concern was that unless the breakout was successfully achieved in the near future, the approaching winter would further slow or even halt the Allied advance, thus enabling the Germans to reinforce in depth. Montgomery, of course, appreciated all of this and was, in fact, preparing to launch his massive armoured offensive: Operation GOODWOOD. Even by the standards set in Normandy, the battle was poised to become bloodier still. Persistent poor weather, however, continued to restrict air operations on 10 July. At 0545 hours, however, Johnnie led 11 442 Squadron Spitfires on an armed recco of the front line. There was little or no enemy activity to report, but the Wing Leader's fuselage was hit by heavy flak. This caused great amusement back at St-Croix, as Johnnie had recently been quoted in the Canadian press as saying he was confident of having never been hit! In his logbook, he wrote, '*Hit by heavy flak in fuselage!!*' The sortie was actually Greycap's last with 144 Wing.

On 12 July, a beautiful day, Johnnie flew to Tangmere, enjoying some well-earned leave before taking on his new post with 127 Wing. Before leaving St-Croix, however, Johnnie typically drove around the airfield, thanking personnel from the various supporting sections for their contribution. Johnnie:

> All of these sections together put our Spitfires into the air, and without them we could not function. I always made sure that my pilots recognised this. It was a shame for the ground people because upon disbandment of 144 Wing they were being shipped back to England, and of course they wanted to stay with 2nd TAF, where the action was, and be a part of the great trek across North-West Europe. Understandably officers and airmen were all downcast and stood around the airfield in groups, waiting for our Spitfires to take off from St Croix for the last time. I tried to give them heart by emphasising that during our short time together we had participated in a tremendous historic enterprise and had shot down seventy-four enemy aircraft. Fourteen of our pilots had been lost, two of whom we knew were safe, so the scorecard was very much in our favour. When I climbed into the cockpit a crowd gathered to wish me luck. I was deeply touched by this spontaneous demonstration. Slowly I taxied onto the runway, opened the throttle and climbed above the haze into the clear sky. For once I was alone. After a slow turn I put the Spitfire into an easy dive across the airfield, seeing the blur of faces when I passed a few feet above their heads!

With an upward roll Johnnie saluted 144 Wing, and was gone.

12

Normandy:
Search & Destroy

127 Wing was located at airfield 'B2', near Crépon and Bazenville, and comprised 403, 416 & 421 Squadrons. On 14 July 1944, these units were joined by Squadron Leader McLeod's 443 Squadron (and 6443 Servicing Echelon) from 144 Wing. Greycap flew into B2 from Tangmere and spent the day settling in. Johnnie also had a long session with the Wing's Group Captain, 'Iron Bill' MacBrien, who expressed concern over a recent spate of flying accidents. Indeed, on 13 June, Johnnie's predecessor, Wing Commander Lloyd 'Chad' Chadburn, had been killed in a mid-air collision with one of his pilots. This loss was deeply felt by 127 Wing, as Chad was a highly popular and respected leader. Then, on 25 June, two 421 Squadron Spitfires, scrambling from opposite ends of the runway, collided and one pilot was killed; the other was seriously injured. The losses of such experienced pilots in flying accidents such as these was clearly unacceptable, and Wing Commander Johnson was tasked with paying particular attention to flying discipline.

16 July saw 403 Squadron destroy seven enemy aircraft, but Greycap missed out on the party, having flown patrols with both 416 and 443 Squadrons, neither of which engaged in aerial combat. That evening, however, Johnnie called all 127 Wing pilots together in the Intelligence Section and gave a lecture on flying tactics and routine. Again, poor weather had reduced air activity for some days, but 17 July was at last fine. Indeed, 127 Wing completed ninety-nine sorties that day. 421 Squadron was the first successful unit and damaged four enemy transports. At 1100 hours, Squadron Leader McLeod called 443 Squadron together to 'determine why this squadron was not destroying enemy aircraft at the same rate or more than other Spitfire squadrons' (443 Squadron ORB). The outcome of that discussion is unknown. At 1600 hours, Johnnie led 403 Squadron up to dive-bomb a railway bridge at Sourdeval. One direct hit was scored on the railway and four near misses on the bridge. After the

attack, Flight Lieutenant Lorne Commerford was lagging slightly behind the Squadron when he was attacked by a lone Me 109 that pounced out of the sun. Commerford was wounded and his Spitfire damaged, although he managed to nurse his crippled mount back to B2. Hospitalised, the Canadian never flew again and his aircraft was considered a write-off. The German pilot believed responsible for having executed the perfect diving pass was Major Klaus Meitusch, *Kommandeur* of III/JG 26. Prior to shooting down the Canadian, III/JG 26 had been in action with other Spitfires and lost four pilots. Some 20 minutes after wounding Commerford, while flying back to Villacoublay, Meitusch was himself shot down, ironically by a Canadian Spitfire of 411 Squadron (126 Wing). The German was wounded but survived the experience, to which he was no stranger: in 452 combat missions he was shot down no less than ten times; with seventy-two victories, he was finally killed by Mustangs in September 1944.

The Allies still needed to expand the beachhead due to cramped conditions and, so far as the Air Marshals were concerned, seize the airfields beyond Caen. On 10 July, Montgomery had outlined his plan for the long-awaited breakout. General Bradley's American divisions would batter their way towards Avranches in Operation COBRA, before dividing to drive westwards into Brittany, and therefore secure the important ports on the Biscay coast, and eastwards towards Le Mans and Alençon to link up with the British and Canadians. Before COBRA, Montgomery was to launch Operation GOODWOOD in the east, the intention being to tie down the German *Panzer* divisions there and thus enable the Americans to make rapid and substantial progress. Lieutenant General Sir Miles Dempsey of the British 2nd Army hoped that in addition to deflecting the *Panzers* away from Bradley's thrust, significant ground would also be gained by GOODWOOD; indeed, he ordered Lieutenant General Sir Richard O'Connor's 8 Corps to drive an armoured division to Falaise. Although Montgomery was more cautious, he admitted to Sir Alan Brooke, Chief of the Imperial General Staff (CIGS), that he had decided that 'the time has come to have a real showdown and to loose three armoured divisions into the open country about the Caen-Falaise road'.

It must be understood that by this time, the Americans had suffered some 37,034 casualties in Normandy, the British 24,698.

The British, however, had been engaged in the global conflict since 1939, and were therefore unable to make good these losses, unlike the Americans, who still had a further nine divisions awaiting embarkation in England. Although the British were short of manpower, Montgomery had some 2,250 medium and 400 light tanks at his disposal. It was therefore decide to plan GOODWOOD with that surplus of tanks in mind, air power beating the way for this awesome array of armour that would advance into the open countryside east of Caen. Although the British possessed sufficient artillery pieces in Normandy, ammunition was in short supply – hence, therefore, the decision to again use heavy bombers in a tactical role. The open countryside between Caen and Falaise was bordered on the west by the Rivers Orne and Laize, and on the east by the River Dives. On the west was the River Orne and its canal, and the industrial area of Colombelles. To the east was the ridge at Bourguébus, occupied by the Germans and from where they could observe the British start line. The high ground was defended by *Kampfgruppe von Luck*, commanded by *Oberst* Hans von Luck. With Tiger tanks, *Panzer* Mk IVs, anti-tank and assault guns, *Nebelwerfer* rocket launchers, infantry and grenadiers, the new commander of *Panzergruppe* West, General Heinrich Eberbach, had cleverly deployed 1st SS *Panzer Korps* and LXXXVI *Korps* in four defensive belts some 9 miles deep – the strongest defensive line so far prepared in Normandy (with a reserve of 60–80 *Panzers* as a mobile reserve). The British expected half that, and moreover German intelligence had predicted a decisive attack from Caen, to the southeast, 'about the night of 17–18 July'.

At 0530 hours on 18 July, in fact, RAF Bomber Command opened another awesome attack on German ground troops. The first wave of bombers dropped a staggering 6,000 1,000-ton bombs and 9,600 500-pounders. By 0700 hours, when the medium bombers of the 8th and 9th US Air Forces attacked, the battlefield was so obscured with smoke, flame and dust that many aircraft were unable to locate and bomb their targets. At 0830 hours, however, the Americans dropped 13,000 100-pound and 76,000 20-pound fragmentation bombs on Bourguébus Ridge. Tiger tanks were hurled into the air and men were driven so mad that many actually committed suicide.

Immediately after this cataclysmic bombardment, the artillery of three entire corps, supplemented by naval fire, loosed approaching

250,000 rounds at the target area. Incredibly, however, this massive barrage failed to destroy all of the German defences covering the British approach from the Orne: the artillery behind Bourguébus remained intact, as did four *Luftwaffe* flak 88s in Cagny. Not surprisingly, as in Caen, the bombing had once more so cratered the battlefield as to impede the Allied advance, and a thick cloud of dust hung over the battlefield, reducing visibility. With only six crossings over the Orne, there was great congestion, this being compounded by the necessity to guide the advancing armour through narrow, safe strips in 'friendly' minefields. The ground attack, however, was launched at 0730 hours by elements of the 11th Armoured Division. At first the Cromwells and Shermans advanced rapidly, everything apparently going to plan, but then, at 1100 hours near Cagny, the initial rush subsided. While checking the damage to his forward positions, Von Luck had happened upon the four *Luftwaffe* flak guns in Cagny, pressing them, at gunpoint, into the anti-tank role. The 88s fired continuously, their salvos parting the corn, and quickly accounted for sixteen tanks of the 2nd Fife and Forfar Yeomanry. Moreover, this delayed the advance of the Guards Armoured Division. With the advance bogged down, a request by the 2nd Army for a further heavy bombing mission that day was rejected, it just not being possible to mount such an operation at such short notice. In the early afternoon, SS *Panzers* engaged 29th Armoured Brigade and began the greatest tank battle of the entire Normandy campaign that pitted outnumbered but superior Tigers and Panthers against Shermans, the so-called 'Ronson' or 'Tommy Cooker', and Cromwells. Fortunately the British tanks were heavily supported by rocket-firing Typhoons, without which their losses would have been even higher.

Naturally, 2nd TAF fighter-bombers were also engaged. 127 Wing carried out twenty-four operational flights on 18 July, although sadly on 421 Squadron's first sortie Flight Lieutenant P. G. Johnson DFC, commander of 'A' Flight, was killed while attacking ground targets; his Spitfire was so low that it hit a tree, crashing and killing the 24-year-old pilot instantly. 403 Squadron flew five missions, all over the front line, dismissively described by the ORB as 'just the good old milk round'. The diary mentioned, however, that 'Those Lancasters which came over to pound Jerry really made a job of it.' Two 416 Squadron aircraft, however, were forced to return early from a patrol having mistakenly been fired upon by the RN. Johnnie flew two front-line patrols with 443 Squadron, the ORB interestingly recording that 'Squadron busily engaged today in support operations to a big army push in the Caen area designed to carry the Allies through to Paris.' That document goes on to say that 'Intelligence reports indicate that the "big push" southeast of Caen is preceding very satisfactorily and ahead of schedule this evening.' That, however, was not so, the confusion having no doubt arisen due to Montgomery's over-optimistic signals sent that day and likewise bad handling of a press conference.

The weather was poor once more, however, this not assisting the 2nd Army in Operation GOODWOOD, still being bitterly contested on the ground. On 20 July, 403 Squadron was given the day off, spending the day getting cleaned up and writing letters, but all 127 Wing pilots attended a 'Gen Session' at 1030 hours, held by the Wing Leader. At 1245 hours, Johnnie led 421 Squadron on an armed recco of the Vire–Argentan area. Greycap damaged an FW 190, which escaped in cloud, but the trip was otherwise uneventful. A combination of factors, including the inclement flying weather, dictated that Operation GOODWOOD was called off that evening. The villages of Cagny, Bourguébus, Bras and Hubert-Folie had been taken by the British, but at a heavy cost: VIII Corps lost over 400 tanks and 2,000 men. In total the 2nd Army had lost 6,000 men, many of them scarce infantrymen. At most the ground gained amounted to 7 miles, and so Dempsey's hope of taking Falaise was dashed. The Supreme Commander, General Eisenhower, was allegedly as 'blue as indigo' over what was considered a lost opportunity. Ike raved that it had taken 7,000 tons of bombs to advance as many miles, and the Allies could just not afford a thousand bombs a mile! That afternoon, Eisenhower and Montgomery met privately at 21st Army Group Headquarters. No record of their conversation has ever been made public. The Air Chiefs were equally furious, if not more so, accusing Montgomery of promising results but then failing to deliver. Johnnie:

> Before leaving the desert, Broady had acquired a captured Fieseler *Storch*, which he used as a personal communications aircraft, which he brought to Normandy. Painted bright yellow and with prominent RAF roundels, the *Storch* was often seen carrying a

VIP passenger in the back seat and observing major attacks. On this particular day all we were told was that Broady was coming in with a VIP and that the Wing was to put up a screen of Spitfires. The *Storch* duly appeared skimming along over the treetops and as it landed and rolled to a stop we were delighted to see that the VIP passenger was none other than the Prime Minister, complete with cigar. And so it was that, on 21 July, we had the rare privilege of meeting Mr Churchill and hearing an impromptu speech on the progress of the war to date.

127 Wing ORB:

The Prime Minister (PM) of Great Britain, the Rt Hon Winston Spencer Churchill, arrived here by air at 1530 hours. The whole Wing gathered en masse at the western end of the runway. The PM stepped out of the AOC's aircraft, followed by the AOC, and was met by Group Captain MacBrien. The Wing Commander Ops and Squadron Commanders were then introduced to the PM. Immediately afterwards the PM moved over towards the assembled Wing. At a gesture from him the PM was immediately surrounded and he climbed onto a dais which had been placed in the centre of the large body of airmen. The PM spoke to those assembled for approximately ten minutes. His speech, and even more his presence, was the cause of great excitement for the Wing. Few persons had previously seen the PM and it was a big day in their lives. The PM thanked the Wing for the splendid work it had done and emphasised the continual need for co-operation between the various services. He mentioned the disruption in Germany and in his amicable style this created considerable laughter. He again emphasised our war aims which amounted solely to the defeat of our enemies and stressed that we had no territorial or other ambitions. With peace we wanted to keep our Empire and run our Empire without anybody else's interference. The Group Captain called for three cheers which were given vociferously by the hundreds of airmen present. Immediately afterwards the PM climbed back into the AOC's aircraft and they took off to visit another Wing. At 1830 hours the PM reappeared, with him this time was Major-General Hastings Ismay, his Military Advisor, and other members of the PM's party. A Dakota aircraft of Transport

Command was waiting to fly the PM back to the UK. The PM
said goodbye to the AOC and Group Captain and climbed on
board and the aircraft took off. The PM was escorted to the UK
by aircraft of 421 Squadron. During the day operations were
uneventful, though two aircraft of 403 Squadron were hit by *flak*
ten miles North of Argentan. Both aircraft returned safely to base
and were categorized Cat 'B'. In all the Squadrons took part in
sixteen shows during daylight.

25 July saw the launch of what would become the greatest American
military achievement in Normandy: Operation COBRA, General
Bradley's long-awaited breakout of the deadly *bocage* country,
south to Avranches. For weeks Bradley's First Army had been
fighting to extricate itself from the hedgerows, countryside entirely
suited to defence, but it was now that Montgomery's strategy paid
off: there can be no doubt that the American success was due in no
small part to the fact that most of Von Kluge's forces were already
engaged with the British and Canadians in the east. The fifteen
American divisions committed to COBRA faced eleven seriously
depleted German divisions, only two of which were armoured,
while the fourteen British and Canadian divisions still engaged
the same number of enemy divisions, six of them armoured. The
objective of COBRA was to turn eastwards once the breakthrough
had been achieved, thus enveloping half a dozen German divisions.
Usually, the Americans preferred to attack along a broad front, but
this time, as suggested by Montgomery, the attack concentrated
upon a front just 7,000 yards wide, yet again preceded by a huge
aerial bombardment, this time by 1,800 American heavies. Fighter-
bombers would then pulverise enemy defences across a section of
battlefield 250 yards wide, immediately south of the St-Lô–Périers
road. The attack would be supported by 1,000 artillery pieces.

The start of Operation COBRA had been delayed by the bad
weather which contributed towards the premature cessation of
GOODWOOD. It had, in fact, been decided to unleash COBRA
on 24 July, but worsening weather meant that General Spaatz's
bombers had to be recalled. Some pressed on, however, and bombed
through cloud, sadly killing many American soldiers and indicating
to the Germans that the breakout was starting. When the attack
proper started at 0700 hours on 25 July, more erratic bombing by

the Eighth Air Force led to the deaths of 111 American soldiers, including Lieutenant General Lesley McNair. VII Corps nevertheless pushed forward, only to discover, as had the British and Canadians in the wake of the GOODWOOD aerial bombardment, that the *Panzer Lehr* Division remained an effective fighting force. In contrast to Von Luck's impressive defence in depth on Bourgébus Ridge, however, COBRA was faced by a crust, which could, and would, be bypassed and outflanked. In the east, the 2nd Canadian Corps again attacked towards Bourgébus, but 9th SS *Hohenstaufen Panzer* Division successfully repelled this new assault.

The launch of COBRA dictated a busy day for 2nd TAF, which not only had to support the Canadian attack but also ensure that no enemy reinforcements travelled West. Such an undertaking by day would, given the Allied air supremacy, in any case have been suicidal for Von Kluge. As it was, 127 Wing flew a total of 27 missions (179 sorties) on 25 July, hammering enemy transports. Anxious to engage enemy fighters, however, Johnnie led 416 and 443 Squadrons on a sweep south-east of Paris. Although it was a long flight, lasting 2 hours and 40 minutes, there was no contact. Johnnie flew an armed recco the following day, with 421 Squadron, but that sortie was also uneventful.

On 30 July, all four 127 Wing Squadrons were actually airborne at 0730 hours, supporting 700 heavy bombers attacking Caumont. The Wing patrolled the Conde–Mezidon and St-Lô–Vire areas until all of the bombers had safely withdrawn. This operation was in support of the British Operation BLUECOAT, launched that day, VIII Corps' southwards thrust towards Vire and the 1,100-foot-high summit of Mont Pinçon. On their right advanced the US V Corps, in support of Operation COBRA, which was reaching a successful conclusion. That day, in fact, the Americans reached Avranches and made their crucial turn east. The British Second Army, however, still pushing slowly forward with heavy casualties continued to face an unbroken German line with far superior armoured strength and fire support than had opposed the Americans throughout COBRA. Whatever the cost, however, the drive was on for Falaise. At 1740 hours Johnnie led 403 and 416 Squadrons on an armed recce over the triangle bounded by Laigle, Mortain and Alençon, but yet again this proved uneventful. Johnnie:

Yes, it could be frustrating, you just couldn't predict when the Huns would be about, so it was again a matter of being in the right place at the right time. Sometimes we were, sometimes we weren't.

From a personal perspective, was the Wing Leader concerned that his own personal scoring had slowed down? Johnnie:

Not at all, and let us get this right. The Wing Leader's job is not, repeat not, to place himself in the prime position to get kills. It was not about that. The object was to lead the formation into the best possible position to attack. The pilot or pilots best placed to intercept would be despatched to do so; others would provide cover. That is the way it worked. It was not about personal scores but about knocking down as many Huns as possible. Obviously that effort could be broken down into statistics for groups, wings, squadrons, flights and sections until you come to the individual. So the individual's score obviously mattered but it was part of an overall effort. Do you see? That having been said, flying up front, it was often the leader who sighted the enemy first and therefore attacked with his Section, covered by those flying behind.

Johnnie concluded his logbook entries for July 1944 with another statistical summary:

Operational hours flown in July 1944:   19.00
Total operational hours this tour: 114.00
E/A destroyed this tour: 10½

Although fresh German infantrymen arrived in Normandy, Hitler had no intention of resting his hard-pressed *Panzer* divisions, from which he now demanded an armoured counter-attack. Isolated from the actual battlefield at his 'Wolf's Lair' at Rastenburg, Hitler decided that General Patton's thrust into Brittany actually presented an opportunity to defeat the Allies in Normandy; the Führer's plan was to assemble all available armour at Mortain and smash through the eastern flank of Patton's advance. Once the *Panzers* reached the sea at Avranches, Patton would be cut off. The crux of the matter was that if Patton succeeded in turning inland, the *Wehrmacht*'s fate in France would be sealed. To prevent this, Hitler had at his disposal six *Panzer* divisions, four of them SS, a total of some 400 tanks. That part of the plan was simple, and perhaps realistic, but Hitler also insisted that the German line from Avranches to St-Lô be restored, to prevent reinforcements reaching the Americans, who were already fast approaching Le Mans. Von Kluge knew instinctively that this was impossible as he had insufficient resources. As withdrawal and failure were forbidden, however, the hapless Von Kluge commenced the necessary preparations for Operation Liege. The German armoured thrust would be undertaken by the six *Panzer* divisions that now formed *Panzergruppe* Eberbach. To General Hans Eberbach's right flank, at Vire, would be 7th *Armee*, now commanded by SS-*Obergruppenführer* Paul 'Papa' Hausser. The Caen front would be held by SS-*Obergruppenführer* Sepp Dietrich's new 5th *Panzer Armee*.

So at the beginning of August 1944, while the British and Canadians continued to make slow progress against determined opposition in the east, and the Americans poured infantry and armour through the Avranches Gap, the Germans prepared the first substantial armoured counter-attack since D-Day. Incredibly it had taken Hitler seven weeks to do so, adding yet another bullet point to a long list of the *Führer*'s military errors. The first day of August 1944 dawned very hazy, visibility being so poor that 127 Wing carried out no flights until lunchtime. From mid-afternoon onwards 443 Squadron provided, on the hour and every hour, a section of Spitfires for beachhead patrol, but these sorties were uneventful. Meanwhile 416 Squadron made no sorties, so the pilots played cards, the 'sharks' of the Squadron, namely Flying Officers Bill Palmer and Ray St George, cleaning out novice bridge player Flight Lieutenant Pat Patterson! At 1800 hours, 403 Squadron were up on an armed recco in the Verey–Flers–Mortain area where a large enemy convoy was sighted and attacked; four lorries were set ablaze, four more and a staff car were damaged, and a motor cycle was destroyed. At this time, the opposing armies were closely engaged, as indicated by the 127 Wing ORB:

> Owing to the see-saw fighting, which at times left bomb line behind our forward troops, the Squadrons were unable to carry out all

the attacks they would have liked, in view of the great danger of hitting our own troops and transport, many of which were sighted having pushed through and in front of enemy troops.

On 3 August, Johnnie and Flight Lieutenant Hank Zary left B2 in their Spitfires, bound first for Tangmere and thence Squires Gate, near Blackpool. The purpose of their visit to England is unknown, but the pilots returned to Crépon the following day. Yet again the weather was poor, but on the evening of 6 August, Johnnie led 443 Squadron on a sweep south of Paris, searching for enemy fighters, but neither were they or even flak encountered. During that first week of August the enemy's efforts were entirely concentrated on preparing for the Mortain counter-attack. Hitler was in favour of allowing Patton to pour even more troops and armour through Avranches, so as to cut off the maximum number of Americans, but Von Kluge disagreed, instead believing that the attack should be launched without delay. The *Führer*, yet again, would not be moved, however, mistakenly believing that Operation LIEGE was blessed with total surprise. That, in fact, was not so, as since August 3rd ULTRA had been decoding German signals. The Allies therefore knew that a substantial counter-attack from Mortain was imminent, and even knew roughly when the operation would be launched. The American General Bradley, in fact, welcomed the German initiative as 'an opportunity that comes to a commander not more than once in a century'. 'Brad' had at his disposal powerful and confident divisions with which he expected to not only withstand but actually destroy Hausser's impoverished formations; the German spearhead committed at Mortain comprised merely seventy-five Mk IVs, seventy Panthers and thirty-two self-propelled guns. Although the *Leibstandarte* was held up due to an Allied aircraft crashing onto its lead tank, the 2nd SS *Panzer* Division *Das Reich* swept through Mortain but was then held by the US 30th Infantry Division, which was dug in on the high ground beyond the town. Once the early morning mist cleared, the Allied fighter-bombers were up over the battlefield in swarms; General von Lüttwitz, commander of the 2nd *Panzer* Division later wrote that 'The planes came down in hundreds, firing their rockets at the concentrated tanks and vehicles. We could do nothing against them and could make no further progress.'

In the Caen sector, *Obergruppenführer* Dietrich's concern – that it had been foolhardy to withdraw the majority of German armour to participate in the thrust towards Avranches and contain the newly won British bridgehead across the River Orne near Thury Harcourt – was being realised. There was nothing left to protect this vital hinge of the German position other than an inexperienced infantry division fresh from Norway as well as the remnants of Meyer's *Hitler Jugend*, which had just forty *Panzers* left out of 214. Unfortunately for Dietrich, at the moment when his forces had been diverted to Hausser's armoured offensive, Montgomery launched the 1st Canadian Army on a major offensive, Operation TOTALIZE, the objective of which was Falaise. Montgomery's strategy was for the Canadians to reach the city of Falaise while the British 2nd Army swept through the *bocage* to the right, before both armies turned left. Concurrently the 1st and 3rd Armies would drive east through southern Normandy, and thus the Germans would be enveloped along the River Seine due to the open south flank. The Canadian advance was, as ever, preceded by a bombardment of German positions by hundreds of heavy bombers.

Surprisingly, the dramatic events unfolding on the ground had little impact on 127 Wing, except that the better weather and greater activity provided more opportunities to batter German troops. The 127 Wing ORB entry on 7 August was as follows:

Heavy ground mist again precluded any operations until early afternoon. Operations for the day consisted of eight armed reccos. 443 Squadron carried out three armed reccos during the afternoon, being airborne on the first at 1224 hours in the Dreux–Laigle area. It was uneventful. On the second recco, the Squadron was airborne at 1717 hours. The area covered was Mayenne–Alençon. The score – two MET smokers, one damaged. The third show in the Domfront–Falaise area, at 2100 hours, was uneventful. Six a/c on each recco carried bombs. One direct hit was obtained on a road bridge and two hits on a road junction. 421 Squadron was airborne at 1500 hours on a recco in the Vire–Mortain area. One MET damaged. Six bombs carried and four hits obtained in marshalling yards near Trouville. 416 Squadron carried out two armed reccos, being airborne on the first at 1435 hours, in the Bernay–Falaise area. Two MET smokers. Six bombs were dropped and three hits made on a road bridge near Melieourt. The second recco, in Lisieux–Falaise area, at 2000 hours, was uneventful. No. 403 Squadron carried out two reccos. The Squadron took off on the first at 1354 hours. The score in MET was three flamers and two smokers. On the second show in the Argentan–Laigle area, one MET flamer and two smokers were secured and one direct hit by bomb on railway bridge near Vimoutiers. One Spitfire Mk VII from Culmhead Wing landed at 1543 hours from a sweep in Auxerre area and refuelled. In all, ninety-six sorties were flown in the day.

The Wing Leader himself, however, did not fly that day. Johnnie: 'Although we were winning, beating the fuckers on the ground, helping the army, it wasn't really what we were all about. We still wanted to engage the German fighters.' Johnnie was occupied with other matters so only flew a 20-minute local flight. The day was, according to the 416 Squadron ORB, a 'scorcher'. All pilots not detailed to fly swam from the nearby beach, and that evening there was a huge thrash in the Mess to celebrate the adjutant's birthday and news of Hank Zary's DFC.

By now, Von Kluge's Mortain counter-attack changed Allied strategic thinking. The opportunity now presented itself to change the proposed long envelopment along the Seine to a shorter one, this effectively being a left-hook to trap the 7th *Armee* between the Canadians, who were advancing towards Falaise, and Patton's XV Corps, which was turning north towards Argentan. The plan belonged to General Bradley, whose forces had to hold the Germans at Mortain for two days, thus permitting Patton to complete his turn north. If the envelopment was successful, the 7th *Armee* would be completely destroyed. By evening on 8 August it was clear that Von Kluge's Mortain gamble had failed: the decisive Battle of the Falaise Gap was now at hand. Although Johnnie himself did not fly on 9 August, 127 Wing was kept busy with the usual round of armed reccos. Before Von Kluge could launch his new attack, however, the Allied offensive was renewed on 11 August with great vigour along the entire German front, which, at last, began to irrevocably crumble. General Warlimont returned to Rastenburg and reported the grim news to Hitler. Ignoring his General's assurance that all involved had done their utmost to make the Führer's plan succeed,

Hitler concluded that the counter-attack had failed purely because Von Kluge had been determined to prove that his orders were incapable of being performed. That day, 127 Wing flew a total of forty-four sorties, 416 and 421 Squadrons again destroying German vehicles. Johnnie led another sweep around Paris and Le Mans, but once more the *Luftwaffe* was not found.

On 12 August, Johnnie's logbook entry is of interest: he did not fly his usual MK392, but JE-J 'Junior', MK329. It has often been written that Johnnie 'often' flew this aircraft, but this statement is not confirmed by Greycap's logbook. On this day, Johnnie flew 'Junior' from B2 to Coltishall, and the following day from there to Rearsby, near his Leicestershire home. There he enjoyed seven days leave before flying 'Junior' down to Tangmere on 21 August, staying overnight and returning to B2 on 22 August. These are, in fact, the only flights recorded by Johnnie in MK329. 'Junior' was actually an unarmed Spitfire made up from damaged aircraft. Breaking just about every rule in the book, Johnnie was extremely proud of this particular machine!

By the time Johnnie returned from leave, the Battle for Normandy had been won, On 13 August, the day after Johnnie went on leave, the OKW at last gave permission for a withdrawal behind the River Seine. It was much too late. A mere 25 miles now divided the British and Canadians from the Americans, and yet the Germans had to evacuate a salient – the Falaise Pocket – 35 miles deep. The race was on to close the gap before the 7th *Armee* could escape across the Seine. Around Falaise, Allied fighter-bombers absolutely dominated the battlefield, their bombs and rockets pulverising the retreating enemy. The *Luftwaffe* had been swept from the Normandy sky, but there was still the occasional fighter combat. 127 Wing, therefore, found itself flying innumerable ground-attack sorties. On 17 August, for example, the 127 Wing ORB reported that the Canadian Spitfire pilots had flown 118 sorties, claiming a total of 196 'flamers, smokers and damaged vehicles, and three tanks destroyed'. On that day, while Von Kluge tried desperately to extricate his troops from the Allied pincer, *Feldmarschall* Model arrived from Russia to relieve him of his command. Having bravely fought both Eisenhower and Hitler, Von Kluge could take no more and committed suicide on the subsequent flight to Berlin. Von Kluge would have died knowing that his 7th *Armee* had lost its race for safety. On the day Model became the third Commander-in-Chief West in as many months, Falaise itself fell to the Canadians, less than 15 miles now separating the two Allied armies. West of that gap were still the remnants of fourteen German divisions, almost 80,000 men, all struggling to make it to the Seine.

In spite of colossal casualties from artillery bombardments and air attacks, until 18 August the German withdrawal had been an orderly, but slow, operation. On that day *Obergruppenführer* Hausser was entrusted with commanding the desperate withdrawal from the Orne salient by the 5th *Panzer Armee*, 7th *Armee* and *Panzergruppe* Eberbach to a position behind the River Dives. For this to succeed, however, it was necessary for the Germans to retake the territory north-west of the small town of Trun, on the Dives. Once achieved, Hausser intended to hold a line south-east of Falaise and north-east of Argentan, and, over a period of several nights, withdraw the divisions lying south-west of the river across the Dives. The counter-attack was to be led by 1st and 2nd SS *Panzer* Divisions, which had already managed to escape from the 'Falaise *Kessell*' (cauldron). Unfortunately for Hausser, 2nd TAF called in all available fighter-bombers to annihilate those Germans still trapped in the Falaise gap. The aircraft flew in pairs, to facilitate a rapid turnaround and return to the killing ground. All pilots knew the area well, so lengthy briefings were unnecessary, this also increasing the number of sorties possible. Whereas the maximum number of sorties per day an individual pilot could be expected to fly would be no more than three or four, even at very busy times, they were now up on six or seven trips a day to the 'Corridor of Death'. 127 Wing ORB:

> It was the busiest day in the history of the Wing. Approximately 290 operational hours were flown by our aircraft. About 30,000 rounds of 20 mm ammunition were expended on the Hun. Nearly 500 enemy vehicles were destroyed or damaged by our squadrons. These enemy vehicles are split up as follows: 160 flamers, 176 smokers, 142 damaged. In addition three tanks were destroyed and fourteen damaged. One engine of a train found in the Bernay area was destroyed. Out of 264 sorties carried out, 192 were armed reccos. At 1800 hours all patrols and readiness were cancelled and a concerted effort from the entire Wing was requested to attack

transport in the Vimoutiers area. From then onwards until dusk every available aircraft, including the Group Captain's Spitfire V, was put into the air. They took off in twos and flew until they had run out of ammunition. They returned to base, were refuelled and rearmed, and were off again. When operations finished, 486 vehicles of one kind or another had been destroyed or damaged, making an average of two and a half vehicles destroyed per sortie flown. A number of our aircraft were hit by flak and several crash landed away from base, but only one pilot, F/O Leyland of 421 Squadron, went missing. A few E/A were sighted but our pilots were unable to make contact.

This was the absolute crescendo to the Battle for Normandy, the terrible proof of tactical aerial superiority. The retreating German troops were completely at the mercy of the scores of Allied fighter-bombers that returned again and again to the battlefield, bent upon their destruction. The daily situation report of 5th *Panzerarmee* despairingly commented that, 'At the exits from the pocket, as well as inside it, constant air and fighter-bomber attacks, even hunting down individual men on foot, make any movement or assembly of units impossible. Our communications systems are largely destroyed.'

The Trun–Chambois road had become a killing ground, dubbed either the 'Shambles' or 'Corridor of Death'. Aircraft from both 2nd TAF and the American 9th Air Force strafed the enemy until it was too dark to see. Complete panic was achieved and the withdrawal became a rout. In total, 83 Group alone claimed the destruction of 1,074 motor transports and 73 tanks. So heavily strewn with dead soldiers and horses was the Normandy countryside that veteran Allied pilots maintain the stench of death was apparent even a thousand feet above the battlefield. The destruction wrought upon the retreating Germans was enormous: 12,369 tanks, guns and vehicles were lost in one of the German Army's greatest defeats, every bit equal to Stalingrad, Moscow and El Alamein. By 19 August, the Germans' escape route was nothing more than a corridor less than 5 miles wide, through the villages of Trun, St-Lambert-sur-Dives and Chambois. The rout saw every man for himself, all command and co-ordination having now deserted the inferno, the crushing effect of tactical air power, which had dominated the entire battle, having won the day. On that day the Polish Armoured Division and US 90th Division linked up in Chambois. Only one road out of the pocket was still open, choked with fleeing transports, the scene all around being one of total chaos and devastation, wrecked and abandoned vehicles and equipment everywhere. The gap was nearly closed, the German army in France finished, including its elite SS *Panzer* divisions.

It was on 19 August, in fact, that Field Marshal Montgomery later considered the Battle for Normandy to have ended; he later wrote, 'On this day we finally cleared up the remnants of the enemy trapped in the 'pocket' East of Mortain. The final victory was definite, complete and decisive.' The victory was undoubtedly 'definite' and 'decisive', but it was not, in fact, 'complete' because it had taken too long to close the Falaise gap. This allowed some 20,000 German soldiers to escape across the River Dives to the safety of the Seine. This was largely because the 4th Canadian Armoured Division, a relatively inexperienced formation commanded by General George Kitching, advanced too cautiously and suffered from confusing orders and poor communications. Moreover, the Polish Armoured Division had mistaken Les Champeaux for Chambois, which was 20 miles away, so the Poles' position was frequently unclear to Kitching. Although the *Luftwaffe* had actually tried desperately to provide air cover for the withdrawal, this was impossible to do. Units were hastily moving, yet again, to bases beyond the reach of Allied fighters, if that was at all possible now, and those fighters of *Jagdkorps* II that did manage to get up were held off by Allied fighters east of the pocket. In fact, only one *Jagdgruppe* successfully attacked Allied fighter-bombers over the Falaise gap, this being III/ JG 27 which, on 17 August, bounced Typhoons of 183 Squadron, and shot down four of them.

On 20 August, 127 Wing pilots reported that although there was still movement down below, frequently upon sighting their Spitfires approaching, the enemy soldiers would endeavour to avoid attack by waving white flags. 421 Squadron reported 150 German troops marching in the direction of Allied lines and prominently displaying a white flag. In any case, Canadian, British, Polish and German troops were now in such close combat that air support was often impossible. Clearly, however, the Battle of Normandy was now over. In this apocalyptic clash of arms the fighter-bomber wings of 2nd TAF had all, without question, performed superbly; during the Falaise fighting alone, 2nd TAF had flown over 12,000 sorties. Johnnie:

> When I got back from leave a few of us went into the 'Shambles' to have a look-see. Having been to Caen and so on we thought that we were prepared for the sights, but this scene of devastation was appalling, much, much worse than anything we had ever seen, or even imagined, before. We went looking for a decent German staff car, a Mercedes or similar, so that we could travel around in a bit more style than afforded by the ubiquitous jeep. But once on the Trun–Chambois road further vehicular passage become impossible as the road was completely choked with wrecked vehicles and debris. Bodies, both human and animal, lay bloating and rotting in the sun, and the stench was dreadful. We found a staff car with the corpse of a beautiful young woman sprawled out across the back seat. It was impossible to extricate any of the vehicles we found, so we left and were glad to do so. It wasn't the kind of place anyone wanted to hang around in. It was quite obvious that what we had seen was the very climax of our air–ground operations in Normandy.

Interestingly, though, after the battle, RAF intelligence officers found few German tanks actually disabled by fighter-bombers – including rocket-firing Typhoons. Many enemy tanks were actually found abandoned, suggesting that their crews had simply abandoned them, so great was the fear of air attack. Nonetheless, whether enemy armour was disabled by rockets or panic was irrelevant: the fact is that an abandoned tank is out of the battle. Moreover, there is no question that fighter-bombers were immensely destructive against soft-skinned and horse-drawn transport – and hence the scenes of devastation in the Corridor of Death. The accounts of all combatant nationalities, in fact, acknowledge that the use of fighter-bombers at Mortain was decisive. Johnnie:

> Ground attack was necessary, of course, effectively supporting the army as flying artillery. The CABRANK system would call us in to attack and neutralise an enemy position, through strafing and dive-bombing. This was quick and effective, meaning that

we could respond to rapidly changing tactical situations on the battlefield. The alternative was artillery, but the big guns were inflexible and slow. It took time, of course, to transport and assemble artillery, and pin-point accuracy was very difficult. So the use of fighter-bombers was the only alternative. Broady and Coningham, of course, had worked it all out in the desert and Italy and it worked very well, really. But as fighter pilots it wasn't what we were about at all. We wanted to be up there engaging *Luftwaffe* fighters, knocking the fuckers down. Beating up the German army was part of our job, but it was a poor substitute for the exhilarating thrill of a dogfight.

When Johnnie returned to 127 Wing on 22 August, it was with renewed vigour and a sustained keenness to search for, find and destroy enemy fighter aircraft. With Montgomery's objectives in Normandy now achieved (the River Seine was, in fact, reached two weeks ahead of schedule), and the requirement for fighter-bomber sorties having abated, the Spitfires were able to resume sweeping the skies in the hope of engaging the *Luftwaffe*. This is what Johnnie was now determined to do.

Jagdkorps II had covered the German withdrawal across the Seine. With the German Army safely across, the enemy pilots' task was not only to maintain their hunt for Allied fighter-bombers, but also to attack Allied troop concentrations on the Seine's west bank, and try to destroy the river's bridges. To this end, the *Werfergruppen* had been added to JG 26, this being a wing of rocket-firing fighters. On 23 August, this *Gruppe* was briefed to attack Allied troops and the Seine bridges, escorted by I/JG 26. Ultimately, however, *Werfergruppen* was scrubbed from the operation, which became a straightforward sweep searching for Allied *Jabos*. Soon after midday, eighteen II *Gruppe* FW 190s rendezvoused above Montdidier with five III *Gruppe* Me 109s, and more fighters from four other *Jagdgruppen*. The enemy formation headed west. Johnnie:

> I got a call saying that the Germans were putting up a fighter screen over the Seine, flying from bases around Paris. The Controller, an excellent chap called Kenway, suggested that if two Spitfire squadrons patrolled the Seine from the east, we might be in luck. This was what I had been waiting for and too good

an opportunity to miss. My pilots were immediately briefed and soon I was leading 443 Squadron, with 421 Squadron stepped up a few thousand feet down-sun. Visibility was perfect. This was more like it!

Johnnie swept well south of Paris before turning north, down-sun, the French capital on the Spitfires' port side. During this leg of the trip, therefore, the Spitfires were vulnerable, as an enemy approaching from their rear would have the all-important advantage of being up-sun. Without mishap, having flown far enough northwards, Johnnie wheeled the Wing gently to port, returning towards the Seine. Suddenly Greycap sighted 'a gaggle of at least sixty aircraft well ahead and the highest of which were at our altitude. A distance of about five miles separated us but as there were so many aircraft I suspected them most likely to be American fighters.' Unable to be sure, Johnnie climbed the Spitfires another couple of thousand feet. The distant aircraft, however, 'milled about the sky ... and were certainly not behaving like our American friends'. Flying further to port, Johnnie cleverly hid the Wing in the sun: 'Greycap to Wing. Sixty-plus at twelve o'clock, three miles. They may be Huns. Green Leader, keep us covered.' Simultaneously with satisfying himself that no enemy fighters lurked above the Wing, Johnnie positively identified the suspicious formation as hostile:

> Recognition came and with it the usual shocked, heart-in-mouth feeling that was always the same ... We were boring into them and I was talking into the microphone to bring the whole Wing down in one fell swoop. As I turned and dived I called the leader of 421 Squadron: 'Green Leader, I'm taking my Section into the top bunch. There's plenty more below. Get in!'

127 Wing bounced the bandits over Senlis. Johnnie ordered 421 Squadron to attack the highest enemy fighters, which were 1,000 feet below the Spitfires, and to remain at that height, about 9,000 feet. To provide top cover, Greycap then led 443 Squadron down to engage thirty to forty enemy fighters flying at about 8,000 feet, and 1,000 feet below him. Higher than the enemy and hidden by the sun, 127 Wing had every advantage: it was the perfect bounce,

achieved through a combination of luck and skill. Johnnie's combat report described events:

> I attacked a FW 190, firing short bursts from line astern, closing to
> 150 yards; E/A caught fire and went down completely enveloped
> in flames. I then chased another 190, flying at ground level and
> opened fire from 300 yards. I saw five or six strikes on the cockpit
> of this E/A and he pulled up steeply before baling out at 1,000
> feet. A series of individual combats ensued as by this time the
> Wing had been split up. I was attacked by six short-nosed 190s
> which possessed an exceptional rate of climb. By turning in to
> each attack I managed to evade most of their fire, only receiving
> one hit in the starboard wing root.

This, however, is worthy of more detailed explanation. After his second combat, Johnnie was

> in an empty sky, but an empty sky is a dangerous sky. I felt it high
> time that I joined forces with a few of my Canadians. I called
> Larry Robillard, reporting my position at 8,000 feet, just east of
> the Seine. Larry replied that he was above, at 15,000 feet. I told
> him to stay there, so as to preserve the advantage of height, and
> started climbing towards the glaring sun. I caught the glint of six
> aircraft, so assumed this to be Larry's Spitfires. I pulled my Spitfire
> well ahead of these fighters and discovered my error the hard way
> when tracer flashed over the top of my cockpit! I broke hard to
> port and over my shoulder saw the lean nose and belching cannon
> of a 109 [although Johnnie's combat report referred to 'short-nosed
> FW 190s']! My fate would be decided by the tightness of our turns,
> and I pulled the stick back so hard that the Spitfire shuddered
> with a warning of the flick-stall. I was blacking out so eased the
> turn slightly so as to recover. Height had to be maintained at all
> costs. The enemy section leader knew his stuff. He had positioned
> a pair of 109s either side of me, whilst he and his wingman stuck
> to my tail. The two flanking pairs began making head-on attacks.
> Fortunately none of the enemy pilots could shoot straight – except
> their leader. I knew that immediately I eased out of the turn he'd
> nail me, but I couldn't turn forever. Somehow I had to climb, so that
> the supercharger would cut in, giving me extra power.

Seconds later the 'blower' did its job. Johnnie outpaced and lost his assailants but discounted the idea of wheeling around to attack their persistent leader: 'Fortune had already smiled upon me and there will be another day,' he wrote.

Squadron Leader Dan Browne: 'One day they caught Johnnie out on the side, on his own, and really gave it to him! When he got out of his Spitfire we all had a good laugh about it. I bet he crapped in his pants that day!' Johnnie:

> I got back to Crepon and asked the Runway Controller to check whether or not my landing gear was fully down, because I didn't know how badly damaged my Spitfire was. It was okay, so I landed and taxied into dispersal where I was met by Robillard. This was the first time I had been hit by an enemy fighter. The vicious fight had shaken me.

Nonetheless, Johnnie had achieved the perfect bounce: 127 Wing claimed a total of twelve enemy fighters destroyed and several damaged; three Spitfires were missing. Of Johnnie's victories, the 127 Wing ORB commented that:

> Wing Commander Johnson destroyed two FW 190s, raising his score from thirty-five to thirty-seven enemy aircraft destroyed. Not so very long our congenial Wing Commander was closing in on first place amongst the fighter boys, now he is pulling quickly away from the next nearest rival, Group Captain Malan DSO DFC, with thirty-two destroyed.

Johnnie:

> Yes, there was more publicity at this time, the papers making a real meal of it all. It was exasperating as they either couldn't or didn't want to understand what I kept telling them. There was no comparison between Malan's effort and mine. Sailor had flown during the dark days of the Battle of Britain when outnumbered by the enemy in defensive fighting. I, conversely, had flown during the offensive operations of 1941 onwards, usually in a Wing of many Spitfires and, since March 1943, at the head of a Wing. So it was ridiculous to compare our two scores.

Nonetheless, with a five-victory lead and with ever-reducing *Luftwaffe* activity – meaning it was less likely that another pilot could catch up, let alone exceed, Johnnie's score – his place in history as the RAF's officially top-scoring fighter pilot of the Second World War appeared likely.

After the action on 23 August 1944, however, the *Luftwaffe* was experiencing an acute shortage of fuel. That evening, while 127 Wing rejoiced at Crepon after its successful action over Senlis, *Oberstleutnant* 'Pips' Priller, *Kommodore* of JG 26, was informed that stocks of aviation fuel had been exhausted. Only ten fighters were operational for the following day, and that had been achieved only through draining fuel from unserviceable machines. The days of great fighter-to-fighter actions were over.

13

127 Wing:
The Long Trek

'Shaken' though he was, having been hit by an enemy fighter for the first time, Johnnie was straight back up in the air, leading 443 Squadron on an uneventful 'Armed Recco'. Upon conclusion, he 'called it a day and went for a drink'. On 25 August 1944, Greycap once more patrolled the Paris area, looking for trouble, but none was to be found. On 28 August, 127 Wing moved to Airfield B26, near Illiers, as the Wing ORB explained: 'B26 is a captured enemy aerodrome at Marcilly-la-Campagne ... approximately eight miles northwest of the city of Dreux, and by air forty miles from Paris, sixty by road.' The tempo of fighting, both on the ground and in the air decreased enormously. The Germans were retreating to bases east of the Rhine while the enemy aircraft industry went into overdrive, achieving a record output of single-engined fighters with which to replenish the *Jagdwaffe*. German pilots from other arms were transferred to become fighter pilots, and with the Defence of the Reich itself now a paramount concern, rebuilding the depleted fighter force became a priority. Johnnie:

> I would be wrong to think that the *Luftwaffe* was a spent force at this time. The Germans did a remarkable job of re-building their fighter-force after Normandy. We began hearing rumours of a fast, jet aircraft, which was the Me 262, of course. We knew that the Germans would defend their homeland bitterly, so the war was far from over.

127 Wing, however, now found itself 300 miles behind the front line, which was now in Belgium and close to the actual German border. Consequently, on 1 September, 127 Wing was advised that it would be downgraded as non-operational on the following day. This was to permit organisation of a move closer to the front, which, by road, would take three days. After the intensive operations throughout

the Normandy campaign, 2nd TAF's aircraft were also in need of attention, so the Wing's Maintenance Section took full advantage of the lull, while the pilots undertook training flights. On 16 September, 127 Wing learned that it was to move to Airfield B68 at Le Culot, near Louvain in Belgium. The Wing arrived on 18 September and it was discovered that 'the Allied air forces had caused great devastation of the strip and buildings' (127 Wing ORB). Indeed, so bad was the damage that none of the buildings were of any use, and the runway had to be much repaired before use. Moreover, engineers were kept busy removing mines and booby traps left as lethal surprises by the retreating enemy. By noon on 19 September, Le Culot was declared operational and 127 Wing's Spitfires flew in the following day. As Johnnie said:

> We had fought our way across Normandy, living a nomadic existence, keeping on the move and flying in support of the army. Initially, living under canvas and operating as a tactical air force came as a bit of a shock to the system, I can tell you, after Kenley and being able to put on your nice blue uniform to get up to the West End for the odd night! But it was all good stuff, good training. I actually enjoyed Lashenden and Headcorn, for example, very much. It was essential experience for Normandy and especially now that our armies were advancing ever eastwards. This was really now the start of what was later described as the 'Long Trek'.

Johnnie:

> On 17 September Operation MARKET GARDEN had begun. Involving more than 1,000 troop-carrying aircraft and 500 gliders, this was the greatest airborne operation yet attempted. The objective was to establish a bridge-head across the Rhine by securing three important bridges over Mass, the Waal and the Neder Rijn. Once these were secured, together with others of secondary importance, the armoured columns of General Horrock's XXX Corps would race up the narrow corridor from Eindhoven to the Rhine, linking up with the airborne forces. There were all manner of problems: the British First Airborne Division was dropped eight miles West of its objective, Arnhem;

their vital radio sets did not work; the reinforcing air lift was delayed by bad weather; the German counter-attack was heavier than expected.

That the German reaction was fierce was unsurprising: Montgomery had ignored intelligence reports that two SS *Panzer* divisions were present in the Arnhem area. These were the 9th *Frundsberg* and 10th *Hohenstaufen* Divisions, re-fitting after the Normandy fighting. The presence of these enemy divisions changed everything. Johnnie:

> Also, the *Luftwaffe* had sorted itself out after Normandy and had plenty of fighters and fighter-bombers, including the new Me 262 jets, with which to attack our lightly armed paratroopers.

When planning the operation, Montgomery had failed to liaise with Air Marshal Coningham and Air Vice-Marshal Broadhurst, which would have dire consequences so far as close air-support would be concerned: even had their radios worked, the airborne troops were unfamiliar with the air-support system in place at that time. Moreover, Allied tactical air forces were prevented from intervening at crucial times because of both the weather and being unable to operate over the battlefield during times of airborne resupply. It was against this backdrop, then, that 127 Wing began operating from its new Belgian base. Johnnie:

> On 21 September, four days after the first drop, we were briefed that the situation at Arnhem Bridge was bad. There, at the northern end, Colonel John Frost's valiant British paratroopers were fighting desperately to hold their position. By then the lead Shermans of the Guards Armoured Division had taken and crossed Nijmegen bridge, but had stalled just six miles away from Arnhem.

By now, the situation on the ground had become confused. The fighting was house-to-house. Even if the Typhoon CABRANK circling overhead could have been called in by radio to intervene, accurate target identification would have been extremely difficult. Instead the Typhoons searched the woods around the town, seeking enemy armour. To facilitate this, the Spitfire wings were briefed to patrol overhead and keep the area free of German fighters. The Typhoons, in fact, only appeared over Arnhem in strength on 24 September, by which time the battle was lost.

On 22, 24, 25 and 26 September, Johnnie led the Wing on patrols over Arnhem. At 1250 hours on 27 September, Johnnie was leading 443 Squadron at 7,000 feet over Rees-on-Rhine. Johnnie:

> I saw nine Me 109Fs flying at ground level immediately below us. I led the Squadron down to attack but E/A saw us and broke upwards into the attack and a general melee ensued. I closed on a 109 turning to port and closed to 250 yards, firing short bursts of cannon and machine-gun. Strikes were seen on port wing of E/A. He peeled away and crashed into the ground.

This – Johnnie's final kill – increased his personal score to thirty-eight and a half enemy aircraft destroyed, placing him even further ahead in the ace race. Additionally, during this action Johnnie's pilots claimed another four 109s destroyed. The operation, however, was not without loss: Squadron Leader H. W. 'Wally' McLeod DSO DFC, CO of 443 Squadron, was missing. After the ill-disciplined Screwball Beurling, McLeod was Canada's top-scoring fighter pilot. Johnnie:

> Importantly, most of Beurling's victories were scored whilst serving in the RAF, as opposed to the RCAF, which is an important distinction. Wally had intended to settle this. Several times I found him sat alone in our cine-projection caravan, analysing his combat film and wondering whether he could have despatched his opponent more efficiently. He had his cannons constantly stripped and checked, his aircraft maintained to the peak of perfection and his sole topic of conversation was air fighting. On his last flight, Wally's Section took on the 109s on our starboard, whilst I engaged those to port. We bounced the 109s perfectly, but the leader was clearly an experienced chap: he immediately climbed vertically. I knew his intention, which was to half-roll off the top of his loop, aileron turn and dive, searching for a Spitfire. As I engaged I shouted, 'Watch that brute, Wally, he knows the form.' Afterwards there was no sign of Wally, and he failed to answer my repeated radio messages. I flew low over the blazing wrecks

of several aircraft but it was impossible to distinguish friend from foe. Back at base Wally's Number Two told me that his CO had gone after the 109 leader but he (the wingman) had been unable to keep up due to high 'g' forces, blacked out and lost his leader. I knew that the 109 was several thousand feet higher, so had a clear advantage. I was not optimistic. A depressed mood soon settled over us all.

Johnnie responded in Johnson-like fashion: a pissup! In short order Johnnie was leading a small convoy of jeeps into Louvain, stopping at Le Café de Sept Coins. Upon hearing that these were Spitfire pilots who had enjoyed success against the hated Germans that very afternoon, the proprietor, Marcel, made the best fare available. High spirits were soon restored, but Johnnie still brooded:

> Wally was not just one of my squadron commanders, he was my friend. With twenty-one enemy aircraft destroyed, three more probably destroyed and eleven damaged – thirteen of them destroyed over Malta – decorated with both the DSO and DFC, he was also an exceptional fighter pilot. We knew, of course, that the end was in sight, which increased my depression. I feared that Wally was dead. After the war I discovered that he had been found in the wreckage of his Spitfire at Duisberg, near Wesel, the scene of our combat. This must have been one of the crash-sites that I flew over that day.

Squadron Leader McLeod had, in fact, been shot down by Major Siegfried Freytag, acting *Kommodore* of JG 77. It was the German's 101st aerial victory – ironically Freytag had been among the leading *Experten* over Malta.

Two days before Squadron Leader McLeod disappeared, the Arnhem gamble had failed. Montgomery's ambitious plan to cross the Rhine and end the war by Christmas had failed. The operation had cost many lives, including those of 8,000 brave British paratroopers. Johnnie: 'Arnhem? It was a fucking disgrace.'

The airfield at Le Culot was becoming overcrowded with fighters, so on 28 September 127 Wing moved to Graves. On that day, 416 Squadron was on patrol over Nijmegen. Orbiting to starboard over the city, the Spitfire pilots sighted one of the new Me 262 jets, which

was diving slightly and travelling at 450–500 mph. Flight Lieutenant
J. B. McColl went after it, diving at full throttle, cut inside the jet's
turn and attacked, closing rapidly from 600 to 200 yards. The 262
pilot took no evasive action but opened his throttle and climbed
away. The 262's maximum speed was some 559 mph, its range 652
miles and ceiling 37,565 feet. Its arrival on the scene represented the
swan song for all piston-engined fighters – including the ubiquitous
Spitfire.

Soon after arriving at Grave, Johnnie was summoned to Air Vice-
Marshal Broadhurst's Eindhoven HQ, there to meet an 'important
personage'. Believing this to be 'Eisenhower, Tedder, Monty, or some
high-ranking politician', Johnnie found the 'guest of honour to be
none other than the King. We had the rare opportunity to meet His
Majesty in a most friendly and intimate atmosphere. The King was
keenly interested in the conduct of the campaign, and as an airman
himself he asked many searching questions about the German jets.'
The jets were, in fact, becoming an increasing problem.

On 2 October, while 421 Squadron encountered '175 plus Me
109s and FW 190s ... North of Eindhoven', destroying three
and damaging several more, Johnnie patrolled uneventfully over
Arnhem with 416 Squadron. Events at Grave, however, were far
from uneventful. Johnnie:

> The Group Captain had gone to England, leaving me in
> overall command, as opposed to just being responsible for the
> flying. I decided to have a look at the airmen's lines but my
> visit was rudely interrupted by the roar of powerful engines
> and the whine of a diving aircraft. This was immediately
> followed by several explosions. We ran out of the Mess
> to see a 262 climbing steeply away, having dive-bombed
> us.

The 127 Wing ORB elaborated:

> During the day, the Airfield was bombed on five separate
> occasions, causing casualties but only a small amount of damage,
> and this to tents and personal equipment only. It was apparent
> that the bombs were of the anti-personnel type and dropped from
> jet propelled aircraft flying at approximately 10,000 feet. The

first attack caused injuries to 127 Wing personnel, due to bombs exploding before anyone realised what was happening. Three pilots were injured, two severely, and, in addition six other ranks and one officer received wounds of a minor degree.

In another attack that day, 126 Wing was hit, the Wing Adjutant and a number of Dutch civilians being killed. The following day, anti-aircraft fire was heard at dusk, resulting 'in a large blinding flash to the North'. It was clear than an enemy bomber had been hit, before dropping its cargo of high explosive. A search of the area revealed just a part of an oleo leg, believed to be from a Ju 88. So great was the explosion, however, that it was believed that 'the Hun had released a composite aircraft against the Wing'. This was another new danger: the so-called *Mistel*, featuring an FW 190 riding piggyback on a Ju 88. The bomber was packed with high explosive and released by the FW 190 pilot to crash on the intended target. This was yet another example of German ingenuity. Indeed, on 8 September Hitler had begun his V-2 offensive, launching rockets against London, Paris and various targets in Holland. Clearly Johnnie was right that 'although the end was in sight the war was far from over'.

After Flight Lieutenant McColl damaged a Me 262 on 28 September, two days later, Flight Lieutenant Ronald Lake of 441 Squadron damaged another, as did Flying Officer Forrest Young of 442 Squadron on 2 October. Eventually a 262 fell to the Canadians' guns on 5 October, when five Spitfire pilots of 401 Squadron shot down *Hauptman* Hans-Christoff Buttman as he attempted to bomb Nijmegen bridge. The successful pilots were Squadron Leader Rod Smith, Flight Lieutenants Hedley Everard and Robert Davenport, and Flying Officers John MacKay and Andrew Sinclair. Squadron Leader Smith described the jet as doing better high-speed rolls than the Spitfire and capable of very high-speed turns. MacKay reported that 'the pilot was hot and put the aircraft through everything in the book'. Johnnie:

One evening Wing Commander Dal Russell called to say that some of his 126 Wing pilots had destroyed a 262. Later, an engineering officer brought me a cannon from the wreck. Then a very polite Canadian officer phoned me saying that as his Squadron had shot down the jet, could he please have the cannon? This Squadron

Leader Roderick Illingworth Alpine Smith DFC travelled to Grave, collected the cannon and became my lifelong friend. 126 Wing put on a great party to celebrate the event, which was a good thing, but it was ominous that the destruction of a single aircraft should receive such acclaim.

On 12 October, a landmark occurred in Johnnie's personal life: Paula gave birth to their first child, a boy called Michael. Paula:

> By then Johnnie was the top scorer, so much publicity surrounded Michael's birth. Because the Group Captain was away and Johnnie was in charge, he couldn't get away until 16 October. Then he flew up to Rearsby and met his new son. There had been complications and I wasn't well. Johnnie came in with lots of lovely gifts for me, including luxurious perfumes. It was wonderful.

On 22 October, Johnnie flew Spitfire MK392, his usual aircraft, to Tangmere, where he left it on 24 October, returning to Belgium as a passenger in an Avro Anson. En route the aircraft was diverted to Brussels-Melbroek Airfield. Les McKellar of 421 Squadron recalled:

> Our former airfield was very advanced, very close to the front, which is another reason why the 262s attacked so frequently. Also it was a grass field and after a period of heavy rain became so rutted that it was virtually impossible to use. So we moved back to Brussels, from where we operated for some months. Flights were therefore longer, using external fuel tanks to extend range. We flew regular patrols, often escorting bombers. Army liaison provided daily information as to where we attacked ground targets. We rarely saw the *Luftwaffe*, which was occupied within the German border.

In such fashion, November 1944 passed without incident for Johnnie, now not only a married man but also a father. The weather in December was poor, which greatly assisted Hitler achieving total surprise when his Ardennes offensive was launched on 16 December. Johnnie:

> Von Runstedt launched three armies on a wide front. The main axis of the armoured thrust was through the Ardennes. Unhampered

by our air forces, the enemy advanced twelve miles a day. Hitler's intention was to capture Antwerp, thereby splitting the Allied armies in two. On New Year's Day 1945, whilst the pilots of 2nd TAF nursed their hangovers, the *Luftwaffe* launched its final offensive: Operation *Bodenplatte*.

At 0939 hours on 1 January 1945, 127 Wing's airfield was attacked without warning by thirty-plus Me 109s and FW 190s. Spitfires of 403 Squadron, returning from a patrol, engaged, destroying several enemy fighters, although Flight Lieutenant Harling DFC of 416 Squadron, who managed to get off during the raid, was shot down and killed. The German attack on Melbroek lasted 12 minutes. Eleven Spitfires were destroyed on the ground, and twelve damaged in addition to eleven vehicles damaged and one destroyed. Johnnie:

> The enemy fighters strafed singly or in pairs. Our ack-ack gunners ran out of ammunition. The enemy completely dominated the scene. There was nothing we could do but shout with rage as our Spitfires burst into flames before our very eyes. The enemy's marksmanship, however, was very poor, many pilots wasting their ammunition by spraying the hangars instead of attacking more profitable targets. They withdrew abruptly and I got a formation of Spitfires up in case another wave appeared. In spite of our losses we had got off lightly: not one Spitfire should have remained undamaged. The Operation was a bold one and did damage 2nd TAF bases, but due to their inexperience the enemy had failed to exploit the advantage of surprise. The shooting was atrocious. Both sides lost about the same number of aircraft, but, as he was operating over our territory, the enemy lost more pilots – and that he was unable to afford. Strategically the attack was mistimed: it should have been the prelude to the whole Ardennes offensive.

On 13 January, Johnnie and Dan Browne were patrolling the St Vith area. In his log, Johnnie wrote: 'Spotted a lot of enemy M/T and put the Wing onto it. Eight-one destroyed or damaged.' Johnnie also had to following to say:

> We were actually after low-flying Focke-Wulfs, which were active again. Suddenly my Spitfire was rocked by an explosion, as I heard

the ugly crunches of heavy flak. The gunners had bracketed my Spitfire. I zoomed away and saw the guns' position. It was a close call. The *flak* gunners, though, were a bit jittery, as their fire drew our attention to a great column of enemy vehicles – tanks, self-propelled guns, cars and half-tracks. This was undoubtedly the spearhead of a *panzer* army. I reported the position to Kenway, who rapidly reinforced us with two twelve Spitfires from two of our squadrons, which met us over Houffalize. For a few minutes Danny and I watched the scene from above before strafing some half-tracks ourselves. Afterwards other Allied fighter-bombers did their grim work, and by evening the enemy column had been destroyed. The snow covered landscape was once more punctuated by fire, smoke and destruction.

Shocking though it first been, by 25 January this, Hitler's last gamble in the west, ground to a halt.

Very little flying took place throughout the rest of January and most of February. On 16 February Johnnie led a three-squadron-strong Wing as escort to 200 Lancasters bombing Wesel, and on 22 February led 421 Squadron strafing 'many ground targets' near Rheine. Johnnie flew further similar sweeps on 3, 9, 12 and 19 March. Johnnie:

> For the last time, group captains and wing leaders were summoned to Group HQ. There Broadhurst briefed us regarding the crossing of the Rhine, Operation VARSITY, which was to go ahead in a few days time. The fighter wings were to keep the air space over the dropping and landing zones clear of enemy aircraft. Rocket-firing Typhoons and light bombers would deal with the *flak* defences. Typhoons would also, naturally, provide close ground support, and fighters would also escort Allied troop transport aeroplanes. Finally, all enemy ground movement was to be harassed and suppressed by armed reccos. It was a good plan.

The air side of the operation was codenamed PLUNDER, this beginning on 24 March. Johnnie led the Wing three times, patrolling Rheine, Osanbrück and Munster. In his logbook, Greycap wrote:

> Operation PLUNDER, first phase of which is to place armies on the East bank of the Rhine. Saw British and American airborne

landings. Many tugs and gliders shot down by *flak*, light *flak* causing most casualties. Group reported no E/A in battle area during the whole day'

Crossing the River Rhine was a great and long awaited occasion. Johnnie:

VARSITY was a complete success. Before we turned in we heard that the situation on the Rhine's far bank was well under control. This final thrust – ending in Germany's unconditional surrender in just six weeks time – had got off to a great start.

On 26 March, Johnnie patrolled the 'Rhine battle area', attacking enemy transport. The end was in sight, for Johnnie in more ways than one. Johnnie:

The following day Broadhurst called to tell me that my days with the Canadians were over: I was to take over 125 Wing at Eindhoven from David Scott-Malden. This Wing was operating the latest Spitfire Mk XIV, and Broady wanted to move it to the first available airfield captured east of the Rhine. Broady was confident that there would be more air fighting. My score remained at thirty-eight-and-a-half, but Broady told me that if I reached forty he would recommend me for a Victoria Cross. Now that, I thought, would be quite something, as only one RAF fighter pilot, James Brindley Nicholson, had received this highest award for gallantry during the Second World War. Anyway, I was to be promoted to group captain, which was all very well because, as Broady reminded me, once the fighting was over I would revert to junior rank. I then drove over to the four squadron dispersals to say goodbye. It was two years since my association with the Canadians had begun. There existed between us that special bond known only to those who have served and fought together. Finally, I shook hands with my ground crew, which had kept my Spitfire sound for the 200 operational flights I had made in her. As Fred Varley, the Labrador and I sped up the cobbled road to Eindhoven, I realised that this was the end of a memorable and significant period in my life.

14

Johnnie Johnson:
Top-Scoring RAF Fighter Pilot

Based at Eindhoven, 125 Wing comprised 41, 130 and 350 (Belgian) Squadrons. The Wing Commander (Flying) was, coincidentally, a Canadian, Wing Commander George Keefer DSO DFC & Bar, who had previously served under Johnnie's leadership. Johnnie:

> George said, 'I suppose you'll want your own Spit, just the same as when you were a wing leader.' I was now the group captain, responsible for every function of the overall Wing, and no longer Wing Commander (Flying), which was George's job. I knew what he was getting at. He was naturally proud of his job and was concerned that if I led the Wing too much it would weaken his authority and damage the important chain of command between the Wing Leader and his squadron commanders. It reminded me of the situation all those years ago with Douglas Bader and Billy Burton at Tangmere. I wasn't about to make the same mistake. I told George that I had no intention of undermining his authority, and that so far as I was concerned there was only one Wing Leader – him. That said, I reserved the right to occasionally lead a section or squadron, and to lead the Wing on its first show over Berlin. It was a compromise that made us both happy, and that was that, the matter never need to be raised again.

Group Captain Johnson chose Spitfire Mk XIV MV268, on which his initials were soon applied. Air Vice-Marshal Broadhurst then called Johnnie again, with news that his Wing was to move to Twente, in Holland but east of the Rhine. The 'Groupie' flew over there on 5 April, but had a nasty shock upon landing:

> I had just switched off the engine when a 109 suddenly appeared low overhead! The Hun saw me and turned for a strafing run.

What a way to buy it, I thought, as, cumbersome parachute still strapped on, I fell out of the cockpit, tumbled off the wing root, hit the ground and grovelled beneath the Spitfire with an airman. We heard two crumps in quick succession, then a large explosion when the 109 hit the deck. Someone produced a jeep and I drove across the airfield to congratulate the RAF Regiment Bofors gun crew which had just saved our lives.

After Johnnie's close shave, the Wing arrived at Twente the following day. Wing Commander Keefer led his pilots on various sorties, sometimes knocking down enemy aircraft but mostly clobbering ground targets. Johnnie contented himself with local flying in his new Griffon-engined Spitfire. On 16 April, 125 Wing moved to Celle – in Germany itself.

At Celle the retreating enemy had once more left behind all manner of booby traps, but these were all safely disarmed by engineers. Johnnie flew over there with Wing Commander Keefer and was astonished at the splendour of the Officers' Mess, in the lavatory of which was a peculiar German bathroom device called a *Brechbeken* – especially for vomiting into! Johnnie:

> When I saw those things I just couldn't believe it, and thought then that we would never understand the mentality of our enemy. But suddenly, now that we were in Germany, the war became more personal. A few miles from Celle was the concentration camp at Belsen. A death camp. A dreadful place. We went there and saw the ghastly ovens and long, filthy, corridors of the prisoners' wooden huts, in which we were unable to distinguish the dead from the dying. We saw the bulldozers pushing hundreds of emaciated corpses into mass graves. The scene defies adequate description, frankly. The attitude of the local inhabitants to all of this infuriated us. We employed some twenty local German girls as cleaners in our Mess. Of course they knew nothing of what had gone on at the Belsen camp! Their elders claimed the same – and this though the camp was but a few miles from the town. Consequently I arranged for some of the locals to be taken there, to see first-hand the effects of Nazi genocide.

On 18 April, Johnnie flew with 130 Squadron on a sweep of Wismar and Bremen. Wing Commander Keefer led the trip and with his Number Two destroyed eleven Me 109s on the runway at Parchim. As the Wing ORB recorded, 'The E/A were apparently ready top take-off and they went up in flames good and proper!' The CO of 350 Squadron, however, Squadron Leader Terry Spencer, was hit while attacking a tanker in Wismar Bay. His Spitfire burst into flame and crashed, it being feared that the popular squadron commander was dead. On 20 April, Johnnie flew again with 130 Squadron. Keefer led the Wing and destroyed a 109. Johnnie – in spite of needing only one and a half more personal kills for Broadhurst to recommend him for the VC – was true to his word.

On 25 April (according to his logbook, but the previous day so far as the 125 Wing ORB was concerned), Johnnie flew with the Wing, leading with 350 Squadron, on what was a momentous occasion: a patrol over Berlin itself. By now the Third Reich was in its death throes in the battered capital below. Hitler and his entourage had long ago retreated to their underground bunker, from where the *Führer* commanded phantom armies and the faithful still believed in miracles. Johnnie:

> We swept to Berlin at a couple of thousand feet. I was flying with an Australian, Flight Lieutenant Tony Gaze DFC, with whom I had last flown in the Tangmere Wing back in 1941. The German capital was covered by thick cloud, forcing us down to a lower level. Masses of refugees filled the roads to the West, all fleeing the Soviet advance from the East. The city burned in a dozen different places and we were suddenly hit by that same stench that permeated the air above Falaise: death. The Russians were hard at it, their artillery pounding the city to rubble while the armour clambered over the debris. Suddenly Tony's voice crackled in my headphones: 'Fifty-plus at two o'clock, Greycap! Same level. More behind.'
>
> 'Are they Huns, Tony?' I asked, as I focussed my eyes on the gaggle.
>
> 'Don't look like Huns to me, Greycap. Probably Russians!'
>
> 'All right chaps,' I said. 'Stick together. Don't make a move.'
>
> They were Yaks, which made a slow turn, which would bring them behind us. There were about 100 of them, then Tony reported

even more above. We held formation. It was very tense. Our respective formations circled each other, cautious and suspicious. When opposite the Russian leader I waggled my wings. He paid no regard but straightened out of his turn and flew off to the East. There seemed to be no pattern or discipline to their flying. The leader was simply in front, his rag-taggle pack following on behind. Every few moments a handful broke away, attacked something in the city, re-joined the main formation and flew on. In this fashion these mechanical buzzards worked their way over the dying city. We were not allowed to fly over Berlin again, which was probably just as well, as in bad weather there could have been an awful mix up with the Russians. So we continued patrolling between Celle and the Baltic coast.

One evening a welcome face appeared unexpectedly in the Mess: Squadron Leader Spencer, CO of 350 Squadron and who had incredibly survived being shot down in flames at low level over Wismar Bay. Group Captain Johnson immediately telephoned the Group Commander, who agreed the award of an immediate DFC for the burned and generally knocked-about Spencer. As the war drew to a welcome close, 125 Wing was still scoring against enemy fighters, but Johnnie was never to get those extra one and a half kills. On 26 April 1945, Group Captain Johnnie Johnson DFC & Bar, DSO & 2 Bars, flew his last operational flight of the Second World War: an uneventful sweep over Wismar lasting 1 hour and 40 minutes. The war in Europe officially came to an end when the Germans surrendered unconditionally on 8 May 1945. Johnnie Johnson, the policeman's son from Leicestershire who had been rejected by the socially elite AAF, had finished his war as not only a highly decorated group captain but the RAF's official top-scoring fighter ace of the Second World War. Johnnie's place in the history books is therefore assured, but as his brother, Ross, commented, 'He was just bloody glad to have survived the war.'

15

Conclusion:
'A Marvellous Life!'

The day after VE Day, 9 May 1945, Johnnie took 125 Wing to Copenhagen in Denmark. That year his association with 350 (Belgian) Squadron led to Johnnie being awarded the Belgian Order of Leopold and Croix de Guerre. He remained in the RAF after the war, and in August 1945 became Station Commander at Lubeck in Germany. On 26 March 1946, Johnnie was permanently commissioned in the RAF, dropping a rank and becoming a wing commander once more. On 1 December 1946, Johnnie and Paula's second, son, Chris, was born. The following year, Paula joined her husband in Canada when he attended the RCAF Staff College. He then served a spell at the Central Fighter Establishment in England prior to being posted to serve with the USAF during the Korean War. Flying the F-86 Sabre and F-80 Shooting Star jet fighters, it is believed that Johnnie saw action against Migs. Unfortunately Johnnie never spoke of this period and frustratingly left behind no written record of his experience over South East Asia. His service with the Americans, though, was recognised by the awarding of the US Air Medal and the Legion of Merit. 1951 saw him back in Germany, commanding the RAF wing at Fassberg before commanding RAF Wildenrath between 1952 and 1954. The next three years saw him in a staff appointment, then on 20 October 1957 he became Station Commander at RAF Cottesmore in his home county. Near the airfield – an all-important Cold War V-bomber station – Johnnie and Paula built a beautiful house overlooking the rolling Leicestershire countryside. It was a happy time that lasted for three years. After attending the Imperial Defence College and serving as Senior Air Staff Officer (SASO) in 3 Group, Johnnie became AOC RAF Middle East, at Aden. In June 1960 he was made a Commander of the Most Excellent Order of the British Empire (CBE) and in 1965 a Companion of the Order of the Bath (CB). Paula: 'By then Johnnie was an Air Vice-Marshal and was disappointed not to have been knighted.' After such long and meritorious service – although it had not gone unrecognised – a knighthood was arguably deserved.

Air Vice-Marshal Johnson retired from the RAF in 1966. He then founded the Johnnie Johnson Housing Trust Ltd, of which he became Chief Executive, providing sheltered housing for the elderly, and was a director of several companies. Today, the Trust manages more than 4,000 properties. In 1967 Johnnie was pleased to be appointed a Deputy Lieutenant of Leicestershire. He also was also a gifted writer, publishing first his wartime memoir *Wing Leader* in 1956, and *Full Circle*, a history of air fighting, in 1964. Several other books followed in later years, all co-authored with another well-known fighter ace, Wing Commander P. B. 'Laddie' Lucas CBE DSO DFC, a former MP and Douglas Bader's brother-in-law.

Johnnie enjoyed attending air force reunions and was always in great demand as a dinner guest and speaker. Today a great cult has built up around the Spitfire, the Battle of Britain and Second World War fighter pilots generally. Since the 1970s, enthusiasts have avidly collected veterans' signatures and ephemera, especially prints of paintings depicting dramatic air war scenes, signed not only by the artist but also by former pilots, and books likewise autographed by the author and veterans. Johnnie was, in fact, instrumental in encouraging this. He recognised, back in the early 1980s, the potential of an artist called Robert Taylor, published by Pat Barnard of the Military Gallery in Bath, and signed various prints which he helped to promote. The enterprise was enormously successful, Taylor still leading the way in aviation art. This new interest also led to Johnnie's sons, Mike and Chris, establishing their own print distribution outlets in both America and the UK. Johnnie was a keynote speaker too at numerous air war symposiums organised by myself throughout the 1990s, and a crowd-pulling guest at book launches and signings promoting our work across the country. He loved being in the company of men who had shared the air combat experience, and, indeed, people who were passionately interested in the subject. To all he was just so special, so... *Johnnie*. Jim Lunney, now Chief Executive of the Johnnie Johnson Housing Trust, and who knew the 'AVM' better than most, remarked that Johnnie was:

possessed of an unlimited lust for life. He cherished its pleasures: fishing, shooting, walking, travel, his dogs, his friends, his family, good food and, indeed, the occasional drink. He was a born warrior, a relentless hunter, whether his quarry was a high flying grouse, an enemy aircraft, or a plot of land for a housing scheme. Negotiating with him, like taking a bet with him, was a mug's game. I once saw him cut a surveyor's bill from £4,000 to a quarter of that figure in two minutes – then sell the poor chap one of his Spitfire prints at full price!

As a leader, many believe that Johnnie was without parallel. The fact that the DSO has never been awarded three times before or since is evidence enough of this. He possessed incredible charisma, charm, enthusiasm and energy. This potent brew combined to naturally inspire others – meaning that Johnnie had that rare ability to get people to deliver their best, because they wanted to – for him – and were not even conscious of it. Johnnie was fascinated, in fact, by the subject of leadership. As a leader there can be no doubt that he possessed that last 'ten per cent' he often talked about and referred to as 'the gift of a great leader, that wins the hearts and minds'. To understand is difficult without meeting the man. It is an intangible thing. But around Johnnie was an aura, no doubt about it, powerful and positive. Indeed, as one reviewer of *Wing Leader* wrote in 1956:

> A number of young men about the same age are trained in the same way in the same kind of skill. They become a team. But whether they are successful or not depends upon something outside themselves – the appearance of a human catalyst, a man with that strange quality which sets fire to the spirit. Such a man was Johnnie Johnson.

Johnnie: 'Douglas Bader, of course, inspired all of us. When my turn came to lead I modelled myself on him, the great man.' With this statement, however, I disagree. The fact that Douglas Bader had no legs made him immensely valuable to the propagandists. Very early in the war he became a household name. Afterwards his story was immortalised by Paul Brickhill in his best-selling book *Reach for the Sky*, later made into a box office hit of the same name starring

Kenneth Moore. Although factually based, Brickhill's book and Lewis Gilbert's film provided a much romanticised view of Douglas Bader. Of course the story of Douglas Bader, a man without legs who became a fighter pilot and leader, is inspirational in itself. But when the layers of legend are peeled back, a different picture emerges. Bader was a snob, a product of the hierarchical society of Britain between the wars. As a graduate of the RAF College Cranwell he was part of a small elite. Bader, in fact, considered himself superior to most, and in many ways he probably was. Certainly he inspired his inner sanctum – young pilots like Johnnie, Cocky and Crow – but many outside the inner circle felt differently. Because Bader always led the Tangmere Wing at the head of 616 Squadron, Squadron Leader Burton was prevented from undertaking his own intended function. Also, because Bader based himself exclusively at Westhampnett with 616, the pilots of the Wing's third squadron, based at Merston, rarely saw their Wing Leader. For those based at Westhampnett, therefore, and especially those of the inner sanctum, a false impression existed as to morale in the Wing as a whole. Moreover, as Johnnie himself said, 'Douglas could have treated the groundcrew better.' George Reid was a member of 616 Squadron's essential ground staff:

> So far as I am concerned, when Wing Commander Bader was shot down, a happy feeling settled on 616, Westhampnett, Tangmere, and, I daresay, Chichester. Good days arrived, the sun came out and life was grand.

Due to his elitist social background, Bader considered ordinary working-class men like Reid inferior and was unable to relate to them in any other way.

Although by his own admission he had been 'inspired' by Douglas Bader, Johnnie actually did everything different when his turn to lead came. He did not exclusively lead his wings with one squadron, section or wingman. In doing so he did not create an elite within an elite, as Bader had at Tangmere. Johnnie, due to his own relatively ordinary social origin, did not consider himself to be socially superior to those in less glamorous but no less essential roles. Before leaving one command to take over another, Johnnie always personally visited and thanked his ground staff. In this way

he welded his wings together, making everyone involved feel valued
and part of a team. In the air, Johnnie was not greedy, either. His
professionalism and leadership qualities were never more evident
than when, as a newly promoted group captain, he did not interfere
with Wing Commander George Keefer's leadership of 125 Wing.
This meant that Johnnie missed out on various opportunities to
personally engage the enemy – at a time when everyone knew that
the war was drawing to a close and Johnnie only needed one and a
half more kills for Air Vice-Marshal Broadhurst to recommend him
for a VC. This, I feel, speaks volumes about the man.

One day, in Johnnie's conservatory office as we talked of the
dramatic past, I challenged Johnnie's claim that he had modelled
his style of leadership on Bader's, pointing out, as I have here, the
fundamental differences between them. Johnnie's response was
'Dunno', and he patently refused to be drawn any further. Something
else very important to Johnnie, this one-time knight of the air, was
loyalty to his friends. And Group Captain Sir Douglas Bader was
Air Vice-Marshal Johnnie Johnson's lifelong friend. As Johnnie said,
'Douglas treated me like a dog, a favourite dog!' – and yet Johnnie
was not only the top-scoring RAF fighter pilot of the Second World
War but had also achieved air rank! Their relationship, of course,
had begun when Johnnie was a very junior pilot officer and Bader
a squadron leader, soon to become a wing leader. The dynamics of
that relationship never changed. Douglas Bader was undoubtedly,
although not flawless, inspirational at many levels, not least to
other amputees and for which work he was knighted. Douglas
Bader died in 1982, after which his family and friends created the
Douglas Bader Foundation, to provide assistance and inspiration
to amputees. Together with Air Marshal Sir Denis Crowley-Milling
and Group Captain Sir Hugh Dundas, Johnnie was among the
charity's first trustees.

What did those who flew with Johnnie really think of him? Group
Captain Sir Hugh Dundas:

> In that long, hot, summer of 1941 at Tangmere, Johnnie and I
> were constantly together, both on the ground and in the air. At an
> early stage Johnnie indicated and showed that he had very great
> courage. Now courage wasn't unique, but it is always remarkable.
> Johnnie had two other things. Firstly he actually hit the things

that he shot at, which was rather important as most of us didn't! Secondly he showed that he had in his personality the terrific gift of leadership, enabling him to lift up the spirits of the people who flew with him and get the best out of them. We had, of course, been set a great example by Douglas Bader, but nobody followed that example better than Johnnie Johnson.

Flying Officer Neil Burns, 442 Squadron:

When I arrived at 144 Wing I was interviewed by Wing Commander Johnson in his trailer. He pointed to the wall behind his desk which contained photos of all the Wing's pilots. He then said, 'One, get your picture taken for my gallery, and two, you will be flying as my Number Two tomorrow. If you lose me you'll be sent back to England.' I was so anxious not to screw up that I stuck indecently close to Greycap throughout that flight! It was quite an introduction to operations for a nineteen year old, but I think it was an example of great leadership: Johnnie had made it clear to me that only the highest standard was acceptable, and so I performed accordingly.

Flight Lieutenant Forrest 'Frosty' Young DFC, 442 Squadron:

I knew Johnnie as Wing Leader of 144 Wing, and I got to know him better on 22 June 1944. Eight of us were scrambled to patrol the Argentan area. I was assigned by my CO, Squadron Leader Dal Russell, to fly as Johnnie's Number Two. Of course I was tense, flying as Johnnie's wingman. Before take off Johnnie took me aside and gave me the word, and I quote: 'You are my wingman. You are to make certain that you stay on my wing. If you don't you will find yourself posted back to England immediately to a bombing and gunnery school, towing drogues.'

What else could I say but 'Yes Sir.'

Off we went, found and engaged the enemy, namely eight 109s and 190s. Johnnie had thirty victories at the time, I had zero. In the ensuing scrap Johnnie destroyed one, I destroyed one, and two others destroyed a couple more. We lost none. Back at base Johnnie said to me 'You done good', or words to

that effect, which I took as quite a compliment from a master
of air fighting.

Flying Officer Ivor Williams, 443 Squadron:

I was a pilot with 443 Squadron, RCAF, which, along with 441
and 442 Squadrons was posted to Digby in February 1944. These
three squadrons had previously been on coastal patrol duties in
Canada, and proceeded overseas together in what was considered
to be a political move to provide a totally Canadian fighter wing
for pre-invasion operations. Soon after arriving at Digby each
pilot was given a short interview with Wing Commander Johnson,
recently appointed as Wing Commander (Flying). Those of us
who had been given an OTU course in Canada (RCAF Station
Bagotville), and who had several months of operational flying
on the Hurricane, were selected to continue as part of the new
Squadron. Those with fewer Hurricane hours or no operational
training were sent off to an RAF OTU for further training. I was
very pleased to be a part of the new Squadron led by Squadron
Leader McLeod and in Wing Commander Johnson's 144 Wing.
Johnnie led us in formation practice and other training flights
until we moved to South Holmsley on 18 March, for operational
duties.

On 28 April I was detailed to perform an engine test on a Spitfire
Mk IX, which had been assigned to me with the identification
21-K. Over the nearby town of Chichester I collided almost
head-on with another Spitfire, losing about twelve inches of fin
and rudder as my aircraft passed under the wing of the other
Spitfire. I was able to return safely to base with the damaged
aircraft, but never had knowledge of the other Spitfire's fate.
Upon landing I immediately reported to Wing Commander
Johnson, who was playing a card game called 'Knock Rummy'
with the three squadron commanders in the farmhouse that
served as Wing headquarters. I saluted Johnson and said, 'I have
had a mid-air collision, Sir.' The Wingco turned briefly and said,
'Congratulations, Williams, I have never known anyone else to
have survived one!' I completed a written report on the incident
which my Squadron Commander, Squadron Leader McLeod,
passed to the Wing Leader with this note: 'Williams is one of

my best pilots and I suggest that no action be taken.' Johnson
returned the note with this comment: 'Williams failed to keep
a proper look out in a high traffic area, and his logbook should
be suitably endorsed.' Operations became more heated at about
this time, however, and no further mention of the incident was
ever made, and my logbook was not endorsed! On numerous
subsequent occasions I flew as Johnnie's Number Two, a position
I always regarded as complimentary to my own flying skills, and
appreciated the fact that my own ability as a fighter pilot was not
questioned because of the earlier flying accident.

Flight Lieutenant Danny Noonan DFC, 416 Squadron, was less
than complimentary:

I flew with Johnnie Johnson in 127 Wing, after 144 Wing was
disbanded, but he was not one of my favourite leaders. Our best
was his predecessor, Wing Commander Lloyd Chadburn – he was
friendly to us all and had a great sense of humour. Sadly 'Chad'
was killed in a collision just after D-Day. In comparison, I am
sorry to say that Johnson was a drunk and egotist.

It is impossible, of course, to please everyone, but the evidence
confirms that overall Johnnie was thought of only in positive terms
by the majority of personnel he commanded.

On 8 May 1985, the fiftieth anniversary of VE Day, Johnnie walked
through Trafalgar Square in London, unaware that his progress was
being filmed and that he had himself become a target. The hunter
in this case was Eamon Andrews, presenter of the long-running
and popular Thames Television series *This Is Your Life*. Achieving
the perfect bounce, Andrews then escorted the surprised Air Vice-
Marshal to the studio. There Johnnie's family filed in, including
his partner, Jan Partridge, sons Mike and Chris with their wives,
and his brother Ross. Even Uncle Charlie Rossell – aged over 100
– contributed to the programme from his Australian home. Dick
Black was there, with whom Johnnie had joined the Leicestershire
Yeomanry all of those years ago, and – typically – his groundcrew
from 616 Squadron: rigger Arthur Ratcliffe and fitter Fred Burton.
French civilians from St-Croix, where Johnnie's Spitfires had been
the first to land in France after D-Day, paid tribute to him on screen

(the French actually awarded him the Legion d'Honneur in 1988). Fighter pilots gathered on stage thick and fast: Air Marshal Sir Denis Crowley-Milling, Group Captain Sir Hugh Dundas (who was, coincidentally, and as Johnnie pointed out to Eamon Andrews, the Chairman of Thames Television!), Group Captains Pat Jameson and 'Hawkeye' Wells, Wing Commander Hugh Godefroy, Squadron Leaders Danny Browne, Jeff West, Terry Spencer, and 'Nip' Hepple, and, indeed, the German ace Walter Matoni. It was a never-to-be-repeated galaxy of Second World War fighter pilots – who afterwards drank the bar dry! Today, the programme provides a unique snapshot of Johnnie's life, and in particular the love and friendship that surrounded him.

A particular friend of Johnnie's was the American Spitfire pilot Dan Browne:

Johnnie Johnson and I met for the first time during early 1943, when I joined 403 Squadron at Kenley. We immediately became friends. Whoever assigned Johnnie to the Canadian squadrons based at Kenley made a match from heaven. There was an instant rapport and the Canadians followed him like wolves in a pack. We pilots had complete trust in and respect for our leader, who was clearly destined for great things. Let us look at a typical sortie from Kenley at that time, led by Johnnie.

Generally, hot steaming tea was brought to the pilots' bedside tables with the words 'Briefing in fifteen minutes'. Those words would shock us into action. We went to the briefing hut, and there would be the clean-shaven 'Wingco' standing in front of a large map. The day's targets and routes would be indicated thereon by red ribbon, and key times would be noted as to when our Merlins would cough and settle into a smooth drone of power. We then went to breakfast, which consisted of sluggish, steaming porridge and kippers, which hopefully stayed put until we returned safely from the show. Invariably we had to cross the Channel, sometimes at wave-top, or climbing to Angels 390, depending on the strategy involved.

During the Second World War, the 'Wingco' repeated this scenario a total of 700 times, surviving every attempt to kill him and the pilots flying with him. He was never shot down, despite having started operational flying in 1940, and still being there on

8 May 1945. During this period he destroyed at least thirty-eight enemy aircraft, a score which officially made him the top RAF fighter pilot. All of his victories, remember, were German fighters, the most difficult opponents of all. In my opinion, Johnnie was *the* epitome of a warrior, *the* outstanding leader, in fact, of both the RAF and RCAF fighter forces throughout the war. He is rightly ranked as one of England's great military heroes. He was truly a giant amongst men. Johnnie knew English history and literature. Everywhere he went in the world he was an unofficial ambassador for Britain.

Johnnie's frequent visits to Plettenberg Bay in South Africa are well known, but an incident occurred when he was past eighty in the Krüger National Game Preserve. We, that being Johnnie, Jan Partridge and myself, were driving through the Preseve and became surrounded by hundreds of wild elephants. We had been told that every herd was led by a big female elephant. I was driving the van, which had a sunroof, and Johnnie was standing on a seat with his head and body outside the van. He decided that he wanted a face-to-face photo of the big herd-leader. He issued an order that I back up on 'Big Mom', 'be prepared for an instant take-off' and 'not to stall the fucking motor!' I stopped the van and began cautiously reversing on 'Big Mom'. In a few seconds 'Big Mom' approached us with her huge ears flapping and a piercing trumpet warning us to stay away. She towered over us and could have flattened us with one foot. Still no orders, though, from the AVM! Finally I heard the camera's click and an order to 'Take-off!' By this time 'Big Mom' was reaching for the back door with her trunk, but I started our retreat – fast! 'Big Mom' seemed satisfied and stopped advancing. Johnnie got his picture and all very happy.

Johnnie and Dan Browne undoubtedly shared a special bond. In 1996, Johnnie underwent successful heart-bypass surgery. In the autumn of 1999, Johnnie, aged eighty-four, and Jan flew to Portugal's Algarve. There they met Dan at a peaceful villa, providing an opportunity for one last, irreverent look back. Referring to Johnnie as 'His Holiness', Dan delighted in telling how during the war he had spent 'most of my time protecting Johnson's arse!' Johnnie's response was typical: 'Don't listen to him, he's one of those

Yanks who would have you believe that *they* won the fucking war!'
This ribald and red-blooded repartee, however, disguised mutual
admiration and respect. Johnnie, out of Dan's earshot, would tell
how Dan, an American, had volunteered for service with the RAF,
and how he had later turned down an offer of transferring to the
USAF (which meant higher pay) to remain with Johnnie and his
Canadians. Dan, likewise, would emphasise that Johnnie's record
in surviving 700 sorties without having been shot down once was
'pretty incredible when you consider the things that the son-of-
bitch used to do'. Clearly, as reporter Len Port wrote of the pair in
the *Anglo-Portuguese News*, 'Old soldiers may fade away: not old
Spitfire pilots!'

Late one afternoon in the winter of his life, Johnnie and I were sat
in his conservatory den after a long session talking about the Kenley
Wing. As the shadows lengthened outside across the Derbyshire
peaks, I asked the now tired and frail Greycap Leader how he
would describe his life. In the gathering dusk, with that irrepressible
Johnson twinkle in his ever-alert eye, he became animated and
answered, 'A *marvellous* life! Well, it was, wasn't it?' Ultimately,
though, Johnnie lost a protracted dogfight with cancer and died
peacefully at home on 30 January 2001, aged eighty-five. Tributes
poured in from across the globe, obituaries quickly appearing in the
world's press. On 25 April 2001, a 'Service of Thanksgiving for the
Life and Work of Air Vice-Marshal James Edgar 'Johnnie' Johnson'
took place at the RAF's adopted church of St Clement Danes, in the
Strand. It was an extremely moving occasion, attended by numerous
of Johnnie's family and friends. Two of the hymns were, I thought,
particularly appropriate: 'Jerusalem', and especially 'I Vow to Thee,
My Country'.

In life Johnnie was passionately enthusiastic about many things,
not least fishing. His favourite trout river, in fact, was the Derbyshire
Wye, and the beat he often fished meandered through the Chatsworth
Estate. It was there that a proud son, Chris, scattered his father's
ashes in the presence of two gamekeepers, with whom, after this
solemn duty, he toasted Johnnie's memory with a 'dram'. For Chris,
his memory of Johnnie is of a man who 'was always a father first'.
Perhaps surprisingly, given this great man's remarkable achievements
and many accolades in war and peace, Johnnie's personal memorial
is a touchingly humble one: a bench placed at his favourite fishing

spot. The inscription reads only 'In Memory of a Fisherman'. Perhaps that is how Johnnie – who achieved his full potential because of a violent war – would prefer to be remembered.

APPENDIX

Johnnie Johnson's Aerial Combat Claims

1941

15 Jan	½ Do 17 Damaged	Spitfire IA	K4477	Nr North Coates	616 Sqn
26 Jun	Me 109E Destroyed	Spitfire IIA	P7837	Gravelines	616 Sqn
04 Jul	Me 109E Damaged	Spitfire IIA	P7828	5m inlnd Gravelines	616 Sqn
06 Jul	Me 109E Destroyed	Spitfire IIA	P7838	S Dunkirk	616 Sqn
14 Jul	Me 109F Destroyed	Spitfire VB	P8707	Fauquemburgues	616 Sqn
21 Jul	Me 109Probable	Spitfire IIA	P7837	Merville	616 Sqn
23 Jul	Me 109Damaged	Spitfire IIA	P7837	10m inlnd Boulogne	616 Sqn
09 Aug	Me 109F Destroyed	Spitfire VB	W3334	Bethune	616 Sqn
09 Aug	½ Me 109F Destroyed	Spitfire VB	W3334	Bethune	616 Sqn
21 Aug	Me 109E Probable	Spitfire VB	W3457	10m E Le Touquet	616 Sqn
21 Sep	2 Me 109Fs Destroyed	Spitfire VB	W3428	Nr Le Touquet	616 Sqn

1942

15 Apr	FW 190 Damaged	Spitfire VB	BM121	10m E Le Touquet	616 Sqn
19 Aug	FW 190Destroyed	Spitfire VB	EP215	Dieppe	610 Sqn
19 Aug	⅓ Me 109F Destroyed	Spitfire VB	EP215	Dieppe	610 Sqn
19 Aug	½ FW 190 Damaged	Spitfire VB	EP215	Dieppe	610 Sqn
20 Aug	FW 190 Probable	Spitfire VB	EP215	Off French coast	610 Sqn

1943

13 Feb	FW 190 Probable	Spitfire VB	EP121	SW Boulogne	610 Sqn
03 Apr	FW 190 Destroyed	Spitfire IX	EN398	E Montreuil	Kenley Wg
05 Apr	3 FW 190s Damaged	Spitfire IX	EN398	Ostend–Ghent	Kenley Wg
11 May	FW 190 Destroyed	Spitfire IX	EN398	Gravelines	Kenley Wg
13 May	FW 190 Destroyed	Spitfire IX	EN398	Berck–Le Touquet	Kenley Wg
13 May	⅓ FW 190 Destroyed	Spitfire IX	EN398	Mid-Channel	Kenley Wg
14 May	FW 190 Destroyed	Spitfire IX	EN398	Nieuport	Kenley Wg
01 Jun	½ Me 109 Destroyed	Spitfire IX	EN398	Somme Estuary	Kenley Wg
15 Jun	2 FW 190s Destroyed	Spitfire IX	EN398	Yvetot	Kenley Wg
17 Jun	FW 190 Destroyed	Spitfire IX	EN398	Ypres–St-Omer	Kenley Wg
24 Jun	FW 190 Damaged	Spitfire IX	EN398	St-Omer	Kenley Wg
24 Jun	FW 190 Destroyed	Spitfire IX	EN398	S of Fecamp	Kenley Wg
27 Jun	FW 190 Destroyed	Spitfire IX	EN398	W of St-Omer	Kenley Wg
15 Jul	Me 109G Destroyed	Spitfire IX	EN398	Blangy–Senarpont	Kenley Wg
25 Jul	Me 109G Destroyed	Spitfire IX	EN398	E of Schipol	Kenley Wg
29 Jul	Me 109G Damaged	Spitfire IX	EN398	SW Amsterdam	Kenley Wg

30 Jul	Me 109 Destroyed	Spitfire IX	EN398	W of Schipol	Kenley Wg
12 Aug	½ Me 109 Destroyed	Spitfire IX	EN398	Axel	127 Wg
12 Aug	½ Me 109 Destroyed	Spitfire IX	EN398	Axel	127 Wg
17 Aug	¼ Me 110 Destroyed	Spitfire IX	EN398	N of Ghent	127 Wg
23 Aug	FW 190 Destroyed	Spitfire IX	EN398	Gosnay	127 Wg
26 Aug	FW 190 Destroyed	Spitfire IX	MA573	SW Rouen	127 Wg
04 Sep	FW 190 Destroyed	Spitfire IX	MA573	NW Roubaix	127 Wg
05 Sep	Me 109 Damaged	Spitfire IX	EN398	Daynze	127 Wg

1944

28 Mar	½ Ju 88 on ground	Spitfire IXB	MK392	Dreux Airfield	144 Wg
25 Apr	2 FW 190s Destroyed	Spitfire IXB	MK392	Laon	144 Wg
05 May	FW 190 Destroyed	Spitfire IXB	MK392	Douai	144 Wg
16 Jun	FW 190 Destroyed	Spitfire IXB	MK392	NE Villers-Bocage	144 Wg
22 Jun	Me 109 Destroyed	Spitfire IXB	MK392	7m W of Argentan	144 Wg
28 Jun	2 Me 109s Destroyed	Spitfire IXB	MK392	S of Caen	144 Wg
30 Jun	Me 109Destroyed	Spitfire IXB	NH380	E of Grace	144 Wg
05 Jul	2 FW 190s Destroyed	Spitfire IXB	MK392	Alencon	144 Wg
20 Jul	FW 190 Damaged	Spitfire IXB	MK392	S of Argentan	127 Wg
23 Aug	2 FW 190s Destroyed	Spitfire IXB	MK392	Senlis	127 Wg
27 Sep	Me 109 Destroyed	Spitfire IXB	MK392	Rees on Rhine	127 Wg

Officially, Johnnie's number of aerial victories was thirty-eight and a half. Johnnie, however, personally approved the list above, compiled from details in his log book. The statistics ultimately arrived at from this data are: thirty-four and seven enemy aircraft destroyed, three probably destroyed with a further two shared 'probables', ten damaged and another three shared; one shared destroyed on the ground. Thirty of Johnnie's aerial combats concerned FW 190s, twenty-five Me 109s, and one an Me 110. Only once did he engage a German bomber, this being his first combat, on 15 January 1941, a kill shared with Cocky Dundas. In total, therefore, Johnnie opened fire on fifty-seven enemy aircraft. His total number of flying hours by 8 May 1945 was 1,741 – 1,628.40 as first pilot and 785.40 of which were operational. This represents some 700 operational sorties.

The foregoing list indicates that Johnnie's most successful combat tour was in 1943, leading what was initially the Kenley Wing and which subsequently became redesignated 127 Wing. During that period, Johnnie claimed fourteen enemy aircraft destroyed while flying Spitfire EN398. This statistic makes that particular machine the most successful Spitfire of all. Unfortunately, however, this historic airframe cannot be found preserved in a museum – it was unceremoniously scrapped in 1949.

Acknowledgements

First, this book could not have been written without the kind co-operation of the Johnson family, particularly Paula, Ross and Duncan, and especially Chris. I must also thank the late Jan Partridge, Lady Bader and Keith Delderfield of The Douglas Bader Foundation.

The following pilots provided essential help and information: Air Marshal Sir Denis Crowley-Milling, Group Captain Sir Hugh Dundas, Air Commodore Sir Archie Winskill, Wing Commander Dr Hugh Godefroy, Wing Commander Charlie Magwood, Wing Commander Bob Middlemiss, Squadron Leader Dan Browne, Squadron Leader Sir Alan Smith, Squadron Leader Lionel 'Buck' Casson, Squadron Leader Rod Smith, Flight Lieutenant the Revd Danny Noonan, Flight Lieutenant Neil Burns, Flight Lieutenant Forrest Young, Flight Lieutenant Ron Rayner, and Flying Officer Ivor Williams.

As ever, Jonathan Reeve and his team at Amberley Publishing have been a pleasure to work with.

Finally, I must, of course, thank my family, especially my wife, Karen, without whom my own spirit and zest for life would not have been re-lit.

Bibliography

Primary Sources

Pilots' Flying Logbooks:
Air Vice-Marshal J. E. Johnson
Group Captain Sir Douglas Bader
Group Captain H. F. Burton

Operations Records Books, preserved at The National Archives:

19 Squadron	AIR 27/252
41 Squadron	AIR 27/425
130 Squadron	AIR 27/938
145 Squadron	AIR 27/985
242 Squadron	AIR 27/1473
350 Squadron	AIR 27/1746
403 Squadron	AIR 27/1783
416 Squadron	AIR 27/1816
421 Squadron	AIR 27/1828
441 Squadron	AIR 27/1881
442 Squadron	AIR 27/1882
443 Squadron	AIR 27/1883
125 Wing	AIR 26/185
127 Wing	AIR 26/187
144 Wing	AIR 26/209

Combat Reports, preserved at The National Archives:

19 Squadron	AIR 50/10
41 Squadron	AIR 50/18
130 Squadron	AIR 50/52
242 Squadron	AIR 50/92
350 Squadron	AIR 50/134
403 Squadron	AIR 50/138
416 Squadron	AIR 50/145
421 Squadron	AIR 50/147
441 Squadron	AIR 50/152
442 Squadron	AIR 50/153
443 Squadron	AIR 50/154
125 Wing	AIR 50/431

127 Wing   AIR 50/433
144 Wing   AIR 50/442

The majority of Air Vice-Marshal J. E. Johnson's Personal Combat Reports
are preserved in AIR 50/402, and can be downloaded online from The
National Archives website.

   Dilip Sarkar Archive: interviews with Air Vice-Marshal J. E. Johnson,
Mrs Paula Johnson & Mr Ross Johnson; Squadron Leader J. D. Brown;
correspondence with former pilots from the Tangmere, Kenley, 125, 127
and 144 Wings.

Published & Secondary Sources

Bader, G/C Sir D. R. S., *Fight for the Sky*, Sidgwick & Jackson, London,
   1973
Becker, C., *The Luftwaffe War Diaries*, MacDonald, London, 1967
Beevor, A., *D-Day: The Battle for Normandy*, Penguin, London, 2009
Berger, M., and Street, B J, *Invasions Without Tears*, Random House,
   London, 1994
Bracken, R., *Spitfire: The Canadians*, Boston Mills Press, Boston, 1995
Brickhill, P., *Reach for the Sky*, William Collins, London, 1954
Burns, M., *Bader: The Man and His Men*, Arms & Armour Press, 1990
Caldwell, D., *The JG 26 War Diary Volume I*, Grubb Street, 1996
Caldwell, D., *The JG 26 War Diary Volume II*, Grubb Street, 1998
Clark, D., *Angels Eight: Normandy Air War Diary*, First Books, Ontario,
   2003
Dean, Sir M., *The Royal Air Force and Two World Wars*, Cassell, London,
   1979
D'Este, C., *Decision in Normandy: The Real Story of Montgomery and the
   Allied Campaign*, Penguin, London, 1983
Douglas-Home, C., *Rommel*, Weidenfeld & Nicholson Ltd, London, 1973
Dundas, G/C Sir H. S. L., *Flying Start*, Stanley Paul Ltd, London, 1988
Fenton, A/C H. A., *The Man Who Holds the Watering Pot*, privately
   published, Sark, 1979
Foreman, J., *1941: Part One*, Air Research Publications, New Malden, 1993
Foreman, J., *1941: Part Two*, Air Research Publications, New Malden, 1994
Foreman, J., *1944: Over the Beaches*, Air Research Publications, New
   Malden, 1994
Franks, N., *RAF Fighter Command Losses, Volume III*, Midland Counties
   Publishing, 2000
Freeman, R., *The Mighty Eighth*, MacDonald, London, 1970
Galland, A., *The First and the Last: Germany's Fighter Force in the Second
   World War*, Methuen, London, 1954
Godefroy, Wg Cdr Dr H. C., *Lucky Thirteen*, Croom Helm, London, 1983
Gooderson, Dr I., *Air Power at the Battlefront: Allied Close Air Support in
   Europe 1943–45*, Frank Cass, Abingdon, 1998
Hall, Dr D. I., *Strategy for Victory: The Development of British Tactical Air*

Power, 1919–1943, Praeger, Westport, 2008

Hastings, Sir M., *Overlord*, Michael Joseph Ltd, London, 1984

James, J., *The Paladins: The Story of the RAF up to the Outbreak of World War II*, Futura Publications, London, 1990

James, T. C. G., *The Battle of Britain*, Frank Cass, Abingdon, 2000

Johnson, AVM J. E., *Wing Leader*, Chatto & Windus Ltd, London, 1956

Johnson, AVM J. E., *Full Circle*, Chatto & Windus Ltd, London, 1964

Johnson, AVM J. E., & Lucas, Wg Cdr P. B., *Courage in the Skies*, Stanley Paul, London, 1992

Johnson, AVM J. E. & Lucas, W/C P. B., *Winged Victory*, Stanley Paul & Co. Ltd, London, 1995

Keegan, J., *Six Armies in Normandy*, Pimlico, London, 1982

Lefevre, E., *Panzers in Normandy: Then & Now*, After the Battle, London, 1983

Luck, H. von, *Panzer Commander: The Memoirs of Colonel Hans von Luck*, Dell Publishing, London, 1989

Meyer, H., *A History of the 12th SS Panzer Division Hitler Jugend*, Fedorowicz, New York, 1994

Margry, K., *Operation Market Garden Volume I*, After the Battle, 2002

Margry, K., *Operation Market Garden Volume II*, After the Battle, 2002

Montgomery, Viscount of Alamein, *The Memoirs of Field Marshal Montgomery*, Fontana, London, 1960

Morgan, E., and Shacklady, E., *Spitfire: The History*, Key Publishing, 1987

Obermaier, E., *Der Ritterkreuztrager der Luftwaffe 1939–45: Band 1 Jagdflieger*, Verlag Dieter Hoffman, Berlin, 1966

Orange, Dr V., *Coningham: A Biography of Air Marshal Sir Arthur Coningham*, Methuen, London, 1990

Overy, R., *The Air War 1939–45*, Europa Publications Ltd, London, 1979

Pallud, J. P., *The Battle of the Bulge Then & Now*, After the Battle, London, 1984

Price, Dr A., *The Spitfire Story*, Arms & Armour Press, London, 1995

Ramsey, W. (ed.), *The Battle of Britain Then & Now, Mk V*, After the Battle, London, 1989

Ramsey, W. (ed.), *The Blitz Then & Now Volume I*, After the Battle, London, 1989

Ramsey, W. (ed.), *The Blitz Then & Now Volume II*, After the Battle, London, 1990

Ramsey, W. (ed.), *The Blitz Then & Now Volume III*, After the Battle, London, 1991

Sagar, A., *Line Shoot: The Diary of a Fighter Pilot*, Vanwell Publishing, Ontario, 1992

Sarkar, D., *A Few of the Many: Air War 1939–45, A Kaleidoscope of Memories*, Ramrod Publications, Worcester, 1995

Sarkar, D., *Bader's Tangmere Spitfires: 1941, The Untold Story*, Haynes (PSL), Sparkford, 1996

Sarkar, D., *Bader's Duxford Fighters: The Big Wing Controversy*, Ramrod Publications, Worcester, 1997

Sarkar, D., *Johnnie Johnson: Spitfire Top Gun, Part One*, Ramrod
  Publications, Worcester, 2002
Sarkar, D., *Johnnie Johnson: Spitfire Top Gun, Part Two*, Victory Books,
  Worcester, 2005
Sarkar, D., *The Few: The Battle of Britain in the Words of the Pilots*,
  Amberley Publishing, Chalford, 2009
Sarkar, D., *The Spitfire Manual 1940*, Amberley Publishing, Chalford, 2010
Sarkar, D., *Spitfire Voices: Life as a Spitfire Pilot in the Words of the
  Veterans*, Amberley Publishing, Chalford, 2010
Sarkar, D., 'Was the Leadership Ability of RAF Fighter Squadron
  Commanders in World War Two Compromised by Socio-Educational
  Prejudice?' (unpublished undergraduate dissertation), University of
  Worcester, 2009
Shores, C., & Williams, C., *Aces High*, Grubb Street, London, 1994
Shores, C., *Aces High Volume II*, Grubb Street, 1999
Shulmaan, M., *Defeat in the West*, Secker & Warburg, New York, 1947
Tanner, J. (ed.), *Fighting in the Air*, RAF Museum, London, 1978
Wells, M. K., *Courage and Air Warfare: The Allied Aircrew Experience in
  the Second World War*, Frank Cass, London, 1995
Wynn, H., & Young, S., *Prelude to Overlord*, Airlife, Shrewsbury, 1983
Wynn, K., *Men of the Battle of Britain*, Gliddon Books, Norwich, 1989

Films
Johnnie Johnson: This Is Your Life, Thames Television, 8 May 1985
Reach for the Sky, directed by Lewis Gilbert, Rank, 1956

Websites
http://www.dilipsarkarmbe.co.uk – Dilip Sarkar's personal website
http://www.jjhousing.co.uk – The Johnnie Johnson Housing Trust
http://douglasbaderfoundation.com – The Douglas Bader Foundation
http://www.nationalarchives.gov.uk – The National Archives

About the Author

DILIP SARKAR has published over thirty books on the Battle of Britain and the Supermarine Spitfire, including a biography of legless fighter ace Douglas Bader and the bestselling *Spitfire Manual*. A retired police officer, Dilip was made an MBE for services to aviation history, and is a Fellow of the Royal Historical Society. In addition to pursuing his historical interests, he is the Angling Trust's Fisheries Enforcement Manager. His website is www. dilipsarkarmbe.co.uk and he lives in Worcester.

Other Books by Dilip Sarkar

Spitfire Squadron: No 19 Squadron at War, 1939-41
The Invisible Thread: A Spitfire's Tale
Through Peril to the Stars: RAF Fighter Pilots Who Failed to Return, 1939-45
Angriff Westland: Three Battle of Britain Air Raids Through the Looking Glass
A Few of the Many: Air War 1939-45, A Kaleidoscope of Memories
Bader's Tangmere Spitfires: The Untold Story, 1941
Bader's Duxford Fighters: The Big Wing Controversy
Missing in Action: Resting in Peace?
Guards VC: Blitzkrieg 1940
Battle of Britain: The Photographic Kaleidoscope, Volume I
Battle of Britain: The Photographic Kaleidoscope, Volume II
Battle of Britain: The Photographic Kaleidoscope, Volume III
Battle of Britain: The Photographic Kaleidoscope, Volume IV
Fighter Pilot: The Photographic Kaleidoscope
Group Captain Sir Douglas Bader: An Inspiration in Photographs
Johnnie Johnson: Spitfire Top Gun, Part I
Johnnie Johnson: Spitfire Top Gun, Part II

Battle of Britain: Last Look Back
Spitfire! Courage & Sacrifice
Spitfire Voices: Heroes Remember
The Battle of Powick Bridge: Ambush a Fore-thought
Duxford 1940: A Battle of Britain Base at War
The Few: The Battle of Britain in the Words of the Pilots
The Spitfire Manual 1940
The Last of the Few: Eighteen Battle of Britain Pilots Tell Their
    Extraordinary Stories
Hearts of Oak: The Human Tragedy of HMS Royal Oak
Spitfire Voices: Life as a Spitfire Pilot in the Words of the Veterans
How the Spitfire Won the Battle of Britain
The Sinking of HMS Royal Oak
Douglas Bader
Spitfire: The Photographic Biography
Hurricane Manual